Psychology

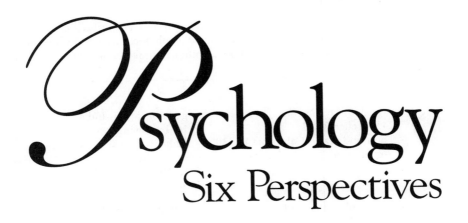

Psychology
Six Perspectives

Dodge Fernald
Harvard University

SAGE Publications
Los Angeles • London • New Delhi • Singapore

For information:

Sage Publications, Inc.
2455 Teller Road
Thousand Oaks, California 91320
E-mail: order@sagepub.com

Sage Publications India Pvt. Ltd.
B 1/I 1 Mohan Cooperative
  Industrial Area
Mathura Road,
New Delhi 110 044
India

Sage Publications Ltd.
1 Oliver's Yard
55 City Road
London EC1Y 1SP
United Kingdom

Sage Publications Asia-Pacific
  Pte. Ltd.
33 Pekin Street #02-01
Far East Square
Singapore 048763

Printed in the United States of America

Library of Congress Cataloging-in-Publication Data

Fernald, L. Dodge (Lloyd Dodge), 1929-
Psychology: Six perspectives/L. Dodge Fernald.
    p. cm.
Includes bibliographical references and index.
ISBN-13: 978-1-4129-3867-9 (pbk.)
   1. Psychology—Textbooks. I. Title.

BF121.F384 2007
150—dc22

                                    2006101378

Printed on acid-free paper.

08   09   10   11   10   9   8   7   6   5   4   3   2   1

Acquiring Editor:	Cheri Dellelo
Editorial Assistant:	Anna Marie Mesick
Production Editor:	Sarah K. Quesenberry
Copy Editor:	Gail Naron Chalew
Proofreader:	Teresa Kay
Typesetter:	C&M Digitals (P) Ltd.
Cover Designer:	Candice Harman
Marketing Associate:	Amberlyn M. Erzinger

Brief Contents

Detailed Contents

Preface

Extending from the natural sciences to the humanities, modern psychology has emerged as a highly diverse, relatively young science. This book offers a broad understanding of the field, using three distinct strategies to promote effective instruction.

First, it respects the advice of the American Psychological Association, offered after its examination of undergraduate psychology curricula throughout the United States. Noting that the instructional goals in courses and textbooks appeared too ambitious, the investigating committee succinctly advised: "Less is more" (McGovern, Furomoto, Halpern, Kimball, & McKeachie, 1991). Thus, this book approaches psychology from the standpoint of six major perspectives. In this way, it recognizes the breadth of the field; at the same time, it sets the boundaries at a half-dozen prominent, alternative viewpoints. In rather brief fashion, these perspectives illustrate the diverse, fundamental ideas that characterize psychology today.

Second, it employs two types of discourse. The fundamental mode of communication in science is rational and direct, guided by logical analysis. Therefore, scientific discourse is the primary means of communication in this textbook. Essential to presenting an accurate, balanced description of modern psychology, it follows the rules and tests of sound thinking exemplified in science.

But the human mind is also disposed to another mode of communication—the narrative method, or storytelling. We tell stories throughout our lives—in families, at work, to friends, on television, even among strangers. Stories are a powerful, universal mode of communication, a natural way of thinking about human behavior (Bruner, 1990). Here storytelling serves as a secondary, intermittent mode of discourse. More holistic and unfolding than scientific writing, it can instruct in ways that are unavailable in traditional textbook discourse, increasing reader interest, comprehension, and recall (Fernald, 1987).

Third, the illustrations deviate from the usual textbook photos and drawings. Instead, the visual images are exclusively diagrams and flow charts, collectively called conceptual models. Devoted solely to instruction, a conceptual model is any graphic display that depicts the relationships between concepts and among their properties.

Overall, this book emphasizes a conceptual understanding of the field, as opposed to knowledge that is more static and factual (McGovern et al., 1991). May this approach provide readers with an opportunity for lifelong learning about psychology.

Acknowledgments

Faculty colleagues and students contributed to this book in the many subtle and inextricable ways that bind all our lives together. They take anonymous places here alongside the reference staffs at the Cabot Library of Science, the Monroe C. Gutman Library of Education, and the William James Psychology Library, all at Harvard, as well as the Wellesley Free Library in Wellesley, Massachusetts. But particular assistance was provided by a half-dozen others who merit more conspicuous recognition.

Bro' Peter, sharing a surname, packet of genes, several editions as co-author of a traditional psychology textbook, and his years of experience on the psychology faculty at the University of New Hampshire, strongly encouraged this briefer, nontraditional textbook aimed at laying a foundation for students' lifelong learning.

As founder, owner, and chief editor of Wordworks, Cherie Potts bridges the gap along the Charles River between Harvard and MIT, processing all manner of manuscripts from both institutions, including several revisions of this one, all the while managing similar requests from all over the world.

Dennis Gaudet, fortified by his irrepressible humor and years of experience as a teaching fellow in continuing education at Harvard, spearheaded the major critique of this manuscript in his usual manner, as a Renaissance man, wide-ranging in thought and eclectic in approaching instruction.

As acquisitions editor at Sage Publications, Cheri Dellelo led the Sage teams involved with this book, providing sagacious macro-level management at each stage of the publishing process. Sarah Quesenberry, in the role of production editor, offered remarkably supportive and judicious micro-level guidance through the editing, design, layout, and related efforts. Together they reflect well Sage's declared partnerships in the complex business of publishing textbooks.

Finally, a faculty member at Massachusetts Bay Community College merits a special salute. Throughout this lengthy business, brown-eyed Jorie not only tolerated this intruder into our private lives but also nourished it—over dinner conversations, during fitness workouts, along the Brook Path, and on the telephone. The presence of this book here testifies to her presence there, throughout our lives together.

1

An Emerging Science

P sychology, a wag once observed, has a long past but only a short history. Its long past extends down through the ages, ever since human beings developed the capacity to ponder their existence. Its short history refers to the relatively brief period since psychology became a modern science.

According to historians, the inaugural event for modern psychology occurred in Leipzig, Germany in 1879 with the founding of the first laboratory for psychological research. It stimulated efforts toward increased precision in the study of human behavior, extending beyond everyday experience and mere speculation. Human activities could be examined through careful observation, description, manipulation, and control—all aimed at measuring and predicting behavior and experience.

Not far from Leipzig and that inaugural event, also in 1879, a young woman reached her 21st year. Born with a silver spoon in her mouth and a riding crop in hand, Anna greatly enjoyed galloping on horseback through the woods near her home in Vienna, often in the early morning hours. This exercise gave her a sense of fulfillment and freedom—and control over her otherwise restricted life. Little did she know that soon she would be forced to abandon this spirited activity.

Talented and attractive, Anna spoke several languages, played the piano, and wrote compelling poetry. She also reacted vigorously in most personal encounters, always ready with a sharp retort, especially to her brother Wilhelm, who was a year younger. They fought relentless sister-brother battles all around the house. Often obstinate, even cantankerous, Anna sometimes seemed to encourage these hostilities.

But she acted quite differently with her parents, for the most part respecting their wishes. And they took extraordinary care to protect their daughter. Even at her age, they restricted her activities outside the home. They insisted that she follow the rigid social codes of their particular culture. One required that young women cease formal education after high school. Another decreed that women from wealthy backgrounds should prepare themselves exclusively for marriage. Her parents' willingness to adopt these codes for her, but not for Wilhelm, aroused her intense frustration, although she showed no overt, outspoken resistance. She had no words to express her conflicted feelings. She suffered an imprisonment—kept apart from full participation in her late 19th-century Viennese society (Breuer, 1895).

Her story provides a backdrop for the instruction in this book. Throughout the world, ancient and modern, Eastern and Western, human beings use stories in this way, as a powerful means of understanding and describing themselves and others (Bruner, 1986). Anna's narrative illustrates and supplements the otherwise rational, direct scientific discourse found in this book and in other traditional psychology textbooks. With its personal viewpoint and orientation in everyday life, her story also increases the potential for readers to remember the work (Sarbin, 1986). It serves well here for more particular reasons too. Anna's early years coincide with the founding of scientific psychology, and most important, the various stages of her adult life become useful settings for addressing the six psychological perspectives examined in this book.

So Anna's story offers a real-life tale of troubles and triumph, told and retold even in this new millennium (de Paula Ramos, 2003; Guttmann, 2001; Kimball, 2000). But the aim here is not to explain Anna. Her presence instead creates a background for the goal of this book—to tell the story of psychology.

This chapter begins with the founding of psychology as a scientific endeavor. Then it turns to the modes of work in contemporary psychology, focusing on two roles: the scientist and the practitioner. It concludes with a description of the great breadth in the field today.

The Founding of Psychology

At the outset, it should be clear that modern psychology reaches far beyond health and illness, mental and physical. Broadly defined, the field of **psychology** is the scientific study of behavior, experience, and mental processes in all living creatures. The two parts of this word *psych-ology,* expressed in reverse order, mean "the study of—the mind." But psychology today extends far beyond the mind in both directions: inward toward the body and outward toward the environment. Its topics of inquiry range from neural messages to cultural influences. Few fields offer such breadth and so many practical applications. Economists concentrate on financial behavior, theologians on religious behavior, sociologists on group behavior, and so forth, but psychology includes the study of the behavior of all living creatures anywhere—a broad mandate indeed.

Sometimes psychologists simply use the term *behavior* to refer to the extensive array of reactions produced by diverse creatures. In such instances, it may include thoughts, feelings, and physiological responses as well.

On these bases, psychology differs sharply from psychiatry. As a specialty within the field of medicine, *psychiatry* deals only with people and only with abnormal behavior. Psychology, a whole separate field in itself, concerns behavior of all sorts in animals and in human beings. One specialty, *clinical psychology,* deals chiefly with the diagnosis and treatment of mental and behavior disorders. Thus, psychiatry and clinical psychology are separate areas within medicine and psychology, respectively. The field of medicine treats illness, usually of the body; the field of psychology addresses all kinds of behavior and experience, normal and abnormal.

In fact, psychology entered the 21st century with a mandate from the American Psychological Association to engage in more intensive study of happiness, fulfillment, and the sense of well-being. Modern psychology seeks to discover and foster the ways in which people and societies can flourish (Seligman & Csikszentmihalyi, 2000).

A Laboratory for Research

Interest in psychological questions, prominent among the ancient Greek philosophers, stretches throughout human history, but psychology became a modern science with the construction of its first research laboratory. In the late 19th century, while Anna pondered the restrictions of her affluent background and fought with Wilhelm around the home, another Wilhelm enjoyed his early success in Leipzig, pursuing a surprising endeavor—or so it seemed at the time.

In a small, empty dining room on the third floor of a university building, Wilhelm Wundt initiated formal research in psychology. It might be said that he replaced forks and knives with tuning forks and color wheels. The building had been there for decades. Wundt had used the room for some time; he had presented lectures on physiology; he had published his own physiological research. But in 1879, a graduate student in that laboratory completed the first published doctoral research, an investigation of human reaction time (Boring, 1950). The publication of that study seemed a fitting event to mark the founding of the laboratory, which in fact occurred over several years.

Possessing a medical degree and training in physiology, Wundt brought a biological background to that laboratory. He adopted apparatus from physiology and physics, and his early research and writing reflected an orientation toward the biological aspects of psychology. With these instruments, he and his followers eventually turned to the study of sensation, perception, attention, and other mental activities. This groundbreaking work, prompted by Wundt's earlier associations with philosophy, suggested that indeed the mind could be measured in a laboratory context. Indeed, psychology could become a science.

Presenting colors, odors, and tones in controlled fashion, Wundt and his colleagues asked observers to report their experiences. They showed a mix of colors on a whirling wheel and asked observers what hues they perceived as the wheel gradually increased in speed. They presented observers with steady clicking sounds from one or more metronomes and asked what rhythms they perceived (Wundt, 1904). Sometimes observers performed similarly and sometimes differently, an outcome that added further challenge to their research.

Especially for some of Wundt's followers, this research involved *introspection,* for the observers looked inward, trying to describe their experience, their mental life at the moment. This work in psychology became known as *structuralism* because the new psychologists were trying to discover the structure, or contents, of the human mind. They aimed to understand a person's consciousness at a certain moment in relation to a specific stimulus. This goal showed an early concern with cognitive psychology.

But studies in Wundt's and other laboratories also produced unpredictable results. For example, when investigators asked a person to lie down and compare the weights of two identical coins placed on his forehead, the person reported a cold coin as heavier than a warm one. In fact, the observer perceived the cold coin as heavier than two warm ones, placed one on top of the other (Boring, 1950; Stumpf, 1930). We know today that the perception of temperature and weight can vary sharply with different tasks in different areas of the skin. In his studies of perception, Wundt was primarily interested in the psychological dimension, not the purely physiological factors.

Wundt ventured into another realm as well. Using homemade instruments, he and his associates presented observers with random letters or actual words at various intervals and examined the contents of their recall. Wundt's broad background and versatility as a scientist-philosopher led him deeply into the study of language and thought, as well as religion, art, and even mythology and morality (Blumenthal, 1997). Altogether, Wundt's wide-ranging works made early contact with what would be known today as biological, cognitive, and cultural psychology.

While Wundt pursued these diverse interests, the method of introspection presented its followers with a major difficulty, casting a shadow over the legacy of the laboratory (Blumenthal, 1975). The observers' experiences were private, known only to them. Because their reports could not be verified by others, the results remained uncertain and therefore unacceptable as scientific evidence. For this reason, the introspective method declined and then, with the rise of other approaches, disappeared.

Four years before Wundt's inaugural laboratory in 1879, an American named William James founded a psychology laboratory, but he used it only for instructional purposes. A weak back, frail constitution, and restless imagination kept him from research; he preferred writing and speaking instead. As America's foremost psychologist, he greatly popularized the field, especially through his lectures and textbooks (James, 1890). But the honor of inaugurating the field goes to Wundt with his studies of mental life in a research laboratory.

Recognizing Wundt in this way, as the founder of modern psychology, creates a distortion in history. No one person inaugurates a field of study, much less by a single act, such as creating a laboratory. Psychology, like other sciences, is a social enterprise. Many people, instruments, methods, and points of view were involved in its founding and development.

Yet it simplifies history to single out a founder of one sort or another. This identification makes it easier to comprehend a broad period of human endeavor. But in addition to physiology and physics, contributions to the field of psychology also came from philosophy, medicine, and even literature.

Empiricism and Rationalism

Beginning with the 17th-century work of Sir Francis Bacon, philosophy exerted a marked influence on the development of all scientific fields, including psychology. In fact, many historians regard Bacon as the founder of modern science. He deflected credit for that accomplishment, pointing out that he merely rang the bell to call the scholars together. He believed that the science of his time relied too heavily on assumptions about human nature and then deducing the facts from these assumptions. Science should proceed in the other direction, Bacon declared, starting with the collection of facts.

This fundamental principle of science, called **empiricism**, refers to the collection of information by direct observation, through experience, rather than relying on personal opinion or the view of some authority. In fact, the concept of empiricism today is loosely synonymous with science. But this experience must be verifiable, available to other observers. They must have the opportunity to make the same observations and decide for themselves. The word *empiricism* means experience; the investigator goes into the field or laboratory and gathers the facts. The surest means of testing almost any idea lies in empirical research.

Empiricism produces instances of factual information called **data**, some of which serve for constructing theories and developing conclusions. The singular of this term is *datum*, referring to one piece of information, but the plural form is commonly used both ways. In any case, psychology includes a large body of data.

A second fundamental principle in science, called **rationalism**, involves the development and elaboration of ideas solely by reasoning, without necessarily conducting empirical tests. Pure mathematics is a form of rational inquiry; through analysis and synthesis, the mathematician uncovers new knowledge. René Descartes, a French philosopher, mathematician, and contemporary of Bacon, became a pioneer in modern science in this way. He pointed to the consistency and certainty in numerical analyses. Applying this philosophical outlook to the study of human behavior, he fostered the development of pre-empirical psychology.

In the humanities today, rational research of an explanatory sort is sometimes called the *hermeneutic approach*, indicating an interpretative study, usually of some text. The investigator begins with information already available and, through logic and creativity, develops a new view. Rationalism is sometimes colloquially and inadequately called library research, for the investigator, rather than going into the laboratory or field, goes to the library or other archival source.

Rationalism can produce a **theory**, which is a group of related principles with explanatory value. It may concern a relatively specific or broad topic. Psychoanalysis, a whole system of thought often described as a theory, actually includes numerous theories—about dreams, human sexuality, maladjustment, personality, and civilization.

Some words, incidentally, are used more loosely in everyday life than in science, and *theory* is one of them. It does not mean simply a thought or a guess: "It's my theory that the bus has been delayed by the parade." Rather, a theory in any science involves a collection of related facts or hypotheses, offering an interpretation about them. It is therefore useful for making predictions about other facts and for developing explanations about how they are related. But the test of a useful theory lies with empiricism. Does it promote the collection of data? If so, it is a worthy theory.

Empiricism and rationalism, fundamental principles in modern science, form the basic themes in this book, along with the concept of multiple causality, considered in detail later. That concept states that numerous factors within and outside the individual typically contribute to any complex reaction. Explicitly or implicitly, these three themes underlie most of the following discussions.

The Nature of Science

On these bases, what is science? The essential characteristic of science is a demand for evidence through empiricism, guided by rationalism. It is a series of logical steps or thoughts based on the observation and interpretation of facts. Yet empiricism alone is insufficient. Otherwise the results from a horse race or observations of the colors of umbrellas might be considered science. The facts must be organized and interpreted in some rational fashion. Science aims not simply at description but also at explanation, prediction, and even control. Science requires empiricism *and* rationalism, data and theory—or at least an interpretation of the data.

This demand for evidence makes science a public activity, not merely because anyone can enter the field but also because scientists must present their work for scrutiny by peers, usually in a written report. This *research report* describes in detail the purpose, methods, and results of an investigation, followed by a discussion of its implications.

To be accepted in the scientific community, this report must appear in a *peer-reviewed journal,* one in which all reports are evaluated by other experts in the field. If these reviewers find a research report acceptable, usually in some revised form, then it is published. The aim is to inform other scientists of the findings and to provide them with an opportunity to criticize and repeat the research, drawing their own conclusions. Without peer approval of this sort, the work is not considered scientific.

Science, in this manner, serves as its own authority. It proceeds in fits and starts and makes mistakes, seeking to correct errors through peer review. It remains unfinished, evaluating the very ideas it has generated. If the new ideas are superior to the old, they are accepted; the replacement is made; and a new cycle begins.

William James described science as "unfinished business" for this reason. Each research discovery paves the way for further research and more discoveries. In this unending process, scientists face the seven-headed Hydra in Greek mythology. For every head they cut off, the monster grows two in its place, and the task becomes ever more awesome. Getting a head simply means more work ahead.

In science, empiricism and rationalism are complementary and intertwined, although empiricism stands ascendant. Observations of some sort commonly precede rational research; the investigator has noted something of interest in the environment and aims to investigate it. And useful empirical research cannot be incidental or haphazard. It must be thoughtfully organized, especially the plans for collecting and interpreting data. Most scientific investigations include both empirical and rational elements.

Respecting the magnitude of Wundt's goal, psychologists today continue to pursue the secrets of human behavior and experience. But they do so with far more sophisticated equipment, and they examine a wider array of influences, ranging from minute biological factors to broad social and cultural forces, largely ignored in Anna's day. They also focus on efficiency in the workplace and worker satisfaction. In the home, they examine parent-child and sibling relationships, both contributors to Anna's frustrations.

At home, Anna led a combative life. She pursued religious instruction only for her father's sake—and deeply resented it. More important, her sibling rivalry with Wilhelm made their home a constant battleground, especially with the increased tension caused by their father's poor health.

Anna also led a dreary life. She had received an excellent education through high school, but with no universities open to women and no thoughts about breaking that barrier, her parents simply withdrew her from further formal education. They even limited her social life almost entirely to family activities.

Her father had developed a serious lung infection the previous summer at Bad Ischl, a celebrated health resort (Guttmann, 2001). His wife, assisted by a nurse, cared for him during the day. Anna took full responsibility alone at night. But illness haunted this family. The second child, Flora, died the year before Anna was born. The first, Henriette, died when Anna was seven years old. The parents were duly concerned about their third and only surviving daughter. And they became proud of their youngest offspring, Wilhelm. He satisfied their wish for a male child (Rosenbaum, 1984a).

So Anna, looking for a quiet solution to her combative, dreary life, entered another world. She nursed her father and daydreamed. She embellished her meager opportunities by creating her own "private theater." Always ready with a reply whenever anyone addressed her, inwardly she was elsewhere, enjoying her fanciful thoughts.

Early in her father's illness, Anna devoted extraordinary efforts to his rehabilitation, fiercely determined to nurse him. She slept in the morning, napped in the afternoon, and stayed awake all night, all the while resenting Wilhelm's complete freedom from nursing responsibilities.

Eventually, Anna needed a longer rest each afternoon. Then, in the early evening, she fell into a fitful, trance-like state. Her habitual daydreaming became her affliction. It laid the foundation for a dissociation, or "split," in her personality (Breuer, 1895). On emerging from this abnormal state, she became agitated and began to cough. The coughing worried her mother, who decided that her daughter had a lung infection, perhaps acquired from her father. So Anna, relieved of her post, tired and sometimes refusing to talk or eat, stayed in bed all day.

The family thereby had a pair of patients, father and daughter, and two caretakers, mother and nurse. Meanwhile Wilhelm pursued his legal studies.

In late November 1881, Anna's mother contacted Dr. Joseph Breuer, an energetic, young physician with reddish-blond hair and a full beard. Breuer knew about this wealthy family, just as its members knew of this kindly, eminent physician. He enjoyed a high reputation throughout Vienna as a medical practitioner and a man of science (Bloch, 1984; Strachey, 1955).

The Work of Psychology

Like Breuer, some psychologists today work both sides of the street, engaging in research and practice. They find the change of focus stimulating. Moreover, research and practice can inform one another. But most professionals today do not have the time, energy, up-to-date training, or appropriate opportunity for steady efforts in both domains.

With the entrance of Breuer in 1881, the sophisticated reader perhaps has recognized the young woman in the story as Anna O. Because she is known throughout psychology as the patient most solely responsible for the origins of modern psychotherapy, many people think that she underwent psychoanalysis. This view is incorrect. She never experienced any form of psychoanalysis and, in fact, vigorously rejected the whole idea later, not only for herself but for others as well (Edinger, 1968; Freeman, 1972).

Breuer gained his lofty reputation through science, not medical practice, and he achieved his first scientific success when still in his twenties. Intrigued because people inhale and exhale so automatically, he wondered how breathing is so well regulated. Like others, he thought the vagus nerve might be influential in that process.

In his first experiments, he studied his own breathing. Then he turned to dogs and cats and even rabbits, blocking their airways, inflating their lungs with a balloon, and so forth. When oxygen was limited, the animals' vagus nerve stimulated increased activity in the respiratory system. When oxygen was plentiful, it retarded activity. Breuer thus established the vagus nerve as the seat of automatic control of breathing. This reflexive activity is now known as the Hering-Breuer reflex in honor of his work with a colleague, Ewald Hering.

After catching his breath, the busy Breuer turned to study the ways people maintain their balance, again in his crude laboratory of homemade apparatus in his attic. This time he began with birds and fish, then progressed to people, examining tiny cavities in the inner ear. These cavities contain a fluid called endolymph. Movements of the head or whole body are registered by the flow of this liquid in the cavity, which bends tiny nerve cells in one direction or another. This discovery, made independently and simultaneously by Ernst Mach, is loosely known today as the Mach-Breuer flow theory of the endolymph in the inner ear (Hirschmüller, 1989).

Scientists and Practitioners

In these instances, Breuer acted as a **scientist,** a person who investigates natural phenomena by using systematic, objective procedures, including empiricism and rationalism. Scientists make discoveries, commonly spurred by technology. Many engage in **basic research,** seeking knowledge for its own sake, aiming to increase our understanding of ourselves and our universe. Others engage in **applied research,** aiming to improve the conditions of everyday life. Scientists of both types seek descriptions, explanations, predictions, and sometimes control. Their work produces the findings and techniques that comprise the field of psychology.

Expressed as a metaphor, scientists pursue both light and fruit. Those in basic research seek light, testing theories and advancing general knowledge. Those in applied research seek fruit, providing new ways and means for society.

Assisting an ill person, Breuer behaved as a **practitioner,** someone who carries out a special service, usually for clients or patients. Practitioners work in **applied psychology,** providing services by using the methods and findings from basic and applied research. But the boundaries between basic research and applied psychology are variable. Applied psychology may create knowledge that is useful in research, as well as vice versa. Through their work, sometimes called **private practice,** practitioners provide various services: as expert witnesses in courts of law, advisors to schools, therapists for adjustment disorders, and especially as consultants for all sorts of marital, family, business, health, career, and even political and performance issues.

In summary, scientists usually study a narrow slice of behavior in many people, aiming to discover a universal law or principle. Practitioners often study a broad array of behaviors in a particular instance, seeking a solution to a specific problem confronted by a certain individual or group.

A universal experience in daily life provides an illustration of this difference between research and practice. We all engage in this activity—sleep.

Years ago, scientists studying infants' sleep came almost by chance on a key to dreaming. They noticed large, coordinated *rapid eye movements,* much like those of a spectator at a tennis match. Thinking this finding worthy of research, they recruited adult sleepers, painted their eyelids black, and then shined a flashlight on them while they were sleeping. The flashlight enabled them to scrutinize the sleepers' eye movements under the eyelids, and the black paint prevented the sleepers from being aroused by the light. The investigators awakened 10 sleepers, sometimes during these rapid eye movements and sometimes when they were not occurring. When awakened during rapid eye movements, nearly 80% reported dreams; when awakened with no rapid eye movements, only about 20% reported dreams (Aserinsky & Kleitman, 1953, 1955). This unexpected finding launched legions of scientific studies on sleep, providing an early means of studying dreams and assistance in identifying various stages of sleep.

Practitioners in psychology, as members of the National Sleep Foundation, have promoted the public understanding of sleep and its disorders: presenting lectures, writing books, conducting workshops, and operating sleep clinics. Naps, for example, have gained a bad reputation. The public considers them something for babies, sissies, and the elderly. The expression "caught napping" reveals this misconception, suggesting that a nap is a sign of laziness, if not poor health. But in today's high-speed, global economy, people facing a demanding circumstance can perform more rapidly, intelligently, and safely after a "power nap" of just a few minutes. Inspired by the National Sleep Foundation, campaigns for napping are making special headway among international travelers, and many computer industries now provide a designated nap room (Dement & Vaughan, 1999).

In their approach to sleep, or any other human activity, scientists are *explorers* in a mental realm. Practitioners are *facilitators* or agents, providing a service. But in psychology, both are called by the same name: *psychologists.*

This condition divides the field, confuses the public, and generally does not occur in other disciplines. Scientists who investigate the human body are known as biologists. The practitioners are physicians; they heal and protect it. Some physicians may engage in research, but biologists do not practice medicine. Scientists who study force and motion are known as physicists; practitioners are called engineers (Hilgard, 1988). In the production and consumption of goods and services, the scientists are economists; the practitioners are businessmen and businesswomen. The public typically recognizes similar divisions of labor between mathematicians and statisticians, sociologists and social workers, and so forth, but not within the field of psychology.

To stay abreast of recent developments, scientists and practitioners in psychology generally confine themselves to one realm or the other, although many become involved in related roles, such as teaching, writing, administration, social reform, and so forth. In any case, referring to scientists and practitioners by the same name—psychologists—contributes to a major schism in a field already marked by diversity. Most psychologists share certain standards of training and knowledge of psychology, but scientists and practitioners use different methods, seek different explanations, and work toward different goals (Kimble, 1984; Rice, 1997).

Psychology's Dual Goals

In understanding psychology's dual goals, two related terms become important. In earlier years, they created considerable controversy; today they provide useful labels for the different works of scientists and practitioners.

Scientists in psychology seek to understand humanity, just as scientists in geology seek to understand the structure of the earth. In all fields, scientists try to discover general principles. In psychology, this endeavor is called **nomothesis,** for it aims to discover the ways human beings are alike—and to describe people in general, or categories of people, such as migrant workers, single parents, practicing dentists, and adolescent girls. The expression comes from the Greek *nomo* meaning law, and *thesis,* meaning to advance or put forth a proposition of some sort. In nomothesis, scientists seek to understand the many; they try to identify universal principles and behaviors occurring in most members of a species. In studying the ways living organisms maintain their balance, Breuer was engaged in nomothetic inquiry, examining birds, then fish, and then people, all to understand basic physical processes in each species.

In contrast, practitioners commonly study a specific case. Often, they aim to solve some practical problem. This work in psychology is called **idiography,** for it focuses on understanding a single instance—a particular person, event, small group, institution, or whatever. The expression comes from the Greek *idio,* meaning individual or particular, and *graphy,* which is a description.

In his attempts to assist Anna with her particular adjustment disorder, Breuer engaged in idiographic inquiry. He focused only on understanding her.

In psychology, nomothesis is commonly the business of the scientist, idiography more often the work of the practitioner. But there are exceptions, and there is an interplay between these dual goals. Findings from nomothetic inquiry become useful in studying a particular case. Whatever is true for the group may be true for an individual. And the reverse sometimes occurs. Idiographic inquiry leads to ideas about people in general. Whatever is true for the individual may be true for the group.

Throughout much of modern psychology, nomothetic and idiographic goals have been regarded as distinct and incompatible, prompting intense debate and efforts to settle the matter (Holt, 1962). Which approach is most appropriate for studying humanity? Recently, the controversy has subsided, partly because the question is no longer regarded as an either-or issue.

Oriented to research, nomothesis prevails in scientific psychology, just as it does in other sciences, ranging from astronomy to zoology. Investigators aim to understand the common properties of a class of events, people, or other phenomena. The focus is on general principles, and this book is directed to that goal. In idiography, investigators move in a different direction, toward the particular. Most practitioners in psychology address a specific problem in everyday life, seeking to understand its distinguishing features, discovering the ways it is typical and distinct among members of its class. The narrative of Anna illustrates this challenge.

In fact, human beings study and explain themselves in both ways. As evident throughout this book, we commonly adopt a scientific approach, organized around careful reasoning and empirical support. That pathway is analytical and direct. As illustrated in the story of Anna, we sometimes employ a more open approach, organized around an unfolding sequence of events over a period of time. That narrative pathway becomes more interpretive, affective, and global (Bruner, 1990; McAdams & Pals, 2006).

In the mass media, idiographic studies, narrative descriptions, and psychologists' practical works often receive greater attention than do the less dramatic, more impersonal nomothetic endeavors. Human beings are ever ready to examine another person's life, especially in a tale of inspirational recovery, awesome heroism, or, alas, hardship and disaster. For this reason, and because both scientists and practitioners are known as psychologists, the public wrongly assumes that psychologists aim to scrutinize people's private lives. But scientists maintain no such professional interests at all, and practitioners do so only when asked to intervene.

Privately a dedicated scientist, Breuer made his living as a practitioner. And in those early days, lacking modern medical knowledge and instruments, he made house calls regularly, as expected at that time. Patients too poor to afford house calls went to physicians' homes for treatment. When they were too rich or busy to be inconvenienced by a doctor's visit, they sent a servant to describe their symptoms and bring back a cure (Holzman, 1984). Physicians abandoned these practices only after improvements in medical equipment made office visits essential.

Breuer visited Anna in the family's luxurious apartment on Lichtensteinstrasse. Immediately, he noticed her cough. It sounded more like a nervous habit than a symptom of an infectious disease. Her face twitched and jerked in painful ways, and something had gone wrong with her vision. She squinted constantly. Breuer diagnosed the cough as tussis hysteria, a nervous reaction, and classified the patient as mentally ill. In fact, he diagnosed Anna's overall condition as hysteria, which meant that she suffered from emotional instability with a variety of unexplained physical ailments.

Indeed, Anna's illness included many of the most dramatic symptoms of her day. At that time, when hysteria appeared more frequently, such a case was not quite so startling as it might seem today. Many components are now diagnosed separately or assigned to other categories. The symptoms remain but not in the concentrated, flagrant form observed earlier (Micale, 2000).

Something else caught Breuer's attention. Anna's dress and demeanor did not reflect her age. In an era when young women usually married in their teens, 21-year-old Anna seemed unprepared for a relationship of that sort. Instead, she acted like a much younger person, displaying no awareness of sexuality.

Today Anna might receive a multiple diagnosis, for she exhibited several categories of symptoms. Among them would be *depression,* which is marked by a sad or irritable mood, no pleasure in life, inability to concentrate, and other signs. Depression has been called the "common cold of modern psychiatry," not because it is of little consequence but because it pervades our society, apparently augmented by the dramatically increased pace and complexity of modern life.

Anna suffered still another problem. Her consciousness alternated between two conditions. In her normal state, she remembered things and followed her usual routines, though she was often sad or anxious. In the other state, she became tormented by melancholy daydreams and vivid hallucinations that left a gap in her memory. Talking incoherently, she would stop in the middle of some words, then resume talking nonsense, only to pause again and again, apparently forgetting what she had just been saying. In her normal moments, she called this second state "time missing."

Breuer began daily visits in November, observing Anna's alternating consciousness. In the abnormal condition, she became rude and markedly disoriented. She claimed that black snakes dominated her life. In her mind, they were everywhere, especially in her hair and ribbons. They even emerged from the ends of people's fingers (Breuer, 1882).

Breuer wondered how far his patient's statements could be trusted. Did she really see black snakes in her hair? Was she unable to hear sometimes? Was she truly unable to speak? He scrutinized his daily reports for consistency and details, and he found no discrepancies. Later he compared Anna's reports with those in her mother's diary, and they too were consistent. Even with his scientific concern for precision, he found no reason to doubt Anna's complaints. She perhaps misinterpreted some of her symptoms, but her accounts were "entirely truthful and trustworthy" (Breuer, 1895).

So Breuer turned to hypnosis. Viennese physicians in the 19th century sometimes employed this procedure in the traditional fashion. Breuer prepared Anna, induced the hypnotic state, and found that she promptly fell into a trance. She also appeared semi-hypnotic after a deep sleep. But in neither state did she emerge from her illness.

Worse yet, Anna vigorously opposed all other therapies. Hypnosis caused no pain, but cold baths, hot showers, electric shock, bitter medicines, and rough massage were another matter. They aroused her very active resistance. Had she been faking, the threat of these drastic treatments surely would have compelled her to abandon any false claims.

In greatly modified form, derivatives of these therapies appear today. Preceded by medication, modern electric shock involves relatively little pain. And it is directed to the central nervous system, not the disabled body part, as in Breuer's day. No longer bitter, current medications are far more effective in suppressing symptoms. Modern science continues to expand the range and effectiveness of all sorts of treatments.

Scope of Modern Psychology

Science advances through the accumulation of reliable research findings, considered the facts of the discipline. Among the older sciences, such as astronomy, it commonly does so within the framework of an overall model, one that structures the way scientists think about their field.

This model, called a **paradigm**, serves a guidance function, presenting a generally accepted approach to the whole field during a particular era. More pervasive and influential than simply a theory, it presents scientists and practitioners with a set of assumptions about what is to be studied and a set of research methods about how those phenomena should be examined. In a broad sense, a paradigm dictates the rules that the whole field follows

(Kuhn, 1970). In metaphorical terms, it can be considered a guiding light for the field, reflecting general agreement on basic issues.

A paradigm serves a science at a certain time in its history. Offering a geocentric view of the earth as the center of our universe, the third-century Ptolemaic paradigm dominated astronomy for hundreds of years. But as astronomers obtained more and more data about celestial bodies, Ptolemaic explanations became increasingly complex and cumbersome. Eventually, this model gave way to the 15th-century Copernican view, which placed the sun at the center of our universe. Advancing the field in this new direction, the Copernican model then became astronomy's paradigm.

In physics, Aristotle's view of the composition of matter prevailed until superseded by Newton's 17th-century mechanical model. That viewpoint, in turn, has been broadly generalized by Einstein's 20th-century relativity paradigm (Watson, 1967). Science progresses through the accumulation of facts, especially when they lead to a new paradigm, thereby inaugurating a scientific revolution (Kuhn, 1970). Scientists in the field then move in the new direction.

The evolutionary viewpoint functions as a paradigm in modern biology, providing a rough map or blueprint of unknown territory. The discovery of DNA has supported this model, offering a mechanism for understanding evolution. But psychology, a near neighbor of biology in some respects, remains without a paradigm. In contrast to the natural sciences, which are older and more basic, it has no unifying model to indicate which phenomena should be studied and how they should be approached. Disagreement continues even about the limits of this broad field. Can it and should it continue to incorporate dimensions of both the natural and social sciences?

Psychological Perspectives

At this stage, modern psychology does not "speak with one mind." Two conditions impede this unification: its immense breadth and its brief history. The challenge is too much for such a short time span. Lacking a paradigm, psychology instead has experienced a series of competing systems or schools of thought, each clearly less encompassing than a paradigm. Almost as old as the field itself, they have been conceived differently over the years, and today psychologists speak of them as trends and perspectives in psychology (Robins, Gosling, & Craik, 1999). Thus a **psychological perspective** presents a point of view and certain assumptions about psychology's goals and methods of achieving them, but its boundaries and assumptions become too confining for most members of the field. Offering no overall guidance, a perspective does not function as a paradigm. It offers instead a particular outlook or approach to the field. Collectively, these successive perspectives might be called "psychologies." Without unifying the field, they provide separate frameworks for organizing data and constructing theories in a coherent fashion (Smith, 2001).

Since the founding of modern psychology with Wundt's first laboratory, a new psychological perspective has appeared approximately every 20 to 30 years. They have often arisen as protests against a preceding perspective regarded as too narrow or based on inadequate premises. Or they have emerged in the context of broad social unrest or change. In either case, the new perspective conceives the boundaries or tasks of psychology differently, setting practical limits within the immense domain of modern psychology. After gaining prominence, each has made an indelible contribution to mainstream psychology. But each, with its parochial view, has failed to achieved the status of a paradigm.

Some perspectives have attained popularity among the public: psychoanalysis, behaviorism, and humanistic psychology. Others, with more rapidly changing boundaries, remain known largely within the field: biological psychology, cognitive psychology, and evolutionary psychology. Each of them affords a different view of the field today.

As with the founding of psychology, the first dates and early leaders of these perspectives are open to some debate. The origins of biological psychology might be assigned to the middle of the 20th century, with the first studies of electrical brain stimulation, or to psychology's earliest days. Wundt came to psychology from physiology and philosophy, calling his early text *Physiological Psychology*, although today we might view it as experimental psychology.

Psychoanalysis became prominent early in the 20th century, followed by behaviorism and eventually humanistic psychology. Then, almost a century after the founding of Wundt's laboratory, modern cognitive psychology emerged, supported in no small way by the development of special instruments for measuring mental activities. In fact, the long-term success of any psychological perspective depends on its capacity for making precise measurements. The most recent perspective, evolutionary psychology, lay fallow until the end of the 20th century, although much earlier Charles Darwin had declared that the theory of evolution offered a new basis for psychology (Darwin, 1859).

After a pair of introductory chapters, this book describes these perspectives chronologically, each in its own chapter. Toward the end, it makes comparisons among them, showing their similarities and differences. In this way, it provides a framework for grasping the field as a whole.

> **2000 Evolutionary**
> Buss, *Evolutionary Psychology*
>
> **1970 Cognitive**
> Neisser, *Cognitive Psychology*
>
> **1950 Humanistic**
> Rogers and Maslow
>
> **1930 Behavioristic**
> Pavlov and Skinner
>
> **1900 Psychoanalytic**
> Freud, *Interpretation of Dreams*
>
> **1870 Biological**
> Wundt, *Physiological Psychology*

Figure 1.1   Overview of the Perspectives. Depicting a trend, inaugural dates have been set at the beginning of the decade closest to the first textbook or other major publication in that perspective. Or they reflect the beginning of the decade that falls between the major works of co-founders. Behaviorism, for example, might be assigned to Watson's earlier work, but Pavlov and Skinner provided the conceptual bases of modern approaches.

Specific dates: Wundt, 1874; Freud, 1900; Pavlov, 1927 and Skinner, 1938; Rogers, 1942 and Maslow, 1954; Neisser, 1967; and Buss, 1999.

These perspectives have created rivalries and allegiances among psychologists, a condition generally regarded as a sign of health in science. As one advances, it challenges another, and a controversy ensues, which is resolved through further research. Eventually some old views become deposed, and some new ones become ascendant and flourish for a time, which is the way of all science (Figure 1.1).

These six perspectives reflect the diversity in modern psychology. Most of them insist on an objective approach, but a few study subjective experience. Some concentrate on narrow aspects of behavior, such as neural pathways and biochemical conditions. Others consider broader issues—family, personal development, aggression, and friendship patterns. In short, these perspectives offer a range of views about human activities and experiences.

Subfields and Specialties

Some of these perspectives, especially behaviorism, remain unmistakably systematic in their research assumptions, methods, and goals. Followers agree on the core concepts, ways of collecting data, and constructing theories. They are sufficiently doctrinaire to be considered "schools" of psychology. Others, such as biological and cognitive psychology, are less systematic, less doctrinaire, and more open to various approaches within their sphere of interest. In this way, they are more like subfields.

Difficult to define, a **subfield in psychology** is essentially a broad area of research interest; its followers are more oriented to that subject matter than to certain core concepts and ways of investigating them. The distinctions between a subfield and perspective at times may be vague or variable, but often a subfield promotes greater latitude in research and less restriction in overall goals. Major subfields include social, developmental, personality, and cultural psychology, as well as psychopathology, formerly known as abnormal psychology.

In the practice of psychology, a certain topical interest is often called a **psychological specialty,** indicating a service or a function to be performed, often narrowly defined. However, clinical psychology is broadly concerned with behavior disorders. More restricted in scope, other specialties range from academic assessment to sports psychology, from genetic counseling to urban planning.

Discussions of perspectives, subfields, and specialties are open to debate; distinctions are sometimes elusive or arbitrary. They point instead to psychology's diverse goals, interests, and areas of endeavor. In this respect, they underscore psychology's **pluralism,** a philosophical doctrine emphasizing the multiplicity and diversity of things in the world at large. No single perspective, subfield, or specialty can account for all the phenomena in any sphere of human life. Contemporary psychology is not a single, coherent system. It is a diverse field, reflecting different perspectives, each aiming in its own way to understand normal and abnormal behavior and experience.

Even today, psychologists would struggle to understand Anna's abnormal conditions. During "time missing," where was her consciousness? What had she been thinking? She began to call these abnormal states "absences" because they left her without any awareness of the preceding interval. With his limited background, Breuer's attempts at alleviation were little more than trial-and-error efforts. He had no theory, much less a therapeutic regimen.

In the middle of one of her absences, he repeated a word she had murmured, and she slowly broke her limited speech. In a halting style, she began to tell him what was on her mind. As she continued, her speech improved; she regained some grammar and pronunciation. When she finished, Anna had fashioned a very simple report, almost like a fairy tale. Most important, she seemed to feel better.

Gradually a pattern developed. As each night wore on, she became increasingly restless and slept poorly. In the morning she lapsed once more into her abnormal state, experiencing hallucinations. Then, in the evening, Breuer arrived. Using Anna's earlier words as start signals, he prompted her to describe the daytime hallucinations, and afterward she seemed relieved again. If Breuer missed a daily visit, causing her to forego a story, she missed the ensuing comfort (Breuer, 1882).

By this time, Breuer had discarded the hypnotic technique. Anna produced reams of material anyway, without the trance-like state. Slowly, her reports progressed to spontaneous storytelling, sometimes even without a signal from Breuer. He simply tried to be a good listener. For three months, Anna kept talking; he paid close attention, and by March, several of her symptoms had diminished, including her difficulties with speech.

She worried constantly about her father and asked to see him. Her mother refused each request, thinking a visit might aggravate her daughter's disorder. For this reason too, Breuer never doubted Anna's symptoms. They prevented her from achieving her passionate, genuine desire—to visit her fatally ill father. Nevertheless, after almost daily therapy, she felt much better. And by April, she left her bed. She had made remarkable progress.

So there stood Anna, experiencing health and fulfillment one moment, illness and frustration the next. Her consciousness fluctuated too, as happens to all of us, although generally to lesser extremes. Human beings are thinking, emotional creatures. Understanding the intricacies of the human mind in its diverse modes has become a monumental challenge for psychology. But the field no longer remains confined to studies of the mind or investigations of health and illness. It stretches across the full range of human activity and experience.

Summary

The Founding of Psychology

For developing a research laboratory in psychology at the University of Leipzig, Germany in 1879, Wilhelm Wundt gained recognition as the founder of modern psychology. Since Wundt's day, the field has expanded enormously, ranging today from the natural sciences to the humanities. As a science, modern psychology relies on empiricism and rationalism in pursuit of its goals. It also relies on peer review of research reports. In this way psychology, like all sciences, serves as its own authority.

Key Terms: **psychology, empiricism, data, rationalism, theory, science**

The Work of Psychology

Unlike most other academic and professional fields, psychology includes both scientists and practitioners. The scientists engage in basic research. They are investigators or finders; they study people or selected groups of people, aiming to understand their behavior. The practitioners apply psychology in everyday situations. They are servers or users; they often study a particular instance or one person, using psychological methods and findings to improve human functioning. These two spheres of work loosely reflect psychology's dual goals, nomothesis and idiography—the search for universals and study of the particular, respectively.

Key Terms: **scientist, basic research, applied research, practitioner, applied psychology, private practice, nomothesis, idiography**

Scope of Modern Psychology

With its brief history and immense diversity, modern psychology has no overall viewpoint, or paradigm, guiding the field. Instead, different perspectives have arisen as guidelines for collecting facts and developing theories about them. The major systematic perspectives today include biological, psychoanalytic, behavioristic, humanistic, cognitive, and evolutionary psychology. With this diversity, psychology reflects pluralism, meaning that no single outlook can account for all its diverse phenomena.

Key Terms: **paradigm, psychological perspective, subfield in psychology, psychological specialty, pluralism**

Critical Thinking

1. A strange sickness has appeared among neighborhood cats. Explain how the combined use of rationalism and empiricism may lead to an understanding of this condition.

2. Suppose a senior citizen consults a nutritionist about chronic fatigue. Indicate why a successful outcome may depend on nomothetic *and* idiographic inquiry.

3. Compare in a general way the work of scientists and practitioners in psychology. Then, using an example, show how research in psychology may inform the practice of psychology and how practice may inform research.

2

Research Methods

M odern psychology emerges from its research. Without formal research methods, psychology would become mere speculation and common sense about human behavior, based on personal experience. In a large measure, the various perspectives in psychology arise from these methods. But which data are obtained? By what methods? How are they analyzed? Answers to these questions shape every perspective. In fact, a major challenge for each perspective, and for psychology in general, is to bring about improvements in research methods.

This chapter begins with the challenge of collecting data, emphasizing the problem of precision in measurement. Then it turns to the basic research methods, experimental and descriptive. The task of analyzing the data concludes this discussion.

The Research Challenge

In any research, the goal is to obtain findings that are reliable, valid, and also substantial. A finding that is stable and dependable shows **reliability.** It reappears consistently with repetition of the same research procedures. In other words, the result is predictable. A finding with high **validity** measures what it purports to measure. It is justified and well-founded. If it claims to show age differences in risk-taking behavior among male human beings, for example, it does indeed reveal a measurable, significant difference between young and old men engaging in unnecessarily hazardous activities.

Of these qualities, validity is the most important. A valid measure includes high reliability, assessing accurately and therefore reliably whatever it is intended to measure. It does not yield markedly different results from one instance to another. Exceptions occur only when the characteristic itself is unstable. For example, mood, hunger, and other temporary conditions may vary unpredictably when measured at different times.

Finally, a substantial finding is widely respected and cited. In fact, it becomes substantial to the extent that it is employed by scientists pursuing related activities.

By today's standards, Breuer encountered no substantial research findings to assist him in working with Anna. Even the few recognized results were of doubtful validity. Moreover, he possessed inadequate research methods and instruments for collecting information about her reactions—physical, mental, and emotional. Indeed, the intrepid Breuer had little but sagacity and perseverance in his favor.

And suddenly his efforts seemed all for naught. Four days after Anna left her bed, her father died, and she relapsed, becoming bed-ridden again, falling into even more profound "absences" and experiencing more terrifying hallucinations.

Anna described how she had been alone one night with her father, frightened and fatigued, awaiting the arrival of a surgeon, with her right arm around the back of a chair. And, alas, she started to fall asleep. In these moments, just before and after sleep, visual images appear most vividly. She suddenly experienced hallucinations of black snakes crawling out of the wall, and she could not drive them away, her right arm having "fallen asleep." Worse yet, her fingers had become little black snakes, and her fingernails had turned into death's heads. Anna had always feared snakes and tried to pray, but she could not speak—until the arrival of the surgeon broke the spell.

Her relations with her mother and brother also had worsened. She could feel a stream of unpleasant heat from her mother; another heat wave, not quite so bad, came from Wilhelm. In English, she called them both "stoves." She claimed she could detect her mother's presence before anyone else sensed it in any way. It agitated her intensely.

Basic Research Approaches

In resuming their sessions, Breuer was continuing his earlier work, not as a scientist but as a practitioner. He sought to provide therapy for a disturbed person, not to study breathing or balance in a certain species.

In his laboratory studies, Breuer-the-scientist had used experimental methods, involving the manipulation of one or more factors and the control of others, to discover what causes what. Manipulation and control form the basis of the experimental method, which often requires a restricted setting. To find out which nerve pathways influence breathing, Breuer manipulated the oxygen supply of animals and people and controlled their exercise. Then he observed the results. Experimental methods show something about the *why* of behavior. They can demonstrate a *causal association*, meaning a cause-and-effect relationship, showing that one event influences another. Breuer found that the vagus nerve causes changes in the rate of breathing.

Occasionally psychologists perform experiments outside the laboratory, taking advantage of a natural setting, which nevertheless limits the manipulation and control of variables. But some limitation occurs in *every* experiment, and indeed in research of any type.

In a restrained way, Breuer used some manipulations with Anna. When she made inadequate progress with traditional hypnosis, he changed to hypnotic suggestion, using it at the beginning of each session. After that effort failed, he spoke relevant words to help Anna begin her story, presenting them as "start" signals. But with little precision and few methods of control, these trial-and-error procedures were not scientific experiments.

Instead, Breuer-the-practitioner used **descriptive methods**, which portray or describe behavior and experience in detail. They depict the reactions of living organisms and factors related to them, but there is no effort at precise manipulation or control. Breuer simply listened to Anna during therapy, observed her outside of therapy, and studied her through the reports of others. Descriptive methods show the *what* of behavior; they depict a person or group through direct observation, self-reports, and other information. They can reveal a *correlational association,* meaning that there is a relationship between two or more events but with no evidence that one causes another. They simply vary together in similar or consistently different ways.

Throughout psychology, research methods often fall into these two major categories, experimental and descriptive. The several experimental methods devote special attention to manipulation and control, gaining a high degree of precision. As a rule, they are used most prominently in the biological, behavioral, and cognitive approaches. The other perspectives employ experimental methods but not with the emphasis observed in that trio.

The descriptive methods take advantage of less controlled, more natural settings, which thereby limit precision. Naturalistic observation is the least controlled method, followed by the case study, prominent in traditional psychoanalysis and humanistic psychology. Like all perspectives, evolutionary psychology uses a range of methods, especially the survey. But in all instances, there are tradeoffs. Limitations occur in every study of any sort. The investigator develops the best possible approach in a given situation, mindful of its limitations (Figure 2.1).

All investigators must be mindful as well of the *ethical standards for research,* a set of guidelines published by the American Psychological Association.

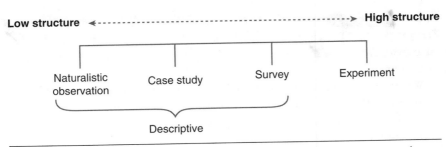

Figure 2.1   **Descriptive and Experimental Research Methods.** Structure refers to the degree of intervention and control by the investigator, which is low for the descriptive methods and much higher for experimental research. Each method includes specific techniques, and sometimes methods are combined.

In conjunction with review boards, these standards establish guidelines for relationships with participants, confidentiality, and related issues (Sales & Folkman, 2000).

If the results of any investigation, experimental or descriptive, appear useful to others in the field, the investigator publishes them in a scholarly journal. Psychology advances through these reports, which include a detailed description of the people or animals that were studied. These reports also describe the apparatus and present a step-by-step statement of the research procedure. In addition, all important terms are precisely defined. Investigations purporting to be scientific must provide unambiguous definitions of the central concepts, enabling peers and subsequent investigators to repeat the research and determine the reliability of the findings.

The Problem of Definitions

All fields of inquiry encounter problems of definition, but they confront them differently. Scholars in the humanities sometimes debate *essentialism,* a philosophical position that concentrates on the indispensable qualities of something—the properties that make it what it is and not something else. This focus on essential properties, as distinct from accidental characteristics, can point to large and perplexing questions: What is the essence of human altruism? Or true love? Or intelligence?

Scientists avoid such questions. They investigate the unknown but not the vague or abstract. They seek instead an understanding about a well-defined object or event or some part of that phenomenon, rejecting any notion that it is a complete explanation. Declarations about "final answers" prompt doubt among scientists.

Instead, scientists seek partial answers. They accept the philosophical principle of *operationalism,* stating that knowledge becomes meaningful only to the extent that explicit procedures for measurement—measuring operations—have been employed. The meaning of something lies within the limits of its measurement.

When these contrasting approaches are compared, essentialism seeks more comprehensive, fundamental definitions, however abstract and elusive. Operationalism strives for more precise, specific definitions, however narrow and incomplete.

On this basis an **operational definition** defines something by measuring it in terms of specific events, procedures, or operations. It relies on the process of *measurement,* which involves a comparison with a standard of some sort. Thus, an operational definition is commonly expressed in quantifiable units or recognized categories, thereby diminishing doubt. The concept it defines can be understood and examined by following the specified measuring operations. For this reason, operational definitions hold a central place in the science of psychology, especially in experimental and survey research.

Consider this human reaction: *Surprise!* John Keats said of his craft: "Poetry should surprise." Exactly what did Keats mean? What is surprise? How might the essentialist respond? In many areas of the humanities, there is little need for precision. In fact, some ambiguity may be desirable—but not for the scientist. In science, even a dictionary definition proves too vague: "surprise—to be caught unawares, to wonder or become amazed about something not anticipated." So the scientist creates a definition, an operational definition consistent with the research goal.

To study surprise, the scientist specifies operations for measuring surprise. These measuring operations might focus on physiological changes—pupil dilation, heartbeat, rate of breathing, and degree of vasoconstriction. Or they might assess surprise in terms of feelings. On a numerical scale from 1 to 10, a person rating herself 8 or higher, for example, might be defined as surprised. Or they might measure specific behaviors: moving the body backward, raising the eyebrows, opening the mouth, and spreading the fingers. Each of these behavioral reactions can be assessed and quantified by a panel of judges viewing a videotape. Or all of these measures can be employed together. Whenever several measurable criteria are included in one definition, they produce a *composite operational definition.*

Similarly, hunger can be operationally defined as the level of blood sugar, loss of body weight, number of hours since last eating, or a person's self-rating on a scale for feeling hungry. Employee attitudes toward work can be defined by the number of absences, promotions, complaints, tardy arrivals, errors on the job, awards for high performance, increases in salary, and the like. All these indicators rely on statistical measures; they can be combined to form a composite operational definition.

Incidentally, the fact that scientists employ operational definitions does not indicate personal disinterest in the broader issues of philosophy, religion, and ethics. They simply use operational definitions to do their work efficiently and productively. Moreover, psychologists engaged in less-structured research may not rely on operational definitions, remaining open to less-precise meanings.

The public sometimes criticizes psychology for its reliance on statistics, operational definitions, and narrowly defined questions, more so than it faults other sciences, partly because psychological questions have more personal significance than questions about such things as geology, astronomy, or physics. The public seeks full and final answers about family therapy, fanatical cults, and fantasy life. But psychology cannot give complete answers any more than modern biology or astronomy can provide ultimate answers to questions about the origins of life or the universe.

Research and Common Sense

The public also chides psychology for another reason. People think long and hard about themselves and their personal relationships. They become much more emotionally involved in questions of human behavior than in understanding why cars run smoothly, foreign governments fail, or crabgrass grows in the lawn. Through these ruminations, they develop a *common-sense psychology* based on personal experience and judgment. It emerges from their own cherished but untested ideas about human behavior, explaining its causes and consequences (Kelley, 1992). On this basis, they may erroneously decide that psychology offers only common-sense knowledge.

Sometimes research in psychology does support common sense. These instances should be gratifying because they suggest that we do learn something about human behavior during our everyday lives. But sometimes research contradicts common sense. Those instances are critical because science is generally regarded as the most reliable pathway to knowledge. A psychology that always supported common sense would be a wasteful enterprise. It would show us what we already know. Yet, a psychology that never supported common sense would be disturbing indeed. It would suggest a reality different from the one we think we know (Fernald, 1997).

Certainly, common sense did not give Breuer anything like a complete answer to Anna's problems, even after daily sessions for many months. Common-sense knowledge ranges from extensive and valid to wrong or useless, but Breuer had few ideas and no direct experience from which to work. He struggled to help Anna in a trial-and-error fashion.

Moreover, he struggled by himself. No colleague offered assistance. This puzzling case carried Breuer further and further into the unknown.

Throughout her unusual therapy, Anna called her monologues "chimney sweeping" because, in her mind, she entered dark, narrow, uncomfortable places, trying to remove the debris, trying to gain some relief from thoughts that caused her stress. Night after night throughout the winter, Anna described her troubling thoughts. After her storytelling, she emerged calmer and more cheerful. But she awoke the next day irritable and again beset by hallucinations. Always, more sweeping was needed, and Breuer came again and again to assist. By these slow, irregular steps, Anna began feeling better and gave this work a more dignified name, the "talking cure." This expression reflected a goal or hope, certainly not an achievement. Anna was far from healthy.

In late May, Breuer decided to transfer Anna to a one-story house in Inzersdorf, just outside Vienna. In this more restful setting, they could take advantage of nearby medical facilities. On nights when Anna was not calmed by the talking cure, Breuer prescribed five grams of chloral, producing a mild intoxication and several hours of sleep. In addition, Breuer could begin more intensive treatment with a medical staff readily available. He urged Anna to relate three to five stories each evening. Less imaginative than before, these stories dealt more directly with her hallucinations. In agitated fashion, she also described her monotonous life around the home. Listening to these extended monologues, Breuer speculated that her depression, self-starvation, and other symptoms arose in the family context.

Experimental Methods

In contrast to Anna's era, psychologists today study home and family influences. Using modern experimental methods, they manipulate one or more factors and control others, thereby examining cause-and-effect relations between family interactions and members' behavior. These methods include the classical experiment and three variations in experimental design.

The manipulated factor is often a **stimulus**, which is any event that elicits action. For example, someone is telling a story. A **response** is any activity that arises from stimulation, such as listening carefully, interrupting the speaker, or looking bored. Several stimuli and responses may be studied in one experiment, depending on the research plan or experimental design.

The Classical Experiment

One such experiment explored family influences on eating, drinking, and personal feelings. Sixty-four women participated. Like Anna, they were young, ranging from 18 to 31 years, and mostly unmarried; many were experiencing bulimia and other eating disorders. The experimenters assigned them randomly to one of two groups. In one group, the experimenters intentionally aroused thoughts of family interactions, the manipulated factor. In the other, they aimed to suppress thoughts of family interactions, eliciting instead random impersonal thoughts (Villejo, Humphrey, & Kirschenbaum, 1997). The purpose of this experiment was to discover whether thoughts of family interactions would influence performance on certain tasks, including eating, as well as feelings about oneself or others.

This experiment is called a **classical experiment** because all presumably influential factors are held constant or controlled except one. This single factor or variable is manipulated in restricted ways to discover its influence on various behaviors.

To maximize the equivalence of the groups, without bias toward one or the other, the group placement of the participants must be accomplished by **random assignment,** in which no known factor except chance alone has influenced the assignment. Or all participants must serve in both conditions, as in Breuer's experiment on breathing. Rarely, experimenters use *matched groups,* formed by creating pairs of participants closely equivalent in all important respects and then assigning each member of a pair to a different group.

The concept of random assignment is readily illustrated. Sometimes each potential participant is designated by a number, and then these numbers are assigned to one group or another by drawing them with a computer, from a hat, or using some other unbiased procedure. In contrast, *incidental assignment* involves no such randomized procedure. The subjects are chosen or assigned haphazardly, on the basis of availability, much as they might emerge from a supermarket. For obvious reasons, incidental assignment does not meet the standards of a true experiment.

After these random assignments, the group exposed to the manipulated factor is called the **experimental group.** The group not so exposed, or exposed in restricted ways, is the **control group,** and it offers a basis for comparison. If the two groups are equivalent in all relevant ways except for the manipulated factor, and if the outcomes for the two groups differ, then these outcomes can be attributed to the influence of the manipulated factor. Thinking about family interaction was the manipulated factor in this experiment.

How did the experimenters in the laboratory arouse these young women to thoughts of family interaction? And how did they observe its influence on eating, depression, or cooperation?

For practical reasons, families cannot be brought into the laboratory for extended observations. Even if they could, the members would not behave in their usual manner. And experimenters cannot regularly enter their homes, asking members to interact in one way or another or to live without any interaction. But in restricted ways, laboratory conditions can evoke responses to family life.

In the first phase of this experiment, both groups completed several challenging physical tasks and then rested while enjoying various foods and beverages. To diminish the likelihood that the participants would guess the purpose of this research, this phase was described as an exercise study.

In the second phase, the experimental group observed 64 statements about family life presented on a screen, one by one, at intervals of 15 seconds each. They read and concentrated on each statement and then indicated whether it was true or false, using a scale of 0 to 100. Some statements were positive: "My mother lets me speak freely and warmly and tries to understand me, even if we disagree." Others were negative: "My father tells me my ways are wrong and I deserve to be punished." Using these statements, thoughts of family interactions were activated in the experimental group.

The control group experienced a comparable procedure, but the statements they rated were impersonal, such as "Chicago is the 26th best metropolitan area in the United States." These neutral statements presumably evoked few or no thoughts of family life.

After the induction of family or neutral thoughts, all participants repeated the earlier physical tasks. As anticipated, after thoughts of family interactions were activated, women with pronounced eating disorders performed more slowly on the tasks, felt more negatively about the research, and showed more hostility in general. Moreover, they experienced greater feelings of hunger than did women without eating disorders or women exposed to neutral statements (Villejo, Humphrey, & Kirschenbaum, 1997). These findings support the view that family interaction may contribute to eating disorders.

In any experiment, there are conventional ways to refer to the basic variables. The manipulated factor is known as the **independent variable** because it is some stimulus under the independent control of the experimenter, which is manipulated according to the purpose of the research. The type of thought, family interaction, was the independent variable in this experiment, manipulated to discover its influence on eating. The experimental group was exposed to this variable, whereas the control group was not. Any difference in performance, therefore, should be attributable to the influence of the independent variable.

The **dependent variable** is some response that presumably depends on the independent variable. There may be more than one dependent variable. In this experiment, performance on physical tasks, feelings of hunger, and resistance to the research were dependent variables, presumably influenced by thoughts of family interaction.

All other potentially influential factors were held constant. Thus, the experiment became a controlled circumstance, not a naturally occurring event. Many laboratory and field experiments are designed in this way, using one independent variable.

In summary, the classical experiment answers this question: What happens when just this one variable—the independent variable—is manipulated? Does it change a dependent variable? The classical experiment is also called a *one-way design*, meaning it has only one independent variable.

There are several approaches to the one-way experimental design. The prior example is known as an *independent groups design* because participants were assigned randomly to perform in one group or the other. Another common approach is a *repeated measures design*, so-called because the same individuals perform under both conditions. They participate twice, serving in the experimental condition and also in the control condition, as their own control.

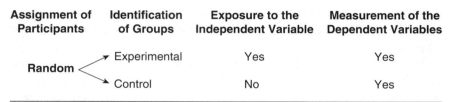

Assignment of Participants	Identification of Groups	Exposure to the Independent Variable	Measurement of the Dependent Variables
Random	Experimental	Yes	Yes
	Control	No	Yes

Figure 2.2   **A Classical Experimental Design.** Participants are assigned randomly to the experimental or control group. Only those in the experimental group are exposed to the independent variable. Afterward, both groups are measured on the dependent variables. Any difference between their scores on the dependent variables may be attributed to the influence of the independent variable.

Variations in Designs

A **research design** is a plan for research stating the expected participants, apparatus, procedures, and results. In the classical experimental design participants are randomly assigned into two groups for the study of one independent variable (Figure 2.2). In other instances, the research design becomes more complex, for the goal of research is to study the interaction among several independent variables, or factors, much as they occur in daily life. An experiment of this sort is called a **factorial design**; a two-way factorial design includes two independent factors or variables, a three-way design involves three independent variables, and so on.

In a factorial study of eating disorders in children, the experimenter might focus on family interaction, type of nutrition, and amount of physical exercise. Statistical analyses would be used to determine the influence, if any, exerted by each of these factors separately and in combination with one another. It might be found, for example, that family interaction is most influential in families with poor nutrition and infrequent exercise. If these conditions are not present, family interaction may have only a slight effect on eating disorders in children.

Sometimes an experiment cannot be performed in a laboratory because it would be too contrived, too artificial. Then a modified experiment might be conducted in everyday life, involving a different design. The experimenter perhaps cannot assign people randomly to different groups and cannot manipulate the independent variable in any precise way. For example, children cannot be assigned randomly to live in a harmonious or disruptive household, and the experimenter cannot control the nature of those family interactions. Recognizing these limitations, an experimenter may identify families already displaying these types of interactions and provide some of them with special activities or dinner guests intended to create harmonious family interactions during mealtime. The other families would be offered different mealtime diversions. After a certain period of exposure or lack of exposure to this intervention, the investigator would assess the eating behavior of children in both sets of families, make comparisons among them, and then draw some tentative conclusions. Research of this sort, based on comparisons between non-random groups, is known as a **quasi-experimental design** because it lacks the random assignments and control required in a true experimental design (Campbell & Stanley, 1963).

As a rule, experiments involve a number of people serving as subjects or participants, but a **single-participant experimental design** includes just one individual. An experiment with just a few participants, perhaps two to six or so, is called a *small-N experiment*, the N referring to the number of participants. Until recently, each individual studied in a research project was referred to as a *subject*. To be more respectful of the individual's contribution to the research, the term *participant* was introduced as a replacement. But the new term sometimes creates a misunderstanding, for all experiments and most research remain completely under the control of the investigator. The participant title overstates the case, especially in research with animals. For this reason, experiments with animals commonly refer to them as subjects.

One of the most renowned experiments in early 20th-century psychology involved just one subject—a horse—and it played a major role in our understanding of the research process. This horse, Clever Hans, apparently possessed some special mental powers, for he could answer correctly questions of all sorts presented by different people, tapping the answers by using a special chart constructed by his master. Eventually, a psychologist named Oskar Pfungst conducted experiments in which the questioner sometimes knew and sometimes did not know the answer to a question he posed for the horse. Thus it was discovered that Hans answered correctly only when his questioner knew the answer. Otherwise, he failed miserably. The horse tapped correctly by observing his knowledgeable questioner's subtle, unintentional head and body movements, unnoticed by human observers prior to Pfungst's research. These tiny cues indicated when to start and stop tapping (Fernald, 1984; Pfungst, 1911).

This finding began a long line of inquiry on non-verbal behavior that continues to this day. It also initiated the study of *experimenter effects,* referring to research outcomes that have been unintentionally influenced by the experimenter's hopes, plans, and personal interests in that research. Unconscious signaling is one such mechanism, prompting research participants to respond in some particular way, thereby favoring the expected outcome (Ambady & Rosenthal, 1993). Experimenter effects might be better called **investigator**

effects, for these unintentional influences on research outcomes can take place in almost any research, whether descriptive or experimental and involving a single participant or a whole group. The competent investigator cannot afford to overlook unintentional influences of any sort.

Breuer's work with Anna was not an experimental investigation, though applied psychologists sometimes do experimental research. His purpose was to help her. Rather than manipulating factors for research purposes, he made whatever adjustments might assist Anna, all the while listening to her endless stories, holding her hand, feeding her, and ruminating on her problems.

Descriptive Methods

As a practitioner, Breuer provided services using descriptive research methods. Less developed in his day, these methods now consist chiefly of naturalistic observation, the case study—which Breuer used with Anna—and also the survey. As a group, descriptive research methods do not offer manipulation and control, but they may take place in more natural, everyday settings.

One evening in her home, Anna told Breuer a story about her stockings. During her father's illness, she occasionally crept down the hall to his room, eavesdropping on his condition. For this purpose, she slept in her stockings. When Wilhelm once caught her listening, he grabbed her, shook her, and left her in an agitated state. After finishing this story, Anna began to cry softly. But she never again wore stockings to bed. In telling the story, she apparently relieved herself of much of the tension of that incident.

On another evening, she recalled one night in Vienna when she sat by her father's bedside, searching for any change in his condition. Concerned about the lateness of the hour, he asked her to tell him the time. With tears of sadness in her eyes, she made a great effort to look at her watch, bringing it close to her face. The watch at that point was blurred by her tears, which prompted her to squint. Attempting to suppress her tears, so they would not be noticed, she squinted again—and again. After she described the incident, her squinting habit receded.

Anna's storytelling was serving as therapy. After she recounted events related to the rise of a certain symptom, that symptom usually disappeared. It could be "talked away."

Breuer's sessions with Anna were not naturalistic observations, for he did more than observe and record. He urged her to talk, administered medications, and at times held her hand or served her food. These responses do not even qualify as participant observation, for Breuer was not simply participating in Anna's activities. Quite the contrary, he was trying to alter her behavior, helping her emerge from her trance-like states.

Naturalistic Observation

When people and animals are studied in their everyday settings, *without* intrusion of any sort, the process is called **naturalistic observation**. The aim is to describe their behavior just as it occurs—on the streets, in the forests, around the dinner table, at work, or anywhere else. The investigator simply observes and records what takes place, using audio–visual equipment or other types of apparatus when ethical conditions permit. Here the investigator has several options. After disclosing his research purposes, he may join the activities of the people he is observing, a procedure called **overt participation**. Another investigator, entering into the activities of her participants without revealing her intentions, engages in **covert participation**. She is obliged to follow precise ethical guidelines, especially in ensuring the anonymity of the participants in any dissemination of the findings. If she declares her purpose but remains apart from the participants, observing only, the procedure is known as **overt non-participation**. Still another investigator may not reveal his research intentions and not engage in any activities with the participants, a procedure called **covert non-participation**, which again raises ethical issues. In fact, all four approaches require careful management of the research data, including each participant's right to privacy.

For an investigator studying adolescents in their school cafeteria, using overt non-participant observation would allow the observer to remain in the cafeteria with them, openly observing and recording all events. But the students may behave differently knowing that they are being observed. The experienced investigator would attempt to diminish this influence by appearing regularly in the cafeteria prior to conducting the actual research, enabling the students to become accustomed to his or her presence. Or the investigator might employ covert participant observation, assuming the role of a new administrator in the school, but again, students might alter their behavior in this context. And the problem of the participants' informed consent must be addressed.

No procedure is perfect. Each has its advantages and disadvantages, and ethical guidelines have been established for each of them.

In all these procedures, the chief advantage of naturalistic observation lies in the setting. Everyday behaviors are observed in their normal or natural context. Investigators sometimes employ this method at the outset of a research program as a means of developing hypotheses for later study by other methods, particularly experimental methods. But the naturalistic method is costly in terms of the amount of information that can be collected within a given period.

These investigations may be idiographic, focused on a particular instance— one specific person, event, or small group. Or they may be nomothetic, studying some psychological characteristic in a large number of participants.

Naturalistic observation has been used to study the family dinner hour. In one instance, investigators employed overt non-participant observation with 20 families for three separate days, focusing on interactions among the members before and during mealtimes. All members agreed to be present without watching television, using the telephone, or having guests. Without any background information on the family, observers recorded the behavior of a specific child every six seconds, noting the ways that the child responded to other members.

Later, when the results were analyzed, the investigators found that the interactions in some families were stressful and negative. The members smiled infrequently, gave relatively little approval to one another, or were uninvolved with family activities—sitting, reading, or working alone. In these unresponsive or stressful families, some children appeared depressed; they cried and complained at twice the rates of children in other families (Messer & Gross, 1995).

These observations suggest a relationship between family interaction and childhood depression, but they do not show that one causes the other. In fact, both conditions perhaps are influenced by still other factors, such as poverty, ill health, and lack of education. The findings only reveal behavior, not its underlying causes and not the unspoken thoughts and feelings of those observed.

Anna's eating disorder and other problems perhaps had their origins in family interactions. But firm cause-and-effect conclusions cannot be derived through naturalistic observation or any other descriptive method, including the case study.

The Case Study

The traditional **case study** is an in-depth examination of a single instance, such as one teenager, a particular group discussion, or an institution. Thus the focus may range, for example, from the rehabilitation of an abused adolescent, to the personal relationships among certain faculty members, to the spectacular success of a specific business, each compiled using diverse methods. The case study may include psychological, biological, social, educational, biographical, and other relevant information. Typically, it employs interviews with the individuals most involved, such as family members, peers, and employers.

Among the major types of case studies, three are named according to the chief source of their data. In a **psychometric case study**, psychological tests and rating scales are administered to one or a few individuals, and the scores are analyzed for trends depicting traits and behaviors, all aimed at yielding greater understanding of the specific person or group. In developing an **archival case study**, the investigator works from files of all sorts, public and private, especially educational and career records, again seeking to identify the prominent factors influencing the behavior of the principal participants. Relatively rare, an **observational case study** is confined to direct observations in one or several settings, often without data from other sources. A fourth type, the **clinical case study**, employs a variety of data sources, especially individual and group interviews, and is typically devoted to assisting someone or some group with a problem of adjustment.

The case study thereby becomes a systematic statement about part of the life of a single unit and is necessarily selective. In fact, the case study is a common form of idiographic inquiry, examining a specific instance. But even when studying just one person or event, the whole story is too detailed or irrelevant for the immediate purpose (Runyan, 1984).

Lacking the rigorous methods of control in experimental research, the case study offers less opportunity for making comparisons and reaching firm conclusions. Diverse explanations become plausible, and the expertise of the investigator remains paramount. Nevertheless, the case study has contributed significantly to advancements in psychology, especially at the frontiers, stimulating hypotheses for later testing by more exact methods. Sigmund Freud's case studies led to psychoanalysis, those of Jean Piaget laid foundations for cognitive psychology, and numerous case studies of brain injury have opened up new lines of thought in biological psychology.

In one case, a teenager had been hospitalized six times for weight loss and rumination, an eating disorder in which a person regurgitates partly digested food, chews it again, and then swallows it once more. This problem began years earlier, when she weighed 120 pounds and entered an exercise program that included six hours of ballet each day. When the rumination appeared, it diminished her consumption of food, prompted chest pains during regurgitation, and contributed to enlargement of her salivary glands. Moreover, it left a foul odor on her breath.

In the hospital, weighing less than 90 pounds, she resisted treatment. She vomited into her clothes, hid food instead of eating it, and feigned increased weight by concealing objects on her person. The staff then force-fed her, but the problem remained.

On her seventh hospitalization, when she weighed only 78 pounds, she participated in family and individual therapy, gained an average of 2 pounds per week, and stabilized at 112 pounds. Although she denied ruminating, the staff found her with cheeks puffed out like a chipmunk, and a videotape showed that she ruminated up to one hour after a meal. She seemed to enjoy both remasticating her food and the reactions of others to this behavior.

On this basis, the hospital staff adopted the simplest of solutions. They offered the patient gum after her meals, and she responded well, chewing vigorously. Within a month, her rumination and chest pains disappeared. In follow-up studies one and two years later, she had not returned to rumination and proudly announced that chewing gum had become habitual (Weakley, Petti, & Karwisch, 1997). The therapists then published this case study as an aid to other practitioners dealing with similar problems and as a contribution to our general understanding of eating disorders.

A case study attempts to answer this question: How do we understand *this* particular instance? A study of Babe Ruth showed his extraordinary perceptual ability and quickness, as well as the capacity of early psychologists to make such measurements (Fuchs, 1998). Social psychologists studied a small religious sect in Chicago before and after their predicted date of world destruction, discovering the ways the members rationalized their behavior after their prophecy failed (Festinger, Riecken, & Schachter, 1956). Continuous studies of a man known as H.M., who underwent brain surgery for epilepsy, have indicated that the hippocampus plays a crucial role in the formation of long-term memories (Milner, Corkin, & Teuber, 1968).

The case study enables a psychologist to describe a person, event, or interacting group, but it cannot demonstrate with scientific certainty *why* a certain person became mentally ill or a particular group responded successfully to a natural disaster. Cause-and-effect answers cannot be obtained because the events, as individual instances, cannot be repeated. Anna cannot relive her life with different parents or without her brother, thereby providing an opportunity to assess experimentally the importance of those factors in her mental illness. The essential investigation cannot be performed, even as a single-subject experimental design.

More than any other method, the conclusions from a case study pertain to *that* particular case. That is its unique contribution and also its special limitation, for it is challenging indeed to determine if the findings can be usefully applied to other cases as well. The conclusions emerge from the investigator's interpretations of the data. They may or may not prove helpful elsewhere.

Survey Methods

A third descriptive method began to emerge around the time of Anna's illness, largely through the efforts of Charles Darwin and his cousin, Sir Francis Galton. Today it is well known. In the **survey method**, investigators obtain information about a large number of people, usually by asking them questions, observing them, consulting records, or examining the ways they respond to their environment. In the most common technique, the **questionnaire survey**, people are asked questions by mail, telephone, electronic means, or personal interview. These questionnaires, which do not require face-to-face contact, often include thousands of participants.

The survey serves nomothetic purposes. The aim is to discover universal principles about human beings or animals or certain categories of people or animals, for example, students in introductory psychology, beavers building dams, pregnant women, or species in other circumstances. No investigator can study all students, beavers, or pregnancies, and therefore sampling becomes an issue.

Survey research also may emerge from old records. These **archival studies** use information about people collected for other purposes. The investigator consults registration files, municipal records, library holdings, and other institutional depositories to obtain information on births, property, social events, crime, and so forth. If the information is not a matter of public record, special permission must be obtained for access, and all data must be kept confidential, ensuring anonymity for the participants.

In a rarer form of survey, called **physical traces**, investigators examine the ways people have responded to their environment by wearing it out or leaving materials after their departure. Museums, schools, zoos, and parks reveal the interests of their users through damaged and missing items, requests for bulletins, pathways in the grass, and so forth. Similarly, trash cans, rest rooms, and public walls show activities and attitudes through residual refuse and graffiti. But in contrast to other survey techniques, investigators can never be certain who left these traces in the first place.

Like all research methods, surveys have both assets and limitations. Their chief advantage is the large number of participants that can be included, especially with the use of electronic techniques for collecting and analyzing the data. But two limitations can be significant. First, in the questionnaire survey some people answer carelessly or incorrectly. Successful surveys require honest, accurate responses by the participants.

Second, a potential sampling problem arises. The value of a survey also depends on who responds to it. Some people who receive a questionnaire do not respond at all. The people who do respond often represent a **sample,** which is just part of a larger group called a population. This **population** includes all individuals, objects, or events in that particular category. A population might include all citizens of Austria as indicated by the 2004 census, all holidays in Vienna for a period of five years, or all foods rejected by a certain woman with an eating disorder. In a survey, the sample should be chosen by random selection, producing a *random sample,* in which every member of the population has an equal chance of being chosen. Or it can include carefully identified, systematic subsamples of the population, selected according to the demographic characteristics of that population. The aim is to obtain a **representative sample**, which accurately reflects the characteristics of the population from which it is drawn.

In one survey, investigators employed a questionnaire to ask a sample of 237 college students about eating disorders, body satisfaction, and symptoms of depression. They hypothesized that eating disorders would be related to body image and depression, as well as failed dieting. In addition, prior studies suggested that such problems would appear more frequently among women than among men.

The results supported these hypotheses and suggested that they applied to college students in general. Students with a negative body image reported more eating disorders and more depression than other students; failed dieting was related to both conditions; and all disturbances were more prominent in women. In fact, depression was a remarkably good predictor of eating problems in women. Western culture idealizes slender women, prompting more women than men to engage in dieting, which is usually unsuccessful for long-term weight control (Koenig & Wasserman, 1995).

Unsuccessful dieting may result in helplessness and depression, which prompt overeating, fasting, and binge-and-purge eating. But in a survey, it is impossible to know which condition—depression or eating disorder—precedes the other. Like other descriptive methods, surveys do not demonstrate cause-and-effect outcomes.

Analysis of the Data

Once gathered, research data must be analyzed to discover their meanings or significance. In other words, the investigator not only collects data but later, in a process called **data analysis,** develops some interpretation of the new information, showing the ways in which it may provide additional knowledge. Thus, data analysis depends in part on the methods by which the data have been collected.

On such bases, experiments and surveys are viewed as **quantitative research,** for they are numerically oriented in the collection and also analysis of data.

Naturalistic observation and the case study are commonly described as **qualitative research** because they are more open and interpretive in data collection and rely more on verbal expression in data analysis.

For example, in an experiment on mood and eating, the investigator must manipulate the participants' moods in precise ways and then obtain valid measurements of their food consumption. In a survey on eating habits, the investigator might use a questionnaire inquiring about the participants' physical health, knowledge of nutrition, and usual eating companions. In both investigations, successful data analysis would require accurate statistical information about the amounts and relationships among these variables.

In contrast, a case study might be developed through several personal interviews with an underweight person, focusing on the meanings that person attaches to food-related events. In another investigation, using naturalistic observation in a high-school cafeteria might provide in-depth hypotheses about the social life of overweight teenagers. In both of these types of investigations, data analysis would include the identification and verbal description of the diffuse themes and patterns embedded within the records of the interviews and observations.

In other words, qualitative research does not impose the rigorous guidelines employed in quantitative research. In fact, qualitative research may incorporate almost any ethical procedures relevant to the investigation (Maxwell, 2005). Both quantitative and qualitative methods may be used in different phases of the same investigation, providing complementary support (Flick, 2006).

Quantitative Analyses

Numbers and measurement are fundamental in science. In quantitative analyses, the term **statistics** refers not only to numerical values but also to techniques for analyzing them. These analyses enable investigators to make precise comparisons among amounts and relationships. In psychopharmacology, for example, the use of certain medications has increased steadily since the middle of the 20th century. Meanwhile, other medications have been employed less frequently or abandoned altogether. With many thousands of participants and hundreds of drugs involved in this research, the trends cannot be readily understood without statistics.

Psychologists use **descriptive statistics** to present an overall view of a group of scores. Descriptive statistics summarize all the scores, showing the *central tendency*, or average, and also the *dispersion*, indicating the extent to which all the scores deviate from the central tendency. Two groups of scores with the same average or mean might show very different dispersions. Breuer noted that Anna's average nightly bedtime occurred around four o'clock in the morning (Breuer, 1882, 1895). But her actual bedtimes varied widely from week to week. For one week, they were widely scattered, occurring both early and late, thereby showing much dispersion. Those for another week were closely clustered around the 4:00 a.m. average, showing little dispersion. For this reason, descriptive statistics depict a group of scores by showing both the central tendency *and* the dispersion.

Descriptive statistics, incidentally, can be used with either experimental or descriptive research methods. There is no necessary connection between descriptive statistics and descriptive research, despite the common name.

Looking over his records, Breuer noted that the dosage of Anna's sedative, chloral hydrate, ranged from 2.5 to 5.0 grams (Breuer, 1882, 1895). With this information, he could think more efficiently about his treatments. Had the chloral dosages been sufficient to induce sleep? Did Anna's bedtime vary with the dosage? Was her day-to-day health improving? Descriptive statistics about bedtimes and dosages enabled Breuer to develop tentative answers to these questions.

Psychologists conduct statistical analyses for a second purpose. They use **inferential statistics** to provide a calculated guess or inference about scores they have not obtained. Inferential statistics involve probability—the chances that a given event, or score, will or will not occur. In these instances, the investigator collects a sample of scores, described with descriptive statistics, and then, by using probabilities, makes a statement about the whole population of scores from which that sample has been drawn. The sample and techniques of inferential statistics enable the investigator to predict scores not yet obtained: the outcomes of using particular medications, health risks with a certain diet, academic achievement, and so forth.

Psychologists use inferential statistics to discover the probabilities that a particular score, such as a sample mean, adequately represents a population mean—a common goal in survey research. They also use inferential statistics to determine the probabilities that a difference between two or more sample means represents the difference between their population means, which is the fundamental goal in experimental research. In other words, experimenters want to know whether a difference between the mean for a sample of participants in the experimental group and the mean for a sample of participants in the control group represents a reliable difference between the means of the two populations from which those samples were drawn.

With inferential statistics, investigators can determine the probabilities that their findings would reappear regularly in repetitions of the same procedures with different samples of participants. They show the likelihood that the same results would be obtained with repeated samples from the same populations.

Qualitative Analyses

Often addressing broad research questions, investigators using qualitative methods may spend extensive time in data collection, gathering masses of non-numerical data, especially verbal reports. Then they face the task of reducing these data to a set of interpretations or findings, an especially demanding challenge insofar as human knowledge is viewed as elusive and personal, changing from one time and place to another (Marshall & Rossman, 2006). Because our knowledge is never fully free of personal concerns, investigators using qualitative methods often place less emphasis on statistical analyses and more on developing thematic interpretations of the data (Hesse-Biber & Leavy, 2006). Sometimes these interpretations move back and forth from parts of the data to the whole and back to the parts, an approach to understanding known as the hermeneutic circle. Hermeneutics are ways of interpreting a text or experience, and the circle refers to the reciprocal movement between the whole and its parts.

Qualitative research therefore employs a flexible plan or design, sometimes called a **research protocol**: a preliminary statement outlining the features of the research. Modifiable during data collection, the protocol might include a list of purposes, research questions, likely sources of data, and proposed research methods (Maxwell, 2005). The protocol may even include some research notes and data that have already been collected. Drawing inferences from these data is sometimes called protocol analysis (Snape & Spencer, 2003).

Qualitative data often appear within a narrative framework as a series of unfolding events: bargaining in the marketplace, children at play, a graduation ceremony, and so forth. Efforts to analyze these cumulative accounts use two basic techniques: coding and connecting strategies.

A concept that appears in quantitative research as well, **coding** is any standardized system or set of rules for achieving uniformity in the collection and analysis of information. It assigns or classifies research observations in a consistent, reliable manner, placing each datum in an appropriate category. In the case study of the teenager suffering weight loss and rumination, the variable "Eating" might be coded for rate: None, Slowly, Normal, Rapidly. These categories might even be defined by numerical intervals. "Eating Behavior" might be coded more descriptively, requiring more judgment by the investigator: Chewing, Swallowing, Spitting, Regurgitating.

In coding, the goal is not to count events but to break the stream of data into categories, facilitating comparisons among them, thereby promoting explanatory concepts (Maxwell, 2005). If the coding system is established before data are collected, the data are gathered in those predetermined categories, increasing precision but decreasing flexibility. Without established categories, data collection proceeds with the opposite assets and limitations.

The **connecting strategies** serve a different purpose, revealing relationships among the data rather than sorting them into separate, coded categories. In one strategy, an interview transcript may be analyzed by detecting associations among the discrete remarks of each participant. In another strategy, transcripts may be analyzed collectively according to similarities among people or events. In still another, the focus may lie with contextual relationships, examining the influence of the surroundings on the underlying patterns and coherence of the entire data set (Maxwell, 2005).

On these occasions, the investigator may seek a *recurrent pattern,* aiming to identify the characteristic ways an individual or group responds in that environment. Among strangers, for example, the issue of leadership often arises. How does a certain participant typically react? How does the group respond? Or a single event may become prominent in connecting strategies. In a *critical incident,* a separate unit of behavior appears to offer special explanatory value. It may be dramatic, or it may be a small triumph or mishap on the part of one participant. It is considered critical when it illuminates or clarifies previously overlooked relationships in the participants' behavior.

No one method always serves best. Ideally, the objective, numerical procedures in quantitative inquiry can become increasingly combined with the subjective, interpretive procedures in qualitative inquiry (Runyan, 1984). Suggestions for their integration include parallel and sequential use in the same research project (Flick, 2006).

The case study and qualitative analyses served Breuer in his work with Anna. He supplemented this approach with a few crude, exploratory manipulations and basic statistics. He conducted tests and read the available records. He kept copious notes and corresponded with colleagues. For 18 months he met with Anna almost daily and sometimes twice a day. Much later, from all this information and his publication of the case, a new approach to therapy gradually emerged.

But Breuer was just in the early stages of understanding what he was doing. And Anna's symptoms did not disappear completely. For a while after a talking session, she simply felt "comfortable."

One evening she described the scene at her father's bedside in Ischl, when they were awaiting the surgeon from Vienna. She heard dance music from a neighboring house and suddenly experienced a wish to be there dancing, not sitting alone at night with a deathly ill parent. Overcome with self-reproach, her mouth dry with fear, she began coughing for the first time. Throughout her illness, she coughed nervously in reaction to dance music or any uncertainty. But she felt more comfortable after describing this incident (Breuer, 1895).

As Anna went on talking with Breuer, her heart went on thumping—partly because of her anxiety in telling these stories. Sweeping her mind clean, she struggled to confront the very events she wanted most to avoid, the thoughts and memories that made her most uncomfortable. But her heart went on thumping for another reason too—at least in a figurative sense. Through their many long evenings together, she had developed a deep affection for Josef Breuer as a person, not just as a healer.

Bright, charming, and energetic, Anna wanted desperately to engage the world outside her home. Along came a sensitive, worldly therapist. In pursuit of better health for her, they became united in a mutual endeavor—she a persuasive young woman who could profit from assistance, he a talented older man who wanted to offer it. Meeting together hour after hour, they struggled with their shared problem.

Anna had recently lost her father, become further estranged from her mother, and quarreled with Wilhelm. In her physician she found a relationship that satisfied emotional needs then unmet in her family. This regular visitor to her home became her savior of sorts, if not her imagined lover, father figure, and maybe even mother-substitute, for he shared her stories, fed her, and put her to sleep (Hirschmüller, 1989). Without doubt, Breuer became the central figure in her life.

Breuer, in turn, became so absorbed with his interesting patient that Mathilde, his wife, became concerned about his evening absences. She grew despondent and jealous as he grew more and more attentive to Anna. As their relationship deepened, the patient and therapist became both bewildered and excited. Neither had experienced an alliance of this sort, and Breuer had no training in understanding their reactions, viewed today as normal processes in extended individual psychotherapy (Holzman, 1984).

When Breuer finally realized the depth of his wife's depression, he realized too that Anna's care burdened him. He was sacrificing his own medical interests to meet this increasingly personal responsibility. Then he left with Mathilde for a month's vacation, apparently in great haste. With his departure he left this talented but troubled young woman to find her own way. They never resumed their relationship.

So Anna continued her disrupted life, and Breuer continued his dual career. In the daytime, he traveled throughout Vienna, making house calls as a practitioner, serving the sick and needy. In the evening, he trudged up to the homemade laboratory in his attic to his life as a scientist, making discoveries about the human body.

Achieving success in both roles—scientist and practitioner—has become far more difficult today, even in clinical psychology, the specialty closest to Breuer's early efforts with Anna. A homemade laboratory in the attic no longer suffices for groundbreaking research; sensitivity to a troubled person remains essential but insufficient for a successful practice in modern therapeutics. For this reason, preparation for clinical psychology has followed a scientist-practitioner model since the mid-20th century. Training in scientific thinking has been conducted chiefly in universities; training in clinical practice has been offered in mental health centers, state hospitals, and related medical facilities.

But spurred by the ever-increasing demands in our society, in recent decades clinicians have shown greater concern for the methods and techniques of practice and diminished interest in research. Today, some university-affiliated programs and free-standing professional institutions offer certified training for professional practice without requiring extensive research experience. This movement has generated a practitioner model for the education of clinical psychologists.

From a more personal standpoint, it remains uncertain whether individuals today in psychology, or any other health field, can embody the fundamentally different personal values, intellectual interests, and social responsiveness required in the very different scientist and practitioner roles (Garfield, 2000). This doubt raises again the question of whether one and the same title, psychology, should denote both scientific and practical work in a field so extensively invading business, education, health, government, and most other aspects of modern life.

Summary

The Research Challenge

Empirical research methods in psychology appear in two broad categories. Experimental methods involve manipulation and control of important factors, thereby showing something about the "why" of behavior; they demonstrate cause-and-effect relationships. Descriptive methods, without precise manipulation and control, show the "what" of behavior; they portray a person, group, or other entity through diverse research methods.

Key Terms: **reliability, validity, experimental methods, descriptive methods, operational definition**

Experimental Methods

In a classical experimental design, one variable is manipulated and other relevant variables are controlled. The aim is to discover the influence of the manipulated variable, known as the independent variable, on one or several other variables, each called a dependent variable. Using a more complex procedure and more sophisticated statistical methods, experiments with factorial designs examine the influence of several independent variables simultaneously. In a quasi-experimental design, the subjects have not been assigned randomly to the experimental and control groups.

Key Terms: **stimulus, response, classical experiment, random assignment, experimental group, control group, independent variable, dependent variable, research design, factorial design, quasi-experimental design, single-participant experimental design, investigator effects**

Descriptive Methods

Naturalistic observation, taking place in everyday settings, involves no disruption in the participants' lives, but the procedures are costly for the amount of information usually obtained. A case study has a different purpose. An in-depth examination of one person, group, or event, it is often the work of a practitioner for purposes of remediation or therapy, rather than the work of a scientist in pure research. The survey can include thousands of participants, but the method of sampling becomes vital regardless of the type of survey: questionnaire, archival, or physical traces.

Key Terms: **naturalistic observation, overt participation, covert participation, overt non-participation, covert non-participation, case study, psychometric case study, archival case study, observational case study, clinical case study, survey method, questionnaire survey, archival studies, physical traces, sample, population, representative sample**

Analysis of the Data

Psychologists employ quantitative analyses throughout research and practice, enabling them to make precise comparisons among amounts and relationships. Descriptive statistics show the characteristics of a group of scores; inferential statistics involve samples of scores and estimates about the probability of other scores based on a sample. Psychologists also employ qualitative analyses, using coding and connecting strategies, seeking recurrent patterns and critical incidents. These quantitative and qualitative procedures can complement one another.

Key Terms: **data analysis, quantitative research, qualitative research, statistics, descriptive statistics, inferential statistics, research protocol, coding, connecting strategies**

Critical Thinking

1. A physician treats people with alcoholism. Present a reasonably valid operational definition of *alcoholism*. Then operationalize *physician*.

2. Imagine conducting observational research on student behavior in the cafeteria: eating a healthy diet, wasting food, or recycling. For your approach, choose overt or covert participant or non-participant observation. Explain your reasoning.

3. The owner of an electronics company decides that work output would increase if all employees took naps. Outline an experiment to test this hypothesis.

3

Biological Psychology

B iological psychology is a useful starting point in the study of behavior. All human and animal activities emerge from underlying biological mechanisms. Focusing on the nervous system, especially the brain, biological psychology examines the ways the organs of the body influence behavior and experience.

In the 17th century, René Descartes greatly advanced the dawn of biological psychology through his inquiry into natural philosophy, meaning a systematic study of nature, especially animal physiology, which was pursued chiefly through dissections. In this way he studied animals and human beings in terms of a machine metaphor. In animals, the mechanical parts were simpler and were activated by a special fluid, which Descartes called animal spirits. In human beings, some mysterious, immaterial substance played a loftier role, for human mental life seemed to be separate from bodily activity. In one way or another, the machine metaphor of the body endured until the contemporary focus on the brain prevailed.

After further comments on the origins of biological psychology, this chapter turns to modern views of the nervous system, organization of the brain, and details of the cerebral cortex. It closes with a discussion of mental disorders and biomedical therapy, followed by a commentary and critique of the biological perspective.

With modern biomedical therapy still emerging in the late 19th century, the Bellevue Sanatorium in Konstanz, Switzerland, developed an enviable reputation for the treatment of brain disorders, now called mental disorders. It resisted the usual therapeutic practices of that day, such as early Hydrotherapy, which was used to shock people out of their illnesses. Suddenly sprayed with a strong stream of frigid water, patients sometimes fainted or experienced even more negative outcomes (Guttmann, 2001).

The Bellevue Sanatorium operated instead on the controversial principle of nonrestraint. In particular, it placed great importance on providing social opportunities for the patients, who came from wealthy families all over Europe. They needed normal human relationships. The Sanatorium encouraged them to mix with the director's family, staff, and visitors, as well as with other patients.

The records of the Bellevue Sanatorium for July 1882 include case 548, which describes the background and mental condition of a young woman named Bertha Pappenheim, born February 27, 1859. According to the report, she entered treatment with a moderately severe hereditary handicap. Her brother and a cousin once prepared a family tree, identifying ancestors who had become mentally ill. They were concerned about genetic abnormalities caused by marriage between close relatives (Guttmann, 2001). Bertha's mental condition was diagnosed as hysteria, a common disorder at that time. But she also suffered involuntary, painful contractions of the facial muscles and an addiction to morphine (Hirschmüller, 1989).

In emphasizing the biological basis of Bertha's condition, this case report adopted an approach to the study of behavior, which is still common today. Some causative factors in mental disorders do lie in the human body. But the evidence for a biological basis varies from one disorder to another, remaining complex and controversial even today.

Origins of Biological Psychology

By several standards the oldest of the modern perspectives, **biological psychology** aims to understand how the mechanisms of the human body make possible our various behaviors and experience. According to this view, the route to psychology goes through anatomy and physiology, especially neurology. Modern biological psychology encompasses the widest possible range of these relationships, and it stands among the most current of all psychological perspectives, steadily advancing its research frontiers. Pursued by scientists with diverse backgrounds, it is sometimes viewed as a broad subfield in psychology, rather than an integrated perspective.

Interest in bodily functions appeared in Wilhelm Wundt's laboratory, and it is of course as old as humanity. However, no one person can be credited with the founding of biological psychology. Wundt serves here as a founder chiefly on the basis of his primacy in the field and training in medicine. But working as a medical doctor did not satisfy his research interests. So he came to psychology from physiology and conducted early investigations on sensory and other bodily processes. His interests shifted later to the study of consciousness.

Wundt and Physiology

Life began in a dismal fashion for Wilhelm Wundt (1832–1920). He experienced little parental love, no close friends, and few playground activities. At age 13, even his teachers openly criticized him. Then he changed schools. In this new environment, he developed a keen interest in reading and began, with much satisfaction, a long life of learning (Boring, 1957).

According to historians, Wundt's early social deprivation and subsequent academic recognition contributed greatly to his prodigious capacity for scholarship. Humorless, tireless, and clearly talented, Wundt not only founded a laboratory but also created a substantial library of books and articles he wrote himself. In his first publication, on the sodium chloride content of his own urine, he noted the change in salt concentration after placing himself on a special diet. Only age 21 at the time, this study began his unrelenting authorship.

He guided his most renowned work, *Principles of Physiological Psychology*, into two volumes and eventually six editions. For decades, this book provided the framework for the emerging interest in experimental psychology. It has been called the most important book in the history of modern psychology (Boring, 1957). Later he contributed ten volumes on social and cultural psychology. He also founded a journal, *Psychological Studies*; the first journal in experimental psychology, it presented the results of his laboratory research. Altogether, his bibliography included 491 entries, averaging about 110 pages each, representing a total of 53,735 pages, including all pages of each revised edition. On this basis, Wundt wrote an average of 2.2 pages per day for his entire career of 67 years (Boring, 1957).

Through his writing, research, and teaching, Wundt greatly influenced many graduate students. After they passed through his laboratory and courses, they returned to their homes, many in the United States, and spread the new doctrine of psychology.

As a distinctive perspective, biological psychology was slow to gather momentum. Introspection and other early efforts, including cultural psychology, intervened. But we can give Wundt credit for being the first psychologist, founding the first laboratory, inaugurating the first research journal, writing the first textbook, and preparing the first graduate students (Boring, 1957). And we can credit him with studying the full range of topics from biology to culture.

His massive *Physiological Psychology* emerged from two traditions. Beginning with the structural elements of the nervous system, it discussed the pathways of neural conduction, the central nervous system, divisions of the brain, and functions of the cerebral hemispheres (Wundt, 1874/1904). In his day, *physiology* referred to experimental or laboratory procedures as well as the study of bodily functions. Thus, the book included methods for experimental psychology. It emphasized that physiological and psychological processes, which were usually separated for purposes of efficiency in teaching and research, occur together in a living human being. Insofar as possible, they must be studied together as a complex but nevertheless unitary entity.

In summary, *Physiological Psychology* became a crossroads book. In it, Wundt moved from physiology to psychology; the field of psychology, in turn, moved away from philosophy toward science.

In this context Wundt noted with some interest the early work of a contemporary Spanish neurologist, Santiago Ramón y Cajal; this work supported his ideas about the structure of the nervous system. At that time, many scientists regarded this new view skeptically, as no more than a hypothesis or theory.

In fact, for thousands of years our nervous system was believed to be one intact, continuous network, an endless matrix of piping that carried messages into every corner of the human body. This view became known as **network theory,** or reticular theory, for *reticular* in Latin means resembling a net. According to network theory, all nerve cells were continuously fused in the brain; they were all interconnected.

Instead, Ramón y Cajal advocated **neuron theory,** which states that the nervous system consists of countless *individual* nerve cells that never actually touch one another. Individual nerve cells are the fundamental units for the transmission of information in the body. Our nervous system is thus not a mass of physically connected cells but rather an exquisitely intricate organization of separated cells. Observing the enormous diversity in human abilities, he decided that no single network could account for such flexibility in behavior.

With his early microscope and staining methods, Ramón y Cajal hit on a promising approach to confirm his view. Because the human adult brain was too densely packed to observe the speculated spaces among its components, he decided to study lower animals in their earliest stages of development, even before birth. Their less-developed brains might be more accessible than mature brains, providing information on nerve growth and the formation of nerve pathways. Working with extraordinary intensity, he examined embryonic chicken brains. In that way, he confirmed the predicted spaces and thereby overthrew network theory (Cannon, 1989).

The delicacy of these cells, and the tiny spaces between them, which somehow must be transcended, greatly impressed Ramón y Cajal—so much so that he called their speculated connection a "protoplasmic kiss." The protoplasm was viewed as a semi-fluid substance essential to life functions; the kiss suggested that adjacent cells somehow made gentle contact through a "lip lock," exchanging that substance with one another (Ramón y Cajal, 1989). We now know that adjacent cells are structurally independent and are functionally connected by electrochemical activities.

Almost single-handedly, he unraveled the *basic* elements of the great raveled knot, as the human brain is sometimes called. Neuron theory no longer remained a theory. The individual nerve cell, or **neuron,** became recognized as the basic unit of the nervous system. Among these billions of nervous mechanisms, investigators might find the physical bases of human thought and therefore the answers to many questions about the biological bases of psychology.

Changing Views of the Brain

Centuries ago, scientists believed that the brain functioned only as a whole. All parts were alike. They responded together and completely or not at all—a capacity called the **principle of mass action.** Furthermore, all parts responded in essentially the same way, a function known as equipotentiality. In short, the brain was viewed as one uniform mass. The highly specialized parts that we know today were not recognized at all.

In the latter part of the 19th century, the idea of mass action became replaced by its seemingly more sophisticated opposite. According to **phrenology,** a person's psychological capacities could be identified in terms of 40 or so highly specific contours or bumps in specific areas of the head—memory emerged from one bump, agreeableness from another, and aggression, reasoning, language, love of infants, and many more from other locations. Enormous interest arose over this long-awaited, apparently successful way of assessing mental functions and personality. The chief concept, *complete localization,* meant that each ability was located solely and fully in just one brain site. But phrenology and its theory of complete localization soon fell out of favor. Experiments with animals showed no relationship between the loss of certain "bumps" and loss of the alleged mental capacity.

Today we regard the human brain very differently indeed, totally unlike what the concepts of mass action and complete localization would imply. Biological psychology today studies the human brain in terms of specialized parts, or systems, and also for their exquisitely complex relationships, both increasingly understood in the context of modularity doctrine. A prominent concept in modern biological psychology, **modularity doctrine** states that for any complex mental or physical activity, units of relatively independent, specialized brain structures become involved in an integrated fashion, with different units in different parts of the brain responding in separate but coordinated ways.

A *module* is a self-contained unit, or it is constructed of self-contained units. Either way, modularity doctrine points to brain systems operating for the most part independently of other brain systems or units. But some units are more autonomous than others, owing to weaker connections with their surroundings. Also, they vary in their integration—the degree to which they are internally coherent. In other words, modules differ in both the integration among their internal components and the strength of their connections with external mechanisms (Schlosser & Wagner, 2004). Information available to a particular module may or may not be available to other modules (Flombaum, Santos, & Hauser, 2002).

On these bases, biological psychologists speak of *modular design,* meaning that some global response, such as viewing a scene, can be achieved by subsystems designed first to react in relatively independent ways to specific information and then to implement that information as part of an aggregate, integrated whole. For a particular scene, individual modules might include color perception, recognition of faces, analysis of space, and language comprehension. Each module would be insensitive to some aspects of the scene but not to others. And some modules could be embedded in others, providing a hierarchical arrangement in the overall response to the visual image (Hirschfeld & Gelman, 1994; Schlosser & Wagner, 2004).

One metaphor for modularity doctrine is an orchestra. Playing in an independent but coordinated fashion, the groups of various instruments produce a complex, integrated outcome. Another metaphor is an ecological system, such as a rain forest, composed of many interdependent parts—plants, insects, decaying trees, birds, and brooks—each influencing the activities of other parts in important, subtle ways. In short, the brain operates not as a whole and not in isolated parts but through exquisitely complex integrations of simultaneously functioning units.

Moreover, the brain constantly reorganizes itself as a function of experience, a condition called **brain plasticity**. These changes in structure involve the generation of new brain circuits and the modification of existing circuits. Alteration in the brain's physical structure is then reflected in the ways it operates. In fact, the capacity to develop new neurons, called *neurogenesis,* has been found not only in birds and nonhuman primates but also recently in certain areas of middle-aged human brains. In particular, studies have shown neurogenesis in the hippocampus (Gage, 2003). If it is to be found anywhere, its presence here is least surprising, for this brain structure is critically important in learning and memory of new information, as noted later. In this respect, the human brain is not a static mass of nervous tissue. Regulated by inborn molecules known as growth factors, and highly sensitive to experience, it undergoes constant modifications on diverse bases.

Influential environmental factors operate throughout the life span, even into senescence. Among the most negative factors, traumatic injury, psychoactive drugs, lead poisoning, and disease can produce profound and irrevocable disruptions. In contrast, a healthy lifestyle achieved through dietary regimens, regular programs of exercise, and challenging mental activities can exert long-term, favorable influences on brain development (Kolb, Gibb, & Robinson, 2003).

Basic Research Methods

Biological psychology expands its knowledge chiefly through experimental methods, supported by clinical case studies. In laboratory experiments with animals, the investigator alters some body part, usually the nervous system, and observes any change in behavior. Or the investigator alters the subjects' living environment and notes any change in the structure or function of the body.

A classic laboratory experiment with animals illustrates this model. Investigators studied rats bred for brightness or dullness, placing half of each group in a restricted environment and the other half in an enriched environment, beginning at 25 days of age. The restricted cages included only a food box and water pan. The same-sized enriched cages also included treadmills, tunnels, swings, seesaws, mirrors, and marbles, in addition to poles with bars for climbing. After 40 days in these environments, all rats were tested in a field maze, which is commonly used for assessing mental ability in animals. The results showed a large difference in ability between the two strains. The bright rats and dull rats from the enriched environments performed much better than both groups of rats from the restricted environments. At both levels of heredity, early experience made a substantial difference in the rats' behavior (Cooper & Zubek, 1958; Greenough & Chang, 1989).

A classic quasi-experimental design demonstrates this approach with human beings. Young children were unintentionally exposed to one of two different environments, enriched or deprived. The former included unexpected, abundant stimulation and child-caretaker interaction; the latter involved the absence of these activities in an early, understaffed orphanage. After approximately two years, the children from these different environments showed clear differences in mental functioning. The enriched group showed an average IQ gain of more than 20 points; the deprived group showed a comparable loss. Marked differences in personal adjustment were observed as well, even in later life, again in favor of the enriched environment (Skeels, 1966; Skeels & Dye, 1939).

In case studies, often with ill or injured people, clinical treatments provide information on the malfunctioning body parts (Rosenzweig, Leiman, & Breedlove, 1996). The procedure involves a comparison of the behavior of the individual before and after the injury.

Phineas P. Gage, 25 years old, had been a healthy, intelligent, respected construction foreman. Working on a railroad in Vermont in 1848, a dynamite explosion sent a pointed, 13-pound, 4-foot iron bar completely through his head. Gage miraculously regained consciousness, then talked and walked around, and later rode in a horse-drawn cart to his hotel. The significance of this case extends well beyond Gage's physical recovery, an outcome meriting attention in the history of biology. Showing no obvious deficits in physical behavior, intelligence, or memory, he became a changed man nevertheless, a result of special significance for biological psychology. No longer respectful of others, he often swore at them instead, becoming obstinate, poorly controlled, and even wildly emotional at times. A person who knew him previously described him as "No longer Gage" (Harlow, 1869).

A full 20 years after Gage's accident, a physician studied his preserved skull and tamping iron and decided that his change in emotional control was caused by damage to the frontal region of his brain. Ten years later, a physiologist speculated more precisely, attributing Gage's misbehavior to damage in the left frontal area of the brain. And in our times, a team of investigators used neuro-imaging techniques with the skull, tamping iron, and its probable trajectory to confirm that Gage suffered damage to the frontal lobes, thereby disrupting his capacity for processing emotional reactions and making rational decisions (Damasio, Grabowski, Frank, Galaburda, & Damasio, 1994).

Despite his emotional outbursts, Phineas Gage's reaction did not demonstrate the role of the frontal cortex in emotional behavior. Rather, it demonstrated that the frontal lobes play a role in rational thought and decision making, thereby exercising control over emotional behavior.

Today, experimental investigations and case studies remain the primary research pathways in biological psychology, but the measurement procedures have improved enormously, entailing little danger for the participants while providing considerable information for the investigators. These devices, collectively called **brain imaging techniques,** produce photographic-like images of the brain's structure or function. Some, like the PET and MRI, do so by monitoring blood flow; others, such as the EEG, do so by measuring spontaneous electrical activity of the brain.

In the *PET scan*, using positron emission tomography, the participant lies with her head in a PET scanner, a framework that includes detectors surrounding the person's head. Then she receives a tiny dosage of a positron-emitting tracer injected into the bloodstream. This tracer enables the PET scanner to assess the blood flow, which signals neural activity.

In an *MRI scan*, using magnetic resonance imaging, the participant places her head into a strong magnetic field, revealing brain images through electromagnetic radiation. The MRI can provide images of brain structure or, indirectly, of brain functions. A functional MRI, or *fMRI,* actually provides images of blood oxygenation that are associated with various levels of neural activities in specific brain regions (Coleman, 2001). A much older technique, the *EEG,* or electroencephalogram, is instead a graphic display of the electrical activity of the brain, sometimes called brain waves, obtained through electrodes attached to the scalp.

In one study, investigators employed the PET scan to examine normal and abnormal brains in living human beings, using a procedure similar to that of the cardiologist who asks a patient to perform various physical exercises, thereby inducing electronically detectable changes in heart functions. These investigators asked each participant to engage in various mental tasks, producing electronically detectable changes in brain functioning. When a participant simply gazed around the room, the PET images showed activities in the visual cortex. When the person listened to speech, the images indicated activity in the left hemisphere but not the right, and vice versa when the individual listened to music. With speech and music together, both hemispheres became active simultaneously. All these responses had been predicted on the basis of prior knowledge. Thus, the PET scan confirmed our understanding of brain regions and normal mental activities without surgery or any other invasive method.

When using a PET scan to assess abnormal brain functions, the investigators proceeded on the assumption that all brain diseases arise from or create biochemical changes in the brain. And they found that the images of abnormal brains revealed specific areas of disturbance in far greater detail than prior techniques, aiding in earlier and more accurate diagnoses of abnormality (Phelps & Mazziotta, 1985).

The Nervous System

Far more than other body parts, the nervous system underlies the riddles of human behavior. As the body's primary communication network, consisting of all organs composed of nerve tissue, the **nervous system** exerts the most fundamental command over the activities of human beings. In fact, it perhaps should not be called the nervous system, for it consists of several intricately connected systems.

Twentieth-century research advanced our knowledge on several fronts. Investigators first calculated the speed of a nerve impulse, known today to be almost 300 miles per hour along some neurons. Then they discovered that this neural message travels across the synaptic gaps between neurons via chemicals called neurotransmitters. Since the identification of acetylcholine, the search for other neurotransmitters has been steady and productive. Other investigators explored the nature of the nerve impulse, which occurs when positively charged ions penetrate the cell membrane, creating a change in electrical potential that travels along the neuron.

Interlocking Systems

Within our vast array of nerve tissue, the integrating and coordinating center is the **central nervous system,** composed of the brain and spinal cord. It is the chief message center. It prepares, receives, and transmits neural messages throughout the body, thereby controlling its activities. In particular, it receives information from the **peripheral nervous system,** which includes essentially all nerve tissue outside the brain or spinal cord. The peripheral nervous system collects information from the outside world and also from inside the body. It is basically a transmission system with two major components.

One part, the **somatic nervous system**, connects with the sense organs for receiving incoming messages and with the voluntary muscles for sending outgoing messages. In other words, it relays to the central nervous system information from the eyes, ears, and skin, and it relays from the central nervous system information for the muscles that move the body. It transmits incoming and outgoing information.

The other major part, the **autonomic nervous system**, connects largely with involuntary organs, such as the heart, lungs, stomach, and various glands, including the adrenal glands. It includes two divisions that increase or decrease the activities of these organs, depending on the individual's interpretation of the circumstances. In perceived emergencies, the *sympathetic division* becomes ascendant, mobilizing the body for action—a fight-or-flight reaction. It accelerates the heart rate, increases the flow of adrenaline, and so forth, as the individual becomes emotionally aroused. The *parasympathetic division* regulates the body in more routine circumstances, conserving rather than expending energy. Heart rates and respiration become normal; digestion commences; and saliva returns to the mouth. The person functions in a more normal manner.

Structure of Neurons

The discovery of neurons, emphasizing that humans have billions of individual nerve cells, had profound implications for understanding the human nervous system. Scientists tried to imagine billions of independent nerve cells somehow making connections with one another. Eventually they discovered *functional* connections, the activities between and among neurons. These connections occur at a **synapse**, a tiny space among adjacent nerve cells where a neural message may or may not pass to countless other cells. The activities in each of these billions of spaces have the capacity to transmit or inhibit messages to countless other neurons, making possible the enormous flexibility of human behavior—from finely coordinated finger movements to unparalleled thought processes. In fact, the process called *learning,* so fundamental in human beings, is based on the capacity of neurons to grow and thereby to create new synapses, new connections among countless other neurons.

If the human brain were one solid mass, like a mound of jelly, we could not originate or transmit the messages behind these activities. We would move in a slow, restricted, repetitive way—or not at all. Our behavior would be extremely limited.

Neuron theory underlies vast areas of biological psychology. The synaptic spaces between cells are so well established and so central to biological studies that this idea is no longer debated and no longer a theory. The individual nerve cell, or *neuron,* is a functionally separate, structural unit in the nervous system, maintaining contact with other such units but not physically connected to them. What we popularly call a nerve or *nerve fiber* is, technically speaking, an extension of the neuron.

Neurologists recognize three major parts of the neuron. The central portion, the **cell body,** is the focal point of the neuron, containing the nucleus. Other nerve tissue is organized around this fundamental component. Two types of thread-like fibers extend from the cell body. The shorter fiber, a **dendrite,** has many branches, all of which carry nerve impulses *toward* the cell body. The longer fiber, an **axon,** transmits impulses *away from* the cell body to dendrites or cell bodies of other neurons. Nerve impulses in axons proceed in one direction only—from dendrite to cell body to axon—which is sometimes called the law of forward conduction and was first demonstrated by Santiago Ramón y Cajal (Figure 3.1).

Moreover, all impulses in axons appear at one level of intensity. This condition, called the **all-or-none law,** means that the nerve responds completely or

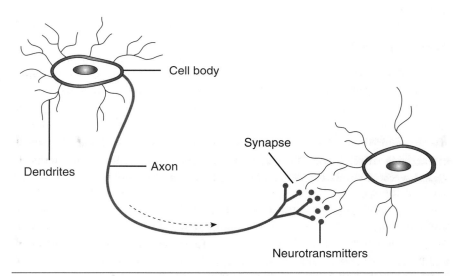

Figure 3.1   A Neuron and Synapse. The neuron's major parts include its dendrites, cell body, and axon. The arrow indicates the direction of the nerve impulse. At the synapse, neurotransmitter substances play a central role in the flexibility of human behavior, stimulating extensive neurochemical activities among the fibers of adjacent neurons.

it simply does not respond. There is no intermediate level of reaction. A doorbell rings or does not ring. A weak press does not produce a weak ring. Why then are some injuries more painful than others? How does someone detect the strength of a stimulus? One answer lies with the number of activated neurons in sensory systems. A stronger or more frequent stimulus causes more neurons to fire, increasing the pain. Or it increases the rate of firing. But it does not influence the speed, direction, or strength of the impulse causing the pain.

A painful condition around the mouth, nose, and face is often associated with the trigeminal nerve. Sudden, sharp aches and twitches occur in this region in a disorder called trigeminal neuralgia. These involuntary movements are habitual and spasmodic; each movement is known as a *tic* and appears as a visible muscle contraction. When admitted to the Bellevue Sanatorium, Bertha Pappenheim experienced tics of this sort.

After a few weeks, Bertha's tics grew worse. By seven o'clock in the evening, animated spasms appeared in the whole left side of her face, especially the jaw. Experiencing no relief, she required more morphine, which extended her addiction (Hirschmüller, 1989).

Tics, and all other responses, are aroused by messages in the nervous system, often originating in the brain. Each message, or *nerve impulse*, involves a brief burst of electrochemical energy traveling along the nerve fiber, much the way a spark travels along an ignited firecracker fuse. Initiated by an adequate stimulus, this shift in energy occurs through an exchange of electrical charges passing in and out of the porous covering of the nerve.

In its resting state, the nerve transmits no message. When the fiber is stimulated, positively charged sodium ions flow inward for an instant, passing through the cell membrane, causing positively charged potassium ions to flow outward. Within nanoseconds, tiny ionic pumps restore the normal balance in that part of the nerve. But this change in voltage initiates a change in the adjacent fiber, and so forth, in successive parts, until this exchange of energy has traveled the full length of the fiber. This exchange of energy in the nerve, known as the nerve impulse, is formally called the **action potential**, emphasizing the change in the polarization of the nerve.

The individual's response to this message is determined by numerous factors. Among them, two are prominent: the sense organ responsible for the initial stimulation—visual, auditory, or otherwise—and the destination of the nerve fiber in the central nervous system.

Three kinds of neurons convey the message. One type, the **sensory neuron**, transmits the nerve impulse from sense organs to the central nervous system, resulting in the experience of pain, vision, hearing, or some other sense, depending on the area of the brain that has been stimulated. Sensory neurons carry information about our world and ourselves. They inform us.

Another type, the **motor neuron**, transmits impulses from the central nervous system to muscles and glands, producing voluntary and involuntary responses. Motor neurons enable us to do something about the information received from sensory and other neurons. These reactions may be involuntary, as in a tic or reflex, or voluntary, such as rubbing the painful spot or requesting medication for pain.

A third type, the **interneuron,** makes connections with sensory and motor neurons and especially with countless other interneurons. Found only in the central nervous system, interneurons often appear with branches, which facilitate these innumerable connections. Thousands of times more prevalent than the other types, interneurons range in number up to many, many billions (Rosenzweig, Leiman, & Breedlove, 1996). Information processing in the human brain takes place primarily among interneurons. They play a vital role in the diverse, marvelously coordinated activities in human thought and behavior.

Neurotransmitters and Drugs

At the center of this flexibility lies the synapse, functionally connecting the neurons. On reaching this space, the nerve impulse releases the chemical bases of nerve transmission from tiny sacs. Each sac contains a chemical substance called a **neurotransmitter,** which travels instantaneously across the synaptic space, exciting or inhibiting adjacent neurons, depending on its fit with the molecular structure of the receiving neurons.

In other words, the nerve impulse does not jump across synaptic space like a spark. Instead, a neurochemical message travels through the fluid-filled synapse.

In some cases, the molecular structure of the particular neurotransmitter matches a receptor site on the receiving neuron, increasing its potential to initiate a nerve impulse, depending on the reactions at other receptor sites. This outcome is called an *excitatory reaction* because it arouses a nerve impulse. In other instances, a neurotransmitter may fit the receptor site, and there is no initiation of a nerve impulse. This outcome is called an *inhibitory reaction* because the neurotransmitter stimulates chemical activity that reduces the propensity of that neuron to arouse a nerve impulse. Still other neurotransmitters become irrelevant, not fitting any site at all. This whole process has been called *lock-and-key transmission,* for the key, the neurotransmitter, must fit the lock, the receptor site, in order to become effective. If it fits, it may open the door, an excitatory reaction, or firmly lock it, an inhibitory reaction.

Some neurotransmitters, rather than being discharged into a specific synaptic space, become discharged into a series of synapses. In addition, they have the capacity to amplify or diminish the capacities of a number of specific neurotransmitters. For both reasons, these modulating neurotransmitters are known as *neuromodulators;* they modify the effects of other neurotransmitters.

This activity takes place among countless neurons simultaneously and almost instantaneously, producing a flood of neurotransmitters into the synapses. For a person to function normally, a delicate balance must be sustained between the diverse excitatory and more prevalent inhibitory reactions. These tiny neurotransmitters, each characterized by its particular chemical makeup, operating in literally billions of synapses, make possible the immense versatility of human behavior.

But what happens to the neurotransmitters after they have served their purpose in synaptic space? How do they leave? In one process, called the *reuptake process,* the neurotransmitter is drawn back into the sending, or presynaptic, neuron from which it was discharged. In another, a *deactivation process,* the neurotransmitter becomes neutralized by cleanup chemicals in the synaptic space.

The number of different neurotransmitters currently remains undetermined, but estimates range upward to 100 or more. Among the most common are glutamate and GABA. Compared with other neurotransmitters, *glutamate* exerts the most widespread influence; it has the potential to stimulate an excitatory reaction in synapses all over the nervous system. In contrast, *GABA,* an acronym for gamma amino butyric acid, exerts a pervasive inhibitory influence, though less extensive than glutamate because it is limited to the brain.

Acetylcholine, whether excitatory or inhibitory, plays a prominent role in learning, memory, and muscular activity. Its release into the synapse initiates a muscle contraction. Its deficit in the central nervous system is associated with Alzheimer's disease, involving memory loss and disorientation. Its deficit also produces paralysis, as demonstrated by a drug known as curare, which obstructs acelytcholine receptor sites, preventing those neurotransmitters from influencing the muscles. When a healthy young man received small amounts of curare, he became completely paralyzed. During the growing paralysis, he spoke as long as possible and then communicated through prearranged muscle movements. After administration of a counteracting drug, he reported that he had remained fully conscious and experienced normal thought processes throughout the paralysis, suggesting that the curare operated on the acetylcholine receptor sites (Smith, Brown, Toman, & Goodman, 1947).

A bedtime snack can stimulate production of *serotonin,* associated with the usually pleasurable activities of eating and sleeping, as well as general arousal. Low levels of serotonin have been linked to aggression and depression; when medication and psychotherapy relieve those conditions, the presence of serotonin is also restored. Also associated with pleasurable activities and psychiatric conditions, *dopamine* influences emotional arousal, rather than general arousal. Special sensitivity to their normal levels of dopamine may appear in people with schizophrenia. Blocking dopamine at the synapses with the administration of psychotherapeutic drugs has proven useful in treating such disorders. In contrast, Parkinson's disease is associated with a dopamine deficiency, resulting in slowness and loss of muscular control. These different responses to the same neurotransmitter in different amounts illustrate the delicate balance among and within these chemical substances.

Finally, *endorphins* are widely recognized for acting as anesthetics or opiates that naturally occur in the body. The term comes from the words *endogenous,* meaning within, and *morphine,* a pain killer. Endorphins become anesthetics by blocking neural impulses for pain much as morphine reduces pain and increases a sense of well-being. As neuromodulators, endorphins operate in a more general way than the traditional neurotransmitters.

The neurotransmitters and neuromodulators together demonstrate that brain chemistry can have both specific and broad functions. In addition, their reactions can vary with different locations in the nervous system. In these ways they exert an enormous influence on the behavior and experience of any human being.

With its billions of separate neurons, their tiny functional connections, and minute chemical messengers, the human nervous system also remains highly susceptible to disorders. As evident with Bertha Pappenheim, conditions can go awry. In her case, endorphins did not suppress pain in the trigeminal nerve, and morphine had become addictive.

But painful tics were not her sole problem. Bertha occasionally experienced serious memory lapses, and she remained depressed for long periods, sobbing over the recent death of her father. She also complained about being in the hospital. Almost daily, she insisted on returning to her home in Vienna to live with her mother.

Returning to Vienna? To live with her mother? Mourning her late father? Suffering from mental disorder?

If Bertha Pappenheim sounds like Anna, the resemblance is not chance. Bertha *was* Anna, and her condition had worsened. After treating Anna—er, Bertha—Breuer later published the case for the benefit of colleagues, referring to her as Anna O., a name still widely recognized throughout psychology. For this pseudonym, he used the letters of the alphabet immediately preceding her initials. B.P. became A.O. Then he selected Anna, which sounds somewhat like Bertha (Jensen, 1970; Pollock, 1984).

Breuer waited 13 years to publish the disguised case in a professional journal, an unusually long time even for introducing a novel therapy. But when he terminated the case, he had nothing to report publicly. The talking cure showed no permanent value at that early point, and he went on to other interests (Hirschmüller, 1989). In fact, he might have refrained from publishing the case at all had not a colleague urged him to do so.

In an earlier, confidential report of 22 handwritten pages to Bellevue Hospital at the time of Bertha's admission, Breuer included extensive details, especially on her tics, which he viewed as strictly a medical issue, not a psychological problem. Thus, he did not include them in the published report of Anna O.

For Bertha's tics, the Bellevue Sanatorium continued to prescribe doses of morphine, numbing the pain. But then she experienced a **drug-induced state,** which is any uncontrollable, often unpredictable, change in consciousness produced by chemical substances. She developed a physical dependence on this drug, called an **addiction,** which included painful withdrawal symptoms when the drug was no longer used.

Morphine quickly becomes addictive. By injection, Breuer had administered large amounts, doses of 0.05 to 0.20 grams daily. The hospital thus pursued both goals: to eliminate the tics and to remove the addiction.

Drugs, natural or manufactured, operate in two broad categories, agonist and antagonist. An *agonist* drug exerts essentially the same effect as the neurotransmitter. It binds to the receptor sites, exciting or inhibiting a reaction, much like a neurotransmitter at that site. An *antagonist* suppresses the influence of an agonist, sometimes by acting at different receptor sites and sometimes by binding to the same receptor sites without inducing excitation or inhibition. The drug nalaxone, a narcotic antagonist, binds to receptor sites that otherwise would be occupied by morphine, thereby preventing the usual effects of morphine (Coleman, 2001).

The hospital staff did not understand how morphine diminishes pain. As an agonist, with a molecular structure much like endorphins, it increases endorphin-like transmission at the receptor. Without the drug, endorphins alone make the transmission. Especially in large amounts, morphine greatly augments pain-killing capacities at those receptor sites.

Breuer also administered chloral hydrate to help Bertha sleep, using doses up to 5 grams daily, many times what might be used today. It produced another addiction. In an effort to wean her, the hospital withheld the drug for four nights, creating serious withdrawal symptoms in Bertha, including *delirium tremens* (Hirschmüller, 1989).

But at totally unpredictable moments, she surprised everyone with her joyful spirits. She even posed for a photo taken by a professional photographer in Konstanz. It showed a healthy-looking, sporting young woman ready to go horseback riding.

Organization of the Brain

Even when Bertha simply posed for a photograph, neural messages excited countless circuits throughout her nervous system. Other messages became activated when she planned a career in nursing and rode horseback in the Konstanz woods. These complex transmissions were coordinated by the brain, which serves as the basic integrating mechanism in the human body. In recognition of the brain's central role, *behavioral* neuroscience has emerged alongside biological psychology, concentrating on the relations between brain functions and behavior. It examines the ways in which the brain influences behavior or, more abstractly, the ways in which the brain, a biological structure, creates the mind, a psychological concept.

Only recently in human history have we viewed the brain as underlying our thoughts, feelings, and behavior. Aristotle assigned this fundamental role to the heart, a much noisier and livelier central organ. The brain, by comparison, appears as an inert mass, crudely described as three pounds of moist rubber, a head of cauliflower, or a deeply wrinkled boxing glove. Unlike the heart and all other bodily mechanisms, it is conscious of itself, and it can understand itself in various ways, one of which involves a self-description in terms of evolution.

Progressing from the upper end of the spinal cord to the very top of the brain, three divisions presumably reflect the evolution of the brain. The lowest portion of the brain, closest to the spinal cord, is called the hindbrain because, for an animal on four feet, it is toward the rear. In an evolutionary sense, it is the oldest part of the brain. The *hindbrain* mediates basic biological functions, such as breathing, digestion, blood circulation, and reflexes. We share the hindbrain with many other animals, including the most primitive aquatic creatures. One major part, the **cerebellum,** called the "little brain" because of its size and location, maintains posture and coordinates sequential movements, making-well practiced habits smooth and precise, as in running, writing, talking, and riding horseback. Adjacent parts play a central role in the regulation of heart rate, breathing, and blood pressure, and perhaps certain cognitive processes as well.

A small area above the hindbrain, the *midbrain,* processes information for the upper brain regions, especially visual and auditory information. And it shares with the hindbrain a group of cells called the **reticular formation,** one part of which serves broadly to induce sleeping, waking, and other levels of arousal. The painful withdrawal from her addiction kept Bertha awake long into the night. When she finally fell asleep, the reticular formation contributed significantly to this quiescent state.

Bertha's thoughts about a career were produced chiefly in the third area, the large *forebrain,* so called because it is situated at the front in four-footed animals. At the top of the human skull, it is responsible for the higher mental processes: our thinking, remembering, perceiving, language, problem solving, and all sorts of experiencing. This portion of the brain makes human beings unique among the species, capable of thoughts and feelings not found in other creatures.

Located in the center of the forebrain, the **thalamus** serves as the main relay center, receiving neural messages from the eyes, ears, and other sense organs and relaying them to higher brain regions where they are interpreted, informing us about ourselves and the world around us. The term *thalamus* means "inner room." Its central location serves well for these activities, playing a major role in human awareness.

These three evolutionary regions provide a rough index of the location of brain organs in relation to their function. The most biological lie at the lowest level, in the hindbrain, also called the reptilian brain. The most psychological occur at the top, in the forebrain, sometimes known as the primate brain. Linking and transfer functions occur in the much smaller midbrain, referred to as the mammalian brain despite its diminished importance in many mammals.

Biological psychology investigates the neural activities within and among these structures. They are specialized to perform one of three basic functions: to obtain information from the environment; to act on the environment; or to transmit information within the body, between input and output, a function of many brain structures.

The following discussion focuses on the forebrain, again in a three-level hierarchy. But here the sequence begins at the lowest level, then moves to the highest, and finishes with a connection between them, providing a conceptual overview of the most complex structure known to human beings.

Maintaining Internal Conditions

In the mid-20th century, partly by chance, investigators discovered some puzzling properties associated with the hypothalamus. In fact, these studies could be considered inaugural moments for biological psychology, for they represented some of the earliest efforts to study specific organs lying deep within the living brain.

The prefix *hypo* means "less" or "lower than." The hypothalamus in human beings lies just below the centrally located thalamus. Using needle electrodes implanted in rats, early investigators delivered electrical stimulation to the *lateral hypothalamus,* at the side of this tiny organ, and they found that it sustained eating, even in animals that were presumably already satiated. And when this area was damaged, the animals ceased eating before their normal needs were met. Despite the availability of food, they became emaciated.

But electrical stimulation of the *ventromedial nucleus,* an area in the lower center of the hypothalamus, produced a very different outcome. Experimental rats immediately ceased eating, even those previously on a food-deprivation schedule. Damage to this hypothalamic region produced marked overeating, resulting in rats three times their normal size. The injured animals simply did not stop eating. Apparently they did not know when they had consumed sufficient food.

Initial interpretations of these findings pointed to the intricate role of the hypothalamus in hunger and eating. However, it alone is not solely responsible for either behavior, nor is any other organ, but it is involved in both reactions. The lateral area prompts eating; if destroyed, eating ceases. The more central region signals the time to cease eating; if destroyed, the stop signal does not occur (Anand & Brobeck, 1951; Mayer, 1956; Miller, Bailey, & Stevenson, 1950). But a major nerve pathway influences such responses, for it passes through the hypothalamus (LeDoux, 2002).

Today we view the tiny **hypothalamus** more complexly as playing a big role in maintaining a healthy body by influencing motivation and emotion and monitoring and regulating our biological drives, including hunger, feeding, fatigue, sexual behavior, and related survival and reproductive activities. Detecting changes in body chemistry and temperature, the hypothalamus has been called the "inner brain" and the "brain's brain," out of respect for its capacity to regulate and maintain appropriate conditions within our bodies, enabling us to respond effectively to the external world (Greenberg, 2004). People who are extremely hungry, tired, weak, hot, or ill are not prepared to carry out their missions in everyday life. The little hypothalamus ensures a healthy readiness to behave effectively.

The hypothalamus maintains this extensive control partly through its direct connections with organs in the autonomic nervous system. In addition, it retains an influence over the **endocrine system,** the body's second major communications network, which is composed largely of glands that secrete chemical substances directly into the bloodstream. These substances, called **hormones,** are carried to various parts of the body, ensuring chemical activities essential for body growth and maintenance. Defects in hormone secretion can have extensive consequences, ranging from sharply stunted physical growth to sudden personality disorders. Malfunction of one element of this system may produce widespread changes in a person's feelings and behavior.

Specifically, the hypothalamus exerts this control through its connections with the *pituitary gland,* the "master gland" in the endocrine system, which in turn regulates the other endocrine glands, involving bodily growth, energy, and even personality. Also known metaphorically as the brain's drugstore, the hypothalamus performs a pervasive maintenance function throughout the body (Greenberg, 2004).

Responding to External Events

In contrast to the tiny, deeply embedded hypothalamus, the large cerebral cortex appears at the very top of the human brain as the brain's covering. A *cortex* is a covering or bark. The term *cerebral* indicates the largest part of the brain, the entire upper portion, both left and right. The **cerebral cortex** covers the whole upper portion of the brain and thereby mediates our sensory and motor contact with the outer world. These functions were first demonstrated convincingly in the latter part of the 19th century.

In the 1860s, two German physiologists resisted the view that the brain operated only as one excitable mass. Prompted by phrenology and more scientific research, they pointed out that the brain's surface had not been examined systematically and that hemorrhages from surgery decreased its responsiveness. With more careful methods, Gustav Fritsch and Eduard Hitzig decided they might be able to show that the brain functions in specialized ways. As a wartime surgeon, Hitzig had noticed that cleaning and dressing soldiers' head wounds sometimes produced a twitching in various muscles. These case studies of human beings laid the groundwork for experimental research with animals.

After some preliminary tests on the cortex of a rabbit, they turned to the Hitzig kitchen table on which they conducted more precise experiments with a dog, using a weak electric current applied directly to the surface of the dog's brain, just as other investigators had done earlier. That current barely evoked a tingling sensation on the human tongue but when applied in a systematic fashion, it worked well. Fritsch and Hitzig found that stimulation at one point on the cortex produced movement in the dog's neck. Stimulation in another region induced leg movements. At still another point, facial movements occurred. Other stimulations brought forth muscle contractions in the back, stomach, and tail (Fritsch & Hitzig, 1870).

The investigators had demonstrated that the human brain was not one excitable mass. Stimulation of certain parts of the brain induced certain body movements. Other investigators advanced this knowledge and within a few years identified most areas of the cortex associated with muscle movements, also called motor control. Study of the sensory areas followed. Sensory studies were initially more difficult owing to the absence of observable movements, but human participants undergoing brain surgery gave reports, facilitating these investigations. Collectively these procedures, called cortical mapping, revealed which areas of the cortex mediated which sensory experiences, such as vision and hearing, and which regions mediated the movements of certain body parts.

We know today that sights, sounds, and experiences of touch are mediated primarily in specific areas toward the rear of the cerebral cortex, just as our responses to such stimuli are organized and initiated toward the front and middle areas. In juxtaposition to the hypothalamus, the cerebral cortex is our "outer brain." The hypothalamus plays a major but not exclusive role in regulating our internal environment; the cerebral cortex becomes vital in managing our responsiveness to the external environment, a complex capacity considered in further detail shortly.

The Limbic Connection

So human beings have brain mechanisms for regulating the body's automatic responses to its internal needs. They also have the apparatus for responding appropriately to external conditions. What more is needed? In fact, the brain requires some linkage between the two—organs to connect our responsiveness to the inner and outer environments. When the deeply embedded hypothalamus signals the need for food or rest, for example, the outlying cortex must make successful contact with environmental events that will satisfy these needs (Greenberg, 2004). The system providing this linkage must be a *subcortical structure,* lying below the cortex, which covers the top of the brain.

The limbic system becomes important here, but it is poorly named. The adjective *limbic* indicates a border, a dividing line, often between two territories. But this system is more like a bridge than a border. A scattered group of brain structures, including the bilateral amygdala and hippocampus, the **limbic system** plays a connecting role in brain functions, especially in the context of emotion and memory. In highly simplified terms, it connects the inner brain of the hypothalamus and outer brain of the cerebral cortex. More generally, it bridges the gap between the deeper subcortical regions and the upper brain areas.

As a limbic structure, the **amygdala** closes the gap partly through its evaluation of emotional experiences, which it does quickly but often inaccurately. In one series of studies, rats learned to fear a sound that had been followed repeatedly by an electric shock. After they acquired this fear, they were denied information about its origins through removal of the cerebral cortex. But they continued to be afraid anyway, even after no longer knowing the prior circumstances. Based on studies of brain anatomy, the investigator pointed out that the amygdala provides a quick but crude appraisal of a potentially dangerous situation, apparently as an adaptive reaction before a more thorough, protracted interpretation is made by the cerebral cortex (LeDoux, 1995, 2002).

Imagine walking in the woods and hearing a growling bear. This stimulus initiates messages that go directly to the amygdala, and you start to run. Your first reaction would be fear, owing to the immediate interpretation of that event as something dangerous. By a longer route in the brain, this strange sound also initiates messages that travel through the cerebral cortex. The slightly delayed interpretation in these areas reveals the stimulus as merely branches brushing against one another in the wind. You smile and begin walking again. As Shakespeare said:

> Or in the night, imagining some fear,
> How easy is a bush supposed a bear.
> (*A Midsummer Night's Dream*)

Both reactions, limbic and cerebral, can be viewed in the context of evolutionary theory and individual survival. The limbic arousal alerts us promptly to possible danger; the cerebral reaction provides a more thorough representation, enabling us to respond more appropriately.

Another major limbic structure, the **hippocampus**, plays a role in the *formation* of memory. Without it we simply cannot create new memories, failing even to recognize someone encountered just minutes earlier, which poses an insurmountable handicap in everyday life.

The role of the hippocampus appeared dramatically and regrettably in the plight of H.M. who, as a young man, obtained surgical relief from constant epileptic seizures. However, the procedure left him with a large deficit in the hippocampal area, after which he could only remember events prior to the surgery. His recall of childhood experiences remains basically undiminished, although he can form no new memories. He has a normal consciousness, but once an event leaves his immediate awareness, he typically cannot recall it. He cannot make new friends because he forgets people after they leave his presence. Over and over, he tells the same jokes, reads the same books, and forgets what he had just experienced. Living in this stressful condition for 50 years, H.M. has offered himself for intensive studies by psychologists (Milner, Corkin, & Teuber, 1968; Postle & Corkin, 1998). They have generated invaluable information on the contributions of the hippocampus to our capacity for memory, although it is not a primary repository of memories.

Much debate still surrounds the functions and even the components of the limbic system. For example, the thalamus and hypothalamus are sometimes included in and sometimes excluded from descriptions of the limbic system. There is, however, considerable certainty that emotional experience involves all of these brain structures, as well as the cerebral cortex and frontal lobes. One inescapable fact about the human brain is its intricate coordination among diverse parts (Figure 3.2).

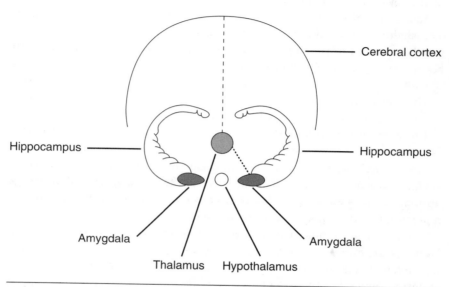

Figure 3.2   **Brain Structures and Fear Reactions.** Shown in cross-section from the front, the brain is largely bilateral, including the almond-shaped amygdala and the hippocampus, resembling the tail of a seahorse. The dotted line indicates the shorter route from the thalamus to the amygdala, providing a quick response to fear. The dashed line represents the longer thalamic route to the cerebral cortex, providing a delayed but more thorough assessment.

All human activity arises from exciting, inhibiting, and reverberating circuits in interconnected areas of the brain. Most synaptic events in the brain are inhibiting, not exciting, even in emotion. Without extensive inhibition, human beings would become inundated by random, redundant, competing neural messages. Brain activities would become chaotic, as in *epilepsy,* when a cascade of neural impulses in a large region produces dizziness, fits, and loss of consciousness.

Tics are a milder, more confined form of this disorder. They reflect a failure of inhibition in a restricted, specific brain area.

Appearing only around the mouth and lower face, Bertha's tics reflected an inhibition failure in those areas of the cerebral cortex. With limited knowledge of tics and limited means of treating them, the physicians at the Bellevue Sanatorium did what they could to ease Bertha's pain. They administered more morphine. But the cost was not worth the benefit. Morphine did not make her comfortable, and because of her increased addiction, withdrawal produced further pain.

She left the hospital anyway after four months of treatment. For case 548, the register at the Sanatorium read: "Condition improved. Discharged" (Hirschmüller, 1989). At her mother's insistence, she went to live with her Homburger cousins in Karlsruhe. There she wrote to Dr. Robert Binswanger, director of the Sanatorium: "As for my health . . . I can tell you nothing which is new or favorable. . . . However, I am glad that I can attend the nursing course which started last Friday" (Pappenheim, 1882).

Bertha never finished that course, but it left its mark, inspiring her with its volunteer opportunities in orphanages, schools for the poor, and soup kitchens. One cousin, Anna Ettlinger, inspired Bertha in a different direction. She had published her recollections and translated foreign prose. After Bertha responded by telling some of her fairy tales from Vienna, Anna advised her to abandon nursing and begin a literary life.

The Cerebral Cortex

All these mental activities—writing letters, taking courses, and telling fairy tales—are centered in the *cerebral cortex*, the much-folded layer of gray tissue covering the forebrain and responsible for many neural connections. In addition to its role in incoming messages and outgoing responses, noted already, this part of the brain is critically involved in mental processes. It serves as our "thinking cap."

As a cap, the cerebral cortex is thin yet large and new yet wrinkled, and these seemingly inconsistent characteristics require some explanation. Only a few millimeters thick, this outer covering represents more of the brain than might be expected or can be observed without pulling the cap apart. The reason lies with its wrinkles, many quite deep. They allow this large surface to fit into a relatively small space, our skull, much as a paper bag can be crumpled up and squeezed into a cup. These wrinkles, or crevices, known as *convolutions,* are less pronounced or absent in animals. Much of this tissue is called *neocortex,* for in an evolutionary sense it is a recent brain development, not shared with many animals. It covers older parts of the cortex.

The two cerebral hemispheres appear essentially alike, and in most activities they operate in a coordinated fashion. Functionally, however, they show important differences called **hemispheric specialization**, meaning that one hemisphere or the other is dominant in a certain activity. They are connected by the corpus callosum, a large mass of nerve tissue lying above the limbic system. Serving as a bridge, the **corpus callosum** transmits information between the hemispheres, thereby facilitating coordination of activities throughout the body. This condition of asymmetry is common in all paired body parts.

The left hemisphere tends to be dominant in language and numbers, the right in synthesizing and using spatial information (Hellige, 1990). For these reasons, people sometimes speak today of being left-brained or right-brained. But these expressions create a distortion, suggesting far greater reliance on one hemisphere or the other than occurs in our reliance on one hand or the other. Despite their specializations, the normal cerebral hemispheres are closely integrated, continuously exchanging information they receive from our many pairs of symmetrically arranged organs.

Primary and Association Areas

In terms of input and output, much of the cortex can be roughly considered as either sensory or motor areas. The sensory areas provide information. Through these regions, located toward the back of the cortex, we learn about our environment. We hear the sound of an airplane. The motor areas enable us to respond to that stimulation. Through these regions, located toward the front of the cortex, we do things about our environment. We look up in the sky.

Each of these regions, sensory and motor, is divided into primary areas and association areas. Here the term *primary* means first in either receiving or sending signals. Thus, the **primary sensory areas** receive information from the sense organs, transmitted via the thalamus. The primary *visual* area, at the back of the head, processes information for seeing. The primary *auditory* area, at the sides of the head, near the ears, receives information for hearing. And the primary *somatosensory* area, at the top of the brain, slightly toward the rear, responds to information about touch, temperature, and other experiences of the skin. The latter term comes from *soma*, meaning "body," and *sensory*, meaning "feeling." Loosely, it refers to touch or skin sensitivity. In addition to vision, hearing, and touch, there are to a lesser degree also primary areas for taste and smell.

These primary areas are often called primary projection areas because they roughly correspond to the regions of the body that they mediate. Thus, adjacent neurons in the retina project their messages onto adjacent cells in the visual cortex. Adjacent regions in the skin project their signals onto adjacent areas of the somatosensory cortex, and so forth. The size of the cortical area does not correspond to the size of the relevant body part, but it reflects the sensitivity of that body area. Thus, the highly sensitive lips and fingers occupy more cortical areas than the less sensitive hips and trunk.

The **primary motor areas** influence body movements, sending information to the muscles and glands via the spinal cord; they initiate walking, talking, and countless other activities. These motor areas are located at the top of the head, slightly toward the front, just forward of the somatosensory areas. As with primary sensory areas, their relationships to the body are *contralateral,* meaning that each hemisphere stimulates or receives messages from the opposite side of the body, a condition found in most nervous systems. And here the body parts are represented in proportion to their flexibility of movement. Again, the tongue, lips, fingers, and other mobile parts occupy large regions; the less moveable torso occupies a much smaller brain region, despite its larger size.

The remaining regions of the cortex are not primary areas. Variously called nonprimary or **association areas,** they retain the effects of prior experiences and thereby play diverse integrating roles, coordinating incoming and outgoing messages for the primary sensory and motor areas and engaging in vast, currently unspecified activities. In short, these cortical regions integrate past experience with new messages. Thus, they provide additional meaning in a given situation. Rarely do adult human beings experience pure, unassociated stimulation. Combining new information with stored information, association areas contribute significantly to higher-level mental processes—perception, memory, and thinking.

Even in routine tasks, such as writing a letter, association areas play a fundamental role. "I hear such good news of my dear mama and my brother," Bertha wrote again from Karlsruhe to Dr. Binswanger, "that it would be irrational of me to be homesick." Reading these words aroused visual impulses that traveled to the primary visual areas and eventually to the association areas where they aroused diverse associations about Dr. Binswanger, his sanatorium, and so forth. Simultaneously, other association areas organized messages for writing more words, coordinated this information, and provided feedback about these activities, which was eventually integrated in the primary motor areas. One defining characteristic of human beings, in comparison with other creatures, is the far greater ratio of brain tissue devoted to association areas of all sorts.

Concept of Localization

Until the 15th century, many investigators understood the human brain differently. As noted earlier, they viewed it like a sponge or muscle, all of its regions similar in structure and operating together in much the same way, as a whole. For any given function, different parts of the cortex were considered equally important. Four centuries later, phrenology made a contrary claim, stating that specific mental functions emerged from bulges in specific areas of the brain. But research eventually refuted this doctrine of complete localization, derisively called "bumpology."

Today we recognize certain brain areas, some called primary, as playing indispensable roles in certain functions, and yet they are complemented by extensive association areas and other brain structures. This viewpoint suggests again *modularity doctrine,* stating that human behavior emerges through largely independent networks of diverse brain structures, or modules, involved in an integrated fashion, with different units contributing in different ways. Some of these units have local functions, others play a more general role, and many of their connections arouse brain regions yet to be understood. Modularity doctrine emphasizes the extraordinary *interactions* among diverse brain structures and functions.

Given this interdependence among parts of the cerebral cortex, localization occurs only in a relative sense. The concept of **brain localization** now means that some areas are especially adapted for specific functions, but it does not mean they are *solely* responsible for them. For example, some areas of the temporal lobes, near the sides of the head, are primary and essential in speech. Without them there is no speech. But even with them, speech also requires responsiveness to the stimuli for speaking, received through sensory channels. It requires associative processes for decisions about what to say. It requires access to memory for the particular words. It requires motor responses to utter them and kinesthetic feedback about which ones we are saying. The temporal areas are necessary for speech, but they are not sufficient. This same condition holds for all other complex mental functions, whether or not they are associated with primary areas.

Thus, the localization of memory, a higher-order cognitive function, consists of numerous lower-order, more specific functions in different brain regions, each contributing to what we call memory: the amygdala in attention and emotional memory, basal ganglia in the acquisition of skills, the cerebellum in conditioning, the cortex in associative memory, and the hippocampus in forming long-term memories. Similar statements can be made for the way the brain manages emotion, problem solving, and other activities. This view of dispersed localization and modularity doctrine has emerged slowly through successive investigations, building on one another and supported today by immense contributions from brain-imaging techniques, including the PET scan, MRI, and others.

As a group, these techniques serve the scientist, who is seeking new information, and the practitioner, who is meeting the personal needs of human beings. Not long ago, the useful options were almost nonexistent. Brain science was confined to autopsies of deceased brains, expanded in Bertha's era to injured and surgically altered brains, and today it includes the study of healthy, living brains, a huge advancement. And the therapeutic treatment of mind-brain disorders also has progressed dramatically, chiefly since the advent of medications in the middle of the 20th century. Practitioners at the time of Bertha's illness possessed only crude methods of drug therapy, evident when she wrote to Dr. Binswanger: "You will realize that to live with a needle always at the ready is not a situation to be envied." Indeed, some of Bertha's symptoms perhaps arose from drug intoxication.

But things have changed. The hospital today would employ much improved medications. Bertha might expect a discharge within a couple of weeks.

Modern Biomedical Therapy

In **biomedical therapy,** the aim is to alleviate psychological problems by altering an individual's physical condition. At the outset the therapist might hospitalize Bertha for diagnostic purposes but would not consider any initial treatment except drugs, perhaps accompanied by psychotherapy. This treatment would be guided by a close monitoring of her condition and vastly greater knowledge of medications than was available to the earnest but ignorant Breuer. With current insurance practices, she would be discharged promptly.

Modern biomedical therapy is known by various names, including *psychopharmacology* and *pharmacotherapy,* owing to the predominance of drug treatments, as opposed to electroconvulsive shock therapy and psychosurgery. Modern drug therapy can be astonishingly effective in relieving even severe symptoms. In fact, drug treatments are so widespread today that many are managed by physicians who are not specialists in psychiatry (Kramer, 2000). In treating a disease about which he had little special knowledge and no training, Breuer would not be so far afield today.

Ideally, the drugs would relieve Bertha's symptoms, enabling her to profit later from some other, less intrusive therapy (Martorano, 1984). This aim is crucial, though not always possible. If the treatment relied solely on medication, Bertha would run the risk of becoming dependent on the drugs. She might never examine whatever psychological issues may lie at the origins of her symptoms, apart from any hereditary disposition. Drug therapy, if required, ideally includes some form of expressive therapy.

Several cautions arise in drug therapy. First, therapists and the public have been bombarded with compelling claims and dramatic reports of their effectiveness in the mass media. As a result, drugs have been overprescribed.

Second, drug treatment avoids a lengthy hospitalization—the positive side. But this prompt discharge leaves many former patients without adequate assistance, and they discontinue treatment—the negative side. In this regrettable cycle, the *revolving-door outcome,* half the psychiatric patients move back and forth, into and out of the hospital—or they remain homeless.

Assessment and Diagnosis

The potency of therapeutic drugs and the ease with which they can be misused have prompted the development of extensive methods for assessing their outcomes. The knowledge gained from these tests is then made available to the individual therapist in the form of a database.

In the most powerful assessment method, the *randomized double-blind technique,* prospective patients are assigned on a chance basis to an experimental or control group. The experimental patients receive the real drug, the control patients a *placebo,* a nonmedical concoction merely simulating the treatment. The technique is called a double blind because neither the experimenter nor the participants know who has been assigned to which group. A third party makes these random assignments, keeps confidential records, and does not participate in judging the outcomes of the tests.

Even as recently as 30 years ago, psychopharmacology was deemed an art, as practitioners struggled to find the appropriate medications for diverse patients. But our knowledge of drugs and ways of evaluating them have grown at an unprecedented rate. Today, with far greater sophistication, drug therapy is a more precise enterprise, practiced not only by physicians but also psychologists with pharmacological training (Kramer, 2000; Nies & Spielberg, 1996). But owing to the unpredictable human element in all patients, it inevitably involves trial-and-error procedures, even in diagnostic efforts.

The Bellevue Sanatorium agreed with Breuer's diagnosis: Bertha suffered from hysteria. Today her diverse symptoms would have produced multiple diagnoses, including depression and some of the following conditions: somatization disorder, dissociative disorder, and borderline psychotic disorder.

As noted earlier, *depression* is marked by sad or irritable moods, poor concentration, feelings of worthlessness, and little pleasure in life. By today's standards, it is perhaps the most encompassing single diagnosis for Bertha.

When diverse parts of the body, or *soma,* become painful or malfunction without any medical explanation, the condition is called a *somatization disorder.* It became another feature of Breuer's diagnosis of hysteria. In addition, she might have been diagnosed with *dissociative disorder*—a sudden, extreme memory loss with no obvious cause. Finally, a *psychotic disorder* includes delusions, hallucinations, and other disorganized behavior, all of which Bertha displayed.

These disorders, described today in the *Diagnostic and Statistical Manual of Mental Disorders—IV,* raise the question about causes of mental illness. In everyday terms, two sets of causative factors can be identified. Some *predisposing factors* may be present well before the outbreak of the disorder, making it more likely. The early deaths of Bertha's two sisters, family discrimination against her, parental overprotectiveness, a possible hereditary tendency, and cultural restrictions in her education all can be viewed as predisposing factors. Then some specific event immediately preceding the illness becomes the *precipitating factor,* the most obvious instigator. Bertha's debilitating effort to nurse her ill father may be regarded as the precipitating factor. Expressed as the vulnerability-stress model of mental illness, predisposing factors make the person vulnerable; then a precipitating factor adds additional, intolerable stress, resulting in the disorder.

Despite her miserable circumstances, Bertha also has been suspected of feigning her symptoms, and perhaps some were of this nature (Borch-Jacobsen, 1996). But to be diagnosed as *malingering,* the patient must feign illness for some personal gain: to collect insurance benefits, evade the law, leave work, or simply to find a bed for the night (American Psychiatric Association, 1994). Bertha gained no such outcomes. She avoided nursing her father and certainly caught Breuer's attention for a while, but her symptoms continued and even increased after both these relationships ceased. To forego the daily pleasures of eating, drinking, talking, sleeping regularly, and even moving about in her environment, and to endure instead incarceration and the threat of treatments with electricity, drugs, and cold baths, as well as surgery, Bertha surely was experiencing a psychological problem of some sort. Amid these stressful, restrictive circumstances, the idea of pervasive malingering gains little significant support.

Moreover, diagnosing mental disorder across cultures and centuries becomes a dubious goal. Symptoms from one time or place cannot be readily interpreted from a different perspective. Legal, institutional, and economic conditions influence diagnoses; even fads may play a role. Seeking a correct diagnosis for someone living years ago in a foreign country is almost impossible. Fortunately, biomedical treatment can be implemented even without a clear diagnosis.

Guidelines for Treatment

Using information from published research, the therapist considers the anticipated effects of administering certain drugs to a particular patient, taking into account the patient's symptoms, age, history, health, genetic background, and a host of other factors (Nies & Spielberg, 1996). Organizing the patient's symptoms into clusters, the therapist begins with the most promising drug for the diagnostic category of the first cluster. If the patient shows improvement, then that tentative diagnosis gains some support. If that drug proves ineffective, the diagnosis remains "uncertain," and the next most-promising drug is employed. This systematic approach is possible because there is a predictable period between the beginning of treatment and the patient's response to a particular drug (Martorano, 1984). That period may range from a few moments to some weeks, depending on the characteristics of the drug.

Many therapeutic drugs fall into one of three broad categories: antianxi-ety, antidepressant, or antipsychotic. For Bertha's symptoms, the initial prescription might be a minor tranquilizer, an **antianxiety drug** designed to diminish tension and sleeplessness. This drug alone probably would not pro-vide a full recovery. It would reduce her symptoms by increasing the action of an inhibiting neurotransmitter. By stimulating a suppressant neurotrans-mitter, the drug would cause the brain synapses to produce tranquilizing effects, enabling her to participate more effectively in everyday activities, perhaps including other modes of therapy.

The probable side effects would include drowsiness and slightly disrupted thinking. A **side effect** is an unintended, usually unwanted, outcome of any therapy, such as increased heart rate, fatigue, or dizziness. Many side effects might be called bad effects. One drug might cause a mildly nauseous condi-tion; another might prompt vomiting; still another might induce dizziness, fatigue, mood changes, or even more disruptive conditions.

If the patient benefited from this medication, her progress would be monitored as a single drug user or multi-drug user. As a rule, the single-drug user does not disrupt the treatment. Multi-drug users are more difficult patients, for they consume whatever other drugs may be available for seda-tive or euphoric effects, complicating the treatment process. Combinations of drugs can create unpredictable outcomes. Bertha's addictive response to morphine in the Bellevue Sanatorium would be a cautionary signal for potential drug abuse (Martorano, 1984).

After using an antianxiety drug for some time, a person may begin to show **adaptation** or *tolerance,* which is a decline in response because the person's body has become accustomed to the stimulus—in this case the therapeutic drug. If adaptation occurs, the drug must be administered in larger and larger doses to obtain the desired outcome, thereby increasing the side effects. The therapist must consider these issues in the later stages of drug therapy.

If Bertha's symptoms instead seemed to cluster around depression, the medication would have been directed to this problem. Following the sys-tematic guidelines, the first question here is whether the depression is re-active or endogenous. As suggested already, a *reactive depression* is a normal but acute response to a traumatic occurrence, such as divorce, bankruptcy, or the death of a parent. A precipitating factor seems clear. The *endogenous depression* has a broader basis and longer history and is not so obviously triggered by a traumatic event. Its more complex origins have earlier roots.

If Bertha's depression appeared to be reactive—essentially a response to arduous nursing and her father's death—the therapist would undertreat it, prescribing small doses of a mild medication that enabled Bertha to obtain a much-needed rest. With an obvious endogenous depression, she would be administered a standard **antidepressant drug**, aimed at stimulating interest in the world. It would do so by increasing the presence of serotonin and certain other neurotransmitters in the synaptic spaces.

Bertha suffered from a traumatic event, but endogenous depression would become the focus of this treatment. This condition had been building for several years—an accumulation of anger, frustration, and feelings of not being truly loved emerging from the obviously preferential treatment given her brother Wilhelm. The therapist would have several choices of medication for endogenous depression, but the lag time for effectiveness might be several days or weeks.

In a broader sense, her diverse symptoms might suggest a psychotic disorder. In fact, Breuer at one point referred to the symptoms of psychosis, noting her hallucinations about black snakes and death's heads. If she were administered an **antipsychotic drug**, used to eliminate hallucinations and disturbed thinking, alleviation of those symptoms would suggest an underlying psychosis, requiring a closely monitored medication.

Many of the most effective antipsychotic drugs diminish the bizarre symptoms by blocking the presence of dopamine in brain synapses. A prominent neurotransmitter, dopamine appears to play a key role in certain psychotic disorders (Davis, Kahn, & Ko, 1991). But antipsychotic drugs can produce highly disagreeable side effects. In addition, they may fail to alleviate many deficits in schizophrenia: diminished speech, thought, and motivation.

But Bertha experienced a combination of symptoms, and here the guidelines become less systematic. If the antidepressant drug did not prove effective, the therapist would be confronted with several questions. Should a larger dosage be administered? Should a different drug be used? Does she need an antidepressant plus another medication for the other symptoms? Fortunately, drugs today contain combined ingredients, eliminating the lag time that would occur in successive treatments with different medications. Moreover, some medications can treat more than one condition.

Considering Bertha's diverse symptoms, a modern therapist certainly would administer a *set* of drugs. But multiple medications raise another pair of problems: patient compliance and drug interactions. Always an issue, *patient compliance* becomes increasingly difficult with multiple medications that may require different doses and different schedules. The treatment plan may become so intricate that the patient does not adhere to it, making the therapy worthless (Kramer, 2000). The second problem, *drug interactions,* occurs when medications consumed by the same patient alter the effect of one another. The combination produces an increased or decreased effect or a totally unexpected outcome, not predicted on the basis of any one drug alone. For example, two drugs may not produce significant side effects when only one or the other is used. When a patient consumes both in the same medically effective time frame, the drugs may generate a marked skin rash, tremor, or other undesirable conditions. Drug therapy requires caution, for it may be prescribed with too little regard for side effects, interaction effects, and long-term consequences. These detrimental outcomes can be cumulative.

Moreover, drugs do not necessarily solve the problem. Often, they simply remove the major symptoms. For this reason, drug therapy is used in conjunction with other treatments, commonly dialogues with a counselor or therapist, along with healthful programs of exercise, nutrition, and rest. In this combined therapy, using two or more treatment methods, each serves a different purpose. The medication provides stability; the dialogues provide an opportunity for exploring possible underlying problems. These patient-therapist dialogues are known as *psychotherapy,* which loosely includes almost any nonmedical conversation aimed at providing assistance. This combined therapy has been found beneficial with some disorders, but not with others.

Modern drug therapy, when used alone, raises still another caution—the absence of sustained contact with a caring therapist. Breuer's regular presence was essential to Bertha and highly unusual. Modern drug treatment tends to be brief and impersonal. A treatment session may last no more than 15 minutes, time enough for the therapist to check some physiological signs and ask a few questions about symptoms and side effects (Martorano, 1984). Even if the therapist demonstrates concern, the patient may feel overlooked and subsequently may fail to comply with the treatment plan. Without a strong patient-therapist alliance, any treatment may become ineffective or ignored by the patient.

Modern medications can provide fast, initial relief. If they had been available, they would have suppressed some of Bertha's symptoms. But they would not have solved all her problems or even enabled her to begin a complementary psychotherapy—because none existed at the time. She became a pioneer in that regard, showing the way through her "chimney sweeping."

Instead, biomedical therapy served Bertha poorly. Without any knowledge of neurons and neurotransmitters, Breuer and others who administered the drugs could not even imagine the blocking and flooding they created in the synaptic connections. Used to diminish her pain or put her to sleep, they sustained her addiction, and they produced powerful withdrawal symptoms. For the overdoses he administered, Breuer today certainly would become liable in a malpractice suit.

But he should be judged by the standards of his day. He used what was available and acceptable at the time. Since then, biological psychology has discovered many new ways of answering old questions—and pursuing the further questions those answers raise. And future investigators will do so too. That is the nature of science. Each generation stands on the shoulders of its predecessors.

Commentary and Critique

Knowledge of brain-behavior relationships takes a vital place in our efforts to understand human behavior and to improve the conditions of life. Biological psychology has made impressive progress toward these goals. But like most of our human-made world, all perspectives and research methods involve assets and drawbacks. In closing this chapter, and those on the other perspectives, it becomes essential to recognize the major limitations of each perspective.

All the perspectives seek findings that are accurate and comprehensive, but they cannot have both at once in any large measure. To ensure accuracy, some address relatively narrow questions or small units of behavior. Sacrificing some degree of certainty in favor of greater breadth, others concentrate on more diffuse questions or larger units of behavior. This dilemma about precision and breadth—the size of the phenomenon to be studied—extends throughout science.

Given that all biological systems are composed of separate but related organs, and that each system is connected to other systems with their own organs, investigators in biological psychology can study the body as a whole or focus on its separate parts. No one investigation can possibly address every aspect of any research question. A choice must be made. And in biological psychology, one choice, called reductionism, has become more popular than the other, variously known as nonreductionism or holism.

The premise in **reductionism** is that complex phenomena are best understood by examining their basic parts. The focus is on **elementary properties,** meaning the most basic, irreducible parts of something. The study of a complex whole is reduced to separate studies of elementary properties because investigating a smaller sphere offers less chance for error than addressing a larger one. The parts are not necessarily simple, but they are more limited than the whole. Scientists commonly tend toward reductionism, investigating narrowly defined topics and hypotheses, gaining precision in exchange for more comprehensive investigations.

In fact, science employs reductionism in two ways: within the same field and to another field. When a question is reduced within the same field, this reductionism might be called narrowness, for it reduces the range of inquiry. In this sense, all perspectives become reductionistic; none can take all factors into account.

Biological psychology illustrates this form of reductionism, investigating narrowly defined hypotheses about the behavioral details of anatomy and physiology. Investigations of the body that do not include a behavioral or experiential element fall outside the boundaries of biological psychology. The other psychological perspectives narrow the scope of inquiry differently. Psychoanalysis focuses on unconscious processes, and behaviorism studies environmental factors. Humanistic and cognitive psychology restrict inquiry largely to mental life in one form or another, and evolutionary psychology examines the implications of our common genetic background.

So much for reductionism as a form of narrowness within the field. It occurs everywhere in varying degrees. And it has been essential to progress in modern science.

Reductionism also occurs when a question is examined in the more fundamental units of a lower-level science, which is its most common meaning. Among all the psychological perspectives, biological psychology, for obvious reasons, most frequently employs this form of reductionism. Here the study of aggression, personality, sexuality, or another psychological phenomenon is reduced to brain physiology, or further reduced to brain chemistry or, once again, to genetics or protein synthesis. This process—moving from behavior, to brain physiology, to brain chemistry, genetics, and so forth—is much like taking a photograph and enlarging it again and again, each time bringing some small part of the picture into sharper and sharper focus (Holzman, 2000). A particular detail becomes increasingly available and thereby can be measured with greater accuracy. But the overall image fades. The periphery of the scene becomes blurry or lost completely.

Reductionism to a lower level does not mean that the question no longer exists at the upper level. It remains, but a narrow part of that question is examined in a more basic form. The question also can be "expanded" back into its original form and studied at that higher level. Especially in biological research, questions often become reduced, not expanded, with the aim of achieving greater precision (Figure 3.3).

But this reductionistic strategy, however compelling, should not lead psychology away from its fundamental goal of understanding human behavior

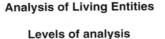

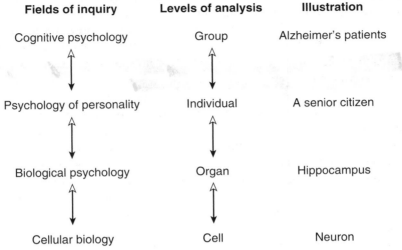

Figure 3.3   **Reductionism in Behavioral Studies.** The fields of inquiry might be extended downward to chemistry and physics or upward toward sociology. They depict a continuum of reductionism, not a series of discrete steps. As illustrated, investigations of memory, for example, occur at various levels of analysis. The open arrowheads indicate the lesser tendency for upward movement, away from reductionism and toward holism (Wahlsten, 2000).

amid the events of everyday life. This larger goal remains. For example, psychoanalysis aims for a grand view of humanity, addressing such broad questions as lifestyle, the unconscious, identity, and sense of self. Like the humanistic perspective, it generally studies the individual interacting in an everyday setting, not in a controlled laboratory environment. This broader aim goes a long way toward capturing the public interest—and poses problems for rigorous science.

Reductionism has played a massive, indispensable role in the advancement of science. As any field matures, it moves not only toward specialization but also toward reductionism, which offers precision and control. But reductionism alone, especially to a more basic science, does not necessarily provide adequate explanations of complex phenomena. Water is composed of two basic elements, hydrogen and oxygen, the former capable of burning, the latter essential for burning. But these basic elements are combined in such a way that water possesses neither characteristic. Similarly, an understanding of the electricity in the circuits of the computer does not explain the machine's problem-solving capacities.

The success of biological psychology's narrowly focused studies of living brains is beyond question. But the extent to which psychological phenomena can be described in neurological terms remains uncertain. At some point the psychological event disappears when examined only in terms of its biological underpinnings.

The **reductionist fallacy** states that phenomena are not always best understood in terms of their smaller, more basic parts. A more complete understanding of the human personality, consciousness, and other psychological characteristics will require something else too. Traditional reductionism does not eliminate the need for insights from other methods and other perspectives at other levels of inquiry (Cacioppo, Berntsen, & Crites, 1996).

Nevertheless, psychologists universally acknowledge the essential contributions from reductionism, especially in understanding the human nervous system. These restricted, precise investigations have formed an indispensable pathway to our ever-increasing knowledge of human behavior and experience.

Summary

Origins of Biological Psychology

In the human body, the nervous system serves as the basic communications network, receiving incoming information, mediating that information, and generating outgoing responses. Modularity doctrine states that any complex behavior requires the integrated contributions of various specific brain mechanisms, or modules. As the second communications network, the endocrine system plays a role in body maintenance, growth, and energy.

Key Terms: **biological psychology, network theory, neuron theory, neuron, principle of mass action, phrenology, modularity doctrine, brain plasticity, brain imaging techniques**

The Nervous System

The human nervous system provides flexibility of behavior through its billions of neurons in the brain, which are especially numerous relative to the size of the body, and through its billions of synapses, which are the spaces between neurons. In these synapses, neurotransmitter substances excite or inhibit connections with countless adjacent neurons, conducting impulses into, away from, and within the central nervous system, thereby enabling human beings to engage in a wide range of reactions.

Key Terms: **nervous system, central nervous system, peripheral nervous system, somatic nervous system, autonomic nervous system, synapse, cell body, dendrite, axon, all-or-none law, action potential, sensory neuron, motor neuron, interneuron, neurotransmitter, drug-induced state, addiction**

Organization of the Brain

The human brain can be viewed in three evolutionary parts: the hindbrain, mediating basic biological functions; the small midbrain, serving linkage functions; and the large forebrain, dominating in thought, memory, language, and other higher-level processes. The forebrain, in turn, can be considered in three levels: at the lower level, the hypothalamus, which plays a vital role in body maintenance; at the upper level, the cerebral cortex, which maintains contact with the environment; and in between them, the limbic system, which serves as a bridge and plays a vital role in emotion and memory.

Key Terms: **cerebellum, reticular formation, thalamus, hypothalamus, endocrine system, hormones, cerebral cortex, limbic system, amygdala, hippocampus**

The Cerebral Cortex

The gray outer covering of the brain, called the cerebral cortex, becomes critical in human mental processes. Its primary sensory areas and primary motor areas play fundamental roles in receiving information and responding to it, respectively. Its association areas serve an integrative function, combining the effects of earlier experiences already stored in the brain with incoming and outgoing information. Modularity doctrine emphasizes that any complex human activity requires an intricate, simultaneous coordination of different brain units, or modules, in various parts of the brain.

Key Terms: **hemispheric specialization, corpus callosum, primary sensory areas, primary motor areas, association areas, brain localization**

Modern Biomedical Therapy

Drug therapy, the most common biomedical treatment today, follows a set of systematic yet trial-and-error guidelines for identifying the most appropriate medication for a certain individual with a specific set of problems. The aim is to stabilize the patient and, ideally, to eliminate the need for medication, partly by encouraging patients to engage in additional therapeutic efforts, such as expressive therapy and programs of exercise, nutrition, and relaxation.

Key Terms: **biomedical therapy, antianxiety drug, side effect, adaptation, antidepressant drug, antipsychotic drug**

Commentary and Critique

Investigators employ reductionism in research by narrowing the range of inquiry and by examining a question in terms of the units of a lower-level science. According to this critique of biological psychology, understanding the operation of the billions of neurons in the human brain will not by itself explain the intricacies of human experience from one moment to another. Nevertheless, reductionism has been essential in the advancement of biological psychology.

Key Terms: **reductionism, elementary properties, reductionist fallacy**

Critical Thinking

1. In order to advance our knowledge of the nervous system, you have been invited to participate in research requiring the sacrifice of part of your brain. You are not suicidal. Indicate your reasons for offering one of these structures: the thalamus or corpus callosum or limbic system. Then state your rationale for keeping the others.

2. Explain the concept of modularity doctrine in brain function by using a metaphor. Think about an orchestra presenting a concert, and then offer a different metaphor.

3. Consider research on depression. Outline a likely reductionistic sequence beginning with culture and proceeding to the synapse. Then describe the reductionist fallacy.

4

Psychoanalysis

Psychoanalysis stresses unconscious mental life. Memories, dreams, and other long-forgotten remnants of earlier conflicts and frustrations presumably lie in this realm of the mind. Outside normal awareness, but not entirely out of one's life, these latent conflicts do not disappear. The anxiety they arouse can reappear in daily life in subtle, disguised ways known as unconscious motivation, the core concept in psychoanalysis and the focus of psychoanalytic therapy.

When Breuer discontinued Bertha's therapy, which was not psycho-analytic, he left suddenly, without warning—today a serious breach of ther-apeutic ethics. After so many intensive sessions together, a contemporary psychotherapist would give notice several months before departure, enabling the patient to prepare for this important event and assisting the patient in gaining contact with another therapist, if that seemed appropriate. Instead, when Breuer left the case, he left Bertha facing still another crisis: how to cope with his abrupt, inexplicable departure.

Much in the fashion of a discarded lover, Bertha had been jilted. According to legend, she responded with an imagined pregnancy and other unconfirmed reactions to their final separation (Jones, 1953). This story, steeped in romance, illustrates unconscious motivation in principle, proba-bly not in fact. The fantasy pregnancy appears fictional—but not the painful parting (Ellenberger, 1970; Hirschmüller, 1989).

The disruption in that parting would not surprise anyone knowledgeable about intensive psychotherapy today. If the therapeutic process goes well, a bond develops, and its unplanned cessation can become traumatic, especially for the patient. Bertha was troubled by her father's death, hostility toward her mother, resentment of her brother, and lack of any close relationship with any other family member or friend, and her contact with Breuer had become the one reliable, supportive human relationship in her life. A strong emotional reaction to this sudden break in intensive therapy would not be surprising at all. In fact, it would be expected—as would various efforts, conscious and unconscious, to ensure its continuation.

The case of Anna O., terminated so abruptly, stands at the beginning of the real-life story of Bertha Pappenheim. And Bertha's fate proved worse than Breuer expected. Their extraordinary therapy seemed to work for a while after each session. But it brought no lasting improvement.

Beginning with the background of psychoanalysis, this chapter then focuses on the structure and development of personality. Afterward, it con-siders the sequence of events creating unconscious motivation and, later, the way unconscious motivation is approached in psychoanalytic therapy. Finally, it concludes with a commentary and critique of the psychoanalytic perspective.

Background of Psychoanalysis

The fanciful pregnancy tale dramatizes the patient-therapist relationship, especially as it develops in the system of psychology called psychoanalysis. The term **psychoanalysis** has two meanings, one referring to a theory of personality, the other to a method of therapy, both emphasizing unconscious conflicts in mental life that are typically shaped by childhood experiences (Freud, 1925b).

Psychoanalysis developed during Bertha's most turbulent years, the last decades of the 19th century, in the Viennese flat of Sigmund Freud (1856–1939). Specifically, it emerged from two places in that apartment at 19 Berggasse: the couch on which his patients reclined in his consulting room and the desk where he wrote in longhand in his study.

The couch stood against the wall in that elaborately decorated room. A pillow lay at its head, some folded blankets at its foot. Using the pillow, a patient could assume almost a sitting position; the blankets offered protection against chilly temperatures. Each patient was instructed to relax and say whatever came to mind, no matter how foolish or embarrassing it might seem.

Sitting most of the day in a green stuffed chair at the head of that couch, out of the patient's line of sight, Freud listened to disturbed people describing their lives. That process was psychoanalysis as a therapy.

Later in the evening, usually after nine o'clock, he retreated to his study at the back of his flat and tried to make sense out of these jumbled monologues. There he sat, in seclusion, for three or four hours. Smoking cigars at the rate of 20 per day, scratching out his manuscripts with pen and ink, he brought forth the ideas for his theory of personality, also called psychoanalysis.

The Freudian Setting

In a sense, psychoanalysis arose as Freud's lofty intellectual protest against his culture and times. The celebrated Viennese society of his day had a dark side. The long reign of Emperor Franz Josef had yielded to favoritism and corruption in city politics, and multiculturalism, responsible for Vienna's cosmopolitan character, had generated political unrest. In fact, cafe society owed some of its popularity to shortages of housing and fuel, which forced people out of their cold, crowded homes and into public places. The city's renowned culture makers—Mahler in music, Kraus in letters, Klimt in painting, and, eventually, Freud in psychoanalysis—were vilified or suppressed. Turn-of-the-century Vienna hardly merited its long reputation as the City of Dreams.

Freud also resisted Viennese culture on more personal grounds. Anti-Semitism ran rampant in the Vienna of his day. He did not practice any religion, but as a Jew he became acutely aware of the indignities suffered by his father. In one instance, unforgettable for little Sigmund, a stranger intentionally knocked his father's new hat into a mud puddle, declaring that people of Freud's ethnic background deserved such treatment.

Graduating from medical school with high promise, Freud had no interest in the practice of medicine. He sought instead a career in laboratory research, which was initially delayed by youthful misadventures. While serving in the military, authorities arrested him for being absent without leave. Absent again later, this time from his laboratory, he lost credit for successful research he had conducted in neurology. Still later he became implicated in a difficult matter involving cocaine and a friend's untimely demise.

But the major deterrent to his research career occurred because Freud, a minority person, experienced discrimination not only in his social life but also in his professional aspirations. Successful in school, Freud nevertheless found himself and other Jews excluded from opportunities at the university. With this barrier, his lack of funds, and a growing interest in marriage, he turned to clinical work to earn a living, though he professed no desire for "playing the doctor game" (1926). Finally, years later, he gained an academic affiliation, working twice the usual period before receiving that recognition.

In the meantime, without access to academic circles, he encountered a research opportunity within his practice as a physician. In this private setting, consulting with people about their personal problems, he developed all sorts of ideas about human behavior. He found himself free to engage in unrestrained flights of speculation on the human condition, calling this decade of the 1890s his years of "Splendid Isolation," for he worked essentially without colleagues. In short, Freud's early poverty, ethnic background, and career frustrations prompted in him an ever-growing resentment against his city and culture. As a result, he completely avoided the political arena. The only favorable characteristic of the Viennese government, he once wryly remarked, was the inefficiency with which it operated. Instead, late at night, in the quiet of his study, he devoted himself to making "explosives"—broadsides directed at the whole way of life he experienced. Slowly, he alone developed psychoanalysis, which can be considered a grand intellectual protest against his time.

Psychoanalysis came not from laboratory studies or other traditional research but instead from a clinical practice, notably case studies. And far more than any other perspective in the 20th century, psychoanalysis arose through the work of one person—"The Professor," as colleagues called him.

As an astute observer of the human condition, Freud's ideas eventually permeated much of the 20th-century outlook on human behavior in Western society, especially with regard to unconscious mental processes and the importance of childhood for the development of adult personality. His work initiated voluminous research in both these areas, which is still vigorously pursued today.

Before Freud, the German philosopher Arthur Schopenhauer ruminated on unconscious mental life. He described human beings as perpetrators and victims of forces they do not comprehend, seeking goals they do not fully understand. But Freud declared that he developed his idea of the unconscious prior to discovering Schopenhauer's work. Yet it is clear that Darwin's work on evolution stimulated Freud's thinking about early experiences and the adult personality. If prehistoric environments influenced current behavior in the manner suggested by natural selection, earlier events in an individual's lifetime also might become powerful influences in one's adult behavior.

Freud's wide-ranging thought created resistance even within his limited circle of early supporters. Later followers were often still more rebellious. Loosely called **neo-Freudians**, they individually reformulated selective aspects of psychoanalysis, generally developing a less biological, more social orientation.

Through the reports of his patients and his own reflections, Freud had decided that even the mind of a child contains hidden sexual and aggressive impulses. This startling announcement in Victorian society brought forth criticism and condemnation in both scientific and public circles. His thinking continues to be controversial, and even his character has been doubted. But prolonged debate arises only over the life and work of people of note (Gleaves & Hernandez, 1999).

Freud's dramatic case studies earned him the Goethe Prize for excellence in literature, the only international award he received in his lifetime. In fact, many observers today view his system of thought as belonging more to literature than to science. As a storyteller, he showed this inclination even in the pseudonyms he chose for his male patients, reflecting their symptoms: Wolf Man, Gingerbread Boy, Rat Man, and so forth. His more restrained pseudonyms for women reflected the gentler social roles assigned to them in Austria and elsewhere at that time: Emmy, Dora, Elizabeth von R., and others.

Practicing psychoanalysts today collect their data in much the same way as Freud did, through case studies, but often without the couch. The analyst listens and observes, gathering information about the patient. But psychoanalytic scientists today also collect data in formal laboratory experiments, studying groups of people in more restricted, controlled ways (Cramer, 2000; Westen, 1998). In both research methods, the exploration of unconscious mental processes becomes a central goal.

Concept of the Unconscious

The concept of the unconscious is the core of psychoanalysis. A generic term, the *unconscious,* or **unconscious mental processes**, refers to the thoughts and feelings of an individual not open to examination by that person. In fact, Freud described two categories of unconscious processes. In one, **unconscious cognition**, mental processes operate outside a person's awareness, but they do not pose any threat to that person. No conflict is involved. They arouse no deep-seated anxiety. The individual therefore makes no effort, intentional or otherwise, to exclude them from consciousness. When hitting a 95 miles-per-hour baseball, for example, the time required to respond precludes thinking in any detail about exactly what to do. Information processing takes place automatically. In a like manner, unconscious cognition does not become a significant issue in psychoanalysis.

The other category of unconscious mental processes does play a vital role in psychoanalysis, however, and here the mental activities do pose a threat. In **unconscious motivation**, certain mental processes instigate anxiety about earlier circumstances, prompting the person to exclude from normal awareness these thoughts and also the relevant feelings and behaviors they may arouse. Psychoanalysts sometimes speak of *unconscious emotion* when emphasizing the feelings; they speak of unconscious motivation with reference to the behaviors and reasons for them. Both types of reactions become unconscious, excluded from awareness because the individual perceives them as threatening.

Unconscious motivation begins with conflict, which occurs in everyone's life. Here **conflict** takes on a broad meaning, indicating a problem of almost any sort producing trauma, indecision, frustration, confusion, abuse—or any other manifestation of anxiety. Bertha undoubtedly experienced anxiety over the conflict with her rivalrous brother, with her overprotective mother, perhaps even with her romanticized father, and definitely with the restrictive gender roles in her society.

To defend against this anxiety, the individual develops various mechanisms, some described later as defense mechanisms. But the chief mechanism, on which all others are based, is repression. In **repression**, a person unintentionally excludes the anxiety-provoking memories, thoughts, and impulses from normal awareness, preventing them from entering consciousness. This concept has become widely debated today partly because of the various ways in which Freud labeled and described this process, partly because of the difficulty in producing this unconscious but motivated condition in laboratory studies (Erdelyi, 2000). But repression takes a primary place in traditional psychoanalytic theory. In a word, the solution for managing these anxiety-provoking thoughts is forgetting. The person forgets the event; it seemingly never occurred. It is kept from awareness by the barrier of repression. Or a whole series of related events are kept outside normal awareness.

However, the anxiety does not disappear. The so-called forgotten problem remains in the background of the individual's mental life, hidden but at the same time seeking expression. Thus, the conflict is only partly or tentatively solved by repression; still deep in the recesses of the individual's mind, it festers and smolders. In short, the individual commonly develops a **fixation**, meaning that the person becomes preoccupied with the unresolved problems, behaving in persistent, puzzling, and generally ineffective ways. A fixated person, intensely concerned with some past event that prompted anxiety, exhibits this tension again and again when confronted with similar events in present-day life. But the individual deals with the problem only indirectly.

These unconscious, anxiety-arousing thoughts and memories may simply appear as an inexplicable nervousness in the individual. Or they may be expressed in an indirect fashion, through an inordinate preoccupation with an almost infinite number of issues: family, food, fantasy, freedom, and friendship, just to name a few. Even in adult life, the person remains fixed on the earlier, unresolved issue, commonly dating back to childhood. Human beings, according to psychoanalysis, spend their lives in an endless struggle, shielding themselves and society from their unconscious fixations. Laid down early in life, they can influence later behavior in unconscious ways.

To portray unconscious motivation in everyday living, Freud used as a metaphor a historical monument, constructed as a memorial to some specific, earlier emotional event. The Great Fire of 1666 destroyed much of London. That fire is over, but the city erected a monument to the catastrophe. Hundreds of feet high, it stands where the fire started. An underground railway station has taken its name, Monument Station, and visitors to London can climb its stairs for a panoramic view of the city.

Suppose a modern Londoner sheds copious tears daily when passing that monument, each time overcome with remorse over the loss of lives and property of his ancestral family hundreds of years ago. Others would view this man with some concern, for he remains fixated on a disaster that occurred long ago. He would be far better served by going about his current business or thinking with pleasure about how London has survived that dreadful event. But many disturbed people behave like this sobbing, impractical man, except they have little idea about what is troubling them. Still dealing with disruptive, unknown events from long ago, they cannot live in a satisfied, productive manner. They neglect what is real and current in their lives. According to psychoanalysis, this fixation with past trauma is the most fundamental characteristic of a disturbed personality (Freud, 1909).

Incidentally, one of Freud's early followers, Carl Gustav Jung, also emphasized our past, but he focused on our distant past, including the experiences of much earlier ancestors. As a neo-Freudian, he conceived of a deeper unconscious, well beyond our personal or individual unconscious. For Jung, the **collective unconscious** contains memories and thoughts common to all people everywhere, described as *archetypes,* meaning mental imprints or patterns to which we are universally predisposed. He found evidence for archetypes and other dimensions of the collective unconscious in human symbols, myths, fairy tales, religions, and other seemingly universal cultural expressions (Rosen, 2000). Critics call for more empirical, controlled support for this theory, but since Freud, the idea of unconscious thought has been pursued vigorously in many directions.

Traditional psychoanalysis approaches personality from the viewpoint of unconscious residues of earlier events in the lifetime of the individual. Prior to Freud, with his emphasis on childhood experience, people commonly explained a disturbed personality in terms of the devil, chance factors, one's constitution, or divine intervention. In particular, the 19th-century outlook explained bad behavior as the result of "bad blood," described by Charles Dickens, George Eliot, and other prominent writers. This preoccupation with blood as the responsible agent did not cease until the 20th century, and Sigmund Freud's concept of the personal unconscious played a very large role in this new line of thought.

Structure of Personality

In psychoanalysis, personality emerges from the interactions of three forces or building blocks, all hypothesized internal structures, within the individual. The first, the **id,** is inborn, part of our biological inheritance; it is the source of all our energies, mental and physical, erotic and aggressive. The id serves as the "motor" of behavior, providing Bertha, for example, with the vitality needed for riding horseback, telling stories, and engaging in her private theater. Following the *pleasure principle,* the id seeks immediate satisfaction of all biological drives, sometimes automatically through sneezing, sweating, and blinking. The satisfaction of other drives—hunger, thirst, safety, and sexuality—requires effort and planning. The individual must find solutions or receive assistance.

From the energy of the id and through the baby's contact with the environment, the second dimension, the ego, emerges. The ultimate task of the **ego,** which is the center of the self or "I," is to preserve the individual; it does so as the executive director or problem solver of the personality. In contrast to the id, the ego follows the *reality principle,* regulating the individual's behavior according to circumstances in the environment. It seeks appropriate ways to satisfy hunger, thirst, safety, and other demands of the id. A strong ego redirects expressions of the id that would be inappropriate in a particular time or place. In the early years, before the ego is adequately developed, an adult must play the ego's role for a child or adolescent, satisfying many of the demands of the id and redirecting others.

From a psychoanalytic perspective, young Bertha lacked the ego strength for coping with her family environment in Vienna. Unable to pursue her personal goals in realistic fashion, she resorted to the fantasy of her private theater. Sad, angry, and confused, she then stayed in bed all day, remained silent, and refused to take nourishment, displaying negative behaviors like those of a small child. She also made suicidal gestures. Her weak ego barely succeeded in the task of self-preservation. Eventually, Bellevue Hospital supplanted Bertha's ego, providing the support and structure she was unable to obtain for herself within her family.

The third force, the superego, begins to develop somewhat later and is significantly influenced by the acquisition of language. As a set of values and standards for behavior in a particular society, the **superego** is acquired through contact with parents, teachers, and other elders. It serves as a moral guide for the individual, developing along two paths. As the child internalizes parental and other social prohibitions, these prohibitions become the *conscience,* that part of the superego placing restraints on "bad" behavior. As the child internalizes parental and other social goals, they become the *ego ideal,* that part of the superego that stresses achievement and other "good" behavior. Both parts of the superego develop through imitation of adults, as well as through direct instruction (Freud, 1925b).

Even as a young adult, Bertha refrained from all sexual expression and all direct confrontation with her overprotective parents. In psychoanalytic terms, this delayed development reflected an overly strong, almost punishing superego. Sex and aggression were "bad" behaviors, and the ego found an escape. Bertha retreated into the fantasy world of her private theater—and then became ill.

As the problem-solving dimension of personality, the ego faces a difficult task. Beset on one side by the urges of the id, on the other by the restrictions and goals of the superego, it must seek effective solutions in a particular environment. An extremely broad concept, the *environment* includes all external factors that have the potential to influence an individual, running the gamut from physical to social, subtle to obvious, family members to strangers, and so forth.

With the support of the Bellevue hospital, Bertha gained some ego strength. She began telling tales again, still dealing with personal problems,

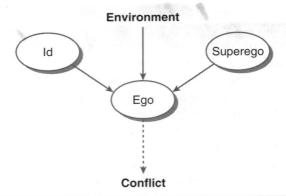

Figure 4.1   Psychoanalytic Approach to Personality. As the executive dimension of the personality, the ego must deal with the requirements of the id, the restrictions of the superego, and the reality of environmental constraints. Not circled as a component of personality, the environment is vital in the development of the ego. In traditional psychoanalysis, a strong ego is a highly desirable attribute, the prime factor in resolving conflict in human life.

but this time with more refinement. Then she began writing some tales. They gave her a way of expressing herself, an opportunity she seized and then lost with Breuer. At first she wrote stories just for herself; later she shared them with cousins; and eventually she authored a small book.

As suggested in these activities, the ego is the problem-solving element in the personality—the responsible agent or self. A resourceful ego directs the individual into successful ways of dealing with problems—writing stories, doing volunteer work, and so forth (Figure 4.1). Bertha published these tales anonymously with her own money. *Little Stories for Children* described lonely people and abandoned babies, hardly the expected themes for young minds (Pappenheim, n.d.). Lonely and depressed, angry at family members, Bertha perhaps wrote these stories as a way of dealing with her own fate. In psychoanalytic terms, her writing was an attempt by the ego to find a solution to her loveless life.

Bertha stayed two months with her Karlsruhe cousins, gaining confidence through her fairy tales and new friendships. Then she spent a short time with relatives in Frankfurt. Afterward, she returned to Vienna. Still experiencing symptoms, she wanted to resume therapy with Josef Breuer. But he refused (Rosenbaum, 1984b).

One of Bertha's Viennese neighbors struggled with these same symptoms— in a different way. He studied them in other people, although he experienced some himself as well. For his ideas, he was scorned by many and then lionized, first in Europe, later in the United States, and finally throughout much of the world. He occupied a flat not far from the center of Old Vienna. These quarters served as the home and offices for Sigmund Freud.

He began his practice with the traditional therapies of his day, all without success, at least by his standards. Gradually, he abandoned these medicines, direct advice, and even hypnosis. Instead, he learned to listen to his patients' innermost thoughts and feelings. These halting, commonly disturbing descriptions revealed the inner workings of the human mind; they became Freud's key to personality and its development.

Scrutinizing himself, his family, and friends, as well as his patients, Freud decided that much of human personality is formed early in life, chiefly during the first five years. The id remains constant, but the ego and superego undergo fundamental, enduring developments in the early years. One of Freud's major contributions to Western thought lay in pointing to childhood as a foundation of adult personality.

Development of Personality

Much of the child's development proceeds through predictable, biologically driven changes, called maturational stages. They occur throughout human life: physical, mental, social, and emotional. A common genetic background underlies most of the rapid developments in infancy, childhood, and adolescence, as well as the slower changes at later ages. From this standpoint, human life becomes a sequence of unfolding stages. But they are modified for each individual by unique hereditary and environmental factors.

The most obvious stages appear in physical developments. In locomotion, the child learns to sit, then crawl, later stand, still later walk, and finally run. In grasping, the child at first can only wave its arms wildly; later it gains control of its arms and hands; still later, it can oppose its thumb to other fingers; and eventually it can use just the thumb and index finger to grasp a cookie crumb or button its clothes.

The Psychosexual Stages

Freud speculated about a similarly predictable sequence in sexual development, defining sexuality broadly to include activities related to ingestion and excretion, as well as reproduction. He also considered the mental and social dimensions to be more important than the physical component.

In physical terms, these developments begin with the alimentary canal, first at the front end, in the lips and mouth. Then they move to the anus and later shift to the genitals. All these developments are the result of biological maturation in what we now call the erogenous zones. These phases of sexual growth, with their mental, social, and physical changes, are known as **psychosexual stages,** and they can have important consequences for the child's emerging personality, depending on the management of tasks that accompany each stage.

The roots of personality lie with these tasks because the erogenous zones provide our greatest sources of pleasure, and yet sexuality is something the child cannot understand or control. Moreover, sexuality involves social prohibitions, thereby creating anxiety in the child. Thus, the child's experiences can leave their marks, especially if performance of the task goes awry. Then the child becomes "stuck" or fixated on that problem (Freud, 1907).

According to psychoanalysis, all normal children pass through these stages. They do so at somewhat different ages, but the sequence is invariant.

The tasks in the first three stages are feeding, toilet training, and adjustment to family life. In each case, the task may generate conflict, depending on the child's readiness to manage it and the caretakers' modes of assistance. The outcomes have implications for the child's feelings of trust and well-being, competence and independence, and capacity for interpersonal relationships.

In the **oral stage,** the infant first derives pleasure through stimulation of the mouth when obtaining food, which in turn produces the energy needed for survival. For this task, the highly sensitive lips and tongue are well suited. The infant enjoys this stimulation, emitting the sucking reflex even in the absence of food. If the infant's nutritional and emotional needs are adequately met during this first stage, the child develops the potential for a confident, trusting outlook on life. If not, feelings of apprehension and dissatisfaction may arise instead. And if repressed, these feelings may become major components of the adult personality.

In the second and third years, with gains in muscular control, the child is confronted with a new and more difficult task: toilet training. Contrary to the feeding task in the oral stage, which is compatible with the demands of the id, the child in the **anal stage** must oppose id impulses, resisting the pleasure associated with elimination. The child must withstand the tension until reaching a proper time and place for excretion. The child who manages this task successfully gains a sense of competence and pleasure in the world. Successful toilet training is most important in developing and strengthening the ego. If instead, the training is too strict, the child's resentment again may become enduring, appearing in adulthood as a rebellious, impulsive personal style or as an excessive concern with correctness. Needless to say, the caretaker's supervision of this task and the child's biological readiness play major roles in bringing about favorable or unfavorable outcomes.

These stages may interact and overlap with one another and with the next stage, which begins around age three—with another shift in erotic pleasure. And here we come to another point of resistance in one of Freud's followers. Freud called this next phase the *phallic* stage, for the child becomes more sharply aware of gender differences and relationships among adults, including the parents' particular roles. Adopting the ways of one or both parents, the child also takes greater notice of the genitals, obtaining pleasure from self-stimulation. The child may engage in related fantasy activities, including a desire for intimate relations, notably with the parent of the opposite sex. According to psychoanalysis, the child's relationships with the parents and siblings at this stage, however stable or turbulent, set the pattern for personal relationships in later life.

But Freud's expression excludes one gender, and Karen Horney raised this issue. As a neo-Freudian speaking of **feminine psychology**, she disagreed with several of Freud's basic concepts, declaring that females must be understood on their own terms, not simply as different from males. Acknowledging Freud's genius and his work in a male-dominated society, she argued that men's exclusion from pregnancy, childbirth, and breast feeding prompted them unconsciously to depreciate women. For these thoughts, she became recognized as the first female psychoanalyst and a pioneer in female psychology (Paris, 2000). Late in his career, Freud turned to female sexuality, but he expressed less confidence about his understanding owing in some substantial measure to the times and culture in which he lived.

Freud had another label for this third stage, when children become more sharply aware of gender differences. He called this condition the **Oedipus complex**, referring to an ancient Greek tragedy in which King Oedipus unwittingly killed his father and married his mother, a potential curse, Freud claimed, laid on every male child. The son directs his first desire for sexual intimacy toward his mother and, accordingly, his first hostile wish toward his father, who has become his rival. The boy wants his mother all to himself; he views his father as a nuisance, feeling resentful about his father's relations with his mother and expressing satisfaction when his father is absent. But at other times the boy feels affection for his father, who protects him and satisfies many of his needs. The result is ambivalence; the child experiences conflict.

Encouraged by Jung much later, Freud incorporated into his thinking a Greek drama about women. In this tale, Electra fell in love with her father and participated in the murder of her mother. Freud regarded the daughter's desire for intimacy with her father and rivalry with her mother as another universal theme, which Jung described as the **Electra complex**, and here the

r experiences conflict. Thus, both boys and girls participate in a
riangle, seeking a special intimacy with the parent of the opposite sex
and adopting a cautiously adversarial stance toward the same-sexed parent.
And when brothers and sisters arrive, this rivalry is enlarged to include them.
With several siblings, all contesting for places in the family, these interpersonal struggles, conscious and unconscious, can exert considerable influence
on the development of personality. These struggles, Freud declared, become
inevitable whenever human beings must live together.

In this context of problems in living together, still another of Freud's
rebellious followers became prominent. In his **individual psychology**, Alfred
Adler stated that each person, in his or her own individual way, strives for
mastery in the environment. This striving becomes the chief force in life
because shortly after birth we all experience *feelings of inferiority,* owing
to our physical limitations with respect to our caretakers, all of whom are
stronger, bigger, quicker, and wiser. Our great deficit in life begins with our
enormous dependence on others. Our enduring difficulty lies with this early
experience of not being a fully capable adult (Adler, 1927).

Freud's emphasis on childhood stimulated these thoughts, but Adler, well
before his time, developed them into topics of considerable modern interest,
such as parenting, family relationships, and living successfully in a community. Among them, *sibling rivalry* and the influence of *birth order* are now
widely recognized and investigated (Stewart, 2000). Today in popular psychology, interest in self-help books on marital relationships, parenting, and
sibling rivalry is exceeded only by the unremitting interest in self-help books
on human sexuality.

Unlike other creatures, Freud continued, human beings begin their sex
lives twice; the first time, like all other animals, occurs early in life, when the
child is only three to six years of age. This effort is a feeble one. Then, after
a quiescent period of several years, in a stage called latency, the sex life
begins again, this time evolving toward sexual maturity. The patterns in this
second instance, beginning at puberty, have already been laid down by the
preceding childhood sexuality. Intense emotional processes accompany these
years of adolescence, reflecting the prior Oedipus/Electra outcomes, and they
function partly outside normal awareness.

Freud described this love-and-aggression triangle as "the romance of the
family" (Freud, 1905). It had more relevance in his Vienna than in societies that
offer more opportunities for diverse, open lifestyles (Malinowski, 1927, 1929).

There are traditional resolutions of the Oedipus and Electra complexes.
Through **identification,** the child adopts the characteristics of someone else,
typically the same-sexed parent, rather than maintaining an adversarial
relationship with that person. The parent thus becomes a model, not a rival.

Identification is the chief but not the only means by which the ego deals with the Oedipus/Electra conflict. In any case, this conflict subsides during a latency of four or five years and then arises again in adolescence. When this second phase goes well, teenagers gradually detach themselves from their parents, ceasing to be children and becoming adult members of society. In adult life, the earlier struggle may be transformed into affectionate and competitive expressions, as well as other derivative forms.

These conclusions about the outcomes in adult life need further empirical support. And times and cultures have changed since Freud's day. But the idea that roots of adult personality lie in the management of childhood conflict has exerted a powerful influence on research in developmental psychology and also in clinical practice.

Fixations in Everyday Living

Life is full of hazards, however. No one makes the journey without some bumps and bruises, mental and physical. Passing through these early stages without any significant disruption requires careful, intelligent caretakers and extraordinarily good luck. Typically the child's needs at some point are unmet or disrupted through negligence or misfortune. Then, as noted already, the outcome may be a *fixation,* in which the gratification of a certain need has been blocked, and the individual becomes controlled or possessed by that issue, overly but unconsciously focused on resolving it. Freud speculated extensively about fixation and its outcomes in adulthood (Freud, 1905, 1909).

According to traditional psychoanalysis, a child in the oral stage is especially susceptible to conflict related to the need for nourishment—when food is not available, not satisfying, not presented in an emotionally satisfying manner, and so forth. As a result, the child may become fixated on these issues later, remaining overly concerned with food, constantly seeking love and support, worried about nutrition, demanding special treatment, and the like. This insecurity, Freud speculated, may remain for the rest of the child's life.

Similarly, if toilet training goes poorly because of the child's lack of readiness, the parents' unreasonable expectations, or any related tension, the child may become fixated at this stage, again becoming unconsciously preoccupied with the problem. Attempting to make amends at later ages, the child may become excessively neat, clean, obedient, and prompt, reflecting an overdeveloped superego. Or, adopting the opposite stance, the child may become messy, tardy, disobedient, and inconsiderate of others. In either case, the frustration over the earlier failure remains. Fixation is a sign of arrested ego development; the person cannot "let go" of the earlier difficulty. Later, even as an adult, the person struggles unsuccessfully to achieve a solution or to retaliate.

And when the great adolescent task goes badly, owing to disturbed ground-work in the Oedipus/Electra stage, issues of sexuality and personal relation-ships appear. Restrictions, punishment, and guilt have left their mark, and again, the development of the ego is arrested. The normal capacity for love is blocked or diverted. The individual may remain for the rest of life overly com-bative, submissive, or otherwise unable to deal with authority, intimate rela-tions, and so forth. On this basis, Freud argued, the Oedipal/Electra stage is the seat of adult personality disorders (Freud, 1917).

The Pappenheims' management of these childhood conflicts and Bertha's response to them remain unknown. But psychoanalysts would speculate that things went poorly. The prevailing sexual code, Bertha's later behavior, and comments by relatives suggest life was not easy for the little girl. In addition to severe restrictions of the superego and the early deaths of two older sis-ters, an unresolved Electra complex perhaps contributed too.

Even in her teens, Bertha displayed some unusual difficulties in everyday liv-ing. For example, Breuer described her sexuality as "astonishingly undevel-oped," and she enjoyed few satisfying relationships with peers, male or female. In a psychoanalytic sense, these problems were remnants of unresolved Oedipus/Electra issues. And some of her tales can be viewed in this way.

In the last of her *Little Stories for Children,* a water sprite lived alone by a pond. As punishment for some misdeed, she was prevented from ever leav-ing her little sanctuary. A great stone head with a forbidding look kept a watchful eye on her. But one night she became uncontrollably drawn out of the pond by dance music. Reaching the dance floor, she met a tall, bearded, blue-eyed man. She became his partner, wrapped in his embrace, dancing to music more and more intoxicating, until it faded. Then the little sprite looked into his eyes. Instantly, a tremor seized the man's body, and he turned away. He knew he had danced with a little sprite; she knew the dance was over and the romance too.

The little sprite crept back to the pond and found it frozen. So she lay down beside the pond waiting for the ice to melt. It snowed and snowed, covering her body. The stone head laughed at her plight. Finally, spring arrived and melted the mantle of snow. Then the stone head, gazing sternly on the scene below, observed a tiny plant. Its solitary white flower sprouted from the place where the sprite had lain beside the pond (Pappenheim, n.d.).

Bertha perhaps composed this melancholy tale from her own life. She too had been prevented from leaving her home. A malicious stone head guarded the water sprite's virtue, just as a death's head, perhaps resembling her over-protective father, threatened Bertha during her hallucinations. And she too heard dance music, which brought thoughts of romance. In coloring and countenance, the water sprite's dance partner resembled Josef Breuer who, in turn, resembled Bertha's father (Hirschmüller, 1989). And that romantic figure disappeared instantly from the sprite's life, just as Breuer had done with Bertha in earlier days.

Written some years after her father's death and her therapy with Breuer, this tale suggests that Bertha still remained disturbed over those earlier events. From a psychoanalytic perspective, that reaction might be expected.

But numerous factors can contribute to any psychological disorder, and early conflict can produce many disparate outcomes. These psychoanalytic stages today are viewed as speculative. More conservatively, it is safe to say that life at times is difficult for everyone, especially in childhood, and that for most of us, some childhood problems persist in adult life. Psychoanalysis is significantly responsible for this view. The importance of childhood for later adjustment and personality is widely accepted today.

By the outset of the 20th century, Freud's work had stimulated considerable support and vociferous objections. Several of his hypotheses and theories have been impossible to investigate scientifically because the underlying concepts are too vague. Others have yielded mixed results, not a surprising outcome, for the value of theory lies primarily in the research it generates. But recent studies in cognitive, social, developmental, and clinical psychology have offered empirical support for the unconscious, which stands as the cornerstone of psychoanalysis (Cramer, 2000; Westen, 1998, 1999).

Crises Through the Life Cycle

Neo-Freudians have modified and extended psychoanalytic theory through the full course of human development. One of them, Erik Erikson, identified eight stages in the life cycle from birth through old age but, like Freud, without impressive empirical support. These stages include a series of tasks or changes in social functioning, called **psychosocial crises,** each involving relationships with other people (Erikson, 1963).

Four crises occur in childhood. In the first, *trust versus mistrust,* the infant develops confidence and optimism, or a negative, distrustful outlook, depending on the caretaker's management of the infant's need for nourishment and support. In the child's second year, the caretaker's task is to allow the ambulatory child as much freedom as possible without endangering itself, creating the crisis of *autonomy versus doubt.* From ages three to six the child is ready to attempt simple tasks, producing the crisis of *initiative versus guilt,* depending again on the caretaker's response to the child's inept efforts. In the final childhood crisis, *industry versus inferiority,* the caretaker guides the child to appropriate tasks, thereby enhancing a sense of achievement, or presents tasks too demanding for the youngster's level of maturity, producing feelings of inadequacy in that child.

With puberty, the teenager's social goals and circumstances change markedly. In this crisis of *identity versus role diffusion,* the adolescent begins an intensive effort to develop a sense of self as an individual, seeking his or her own pathway in life. Erikson called this challenge of moving away from the family the *identity crisis,* a time of personal upheaval and uncertainty.

Bertha Pappenheim experienced much emotional turmoil in late adolescence. One might speculate that her parents and culture forced her toward an identity that she could not accept—that of a dependent housewife.

The tensions aroused by moving away from one's family create in young adulthood the crisis of *intimacy versus isolation.* If this crisis is successfully managed, through a close relationship with someone else, the person feels supported rather than alone and alienated. The crisis of *generativity versus stagnation* occurs in middle adulthood, raising the challenge of progressing beyond intimacy and one's own welfare to a broader concern for humanity. In the final crisis, called *integrity versus despair,* the individual looks back on his or her life and finds meaning and satisfaction or disappointment and despair. Integrity here refers to emotional integration, and the issue is not what has happened but rather how a person feels about those earlier events.

Like many theories, Erikson's work has been criticized as lacking precision and empirical support, especially in the later crises. But in emphasizing the full life cycle, social development, and an identity crisis, this theory offers useful points of departure for the study of adjustment and maladjustment. At the core of this view, founded on Freud's work, stands the notion of fixation. Unresolved childhood social crises can become core aspects of the personality later in life.

Expressions of the Unconscious

This concept of the unconscious can incite disagreement. As something apart from normal awareness, something not available through ordinary introspection, its presence or absence cannot be proven directly. Instead, evidence can be collected for or against the presence of unconscious mental processes, and in each instance, a case must be built. Seeking degrees of certainty, psychoanalysis often makes such a case (Schwartz, 2003). And support has been gained from investigations outside the traditional psychoanalytic context, revealing empirical evidence for unconscious thought in cognition, motivation, and emotion (Westen, 1998).

Symbolism in Behavior

Unconscious motivation occurs when someone behaves in certain ways, but neither these actions nor the reasons behind them are open to direct, conscious scrutiny, though they may convey traces of their origins (Freud, 1915, 1917). And here a brief review is in order.

Psychoanalysis is sometimes called the study of personality from the viewpoint of *conflict,* referring to the incompatible urges and tendencies that pervade human life. Our biological requirements and interests are commonly at odds with the restraints imposed by civilization. The struggle for survival continues in all cultures. At a more personal level, we experience ambivalence toward those people most important in our lives—those who have loved and protected us during our earliest, most vulnerable years. At one time or another, our interactions with them became frustrating and painful—for example, when we were punished for something we did not understand, when we were denied requests that seemed perfectly reasonable, or when we were ignored when we needed assistance. Emotional closeness in a family inevitably produces a great variety of feelings within each member, including tenderness, rivalry, fear, respect, and other incompatible feelings.

The individual is most vulnerable to conflict during the early years. Too weak to fight, too small to threaten, too ignorant to scheme, too clumsy to flee, too speechless to explain—the child is at others' mercy. Despite the most watchful caretakers, childhood traumas are almost inevitable. For little Bertha, the early deaths of her siblings certainly had this potential, as did her later quarrels with Wilhelm, restrictions in sexual expression, and the cultural discrimination against females.

Conflict, then, sets the stage for something to follow—the ego's effort to cope with conflict and the anxiety it generates. What happens when the ego cannot manage this task directly? In psychoanalysis, the answer is clear. The ego solves the problem indirectly.

In *repression,* a controversial concept, anxiety-provoking thoughts are excluded from consciousness through unintentional forgetting. In psychoanalysis, repression is the primary defense mechanism of the ego. Fearing reprisal for forbidden impulses, a person may repress the whole experience, thereby diminishing the overt anxiety. But repression is only a partial solution. The conflict is not truly resolved; the anxiety does not disappear completely.

In dealing with this persistent, puzzling anxiety, the individual develops a *fixation,* becoming overly and unconsciously concerned with the unknown problem. The person becomes "possessed" by it. Coping with it in the back of the mind, the person's effectiveness in daily life is thereby reduced (Freud, 1915).

This fixation occurs because repression is not a static state, like a lid screwed onto the top of a jar. It is instead a bubbling cauldron in which highly emotional conflicts seek expression, kept from daily awareness at the cost of considerable psychic energy. When these conflicts threaten to break the ego's barrier of repression, the fixation appears in indirect and unexpected ways called symbolic behavior. In other words, **symbolic behavior** is any disguised expression of some fixation; it is the behavioral manifestation of a partly repressed thought or feeling. Thus, fixation is a process, referring to the covert, internal state of tension. Symbolic behavior is an outcome, referring to any presumably disguised expression of that internal state appearing in dreams, mistakes, adjustment reactions, and other forms.

Unlike typical symbols, such as a wedding ring or a person's signature, symbolic behavior becomes a representation *and* a misrepresentation, a compromise between the underlying impulse and its complete denial. Especially in the context of maladjustment, a symbolic behavior is sometimes called a *symptom,* meaning any overt condition that suggests an underlying disorder.

Symbolic behavior can appear, Freud emphasized, in people in any condition—ill or healthy. Moreover, different symbolic behaviors can represent the same or different fixations in a particular individual. For the observer of human nature, Freud concluded, symbolic behavior can convey all sorts of information—at times more than the observer wants to know (Freud, 1901). But these behavioral expressions are most likely to occur when a person is sick, tired, under emotional strain, or in an otherwise weakened condition.

Still sick and experiencing emotional strain, two years after completing *Little Stories for Children* Bertha published another book, this one for adults. Again, writing these tales could be considered symbolic behavior, revealing something about her personal issues, conscious or unconscious. But this time she became more open about herself, perhaps showing further signs of growth. She used a pseudonym with obvious elements of her own name, P. Berthold, and told a collection of stories through a collection of junk, calling the book *In the Junk Shop* (Pappenheim, 1890).

All the characters in these stories remain lonesome souls. In a junk shop, they are not suited for everyday life. And they betray one another, or some chance factor disrupts their bond, perhaps symbolizing what happened to Bertha.

According to psychoanalysis, Bertha's depression, paralyses, headaches, anesthesia, and other symptoms were partial expressions of buried conflicts—childhood concerns about love, sex, rejection, anger, and relations with parents and siblings, all thrust into an unconscious realm at the price of these debilitating symptoms. Psychoanalysts regard such symptoms as possible symbolic behavior—clues to underlying emotional disturbance (Muroff, 1984). Freud, in particular, pointed to the symbolism in dreams, odd mistakes, defense mechanisms, and adjustment reactions, as well as one's overall lifestyle (Figure 4.2).

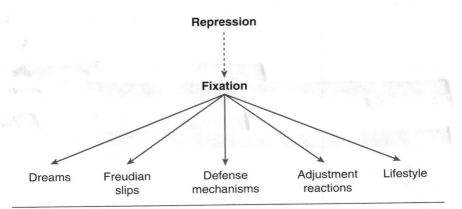

Figure 4.2   Forms of Symbolic Behavior. When the ego cannot manage a conflict directly, it may seek an indirect solution through repression, resulting in a fixation. Signs of the unconscious fixation may appear later in various symbolic forms, ranging from dreams and everyday mistakes to an unusual lifestyle.

Dreams and Mistakes

In the study of symbolism, Freud developed an elaborate theory of dreams, the intermittent visual and auditory images occurring in a semi-narrative sequence during sleep. He postulated that the ego, less vigilant in sleep, allows repressed conflicts to escape from the unconscious and appear symbolically in the dream story (Freud, 1900). This dream story, however incoherent, is the *manifest content* of the dream, the obvious sequence of events depicted by the visual, auditory, and other dream images. Freud's interest lay instead in the **latent content of dreams**, the underlying, unconscious meaning, which is partly symbolized and partly hidden by the manifest content. The latent content becomes available only through careful inquiry into the dreamer's recent and earlier experiences and into the dreamer's spontaneous reactions to specific elements of the manifest content. In other words, any dream interpretation requires carefully obtained background information about the dreamer.

One night Bertha dreamed that she had tamed two jackals and kept them each on a leash. Reeking with an offensive odor, these animals turned into a pair of men she recognized as her neighbors in Vienna. She controlled them by pulling on their leashes, which concluded the manifest content of the dream. Some observers might view these actions as symbolically sexual, aggressive, or both on the part of the dreamer, perhaps elements of the latent content. But according to psychoanalysis, no dream interpretation can be of any use whatsoever without a detailed knowledge of Bertha's life at the time and without her unrestrained thoughts about the dream, called free associations. Freud remained emphatic on this point, which is constantly overlooked by enthusiastic but unenlightened followers.

Especially in dream interpretation, Freud made extensive use of universal symbols. Transcending culture, a *universal symbol* conveys the same meaning or the same set of meanings for all people everywhere, regardless of background. These symbols presumably have existed down through the ages. In contrast, an individual or *private symbol* carries a specific meaning for a particular person, which is not necessarily shared by others. According to Freud, most symbols, especially those that are universal, pertain to relatively few topics: the human body, family members, birth and death, nakedness, and sexuality (Freud, 1916).

Freud's approach was highly speculative and included dozens of universal symbols for male and female genitalia (Freud, 1916). But simply enumerating these symbols does no justice to Freud's thought. Even discussing his ideas in one or two paragraphs produces an inadequate account, almost a caricature. His range of interests and emphasis on human beings as symbolizing creatures have been of major importance in literature, art, drama, and other humanities. But by today's standards, this thinking lacks the empirical support considered essential in science.

Freud spoke of *The Interpretation of Dreams* as his most important work. The text of this book shows a logical, step-by-step organization befitting a scientific report. The illustrations, often of Freud's own dreams, reflect a series of disparate but personally important themes in his life. Thus, at the first level the book takes readers ever upward to increasingly sophisticated dream analysis. At the second and lower level, the illustrations transport the reader ever downward into increasingly deeper reaches of Freud's unconscious mind (Schorske, 1979). Owing to its magnitude and dual content, this work best illustrates Freud's thought and stands as the masterpiece of his writings, though the theory still lacks convincing support.

The unconscious appears in dreams, Freud speculated, because the ego becomes less vigilant during sleep. But symbolic expressions of the unconscious also appear regularly throughout waking life, he declared. In daily behavior, we sometimes do or say things incorrectly or clumsily because unconscious conflicts break the barrier of repressions, revealing our inner concerns and unacceptable wishes. In fact, the popularity of psychoanalysis in public life centers around the attention it devotes to dreaming and to these lapses in appropriate behavior.

Sometimes a mistake in everyday life is popularly called a **Freudian slip** because Freud regarded many such errors, but not all, as symbolic behavior—further expressions of the unconscious. They include temporary forgetting, errors of the tongue or pen, accidental self-injury, and various bungled actions. Bertha injured herself by nursing her father in a needlessly strenuous fashion, though her wealthy family could readily afford full-time help.

Why did Bertha place such unreasonable demands on herself? Did this "accidental" self-injury serve some unconscious purpose in her life? Was her overly stressful nightly nursing driven by unconscious conflicts? In traditional psychoanalysis, her totally unnecessary sacrifice perhaps became her way of seeking assistance for her own personal problems.

With the widespread interest in *The Psychopathology of Everyday Life*, his book about errors in everyday life, Freud became jubilant. He called it a triumph for psychoanalysis; the gulf between normal and abnormal mental life had been narrowed (Freud, 1901).

Defense Mechanisms

Another sign of the unconscious appears in a **defense mechanism**, a way of thinking or behaving that enables a person to avoid awareness of anxiety-arousing thoughts. Formally, these reactions are called the *ego's mechanisms of defense* because the ego defends against unwanted thoughts by deceiving itself. This idea, that people unconsciously avoid what they do not want to know, became so popular that the public and psychologists themselves lengthened Freud's list of defense mechanisms, often incorrectly. Anna Freud, his daughter and noted psychoanalyst, deserves much credit for clarifying and elaborating the defense mechanisms. In contrast, *coping mechanisms* are employed consciously to deal with stress. They include thinking about the situation in a more positive way, focusing attention elsewhere, and relieving stress through relaxation techniques and physical exercise.

In defense mechanisms, the individual defends *without* awareness of the real problem, as in the following: *rationalization,* by concocting plausible but false explanations; *reaction formation,* by taking a stance opposite one's deeper feelings; *displacement,* by directing an emotional reaction onto something or someone other than its appropriate target; and *sublimation,* by engaging in socially acceptable behavior as an indirect expression of socially unacceptable impulses. There is no intent to be deceitful in any of these mechanisms. The individual's conflict remains unconscious. Repression, the basic defense mechanism, underlies all others.

Bertha's passionate declaration of love for her father may be viewed on this basis. It perhaps had origins in displacement, whereby she directed onto him the love she wanted to express toward a male peer. It may have involved reaction formation, whereby she disguised even from herself the hostility she felt toward her father because of his overprotectiveness, which prevented her from establishing close relationships with peers. These statements are consistent with psychoanalytic theory, but without more precise information, they remain mere conjecture.

In one study of defense mechanisms, two groups of 10 children each were examined four times over a two-year period. Beginning at age six years and six months, each child individually told stories in response to a traditional projective test. Altogether, 134 stories were recorded, coded, and randomized to make identification of the author and date impossible. Then they were scored for use of three defense mechanisms: *denial*, refusing to acknowledge disturbing events; *projection*, attributing one's undesirable traits to others; and *identification*, accepting as one's own the goals and ideas of another person.

It was predicted that denial, the simplest mechanism, would decrease as the children gained increased cognitive development; that it would be replaced by projection, which assigns the blame to others; and that identification would show a gradual increase, presumably reaching a peak later, in adolescence, when the individual encounters the identity crisis. All three predictions were confirmed, providing further evidence that children do not suddenly adopt and discard defense mechanisms. Instead, they experience shifts among them almost automatically, reflecting the usual patterns of cognitive development (Cramer, 1997).

Adjustments and Lifestyles

From a psychoanalytic standpoint, the unconscious sometimes emerges dramatically in an **adjustment reaction**—a disturbed condition that may include diverse symptoms, ranging from personal discomfort to socially disruptive behavior. Bertha's phobia about black snakes, her puzzling cough, inexplicable deafness and blindness, and paralyses with no medical bases revealed adjustment reactions described today in the *Diagnostic and Statistical Manual of Mental Disorders—IV*, cited earlier as the basic guideline for clinical diagnoses in our times. In psychoanalysis, such instances of anxiety and inexplicable illness, formerly called *neuroses*, may be viewed as symbolic expressions of unconscious conflicts that partly burst through the repression.

Even a person's lifestyle may reflect unconscious motivation, as Alfred Adler suggested. Here **lifestyle** refers broadly to a person's way of living—the activities, friends, possessions, and entertainments one chooses to pursue or ignore.

Repressed conflict in the oral state, Freud speculated, may result not only in a dissatisfied, distrustful outlook on the world but also in more specific lifestyle patterns. Years after deprivation of oral needs in childhood, an adult may display an *oral-passive* character, evident in excessive eating and drinking, special concerns about nutrition, persistent demands for love and attention, and a marked dependency on others for support. Another adult, also deprived in the oral state, may exhibit instead a resentful lifestyle, called an *oral-aggressive* character: prone to hostility, envy, argument, and a generally contentious demeanor. In traditional psychoanalysis, both these very different overt reactions may be symbolic expressions of a fixation at the first psychosexual stage.

In the anal stage, conflict over toilet training may result in a fixation. After experiencing overly strict training procedures in childhood, a person may become unconsciously defiant, exhibiting an *anal-expulsive character* in an incurably messy, tardy, irresponsible mode of life. Or, to make amends for earlier training failures, an *anal-retentive character* may demonstrate an excessively clean, prompt, trustworthy lifestyle. For any fixation, symbolic expressions may vary from one individual to another.

Many modern psychologists resist these specific conjectures about psychoanalytic "characters," for they lack substantial empirical evidence. But most accept the broader, *general* implications: Childhood experiences can shape adult lifestyles. As for Freud, he extended this thinking into the Oedipus-Electra stage, as noted earlier.

Bertha's overly strenuous nursing at the time of her father's illness depicts a temporary lifestyle, lasting a few months, and suggests an Electra theme. Despite her family's wealth, she chose this sacrificial role, which justified her nights alone with her beloved father, the only man toward whom she showed deep affection. She experienced intimacy through nursing, bathing, and perhaps even toileting him. Without full awareness, this devoted daughter partly fulfilled the Electra wish. In addition, this lifestyle offered self-punishment for her aggressive impulses toward her parents, who favored Wilhelm and restricted her social life. Bertha described her mother as a stove, too hot for close comfort. From the psychoanalytic perspective, unconscious sexual and aggressive urges lay behind her martyrdom for her father and resistance to her mother (Noshpitz, 1984).

A more enduring dimension of Bertha's lifestyle occurred in her efforts to control virtually everyone with whom she associated. Earlier, in Vienna, she totally controlled polite conversations, even in gentle social gatherings. She controlled her therapy with Breuer, setting an entirely new direction—until it overwhelmed him. She controlled her father's nightly care—until it overwhelmed her. Around-the-clock nursing would have left her and other family members free for more personal companionship with him. The fact that they accepted her sacrificial role bears further testimony to her capacity for control. She demanded and obtained this self-destructive lifestyle (Noshpitz, 1984).

And when she became ill herself, she controlled the family in a very different way, forcing the members into caretaking roles for her—or at least forcing them, even Wilhelm, to behave in ways properly respectful of a sick person. From the psychoanalytic perspective, these efforts at sacrifice and control, both direct and indirect, stand as symbols of Bertha's unconscious struggle against the gender restrictions and discrimination she experienced with her parents, her brother, and her culture. These efforts continued as a lifestyle throughout her adulthood, even into her later years.

Totally alone during his early work with Bertha, Breuer had available no theory of personality, especially concerning her control efforts and the erotic nature of her fantasies (Holzman, 1984). She was sexually naïve, and Breuer was naïve about her undeveloped sexuality and its possible contribution to her illness. Through the storytelling procedure, he relieved Bertha's painful feelings stemming from recent events—her father's illness and death, abuse by Wilhelm, and an overprotective mother. But those stories never became pathways to deeper explorations of earlier events. Breuer's therapy remained essentially on the surface.

Several years later Freud constructed an extensive theory of personality from which to work. With this background, he helped his patients to retrace earlier events, beginning with the unconscious conflicts that brought the person to therapy in the first place. Then he guided the patient in the difficult process of moving through the barrier of repression, aiming to encounter the earlier traumatic events that usually had occurred in childhood. Possessing a more mature ego than in childhood years, the adult in therapy has far greater promise for viewing long-forgotten childhood conflicts with greater understanding, tolerance, and acceptance (Figure 4.3).

Psychoanalysis as a Therapy

Neither Freud nor Breuer nor anyone else employed psychoanalytic therapy with Bertha. Her troubles antedated the theory and therapy. Freud was advancing toward these ideas; Breuer went on to other interests; and Bertha was showing some improvements in her health.

In the meantime, Freud learned about Bertha from two friends, one younger and the other much older than he. The first, Martha Bernays, later became his wife. She had known Bertha since their schooldays, and the young

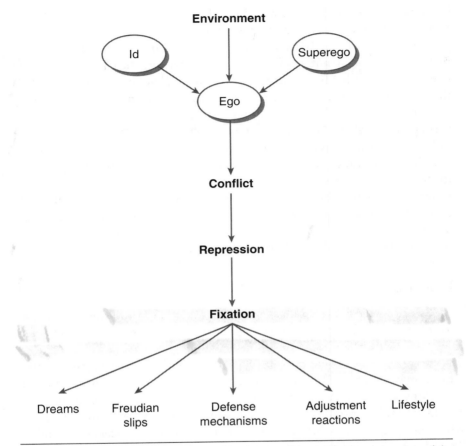

Figure 4.3   A Theoretical Foundation for Psychoanalysis. The upper portion of the figure shows the demands on the ego in managing conflict. The lower portion shows the behavioral expressions of repressed conflict. The darkened sequence—conflict, repression, and fixation—depicts the core of unconscious motivation, standing at the center of psychoanalytic theory, holding the pieces together. The arrows show the sequence of events in the origins and outcomes of unconscious motivation. A person in therapy progresses in the opposite direction, working upward against the arrows.

women met on several occasions. The second friend told Freud about Bertha in professional dialogues. Freud's older friend in this instance was none other than Bertha's former therapist, one Josef Breuer.

By this time, Breuer had concluded that hysteria was not caused by some physical defect, especially when none could be found and the illness moved from place to place in the person's body. He decided instead that extreme psychological stress could cause these problems and that a release from this stress could cause the symptoms to disappear.

Fascinated by Breuer's account, Freud declared that he would have continued treatment, if not for the sake of the patient, then for the sake of science. He regarded Breuer's approach as incomplete. It did not go *beyond* the symptoms to predisposing factors in childhood. In particular, Breuer never considered Bertha's unconscious conflicts.

So psychoanalysis did nothing for Bertha. It came after her illness. But she did something for psychoanalysis. Through Breuer, she stimulated Freud's thinking about these disorders and their treatments, thereby pioneering in the foundations of psychoanalysis as a psychotherapy.

But what would have happened if Bertha experienced her adolescent upheaval 15 years later? With her family's wealth, their Viennese background, and her mother's insistence on the very best treatment for her daughter, Bertha might well have become a patient in psychoanalysis.

Use of Free Association

Psychoanalytic therapy offers no certain route to the truth, but in contrast to other psychotherapies, it aims at uncovering unconscious thought. The analyst assists the patient, called the analysand, by offering a safe, facilitating environment for these explorations, enabling the patient to gain greater freedom of thought and action. Through these self-explorations, the patient develops self-understanding and increased mastery in the environment.

In traditional psychoanalysis, the sessions would be very different from those she experienced with Breuer. Like the archaeologist seeking to understand a buried civilization, the psychoanalyst searches *beneath* the surface, exploring long-forgotten roots of personal problems. The bowls and busts, ornaments, and other artifacts from ancient civilizations that littered Freud's consulting room gave testimony to his passion for the archaeologist's method. Much like the study of past life in a buried city, Freud and his patient painstakingly reconstructed an earlier scene from her life, piece by piece, using only fragmentary evidence—symptoms of one sort or another. For Freud, this task became inspiring and tedious; for the patient, it provoked distress. She was hard at work against herself, trying to bring forth the very experiences she wanted most to forget.

Freud stressed the search for a *set* of determinants. Seldom does the patient's problem arise from a single traumatic event. Instead, a number of smaller incidents become a group of provoking causes (Breuer & Freud, 1893). Sometimes the first incident leaves no mark and a later one of the same kind produces symptoms, and yet those symptoms would not have appeared without the earlier provoking incident. Hence, in removing the symptoms, all the provoking incidents must be taken into account.

In Breuer's presence, Bertha considered numerous emotional incidents directly, thereby weakening or eliminating the anxiety associated with them. But merely working through the symptoms in this way, without considering their underlying causes, produced little long-term gain and no fundamental change in personality.

For probing beneath the symptoms, the chief psychoanalytic techniques include free association and interpretation. Freud discovered the first of these methods by listening to his patients.

Abandoning the traditional herbs, baths, electrotherapy, and even hypnosis, he tried to work with his patients' memories. As his patients lay on the couch with their eyes closed, he demanded that they recall some elusive event. He pressed for an answer, verbally and even physically, pushing with his hand on their brows. One patient rebuked him for this technique; he made her forget something she was just about to remember! After that, Freud became less intrusive and more dependent on the meanderings of the patient's mind. Later patients taught him to go even more slowly and to take these mental wanderings very seriously.

Eventually, Freud presented each patient with simple, explicit instructions. He told them to be completely straightforward; just say whatever comes to mind; never omit anything too embarrassing or painful to share with others. Throughout his psychoanalytic sessions, he reminded his patients of this pledge, required of anyone who participated in his psychoanalytic therapy (Freud, 1926).

This unrestrained expression of ideas, letting one thought lead to another, that to another, and so forth, is called **free association**. Here the word *free* means free from any instructions. These uncontrolled thoughts and memories, encouraged by the relaxing freedom of lying on the couch, became the primary material in psychoanalysis as a therapy. With this method, Freud claimed a technique for exploring the unconscious.

But free association is never entirely free. Inevitably, the analysand engages in some sort of selection process. Complete honesty is also an impossible task. The overall aim is to speak as freely as possible.

Trying to put aside every reservation, patients attempt to report all their thoughts, no matter how stupid, insulting, or strange they seem. Of course they resist sharing some of them, and they are unable to retrieve certain memories. In this difficult and taxing task, honesty is the key factor. Nothing must be consciously withheld, nothing censured.

In the process of **interpretation**, the analyst encourages the patient to examine carefully the thoughts brought forth in free association and to search for any unexpected or symbolic meanings. The patient tries to think beyond the mere facts, or perceived facts, and discover their meanings, their particular importance in one's own life. At appropriate moments the analyst encourages interpretations, raises a question about the patient's reports, or simply supports further inquiry. Often, these efforts at interpretation lead to new views of the free associations, which sometimes concern earlier conflicts that have been disguised through repression by the childhood ego. To be resolved, the conflicts must be identified, re-experienced, and then accepted by the more mature, adult ego.

Among all the techniques in psychoanalytic therapy, interpretations are the most susceptible to investigator bias. Events are viewed as endowed with meanings about which even the behaving individual may be unaware. Symbolism becomes a central concern, and the interpretation of these symbols remains a speculative endeavor. The analyst may interpret events in therapy in ways consistent with his or her own wishes, expectations, or hypotheses, unintentionally or otherwise misconstruing the data in various ways. In the context of investigator bias, the analyst has the potential to influence the behavior of the analysand, the collection of data, and the interpretive process.

When Bertha sat alone with her father on that fateful night in Ischl, awaiting the surgeon, she experienced for the first time her most frightening dreamlike hallucination—a black snake crawling toward her father, followed by many black snakes crawling out of the walls. Breuer never encouraged any interpretation of this recurring, possibly phallic, image. Had he done so in the classical psychoanalytic manner, which was not then available, Bertha's concerns about sexuality might have come to the fore. Acknowledging these feelings would have created opportunities for Bertha to begin to incorporate adult sexuality into her own life. Instead, these feelings were displaced onto Breuer who, as a surrogate parent, also was unprepared to deal with them.

Bertha had never been in love—at least to the point that it replaced her relationship with her father. Instead, things seemed to be reversed. Her relationship with her father remained ascendant over all potential love relationships with peers (Breuer, 1882). If she ever reached this idea in therapy, the interpretations presumably would have revealed Electra themes.

Resistance and Transference

In therapy, the most important interpretations focus on two events: resistance and transference. They suggest promising sites for exploration of the unconscious.

Resistance is understood as patients' unwillingness to examine their behavior. Anything that patients do to obstruct access to their unconscious constitutes

resistance. Because of shame, distrust, or any other reason, patients may prevent further progress in therapy by remaining silent, rejecting the analyst's views, missing appointments, arriving late, forgetting things, speaking to other issues instead, or becoming more disturbed and thereby avoiding the responsibilities of free association. These acts arise when their confrontations with the unconscious become too intense. They are the ego's attempts to maintain repression.

The analyst aims to clarify these avoidances in patients' free associations. More subtle resistances involve various defense mechanisms of the ego. They make interpretation a challenging task. If interpretation becomes abrupt, confrontational, or highly speculative, it may simply increase, rather than diminish, patients' resistance.

When successful, the interpretation of resistance increases patients' awareness of themselves and competence in free association. At the same time, it increases the sphere of activity outside therapy (Schwartz, 2003).

If Bertha had been in psychoanalysis during her illness, some of her bodily symptoms might have been interpreted as resistance. They would have prevented her from engaging in therapy, as they did at times with Breuer. When Bertha could hardly speak, even in her native tongue, she certainly could not have entered into a psychoanalytic dialogue. When she became intermittently deaf and blind and unable to move, she was shielded from family activities, potential topics of conversation in therapy. Her extensive loss of memory would have further precluded participation in therapy (Noshpitz, 1984). These massive, inexplicable adjustment reactions suggested a resistance not only to therapy but also to life itself.

Resistance and transference can be usefully compared. In resistance, patients hold back. They do not confront their problems. The existence and nature of those problems are inferred on the basis of patients' avoidance reactions. In transference, patients express their problems, consciously and unconsciously. They re-enact earlier issues, using the therapist as a substitute for other people.

Bertha's fantasy pregnancy probably did not occur, but other evidence suggests that she developed a strong affection for Breuer. The pregnancy myth dramatizes the intimacy in the patient-therapist relationship, which creates the potential for transference—a subject of intense interest in psychoanalysis.

"This personal influence is our most powerful dynamic weapon," said Freud, speaking of that relationship (Freud, 1926). He was referring to **transference,** a process in which patients direct toward the analyst emotional reactions originating with other people in their lives, often their parents. The analyst does nothing explicit to provoke these reactions. But by maintaining an appropriate reserve, the analyst creates opportunities for transference.

Most analysts readily accept transference. The patient needs to re-experience some unresolved emotional problems, and the transference relationship supplies an opportunity to do so. It meets earlier needs still active in the patient.

To facilitate this process, the analyst maintains neutrality, engaging in neither scorn nor praise, not taking sides in any expression of conflict. Under these conditions, the patient's unconscious concerns are most likely to emerge. The analyst also refrains from self-disclosure, which may obstruct transference and thereby hinder the analytic process. Even sitting face to face during the therapy sessions may diminish the analyst's neutrality. Bertha developed a transference reaction toward Breuer who, in fact, did go beyond the bounds of neutrality. Today the therapist is expected to keep a certain distance from the patient, but the transference relationship develops anyway, regardless of age, gender, or social class. It is a compulsive kind of love, anger, admiration, fear, or whatever, expressed toward the therapist.

"One would have thought that the patient's relation to the analyst calls for no more than a certain amount of respect, trust, gratitude, and human sympathy," Freud continued. "Instead, there is this falling in love, which itself gives the impression of being a pathological phenomenon" (Freud, 1926).

This love grows insistent, resulting in affection and satisfaction, called *positive transference.* It shows its opposite as well, a readiness to hostility and revenge if thwarted, known as *negative transference.* In both instances, the patient displaces or projects onto the analyst unconscious thoughts and feelings originating with earlier figures in his or her life and intimately connected with the origins of personal problems. The transference process, another form of symbolic behavior, brings this repressed material into awareness, where it can be reconsidered and understood, intellectually and emotionally.

By responding emotionally to the undemonstrative analyst, patients reveal formerly hidden aspects of their reactions toward other people. They reproduce them tangibly, as if they were occurring at the moment, rather than arising through memory.

By his age and experience, Breuer partly replaced the father that Bertha had so recently lost. Providing sleep, nourishment, and the occasion for bedtime stories, he also replaced a nurturing mother. As a devoted, appealing personality, he offered the image of an imagined lover. With this potential for meeting several unmet needs in Bertha, it was almost inevitable that she would displace onto him all sorts of feelings originating with her father, mother, Wilhelm, and other important persons in her life. If Breuer had remained as therapist and allowed this positive transference to continue, Bertha might have experienced differently that traumatic dream about the snakes at her father's bedside. In addition, she might have perceived in new ways scenes from her childhood—scenes in which she experienced anger over Wilhelm's preferential treatment, resentment of the restrictions on her social life, fear of separation from her father, hostility toward her mother, and perhaps guilt over the deaths of her sisters, all likely remnants of repressed childhood conflict.

When successfully interpreted and incorporated by the patient, transference, like resistance, increases the person's self-awareness and competence. It creates psychological freedom, especially when there are opportunities for practice outside the psychoanalytic setting (Schwartz, 2003).

But transference had not been recognized in Breuer's time. He had no idea that he had accidentally discovered this condition, a most fundamental phenomenon in psychoanalysis and commonly observed in many psychotherapies today. He thought Bertha's affectionate response was unique to their relationship. He certainly did not view it as a therapeutic opportunity. Had he seen its potential and worked with this powerful opportunity, the whole outcome of her therapy might have been different. Eventually she might have confronted her restricted sexuality as well. Rather than achieving temporary relief from symptoms, she would have gained a more permanent alleviation of her illness.

Instead, Breuer's abrupt departure made Bertha worse. He left her in the midst of these emerging feelings.

Breuer had developed a special affection for Bertha and made a sustained commitment to her, one that increased during the therapy. His final report described her "remarkably shrewd powers of reasoning ... highly developed gifts of fantasy and poetry ... and very lively compassion" (Breuer, 1882). His interest in her went beyond the normal call of duty.

Such reactions on the part of the analyst may impede the treatment process. In **countertransference**, the therapist develops a strong emotional reaction to the patient, experiencing feelings aroused by the patient. These responses may disrupt the therapist's neutrality. As the therapist's reaction to the patient's transference, countertransference is not a therapeutic technique. It can become a serious obstacle in therapy.

But the analyst who can manage countertransference may find it useful. By observing his or her own feelings, the analyst may gain insight into the reactions the patient arouses in other people. The analyst may understand how the patient makes others feel when they become associated with that person.

In any case, the therapeutic relationship is not intended to be romantic or sexual. In fact, there is tacit agreement that it must be asexual. If it becomes sexual, it changes dramatically and irreparably. A therapist who becomes a lover cannot be endowed with other roles according to the patient's diverse needs.

"To yield to the demands of the transference," Freud cautioned the therapist, referring to its sexual potential, " ... is not only justly forbidden by moral considerations but is also completely ineffective as a technical method for obtaining the purpose of the analysis" (Freud, 1926).

Freud spoke here not only about love but also about anger, resentment, and related feelings. The therapist cannot succeed by submitting to these entreaties or by striking some compromise with the patient. The only useful solution is to trace these emotional reactions back to the patient's past, confronting them as they were originally perceived by the patient. As a rule, the prototype of the transference reaction has occurred in the patient's childhood relationship with one or both parents.

Even more than the other techniques in psychoanalysis, transference can foster a **catharsis**, which is a release of deep emotional tension. A catharsis offers a discharge of anxiety, a purging of feelings, a sense of relief.

Metaphorically speaking, the goal in therapy is to give that distracted Londoner, daily passing a memorial to the Great Fire, a prolonged safe cry, enabling him to confront fully his disruptive past. He does so as an adult, yet in the security of a confidential relationship. Under these conditions, he becomes able to understand and accept what has happened and to look to the present and future. He passes the monument without turmoil.

In a therapeutic catharsis, age works in a person's favor. An event from which a childish ego might have retreated in fear years earlier may seem to the stronger, adult ego as far less important, even trivial (Freud, 1926). The anxiety associated with the experience thereby becomes weakened or eliminated.

Through this expressive process, Bertha's ego presumably would have been released from its vigilant repression of childhood conflicts and restored to its command over the id. With her ego freed for more productive adult tasks, she would have become more openly concerned about her delayed sexuality, insistence on control over others, resentment of gender discrimination, and her irrational demand for the sacrificial role. With this increase in self-knowledge, she would have attained greater satisfaction and competence in life.

Breuer's method was cathartic. It enabled Bertha to re-enact the traumatic events in her father's illness, relieving some of her symptoms. But it was not a deep excavation. It did not go into the unconscious origins of her problems, including sexuality. It was not psychoanalysis.

Yet Freud openly regarded Bertha's case as the beginning of psychoanalysis. He and Breuer co-authored a major early book beginning with her case. She is the patient who, as Anna O., prompted the development of depth therapy, thereafter called psychoanalysis. She is the patient who, through Breuer's work and Freud's influence, stimulated the whole broad movement of modern psychotherapy, insight therapy, or personal counseling, as the many different "talking cures" are known today.

"Much is won," exulted Freud, speaking of his therapy, "if we succeed in transforming hysterical misery into common unhappiness" (Freud, 1895).

But after Breuer's abrupt departure, Bertha experienced more than common unhappiness. She experienced relapses.

Would psychoanalysis have altered this pattern? Would breaking the barrier of repression have alleviated some of Bertha's problems? Of course we cannot know. She never even began psychoanalytic therapy. But Freud, in simple terms, reminds us of its basic goal: to make the unconscious conscious.

Commentary and Critique

Any effort to understand what has made our conception of humanity in the 20th century distinct from the views in preceding eras must give attention to psychoanalysis. It presented a whole new and dramatic outlook on the human condition. But despite his extensive scientific training and early success in laboratory research, Freud promoted psychoanalysis without the usual scientific caution, even for his day. Perhaps he viewed his unrestrained literary approach as necessary for the prompt response he sought. In any case, this literary approach raises the major objections to psychoanalysis today.

Critics view psychoanalysis as more art than science, and indeed Freud was a gifted writer, who was awarded the Goethe Prize in 1930, recognizing outstanding achievements in literature. Resistance to Freud's science arises largely on three related bases. First, it falls short of the usual standards for empirical research. Second, it appears to be contaminated by investigator effects. Third, it raises the issue of falsifiability.

With regard to research standards, Freud used the time-honored case study, but he collected and reported presumably empirical data in casual fashion. He did not study representative samples of people, collect data rigorously, maintain systematic records, or use statistical measures to evaluate the outcomes. Moreover, he did not show the usual scientific caution in reporting his findings. Rather than using tables and graphs and objective prose, he argued by analogy, metaphor, and storytelling, speculating about unseen forces in the lives of his patients, giving free rein to his creative imagination. His compelling language made persuasive reading for his literary-minded audience, but it raises objections today among more scientifically inclined people.

In fact, Freud's case studies of therapy served as the only evidence of his major findings. But even favorable therapy outcomes do not validate psychoanalysis as a theory or a therapy. A patient can show improved adjustment without any therapy at all—and for any number of other reasons ranging from improved finances to increased friendships. Traditional case studies simply do not include sufficiently controlled conditions to permit substantial scientific conclusions about cause-and-effect relationships.

A second point of resistance to Freud's research methods arises from *investigator effects*. Without awareness, the investigator may foster the outcomes he or she expects to obtain, making the research results unreliable. They are not attributable solely to the events under investigation.

Investigator effects stem from three types of errors. In errors of observation, even conscientious and careful investigators may make mistakes, seeing whatever they hope or expect to see, rather than what actually happens. In errors of interpretation, they may unintentionally reach conclusions not warranted by the data, such as Freud's overgeneralizations from his own self-analysis. And in errors through cueing, investigators' personal style and nonverbal activities, without their awareness, may inform the participants about the responses they seek and anticipate. Thus, critics have declared that, amid the compelling setting of his consulting room and his determination to develop an extensive system of psychological thought, Freud could not avoid guiding his patients' thinking, making suggestive comments or inquiries, and recalling their monologues in a manner consistent with his own thinking. These errors were most likely in discussions about sexuality, which Freud deemed most important in the development of personality (Crews, 1998). And they become evident through the feminist critique of the gender bias in Freudian theory.

Resistance to Freud's science also arises from some of his hypotheses and theories, apart from his research methods. Here we encounter the third problem, testing his ideas. Some cannot be verified or refuted. This condition, called the **falsifiability problem**, occurs when there is no possibility of demonstrating that a particular hypothesis or concept may be wrong. There is no way to test the hypothesis. It is untestable.

The potential for refutation, or falsification, plays a central role in research. A testable hypothesis can be shown to be true or false. Consider this hypothesis, "The devil can dance on the head of a pin." That untestable and therefore irrefutable hypothesis has no place in scientific inquiry. It demonstrates the falsifiability problem. No scientific procedure can show it to be incorrect.

Behind every dream, Freud hypothesized, lies an unfulfilled childhood wish. He knew this dramatic statement about childhood and childhood sexuality would be criticized. And that has been the case; it raises the falsifiability problem. Imagine the difficulty in demonstrating that an adult dream does not inevitably date back to some obscure, unfulfilled wish in childhood.

The concept of repression, in particular, limits the falsifiability of certain psychoanalytic ideas. If someone behaves aggressively, she has a problem with aggression; repression has been unsuccessful. If a person never displays even a mild form of aggression, then she too may have a problem—which has been repressed. If someone shows a normal amount of aggressive behavior, then repression has produced a balance between aggressive and socially constructive impulses. The concept of repression has stimulated much research on unconscious mental processes, and that stands in its favor. But with no clear limits, it cannot be readily refuted.

Broadly accepted among the public, repression has received only mixed empirical support. Many difficult experiences are remembered quite clearly, suggesting that repression is not an automatic phenomenon. Difficult to test experimentally, it tends to be more impressive in postdiction—explaining something after the fact—than in prediction, one of the basic aims of science.

Without firm, empirical support, a perspective tends to lose its focus. Rationalism then proceeds in diverse directions. Psychoanalysis became increasingly fragmented on this basis and has been evolving since Freud's day. Numerous divergent theories now contribute to this perspective, as noted in the works of Jung, Horney, Adler, and Erikson.

In fact, the most substantial modification of psychoanalytic thought today lies in **object relations theory**, which emphasizes the emotional bond that human beings form with other "objects"—anything in real life or fantasy, including other people. Object relations include the capacity for loving relationships with other human beings, juxtaposed to self-interest and self-love. But the specific influences of this concept become difficult to assess because it is used in so many different ways and different contexts. In psychoanalytic theory, it represents a shift away from Freud's basic drives of sex and aggression toward the importance of relationships with others. In practice, the movement is away from the analyst's remote neutrality and toward a therapeutic alliance, recognizing the emotion in the therapeutic relationship and the here-and-now experience in this one-to-one encounter (Mitchell, 2000).

Today these derivative viewpoints, including those of neo-Freudians, stand as testimony to the influence of Freud's thought. Collectively called **psychodynamic theory**, they comprise a loose collection of approaches to personality and human development evolving from psychoanalysis. Compared with traditional psychoanalysis, they are primarily concerned with adult life, as opposed to childhood, and with the whole range of social responses, as opposed to the primacy of sexuality. The term *psychodynamic* is used broadly today to refer to any concern with the urging and checking forces in unconscious motivation, within or apart from theory or therapy. In this respect, modern psychoanalytic thinking is no longer the work of one person—Sigmund Freud.

In therapy, Freud expected to assist people in a matter of months, without requiring daily sessions. But shortly after his time, analysts began meeting their patients for several 50-minute sessions each week over a period of years. Recently, insurance companies and others have demanded a shorter, less extensive, less expensive therapy. Many contemporary analysts therefore have adopted modified psychoanalytic procedures. Known as **psychodynamic therapy,** most of these modified procedures are based on the assumption that awareness of unconscious conflict is essential to improvement in adjustment. However, these procedures focus more on the patient's present situation and less on the past, more on everyday relationships and less on early sexual matters, a therapy sometimes called "re-parenting." These therapists often abandon the couch, partly to observe better the patient's gaze and body movements. But whatever the patient's demeanor, the emphasis on unconscious conflicts—the so-called depth factors—continues as the hallmark of this therapy.

Freud's supporters point to these diverse accomplishments, saying that it was not his purpose to develop an empirically based system of thought. That approach to human understanding was too slow for him. He left systematic research to others. In a more speculative style, he preferred to ask the right questions rather than to engage in the painstaking task of finding well-supported answers. His contributions lie in the first of the idealized stages of modern science: forming hypotheses. His major ideas focused on unconscious mental processes, a broad and lively concern in current psychological research; childhood experiences, considered in the Western world today to have a long-lasting impact on the adult personality; and the inescapable role of conflict in the adult personality. He had no intention of completing the second and third of the idealized stages himself, testing and verifying these hypotheses. He laid the rational groundwork for countless follow-up investigations, an essential condition for successful science.

A pair of examples illustrates current empirical research on unconscious mental life. In the first, focusing on *unconscious emotion,* investigators interviewed 50 college students individually about their attachment experiences in childhood. Throughout each interview, which lasted approximately an hour, each participant wore a small, painless skin-conductance device on the dominant hand, yielding a completely unobtrusive measure of emotional arousal during discussions of childhood experiences. These discussions included early relationships with parents, incidents of distress, separation from parents, rejection by parents, and the consequences of these experiences on their personality. A careful debriefing followed, and as predicted, many participants who seemed most unperturbed, overtly indicating that they had no difficulties with parental separations and rejections, showed substantial physiological reactions to these questions. The investigators concluded that such participants effortfully engaged in activities to diminish awareness of disruptive earlier experiences (Dozier & Kobak, 1992). But the unconscious emotion apparently became expressed inwardly, if not outwardly.

A second illustration focuses on *unconscious motivation*, the thrust of psychoanalytic inquiry. Here college students completed individually a priming task, identifying among a list of words those related to achievement, such as "strive" and "success," or to affiliation, such as "sociable" and "friend." Then each participant worked as a partner with another person, presumably another participant, searching for unrelated words in five additional lists. But that "teammate," an accomplice of the experimenter, intentionally performed at a very low level, seeming to become more humiliated as the experiment progressed, thereby placing the actual participant in a conflict situation. Each participant could attain a high achievement score by working hard alone or could respond to affiliation needs by slowing down to the pace of the presumed teammate. The results showed that the participants primed earlier with achievement-related words performed at a much higher level on the teamwork task than did the participants primed with affiliation-related words. Moreover, during the debriefing process, the participants showed no awareness that the priming task perhaps influenced their performance (Bargh, 1997).

As suggested by these experiments, Freud established major beachheads for many new lines of inquiry, ranging from the role of the unconscious in everyday life to childhood influences on the adult personality. More rational than empirical, he developed many hypotheses, but he did not test them in any substantial way. To expect him to accomplish the extensive, often tedious empirical research as well, after producing this provocative view of humanity, is asking too much of one human being. Freud did not promote psychoanalysis as a scientific enterprise. He described the grounds on which he arrived at his psychoanalytic conclusions.

Summary

Background of Psychoanalysis

Psychoanalysis emerged through the work of Sigmund Freud around the beginning of the 20th century, largely through his interpretation of the memories and dreams reported by people who lay on a couch as patients in psychotherapy. For Freud, a historical monument to some tragedy serves as a metaphor for psychoanalysis, which focuses on unconscious mental processes. The event is long past and poorly remembered, but it may evoke deep feelings, much as the unconscious memories of private difficulties can disrupt the routines of an individual's everyday life.

Key Terms: **psychoanalysis, neo-Freudians, unconscious mental processes, unconscious cognition, unconscious motivation, conflict, repression, fixation, collective unconscious**

Structure of Personality

In traditional psychoanalysis, personality emerges from the interactions among three intrapsychic forces or components: the id, with its biological requirements; the superego, imposing social goals and restrictions; and the ego, which is the executive director of the personality, responsible for solving problems and thereby preserving the individual. The ego faces a clear challenge. It must deal with the demands of the id, standards of the superego, and also the limits of a specific external environment.

Key Terms: **id, ego, superego**

Development of Personality

Psychoanalysis emphasizes the importance of childhood experiences in the development of the adult personality. Among them, the tasks associated with sexual development become particularly influential because our greatest sensitivities and pleasures lie with sexuality, which develops through a series of early stages: oral, anal, and Oedipus/Electra. The child's frustrations in these developmental tasks, if repressed, can become fixations, establishing patterns of unconscious motivation in later life, extending into adult personal relationships and the various psychosocial crises.

Key Terms: **psychosexual stages, oral stage, anal stage, feminine psychology, Oedipus complex, Electra complex, individual psychology, identification, psychosocial crises**

Expressions of the Unconscious

Unconscious motivation arises from three sequential events often occurring in childhood: conflict, repression, and fixation. When a conflict or other traumatic event cannot be managed directly, it may be managed indirectly by the individual through unconscious forgetting, called repression. But repression is not complete and occurs at a cost. The repressed conflict seeks expression in disguised or symbolic form in everyday behavior: through dreams, inexplicable mistakes, defense mechanisms, adjustment reactions, and even the individual's lifestyle.

Key Terms: **symbolic behavior, latent content of dreams, Freudian slip, defense mechanism, adjustment reaction, lifestyle**

Psychoanalysis as a Therapy

In psychoanalytic therapy, the patient uses free association to say whatever thoughts come to mind, no matter how repugnant, with the aim of bringing forth repressed conflicts. By interpreting these free associations, the patient attempts to understand their deeper, personal significance. The patient's resistance to discussing certain events and his or her transference of emotional reactions onto the analyst provide promising pathways into the unconscious conflicts. The overall aim is to enable the patient to break the barrier of repression, making the unconscious conscious and thereby leading a freer life with less tension.

Key Terms: **free association, interpretation, resistance, transference, countertransference, catharsis**

Commentary and Critique

The view of humanity presented in traditional psychoanalysis arose through doubtful science, based on informal ways of collecting and reporting the data in case studies and with the potential for investigator effects influencing the research results. In addition, certain psychoanalytic theories raise the falsifiability problem, for they are untestable. They cannot be demonstrated as correct or incorrect.

Key Terms: **falsifiability problem, object relations theory, psychodynamic theory, psychodynamic therapy**

Critical Thinking

1. To enhance team unity, a professional baseball team recently posted this sign: "No egos allowed in this clubhouse." Based on Freud's original conception of the ego, indicate your reaction to this prohibition.

2. A man in psychoanalytic therapy becomes angry with his analyst about an irrelevant, minor issue. What process may be taking place? How may it foster the therapeutic goal?

3. Does the falsifiability problem seem more prevalent in psychoanalysis or in biological psychology? Support your opinion.

5

Behaviorism

B ehaviorism investigates the ways in which events in the environment modify our behavior. We experience delight, become afraid, or feel sentimental at the sound of certain music, sight of some building, or odor of a particular perfume. The environment evokes these emotional reactions on the basis of an individual's prior experiences with these events.

Other environmental stimuli signal the occasion to emit a certain behavior. We await the WALK sign and cross a street, answer a ringing telephone and speak with a friend, or look away when our boss appears, perhaps avoiding a reprimand. When these events occur—the WALK sign, ringing phone, and the appearance of the boss—we generally behave in a manner that yields positive consequences. The environment influences our behavior in both these ways: through signals of impending events and through the consequences of our behavior.

This chapter concentrates on environmental influences known as classical and operant conditioning. It addresses them separately and then together in two-factor theory. As with all chapters on the perspectives, it includes a discussion of therapy and closes with commentary and a critique. The emphasis throughout all discussions is on environmental events.

The most important elements in our environment are other people. They influence our behavior in profound ways, especially early in life. This condition was true for Bertha Pappenheim, and it is true for the rest of us. Discouraged by her daughter's regular relapses, hopeful that another environment might prove beneficial, Recha Pappenheim decided they should move to Frankfurt, her childhood home and the birthplace of her parents and Goldschmidt grandparents. As the only person who regularly overruled Bertha, she insisted that they move. Once again, Bertha would be living among cousins. Wilhelm would stay in Vienna.

Bertha resisted, but Recha prevailed. They moved into a spacious apartment on Leerbachstrasse, bringing with them their cherished furniture and antiques, including a black Biedermeier cabinet and gold and silver goblets. Bertha had a special name for this expensive treasure, calling it her "comforter." In its presence, she experienced an unusual sense of pleasure and contentment.

In another part of town, marginal members of society starved and shivered. Refugees from all over Europe, destitute and displaced, they needed food, shelter, and support. No welfare programs existed. These penniless souls depended entirely on contributions from private citizens and religious institutions.

The Goldschmidts assisted in these altruistic endeavors. But like other members of the upper class, they did so by sitting on advisory boards, planning programs, or offering financial aid out of their own pockets. People from these circles never rubbed elbows with the downtrodden—serving soup, wrapping wounds, mending clothes, and so forth.

Among Bertha's cousins, Louise Goldschmidt was involved in this volunteer work and was more than a cousin to her. Six years older, she was also Bertha's aunt, for she had married her own uncle, a man who was Bertha's uncle too. Gradually, this double kinship developed into a friendship. Bertha began to learn some of Louise's ways, especially in volunteer work (Hirschmüller, 1989). And that became a healthy influence.

Beginnings of Behaviorism

Behaviorism focuses on learning—on creating and changing behaviors. As a system of psychology, the only appropriate aims in **behaviorism** are studies of overt behavior and environmental events; behaviorism investigates the ways they interact to produce learning. The concern lies with *overt* activities, rather than memory, thinking, and other mental processes, which cannot be observed directly.

In studying Bertha's adjustment to Frankfurt, behaviorists would not speculate about her mental states or hereditary influences. Instead, they would examine external, observable events—her overt behavior and relevant environmental factors. They do so because they place the highest value on objectivity. Influenced by this emphasis on objectivity, countless psychologists today study behavior, although they are not necessarily behaviorists.

One long line of pre-empirical thought influenced some American psychologists to adopt this perspective. Since René Descartes, philosophers and scientists had described the human body as a machine, though certainly an extraordinary one. This analogy facilitated explanations of human beings—up to a point—and it fostered a practical outlook compatible with behaviorism.

Two streams of later thought contributed markedly to the rise of behaviorism. Evolutionary theory in biology stressed the role of the environment in shaping the physical structure of organisms over the millennia. According to behaviorism, the environment plays a similar role in shaping the behavior of any species over the millennia, as well as the behavior of an individual over his or her lifetime. Behavior is selected or molded by its antecedents and consequences in the environment.

The other stream, operationism in philosophy, emphasizes that the only concepts suitable for scientific study are those defined by the operations for measuring them. The precision in operational definitions appealed to behaviorists, and their use spread throughout psychology, contributing to behaviorism's eminence in the field.

Conditioning as Learning

In some respects, behaviorism began in the United States in 1913 with a call to arms by the colorful and controversial John B. Watson, who published a paper entitled *Psychology as the Behaviorist Views It*. He rebelled against introspection and other studies of consciousness from Wundt's laboratory, arguing that psychology should abandon all introspective efforts to examine the mind, which is observable only by the experiencing individual. His approach, called *methodological behaviorism*, rejected the study of any events that could not be investigated by the more objective methods of the natural sciences. Like physics, physiology, and other natural sciences, Watson argued that psychology should study publicly observable events, not mental activities, whatever they may be. But not long after his dramatic protest, Watson left the field, his university, and academia altogether, all on a scandalous basis—at least in those days. He moved into the expanding field of advertising, where he again became prominent.

A number of different behavioristic approaches then emerged, collectively called *neobehaviorism*. The prefix *neo* means "new," and some did not endure, including those with the cognitive underpinnings that Watson so vigorously spurned.

On other bases, behaviorism's more enduring inaugural moments could be set later, somewhere between the 1927 publication of Ivan Pavlov's *Conditioned Reflexes* and B.F. Skinner's first major work, in 1938, *The Behavior of Organisms*. These more fully developed approaches eventually dominated the field. With Watson's early departure, and especially with Skinner's later eminence, the more influential beginnings of current behaviorism can be assigned to the 1930s, when Skinner began to distinguish his work from that of Pavlov, thereby setting the major guidelines for behaviorism as it is known today.

In fact, as a young college graduate facing an uncertain future, Skinner turned to psychology and behaviorism after reading Watson's book. Later, as a graduate student, further reading prompted him to incorporate some of Pavlov's basic terms into his own work, although he pursued a different research goal, partly by using different equipment.

In his approach to behaviorism, called *classical conditioning*, Pavlov (1849–1936) examined the behavior of dogs by studying each experimental animal in a separate room, each restrained by a noninvasive harness limiting the animal's movement. In this way, he could study precisely the influence of a specific stimulus on the animal's response—typically salivation. A Russian physiologist who turned to psychology through this work, Pavlov's experimental principles and techniques became widely adopted by later behaviorists. In fact, the term *classical* means "in the established manner," in this case the manner established by Pavlov. But his apparatus has been abandoned.

Quite the opposite has been true for the apparatus in *operant conditioning,* developed by B. F. Skinner (1904–1990). He constructed an enclosed space in which a rat, pigeon, or other small animal could roam freely. He studied animals because they were readily available, efficient to use, and, most important, could be examined in a controlled environment. Human beings would not participate in such experiments, which lasted for weeks, months, and even longer periods. When placed in this special space, a deprived animal, not restrained in any way, could gain access to food by pushing, pecking, or responding in some other fashion. This apparatus, which Skinner appropriately called an *operant chamber,* proved so popular in animal laboratories that it became known as a "Skinner box."

This difference in apparatus reflects a profound difference in the conditioning processes investigated by Pavlov and Skinner. In studying freely emitted behavior, rather than the confined reflexes Pavlov examined, Skinner greatly broadened the scope of the behavioristic movement and became its undisputed leader.

All studies of conditioning involve stimuli and responses, and early investigators focused on highly specific responses, such as salivation, the eyeblink, knee jerk, and other largely reflexive reactions, prompting critics to call early behaviorism "muscle-twitch psychology." Later investigators studied broader, more intentional behaviors, such as assertiveness, social skills, and school learning. Today the units of analysis in behaviorism range widely in scope.

These investigations have produced considerable information on the principles of **learning,** which is any change in behavior not due to maturation, illness, injury, or other disruptive factors. A relatively simple form of learning, **conditioning** occurs through associations among stimuli and responses, resulting in acquired behavior patterns of one form or another. Adopting Pavlov's expression, Skinner described his behavioral studies as investigations of conditioning, and the term refers to both approaches today. But the operant processes are also known as operant learning (Catania, 1998).

Respondent and Operant Behavior

Pavlov and his followers studied **respondent behavior,** meaning inborn behavior *elicited* by a specific stimulus; it occurs as an involuntary response to that stimulus. Thus, classical conditioning is also called *respondent conditioning*. The individual has little or no control over this reaction. A particular sound, sight, odor, or other stimulus automatically elicits a change in breathing, heart rate, salivation, or perspiration, or it produces a "lump in the throat." These reactions are often emotional, involving reflex physiology. The response is extracted by the environment.

Skinner and his followers focused instead on **operant behavior**, which is *emitted* by the individual as a learned response, not as an automatic, involuntary reaction to some specific stimulus. It is sometimes called a *free operant* because the organism emits the behavior, which is guided but not automatically elicited by environmental factors. Typically mediated by the striped or skeletal muscles, operant responses are the ways people cope with their needs and environments: by catching frogs, dousing fires, attending meetings, and endless other overt reactions. Some are repeated and elaborated; others are discarded, chiefly on the basis of their consequences.

In other words, respondent and operant behaviors exist on a reflexive-nonreflexive continuum. They differ in the degree to which they are under external, environmental control. At the reflexive end, respondent behaviors are readily and immediately elicited by a given stimulus. At the non-reflexive end, operant behaviors are influenced by antecedent stimulation, but they are not inevitably elicited on that basis. This distinction indicates a difference in the degree of stimulus control.

Expressed differently, respondent conditioning emphasizes the antecedent stimulation, which automatically elicits the response. Operant conditioning emphasizes the consequences of the response, which support or disrupt the response. But antecedent conditions also play a role, signaling the occasion to emit that response.

In both instances, especially operant conditioning, reinforcement is a key concept. In fact, Pavlov brought the term "reinforcement" into behaviorism—well before it became widespread through Skinner's work in operant conditioning. For Pavlov, *reinforcement* occurred whenever an automatic stimulus, such as a loud clap of thunder, follows closely after a neutral stimulus, in this case lightning. As described shortly, the thunder reinforces the capacity of lightning to elicit a startle reaction (Pavlov, 1927). In operant conditioning, **reinforcement** designates any event following a response that increases the probability that the response will be repeated. A child who says "Please" and always receives a cookie is likely to keep asking with "Please." Operant responses are supported, or reinforced, by their consequences (Skinner, 1953).

In operant conditioning, the **reinforcement principle** states that behaviors tend to appear, disappear, or become otherwise modified according to their consequences. Behaviors are commonly repeated and elaborated when followed by praise, freedom, sustenance, or other positive outcomes. They are likely to be discarded when ignored or followed by punishment. The reinforcement principle focuses on the consequences of a certain response in a particular environment, but antecedent events cannot be overlooked. They set the stage for responses.

Skinner's Radical Behaviorism

Skinner's interest in apparatus and animals emerged in his youth on the banks of the Susquehanna River in Pennsylvania, where he caught and trained all kinds of creatures. There he also constructed all kinds of contraptions, including a steam cannon made out of a discarded water boiler. With it, he harassed the neighbors by shooting vegetables over the rooftops of their houses (Skinner, 1976).

At a county fair, a fire in a toy building left a deep impression on him. As smoke poured from the roof, a pigeon poked its head out a window, seemingly trapped on the second floor. Then a whole team of pigeons arrived for the rescue, some pulling a fire engine, others riding on it while wearing red hats and one, tugging on a string, ringing a bell. One of the fire pigeons ascended a ladder to the second-floor window, and then it descended, followed by the "rescued" pigeon, previously unwilling to leave the burning building (Skinner, 1967).

Hearty applause from the crowd strengthened Skinner's interest in this event, the memory of which lasted the rest of his life. Eventually, he and his followers completed extensive research projects and practical applications with animals, teaching them to work for their food, do tricks, play games, and perform labor-saving activities for human beings.

Behaviorism developed most rapidly in the United States, offering opportunities in basic research with animals and human beings; such research was eventually called the *experimental analysis of behavior.* In everyday life, it offered research with practical applications, later known as *applied behavior analysis.* It was not immediately off with an old love and on with the new, but behaviorism clearly adopted a position contrary to introspection and psychoanalysis. It examined observable behavior, not the unobservable recesses of the mind.

Today B. F. Skinner's radical behaviorism, including operant conditioning, is virtually synonymous with modern behaviorism. Contrary to popular belief, it does not deny the mind or the existence of thoughts and feelings; rather, it denies the value of explaining behavior on these bases. As a philosophy of science, **radical behaviorism** advocates the study of behavior on its own, as a separate phenomenon, without regard for explanations based on internal factors, mental activities, or physiological events (Skinner, 1989). Thus, it does not study mental processes. Or it examines them only as behaviors to be explained. And it does not study bodily processes, except as behavior. Mental and bodily states certainly occur, but from this viewpoint they are more profitably regarded as behavior to be investigated, rather than as the explanations of behavior.

The term *radical* means extreme; it indicates a considerable departure from tradition. Skinner used it to distinguish his approach from the earlier neobehavioristic viewpoints, both in terms of research methods and goals.

Contrary to traditional experimental methods, Skinner sometimes conducted single-subject experiments, examining a number of individuals separately with respect to the same thin slices of behavior, such as lever pressing and disk pecking. Using only elementary statistics, he compared different subjects and even different species, leading to the discovery of such general principles as reinforcement, extinction, spontaneous recovery, and many others, all of which are considered later in this chapter. Skinner recognized the value of working with groups, but he remained concerned that group data obscured individual performances by combining them into averages, deviations, and probabilities.

As for his research goals, Skinner viewed mental activities as internal behaviors eventually to be studied by psychologists and others with more appropriate equipment than existed in his day, some of which has appeared in our times. He wanted to separate his approach from those of neobehaviorists who refused even to recognize internal states and activities unavailable to direct observation. But rather than calling his work radical behaviorism, using a less polarized expression, such as *inclusive behaviorism,* would have created a more user-friendly image, at the same time avoiding the separatist position of methodological behaviorism.

Radical behaviorists and others object to the basic assumption that the mind is composed of something other than physical entities. This approach, thinking of the mind as a phenomenon of a different order, at least partly non-physical, raises the question of a different reality. The mind becomes a mysterious agent of some sort, directing and controlling an individual throughout life, for better or worse. For radical behaviorists, this assumption produces an unnecessary detour, complicating our study of behavior.

In taking this position, Skinner pointed to a pair of unavoidable gaps in any account of human activity from the perspective of behaviorism. One lies between the stimulus conditions in the environment and the response of the individual. The other lies between the environmental consequences and the subsequent change in behavior. Only brain research, Skinner declared, can fill those gaps, thereby completing the account of behavior. The biological approach does not provide a new or different account. It simply adds to the explanation. Human behavior, according to Skinner, eventually will be explained by the collective action of brain science and behavior analysis, along with ethology (Skinner, 1989). Speculating about the mind as an over-all *controlling* agent takes psychology in the wrong direction.

With regard to internal states, Skinner made a distinction between thoughts, which are imagined or simulated behaviors, and feelings, which are private behaviors with a physical basis. In particular, he did not view thoughts as *causing* an organism's response. They too are determined by interactions with the environment. An athlete explains that she performed well because she knew she was better than the competition. But radical behaviorism states that influential events in the environment preceded both her positive thoughts about herself and her successful performance. A depressed individual might go on a shopping spree and alleviate his feeling of depression. According to radical behaviorism these outcomes also have been precipitated by prior events, such as unkind remarks, which prompted both the depression and the shopping spree.

This position is at odds with the widespread view of the mind as *the* determinant of behavior. In fact, the public expects and seeks cognitive explanations. In opposition, radical behaviorism shuns mentalistic explanations, those that refer to the mind. It does not study people in terms of two separate systems—mental life and overt behavior. Thoughts and feelings are private behavior; actions of the muscles and glands are more public behavior. Both types of responses, mental and physical, need to be explained. Radical behaviorism approaches living organisms as indivisible wholes interacting with their environments (Chiesa, 1994). Internal events, to the extent that they can be studied, are simply part of the larger, unified system, yet to be understood.

Many people think that Skinner completely ignored the mind or said that private experience did not exist, neither of which is true. Instead he declared that the mind is not an agent causing behavior; there is no "little person" inside us dictating our ways. Rather, our mental activities, just like overt reactions, are behaviors to be explained, chiefly by studying the environment as well as human physiology.

In all instances, behavior is the fundamental unit of analysis, much as a specific physiological process becomes the basic unit of analysis in physiology. Both fields investigate human activity—physiology focusing on the smaller, underlying bodily responses and behaviorism on the larger, more overt reactions.

Behavioral Science and Society

Resisting the mind as the guiding force in human activity, Skinner instead described the environment as the influential agent. Through his science of human behavior, he wanted to discover and systematically apply these environmental principles for the benefit of society.

His convictions about the potential of these principles led him to write a controversial utopian fiction, known as *Walden Two,* which urged their use for developing a more communal, less competitive human society (Skinner, 1948). Years later, he restated this belief from a different perspective in *Beyond Freedom and Dignity,* describing how the major problems in modern societies arise through inappropriate use of these same principles (Skinner, 1971). Carrying on this tradition, followers today continue to view applied behaviorism as the most promising means for improving the human condition, whether through education, medicine, parenting, government, or other means (Cautela & Ishaq, 1996).

Skinner's interest in controlling human behavior through changes in the environment also raised opposition; the media sometimes portrayed him as tyrannical and manipulative, a threat to freedom in American life. In response, he pointed out that teachers, coaches, priests, politicians, parents, police, salespersons, supervisors, siblings, spouses, friends, neighbors, therapists, counselors, advertisers, and countless others constantly try to influence human behavior. And all of us do so whenever we ask for a favor, give advice, or vote for a candidate, just as cousin Louise encouraged Bertha to engage in volunteer work. Efforts to control others are *everywhere,* often applied in a haphazard fashion.

The Bellevue Sanatorium certainly controlled Bertha's behavior. She wanted to assist underprivileged people, but the staff prevented her attempts to do so. In Karlsruhe, she began a nursing program, but her mother moved her back to Vienna before she could finish the course. In Frankfurt, Bertha observed Louise's charity work. Later, she met some volunteer workers, listened to lectures, and then attended some meetings describing opportunities for serving the needy. With this stimulation, Bertha's efforts to enter the field became supported and augmented by their consequences in that environment. So sayeth the behaviorist.

One day she found herself in a soup kitchen, doling porridge to the destitute. No longer with privileged women in a drawing room, Bertha had entered the arena directly, assisting the downtrodden herself. That event became a notable achievement for her, and it also violated a social norm. People from her favored background did not associate with the impoverished population in any personal way.

In the absence of specific details, the behaviorist would employ a limited metaphor to account for any gradual change in behavior, such as Bertha's transition from sanctioned leisure to soup lines. The environment shapes behavior in much the same way a sculptor shapes clay. Beginning with a formless lump, the sculptor pushes and pulls, twists and squeezes, smoothes and wrinkles parts of the clay, advancing toward the final outcome. Sometimes the successive stages show little change; at other stages, the sculptor's work becomes more dramatic. In the same way, environmental events mold behavior. Antecedent stimuli and the consequences of behavior prompt and prod the individual in one direction or another. In small steps or large, through rules and accidents, prizes and punishments, the environment continuously shapes behavior into well-established patterns (Skinner, 1953).

But Skinner's metaphor has a major limitation. As the metaphorical sculptor in everyday life, the environment does not encounter each person as a completely new, untouched piece of "clay." Each of us has a reinforcement history. Except for the newborn, the environment shapes used clay, which has already been bent, twisted, and otherwise molded in one way or another by earlier environments. In contrast, the sculptor sometimes works with fresh clay; it has not been shaped previously.

Nevertheless, the metaphor becomes useful in a more subtle, vital way. The behaviorist studies functional relations between environmental events and behavioral outcomes. The action occurs in *both* directions, from the sculptor to the clay and vice versa. In small ways, according to its consistency, temperature, color, and other characteristics, the clay requires the sculptor to respond in certain fashion. The clay exerts some control over the sculptor, just as the sculptor exerts control over the clay.

In other human endeavors, the mutual influences appear more clearly in both directions: back and forth between behaving individuals and environmental conditions. People do things to the environment—build bridges, pass laws, and plant corn—and the environment does things to people, prompting them to drive over bridges, obey laws, and eat corn. Thus, Skinner did not view the environment as an independent force or agent. Rather, his radical behaviorism focuses on the *functional relations* between behavioral and environmental events, meaning the tendency of one event to change in some consistent manner with changes in one or more other events. The interest lies with the *interactions*, the mutual influences, between behavior patterns and events in the environment.

The refugees—an important part of the environment for Bertha—influenced her behavior, just as she shaped their behavior. Each party, the server and served, became a prominent element in the other's environment.

A traditional behaviorist would not speculate about the thoughts or social conscience that brought Bertha back daily to the soup kitchen. Those mental events did not cause her behavior, and anyway they lie outside the domain of traditional behaviorism. The behaviorist would note instead that she arrived at the refugee camp with increasing frequency, an overt response, and would assume that something in that environment strengthened the probability of this behavior—perhaps the smiles, hugs, and words of gratitude from the ill and illiterate, old and weary, and other refugees. Then too, the food, instruction, clothing, and medicine Bertha gave to the refugees perhaps sustained their interest, bringing them back day after day. According to behaviorism, she and the refugees each supported one another's habit of returning to that kitchen. And Bertha found a place for herself.

Owing partly to its focus on the environment and partly to its explicit procedures, the behavioristic tradition continues to be a popular approach to solving everyday behavior problems, emphasizing the functional relations between behavior and environmental events. But especially with the development of electronic brain scanning devices, many behaviorists now take a less extreme position. Focusing on interactions with the environment, they may recognize or employ mental events, including self-observation. The concern, however, is not with judging, imagining, worrying, remembering, deciding, and other mental activities. It remains on the behavioral manifestations of these reactions—concepts and terms that refer to overt behavior and events in the environment (Skinner, 1971).

On this basis, research in operant and classical conditioning no longer maintains the premier status it held in the mid-20th century, but it does continue to influence research in the field, often by supporting research from other perspectives. In particular, it has provided unprecedented frameworks for studies of animals and human beings in biological and cognitive psychology.

Classical Conditioning

In Pavlov's early work as a physiologist, an unplanned event with dogs changed his whole research program. After many days in the laboratory, these animals salivated at the sound of the keeper's footsteps, even before the arrival of food. This sign of anticipation, already well known, disrupted his laboratory studies of digestion. So Pavlov redirected his research. He turned from the physiology of gastric secretions to the psychology of learning.

In controlled trials, he regularly sounded a buzzer just before serving his dogs their meal. Soon the dogs began to salivate when they heard the buzzer, before the food arrived (Pavlov, 1927). A buzzer, as opposed to a bell, gave Pavlov greater control over the sound—a buzzer stops abruptly; the sound of a bell fades away gradually. This approach gave greater precision to his studies. But the idea that he used a bell appears throughout psychological and lay thought, perhaps because a dinner bell for dogs makes a more compelling tale.

The Classical Process

In this process, food is an **unconditioned stimulus,** an event that auto-matically elicits the response in question; no learning is involved. Salivation to food is an **unconditioned response,** a relatively simple, automatic reaction to an unconditioned stimulus. Unconditioned means unlearned. The food-salivation association is inborn; no learning is required.

Learning occurs when a neutral stimulus becomes involved. A *neutral stimulus* has no capacity to evoke the response in question. But in **classical conditioning,** a neutral stimulus, after being paired with an unconditioned stimulus, develops the capacity alone to elicit a certain response, commonly with physiological or emotional components. The sound of a buzzer, a for-merly neutral stimulus, evoked salivation after being paired regularly with food. The sound of the buzzer thereby became a conditioned stimulus. A **conditioned stimulus** is a previously neutral stimulus that has become capa-ble by itself of eliciting a certain response. That reaction to a conditioned stimulus is known as a **conditioned response,** which is similar to the uncon-ditioned response (Pavlov, 1927). The appearance of the involuntary condi-tioned response has led some people to refer to this classical process as respondent conditioning, emphasizing respondent behavior (Figure 5.1).

At one point Pavlov called classical conditioning "stimulus substitution," for a formerly neutral stimulus took the place of an unconditioned stimulus. In restricted ways, the buzzer does become a substitute for food, eliciting the response of salivation. But the buzzer is not food. So the subject simply

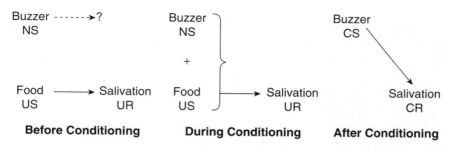

Figure 5.1   Process of Classical Conditioning. Before conditioning, the sound of the buzzer, a neutral stimulus (NS), does not cause the dog to salivate; food, an unconditioned stimulus (US), automatically causes salivation, an unconditioned response (UR). During the conditioning process, the buzzer is paired with food. After conditioning, the formerly neutral stimulus, the buzzer, becomes a conditioned stimulus (CS), eliciting salivation, known as a conditioned response (CR).

develops an expectation about the presence of food. On this basis, the buzzer may elicit a conditioned response somewhat different from the unconditioned response. That conditioned response may include anticipatory reactions not elicited by the unconditioned stimulus alone, such as pricking up the ears, and abbreviated responses, such as weaker or less salivation (Rescorla, 1988). In other words, classical conditioning merely provides the organism with helpful information about the possible presence of some object or event.

Thus, the acquisition of a classically conditioned response can be viewed as a two-unit sequence: antecedent stimuli and a response. As a rule the neutral stimulus must be paired several times with the unconditioned stimulus before it alone acquires the capacity to elicit the conditioned response.

A child suffering a bladder ailment illustrates this process in everyday life. She received medical attention every three weeks. The doctors at the hospital wore long, white coats, and the little girl went through much discomfort. On each appointment, she saw those long, white coats and then experienced the painful examinations and treatments. On the first visit, the white coats had little meaning. The next time she went to the hospital she became fearful as soon as the doctors appeared wearing their coats. And on the third visit, she let out a loud scream as soon as she saw the long, white coats. Those coats signaled for her the start of a very painful experience. They became the stimulus for her response of screaming and crying (Fernald, 1997).

This circumstance depicts the sequence of events in classical conditioning. The neutral stimulus occurs first, followed by the unconditioned stimulus. The white coats, with no meaning on the first visit, appeared *before* the medical procedures. In this way, the white coats became the signal for a forthcoming event: the painful examination and treatment.

This sequence—first the signal, then the unconditioned stimulus—represents the usual sequence in classical conditioning. It is called **delayed conditioning** because the neutral stimulus, the white coats, appears before the onset of the unconditioned stimulus, the medical treatment. Then both stimuli continue to be present together for some period. Delayed conditioning is generally the most powerful form of classical conditioning. The neutral stimulus also appears first in **trace conditioning,** but it disappears after an interval, prior to the presence of the unconditioned stimulus. As a rule, the briefer the interval, the stronger is the conditioning, but there are exceptions, especially in the conditioning of food aversions. The term *trace* emphasizes a memory trace essential in the pairing of the neutral and unconditioned stimuli.

Sometimes the neutral and unconditioned stimulus occur together, a process known as **simultaneous conditioning.** In this case, the white coats would appear only when the physicians commenced their work. This pairing results in weaker conditioning because the signal does not appear in advance.

And when the neutral stimulus occurs *after* the unconditioned stimulus, it cannot function as a signal at all. There is no substantial conditioning.

Classical conditioning enables an individual to learn the meaning of a particular stimulus. The individual develops an attitude or emotional reaction about some impending event (Kohn & Kalat, 1992).

Bertha developed a special affection for her father's Biedermeier cabinet, which she brought from Vienna. How did that happen? How did this furniture become her "comforter"?

We cannot know, but we can enumerate from psychological research three major possibilities, three ways in which people acquire attitudes and emotional reactions. First, they may do so through direct instruction. Told that a certain food causes cancer, a person may develop an aversion to that food. The instruction suffices. Bertha's father perhaps instructed her about the value of the cabinet, causing her to cherish it as a means of security.

Second, people develop emotional responses by observation, without any instruction. In this process, called modeling, or observational learning, a person may become fearful of a certain tool after watching someone else suffer an injury when using it. Intentional or otherwise, a demonstration sometimes can be sufficient. Without saying anything, Bertha's father perhaps behaved in ways that showed how much comfort he gained from that cabinet.

Extensive research has supported instruction and observational learning as ways to develop and change attitudes. Both can be effective, separately or together.

A third way, viewing this outcome in the context of classical conditioning, has special appeal for the behaviorist. The behaviorist would note that the cabinet by itself—hard wood, painted black—did not have any natural features of an *un*conditioned "comforter." It could not be mistaken for a child's soft security blanket, a mother's warm and tender hug, or even a father's lap. But this large piece of furniture in the drawing room certainly would have been noticed by anyone experiencing warmth, hugs, food, and other comforting events in that room.

In fact, Bertha suggested that this cabinet had been regularly associated with pleasurable stimuli in her early life—food, drink, rest, cuddling, and play with her father. Through these associations with these positive, unconditioned stimuli time and again, the cabinet perhaps became a conditioned stimulus for feeling comforted. This process would involve delayed or simultaneous conditioning. The cabinet would have gained its comforting qualities by its presence on these occasions with food and drink and hugs in the drawing room.

We cannot know for certain how that dark, hard piece of furniture became a comforter. There is no evidence that anyone used direct instruction for this purpose. Observational learning seems a better possibility, and it could have occurred amid a conditioning process. Both techniques are often used today in behavior therapy.

In any case, years later and miles away on Leerbachstrasse, that cabinet elicited in Bertha a strong, favorable reaction. Even after Willie took away the goblets, it remained her comforter (Edinger, 1968).

Classical Conditioning Principles

Principles of classical conditioning are widely used to explain the development of emotional reactions in everyday life. On passing a tree from which she fell as a youth and sustained serious injury, an elderly woman still shudders a bit. A man enjoys a slight flash of excitement on walking in a park where he encountered his first love on summer evenings. Someone who becomes violently nauseous while dining at a certain restaurant or using a certain medication tends to re-experience some of that illness on confronting the relevant stimulus again. Classically conditioned responses of this sort appear throughout daily life. Within psychology, no other theory or perspective offers an equally compelling explanation of unusual, individually acquired fears and preferences.

Sometimes a stimulus that is merely similar to the conditioned stimulus elicits the conditioned response, an outcome called **stimulus generalization.** The new stimulus is not the same as the conditioned stimulus—but is enough like it to call forth the response. A cabinet similar to Bertha's Biedermeier might evoke a positive emotional response in her. A setting similar to their soup kitchen might have elicited a positive emotional response among the refugees.

The little girl who became fearful of doctors' long, white coats one day was taken to a restaurant and observed the waiters wearing short, white coats. But the length did not matter. Immediately, she started crying and screaming. Stimulus generalization had occurred. The short, white coats were enough like long, white coats to elicit the fear reaction (Fernald, 1997). That was the long and short of it.

As a rule, the individual eventually learns the difference between relevant and irrelevant stimuli, such as long and short coats. The process of responding only to the correct stimulus, and not to others that appear similar, is called **discrimination.** In the early stages of classical conditioning, discrimination may not take place. The individual responds in a more random manner, suggesting stimulus generalization. But if the unconditioned stimulus is paired with the conditioned stimulus, and not other stimuli, then discrimination will appear at some point.

Classical conditioning, also called Pavlovian conditioning, produces both positive and negative emotional reactions. But the latter appear more frequently, owing to the numerous possibilities for stress in our lives. Breuer described Bertha's nervous coughing in this way. She could not understand how the sound of dance music made her cough, but she heard that music at an extremely stressful time in her life—when she was sitting by the bedside of her dying father, awaiting the arrival of the surgeon. The muscle tensions and twinges she experienced while waiting with him during that traumatic period were unconditioned stimuli for a cough, a normal muscle spasm of the glottis. By coincidence, she heard the dance music at just such a moment (Breuer, 1895). This reflexive cough, occurring at the same time she heard the music, apparently transformed that music into a conditioned stimulus for nervous coughing.

This outcome, **one-trial conditioning**, occurs through a single pairing of a neutral and unconditioned stimulus. It can be demonstrated in the laboratory, and it can occur spontaneously amid the events of everyday life, especially with strong stimuli.

But conditioning sometimes disappears. If the conditioned stimulus appears repeatedly without the unconditioned stimulus, eventually the conditioned response does not occur, an outcome known as **extinction**. The conditioned response becomes inhibited. If the little girl were regularly exposed to white coats in her everyday life, without any negative incidents, then her anxiety would gradually disappear.

The extinguished response may reappear, however. If the individual has not been in the original conditioning situation for some interval, and the conditioned stimulus has not been present during this period, the previously extinguished conditioned response may reappear on exposure to the conditioned stimulus. Without encountering white coats of any sort for some time, the little girl may experience a fear reaction on seeing them once again. The conditioned response may re-emerge. This phenomenon, called **spontaneous recovery**, becomes weaker and weaker with each subsequent presentation of the conditioned stimulus alone. In the long run, the conditioned response disappears completely.

One other principle deserves special mention because it has the potential to greatly expand the influence of classical conditioning. Known as **higher-order conditioning**, it occurs whenever a neutral stimulus becomes a conditioned stimulus without being paired previously with an unconditioned stimulus. It is paired instead with a conditioned stimulus. In Pavlov's laboratory, the sound of a buzzer became a conditioned stimulus through pairing with food, a procedure called normal or *first-order conditioning*. Then Pavlov several times paired a light, a neutral stimulus for salivation, with the buzzer eliciting salivation, and eventually the light became a conditioned stimulus—without the use of food or any other unconditioned stimulus—in a process called *second-order conditioning*. If a tap on the nose, regularly paired with the light but never with food, then alone elicited salivation, the result would be *third-order conditioning*, and so forth.

Investigators have experienced difficulties proceeding beyond second-order conditioning, especially with animals, because any conditioned stimulus can become extinguished after many presentations without an unconditioned stimulus. Moreover, a higher-order conditioned response is weaker and more readily extinguished than a first-order response. Pavlov believed higher levels are possible with human beings, and certainly advertisers, politicians, and many others today try to associate themselves or their products repeatedly with popular people, prestigious events, patriotic symbols, and other conditioned stimuli that elicit positive emotional reactions. In turn, they try to depict their rivals as associated instead with negatively conditioned stimuli.

From the behavioristic viewpoint, the environment shapes behavior—much as the sculptor shapes clay. The sound of dance music, the sight of an old cabinet, cooking odors, soup bowls—all can become conditioned stimuli through their associations with certain events. In this way, they acquire the capacity to elicit emotionally toned responses.

But these conditioned associations are not completely random, a point that needs emphasis in closing this discussion. Certain associations develop more rapidly than others, depending in part on the species involved. This phenomenon, called **biologically prepared learning**, means that an organism is biologically predisposed to develop conditioned reactions to certain stimuli and not to others, owing to "hard-wired" elements in its nervous system.

In a classic experiment, rats drank water paired with three simultaneous stimuli: bright light, a clicking noise, and a sweet flavor. Later, half the rats experienced an electric shock whenever they drank this water, and then the experimenters tested them for their response to the previously neutral stimuli, one by one: bright water, noisy water, and sweet water. What would the rats do? Had they developed a conditioned aversive reaction to one or more of these stimuli? As it turned out, they avoided the bright water and noisy water but not the sweet water. In other words, with electric shock as an unconditioned stimulus, the light and sounds became conditioned stimuli, but the flavor remained neutral. It did not become a negative conditioned stimulus.

The experimenters treated the other half of the group differently. While these rats were consuming the bright-noisy-sweet water, the experimenters exposed them not to electric shock but to radiation, an unconditioned stimulus for nausea. Then, when they tested this group for each stimulus separately, they found that these rats avoided the sweet water but not the bright or noisy water. In other words, with nausea-inducing radiation as an unconditioned stimulus, only the flavor of the water became a conditioned stimulus

(Garcia & Koelling, 1966). Thus, flavors and odors tend to become conditioned cues when the unconditioned stimulus causes gastrointestinal discomfort. Sights and sounds become conditioned cues when the unconditioned stimulus causes externally experienced pain.

Apparently natural selection has prepared organisms for these adaptive associations. Animals and human beings with these adaptive tendencies are more likely to survive and reproduce. Among human beings, for example, stimuli associated with snakes and spiders elicit more fear reactions than those associated with flowers (Marks, 1969; McNally, 1987). In short, the associations in classical conditioning tend to be biologically based, especially in animals. In human beings, who have greater potential for learning, conditioned stimuli are more diverse.

Operant Conditioning

In a different type of conditioning, the responses are not elicited by conditioned and unconditioned stimuli in the environment. They are instead emitted by the individual. The metaphor of the sculptor applies to both types, but it is even more applicable in operant conditioning, as developed by B. F. Skinner.

The Operant Process

Behavior followed by positive consequences tends to be repeated and elaborated. Behavior followed by no obvious consequences or aversive outcomes tends to be discarded. In **operant conditioning,** or *operant learning,* responses emitted by the individual are developed, sustained, and elaborated by their consequences, as well as by the antecedent conditions in the environment.

Bertha's activities supported the behavior of some of the refugees. They came hungry to the kitchen, she doled out soup; they said they were cold, she gave them blankets; they tried to speak German, she assisted them with their new language. These consequences increased the probability that the refugees would repeat those behaviors. Prior to Skinner's work, this relationship was called the *law of effect,* indicating that the consequences of behavior strengthen or weaken its recurrence. As Skinner emphasized, the consequences strengthen or weaken the *probability* of the response occurring again, not the strength of the response.

Thus, the acquisition of an operantly conditioned response is not viewed as a two-unit sequence—stimuli and response. Rather, it involves a three-unit contingency: the antecedent stimulation, the response, and its consequences.

These consequences, reinforcement or punishment, influence the relationship between the first two units—the antecedent stimulus and the response. They alter the significance of that stimulus, making it a signal that precedes and therefore guides the response (DeGrandpre & Buskist, 2000). In fact, reinforcement refers to the strengthening of that relationship.

In a laboratory demonstration, a food-deprived rat or other animal is placed in a Skinner box with a lever that, when pressed, dispenses food or water. The investigator has no special interest in lever pressing per se, just as Pavlov had no continuing interest in salivation. However, both behaviors are useful in studying conditioning processes. Free to move within the confined area, the rat engages in incidental behaviors, including intermittent lever pressing, obtaining food on each occasion. Eventually, the animal presses the lever regularly until it becomes satiated. This behavior, lever pressing, is called an **operant response** (R^O), or operant behavior, because it is learned and merely guided by the stimulation. Unlike respondent behavior, it is not innate and automatically elicited by the environment.

Then the experimenter alters the apparatus, dispensing food only when a light is lit. Soon the rat presses the lever when the light appears and ignores the lever otherwise. When the light reappears, the rat returns to work. The light has thereby become a **discriminative stimulus** (S^D), indicating that reinforcement is available if the proper response is emitted. And the food, appearing immediately following the correct response, serves as a **reinforcing stimulus** (S^R), increasing the probability that this operant response will be repeated or modified in some way. This laboratory procedure illustrates the basic components of the operant model, used to investigate the numerous principles of operant conditioning (Figure 5.2)

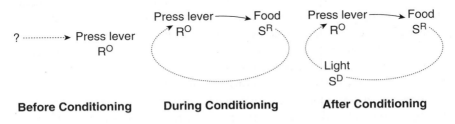

Figure 5.2   **Process of Operant Conditioning.** Before conditioning, the initial stimulus is uncertain. During conditioning, pressing the lever, an operant response (R^O), may result in food, a reinforcing stimulus (S^R). The availability of food may be signaled by a discriminative stimulus (S^D), such as a light. After this discrimination training, the rat presses the lever only when the light appears. The reversed order of the symbolic letters and the superscripts distinguish this notation from that used in classical conditioning.

When the organism emits a response that is followed by the *appearance* of positive consequences, such as food or an increase in salary, the outcome is called **positive reinforcement**. These consequences increase the probability that the prior response will be repeated in the presence of that same stimulation. Similarly, when the response is followed by the *disappearance* of some aversive event, such as a bitter taste or potential loss of a job, that outcome is known as **negative reinforcement**. These consequences also increase the probability that the prior response will be repeated in those circumstances.

All reinforcers, positive and negative, increase the probability that the prior response will be repeated or elaborated. In positive reinforcement, a satisfying event appears; in negative reinforcement, an aversive event disappears. The vital point here is that negative reinforcement is not a bad outcome. It is instead a favorable event, the removal of a potentially disagreeable circumstance. Behaviorists use this term for this specific meaning. Contrary to popular speech, negative reinforcement does not mean punishment. All reinforcement increases the probability of a response, and the term *reinforcement*, when used alone, almost invariably indicates positive consequences.

But the acquisition of an operant response cannot be explained solely by its consequences. It must also be understood in terms of the antecedent stimulus, which exerts a measure of control over that response. The organism learns something about a stimulus in its environment; it makes an interpretation and then responds accordingly. If the contingency relationship is simple, such as the light in the Skinner box, the learning is simple. If it is more complex, involving comparisons and abstractions, the learning is more complex, involving more cognitive components (DeGrandpre & Buskist, 2000).

The first element in this three-unit contingency, the discriminative stimulus, becomes vital, for all behavior occurs in some context. In classical conditioning, the behavior is elicited solely by a conditioned or unconditioned stimulus. In operant conditioning, a certain stimulus alone is an insufficient context. The behavior is evoked by a *combination* of the antecedent stimulus and prior consequences of that behavior. The antecedent stimulation merely signals an occasion for the operant response; it does not elicit that behavior. Red traffic lights do not make motorists stop, but they do influence this response. Prior consequences, such as a previous accident or traffic ticket for running a red light, also increase the probability of stopping.

In operant conditioning, behaviorists refer to this combination of antecedent stimulation and prior consequences as **stimulus control**. The stimulus implies a specific context; the control refers to the likelihood that the response will appear in this context. When the light changes to red, motorists typically apply the brakes, but they are not compelled to do so in the way an odor makes us salivate and dust induces an eyeblink (Baum, 1994).

An operant response may come under stimulus control through trial-and-error behavior. A cook gradually discovers the oven temperatures that prove most successful for preparing a certain specialty. A child learns to whine for privileges from his parents but not from his teacher, who pays no attention. These responses are called *contingency-shaped behavior* because they emerge through their consequences, apart from direct instruction.

Other operant responses come under stimulus control on the basis of some instruction, law, advice, or other explicit statement about how to behave. In these instances, called *rule-governed behavior,* the response and its likely consequences are known in advance. The teacher has told a child: If you whine, you cannot go outside for recess. The child knows the probable reinforcing or punishing consequences of following or breaking the rule. In daily life, people learn by both means, moving back and forth between rule-governed and contingency-shaped behavior (Skinner, 1989).

In either case, stimulus control in operant conditioning is conceived and labeled differently from that in classical conditioning. In classical conditioning, the newly eliciting stimulus, formerly neutral, is called a conditioned stimulus. It has become capable of generating the response by itself. In operant conditioning, the capacity of the discriminative stimulus to evoke the response depends on the prior consequences of that response.

In other words, the first and third units in the operant process are stimuli, occurring before and after the response, respectively. When the first unit is present, a correct response yields reinforcing consequences, such as a smile, food, money, or other positive outcomes. Thus, the third unit, the consequences, is often called a *reinforcing stimulus.* But sometimes the operant response is not correct, and therefore does not yield a reinforcing stimulus. Instead, a *punishing stimulus* decreases the probability that the response will be repeated. It may be an illness, spanking, loss of money, or detention after school. In short, the consequences strengthen or weaken the potential of the discriminative stimulus to evoke the response.

For another reason too, the consequences may not be a reinforcing stimulus. Suppose, for example, that children are running wildly in the school building. In a program of behavioral modification, they can be instructed to sit quietly for just a few moments, and then, if they do so, they are rewarded with a legitimate opportunity to run freely around the gymnasium. In weekly or longer intervals, the length of the required quiet period is gradually increased, each time rewarded by a period for running. Thus, running—a behavior, not a stimulus—constitutes reinforcement for another behavior, sitting quietly. To be loosely consistent with the idea of a consequent stimulus, it might be claimed that the room with no rule against running temporarily becomes a reinforcing stimulus.

In any case, the fact that a high-frequency behavior can serve as reinforcement greatly extends the usefulness of operant conditioning (Premack, 1965). Thus, the terms *reinforcing consequences* and *punishing consequences* might serve better, avoiding perpetuation of the myth that some physical "prize" is essential as the third unit in operant conditioning. That misconception has become a substantial source of public resistance to operant conditioning.

In another misconception, the public often fails to understand that intentional reinforcers can be gradually reduced and eventually replaced by natural reinforcers. A child learning to write the alphabet or an adult learning ice skating may need consistent, extrinsic reinforcement at the outset simply to persist at the task. But once partial mastery is achieved, the intrinsic, natural reinforcers of writing one's own name or gliding across the ice begin to become ascendant, sustaining the behavior for its own sake, apart from prizes or other arbitrary consequences.

And in everyday life, discriminative stimuli are usually more complex than a green light for a pigeon to peck a disk, a red light for a motorist to press the brake, or a growling dog for a pedestrian to stand still. They may involve several elements, past and present. And again, when discriminative stimuli are combined with prior consequences, the result constitutes stimulus control. A woman invites a man to meet her for dinner at 6:00 P.M. on Tuesday at Peter's Place, providing he can obtain theater tickets. For the man, the discriminative stimuli include the availability of tickets, Tuesday, 6:00 P.M., Peter's Place, and of course the original invitation (Baum, 1994). But the prior consequences also play a role. If the woman issued a previous invitation to this man and did not appear herself at the appointed time and place, the man may well stay home instead. Stimulus control would be weak in that instance.

For radical behaviorists, the individual's reactions to the discriminative stimulus pose no special concern. They are viewed as responses to the preceding stimuli. But for other psychologists, they raise questions about the cognitive bases of behavior (Rescorla, 1988, 1992).

In exploring these relationships, Skinner at times focused on a single participant because the significance of the discriminative and reinforcing stimuli may vary from one individual to another, depending on each individual's personal history and genetic background. In behaviorism, personal history refers to a person's history of reinforcement. Which behaviors have been most reinforced? By which consequences? Which discriminative stimuli have preceded these behaviors, signaling an occasion to emit the response? A behaviorist would ask such questions in attempting to understand any persistent behavior in any individual.

These questions can be extended to the soup kitchen where Bertha offered food, clothing, and other supplies to the refugees. Did their arrival become for Bertha discriminative stimuli to serve soup and provide other help? Did their smiles, thanks, and other reactions become important consequences for her? Later, she helped them learn basic expressions in German and find their way around Frankfurt. The details remain unknown, but from a behaviorist viewpoint, relevant stimuli and consequences played a fundamental role. Bertha returned to the soup kitchen again and again.

Operant Conditioning Principles

Thirty little girls lived in an orphanage attached to that soup kitchen; most were illegitimate and all were assigned to the state and in need of assistance. Occasionally Bertha observed them at play. At one point, she became more active, reading to them and telling stories from *In the Junk Shop*. Then she encouraged her little listeners to tell their own stories, which were often quite sad (Guttmann, 2001). Later, she served snacks to the children and learned the procedures for assisting them at mealtime, bedtime, and playtime. Eventually, she moved completely out of the kitchen and into the orphanage. There she fed toddlers, taught sewing, and organized a club for adolescents. In this environment, she acquired basic skills in what would be known today as child care and social work.

From the standpoint of operant conditioning, acquiring any skill occurs most rapidly with constant reinforcement. More precisely, it is called **continuous reinforcement** because every correct response is followed by an event, such as a child's hug or adult's gratitude, which increases the probability that the response will be repeated. Continuous reinforcement is most important in the early stages of learning. After the skill has been acquired, partial reinforcement may be equally or more effective. In **partial reinforcement**, only some correct responses are followed by consequences that increase the probability of repetition. Reinforcement does not occur after every correct response.

In one form of partial reinforcement, called a *fixed-interval schedule,* reinforcement becomes available only for the first correct response after a certain period of time, such as every 30 seconds, regardless of the number of correct responses. In laboratory studies of this schedule, an individual eventually emits a burst of responses toward the end of each 30-second interval. In daily life, with a statistics quiz every Friday morning, students are likely to ignore statistics during the week, engaging in a "cram session" every Thursday evening. In another fixed schedule, the *fixed-ratio schedule,* reinforcement becomes available only after a certain number of correct responses, such as every 3rd or 15th response, regardless of when they are emitted. Under this schedule, the individual eventually emits responses in clusters of 3 or 15, matching the ratio required to earn a reinforcer, a condition sometimes called *piece work.* People in rigorous routines of physical fitness give themselves a rest after a certain number of stretching exercises in each position or a certain number of repetitions lifting a particular weight.

In partial reinforcement on a *variable-interval schedule,* reinforcement becomes available at random, unpredictable times but reflects an overall average. In a variable-interval schedule of 10 seconds, reinforcement might become available for the first correct response after 4, 18, and 8 seconds, representing an overall average of 10 seconds. The bartender, reference librarian, and firefighter never know when the next patron or emergency call will appear. In another variable schedule, a *variable-ratio schedule,* reinforcement becomes available after an unpredictable number of correct responses, but again an average is involved. In a variable-ratio schedule of 7, reinforcement might become available after 3 correct responses, then 10, and then 8, representing an overall average of 7. Gambling activities illustrate the variable-ratio schedule. Variable schedules of either type generate high, steady rates of response because, with the occasion for reinforcement unknown, greater effort is expended for each reinforcement (Skinner, 1953).

In research and practice, behaviorists amplify or diminish reinforcement in subtle ways as well. In teaching self-control to hyperactive children, for example, they offered each child a choice between a small bit of cookie immediately or the whole cookie later. The children invariably chose the small, immediate reinforcer. But when the trainer, during the period between the response and the reinforcement, simply talked to the child about something else, the child showed increased self-control, choosing the whole cookie after the longer period of time (Binder, Dixon, & Ghezzi, 2000). Mentally disabled adults have shown similar self-control. Simply having a task to complete enabled them to accept delayed reinforcement (Dixon & Holcomb, 2000).

If reinforcement disappears entirely, eventually the response disappears too. This outcome is called *extinction,* meaning that the conditioned response has failed to occur. Extinction is commonly used in clinics to eliminate shouting, aggression, messiness, complaints, and other undesirable responses. A previous schedule of variable reinforcement, incidentally, makes any response resistant to extinction. The individual becomes accustomed to some or many non-reinforced responses and therefore continues responding for some time when no reinforcement is forthcoming at all.

But does the extinguished behavior disappear in a gentle fashion—going quietly into the night, so to speak? Does any other behavior emerge? Is there unfinished business? In research, there is always unfinished business, even with extinction.

Unwanted outcomes often accompany the extinguished response. One, called the *extinction burst,* involves a sharp increase in the response undergoing extinction. In another, extinction-induced aggression, the individual responds with hostile physical behavior.

Investigators have tried to eliminate these side effects, and in one instance they studied people receiving treatments for self-injurious behavior—scratching, hitting, and biting oneself. Their ages ranged from 18 to 54 years. They were treated in three groups: 10 people exposed to extinction alone, 9 exposed to extinction combined with reinforcement for unrelated desirable behaviors, and 11 exposed to extinction and reinforcement not directed toward any specific behavior. Analysis of the results showed that half of the participants displayed at least one side effect, with extinction-induced aggression more common than the extinction burst. However, both responses decreased substantially when extinction was combined with reinforcement for other behaviors. Moreover, the group that received reinforcement for unrelated desirable behaviors displayed the least disruption. Only 20% showed any side effects when extinction was supplemented in this way. When it remained the sole technique, 62% displayed side effects (Lerman, Iwata, & Wallace, 1999).

In addition to acquisition and extinction, classical and operant conditioning share other basic principles, notably spontaneous recovery, stimulus generalization, and discrimination. After extinction and a sufficient interval, a conditioned response may reappear without further training, an outcome known as *spontaneous recovery*. And a stimulus that is merely similar to the discriminative stimulus, but not identical, may evoke the conditioned response, demonstrating *stimulus generalization*. When the individual responds only to the original, discriminative stimulus and not to others that may be similar, the phenomenon is called *discrimination*, which is essentially the opposite of stimulus generalization.

These principles, common to classical and operant conditioning, sometimes obscure the difference between them. In classical conditioning, the reinforcer is paired with a neutral stimulus. Food and drink accompanied the Biedermeier cabinet in Vienna, and later Bertha felt comforted merely by the presence of that dark, wooden structure. In operant conditioning, the reinforcer is contingent on a certain response. When Bertha moved from Vienna, she brought that cabinet along; then she could enjoy it in Frankfurt too.

At the orphanage, the board of directors noticed Bertha's effectiveness in self-appointed managerial roles. She guided the children and also the staff—even without formal requests to do so. Some people described her as "bossy" because of her tendency to take control. But she managed the work well.

Searching for a new director, the board made a surprising decision, selecting a headstrong young woman relatively new to the institution. This choice surprised even Bertha herself, for she had no formal experience in administration and maintained meager relations with other staff members. Bertha was lonely and aloof, and the orphanage apparently served as a diversion in her otherwise privileged, reclusive life (Edinger, 1968). Apparently she found the work satisfying, for she certainly did not need the salary.

For the formerly ill daughter in an upper-class Viennese family, opportunity had knocked. This position offered an entirely new start for 36-year-old Bertha, but she kept one foot in her previous life. She rejected the third-floor bedroom occupied by her predecessor, staying instead with her mother in the center of Frankfurt, walking a half-hour each way from their elegant apartment to the modest, crowded orphanage on the outskirts of town (Freeman, 1972; Guttmann, 2001). In this way, she accepted the challenge.

She began her new role thinking well beyond the physical needs of her 30 children, aiming to foster their education and social development as well. These girls would be her "daughters." She wanted them trained to take useful and satisfying places in society.

In training anyone for complex behavior, the skilled instructor begins with easy, small steps. In this operant method, known as **shaping**, each task or step is only slightly more difficult than its predecessor, and reinforcement is always available immediately after each success. Hence, the individual usually succeeds at each new step, gradually developing increased proficiency. Each of these steps, called a **successive approximation**, is just a bit closer than its predecessor to the final step, or goal, which may be quite different from the starting point.

In working with numbers, the child first learns to count, then add, later subtract, multiply, and other mathematical procedures. At each level, even smaller steps are established, moving from single digits, to double digits, to "carrying" remainders, to triple digits, and so forth, and in every instance, reinforcement is contingent on success. Gradually in this step-by-step fashion, the learner acquires full mastery of arithmetic or some other complex subject. Long division, fractions, and algebra, for example, require mastery of many responses at prior levels.

As Skinner pointed out, the fire-fighting pigeons learned their jobs through shaping. In teaching the bird to ring the bell, the first step, or approximation, was to bring the bird close to the string. To do so, the trainer presented a food pellet as reinforcement whenever the bird moved into that vicinity. After several reinforcements for this behavior, the bird remained near the string. Then the trainer moved to a second approximation. The pigeon received no further reinforcement until it touched the string, perhaps pecking it lightly. After sufficient reinforcement for touching the string, the next successive approximation was established. The bird was required to pick up the string in its beak in order to receive a reinforcer. After it did so regularly, it received no more food for merely taking the string in its beak. That criterion had been reached. For the fourth approximation, the bird had to pull on the string; only these responses were reinforced. And eventually the pigeon reached the final criterion, pulling on the string with sufficient strength to ring the bell, thereby earning a reinforcer.

With animals and people, operant conditioning involves two types of reinforcement, primary and secondary. Any event that automatically satisfies some inborn, biological need is known as **primary reinforcement**. Food, drink, and fresh air serve as primary reinforcement; they satisfy bodily requirements. After the children showed the expected behavior on field trips, Bertha offered them tasty snacks. In contrast, **secondary reinforcement** is any event, not *originally* associated with biological needs, that satisfies an acquired motive, such as the desire for recognition. A colored sticker, a word of praise, a high grade—all serve as secondary reinforcement for success in education (Skinner, 1953).

The concept of secondary reinforcement occupies an important place in the behavioristic outlook. It offers some understanding of what keeps people at their tasks, hobbies, and other routines without the direct satisfaction of biological requirements. In many respects, it bridges the gap between the use of intentional, primary reinforcers, such as food, and the appearance of natural reinforcers inherent in successfully performing a certain task. When primary reinforcement is inconvenient, unavailable, or inappropriate, a smile or word of encouragement may sustain the response until sufficient mastery results in intrinsic reinforcement.

However, most responses do not occur in separate segments. Observe a child eating a snack, an adult balancing a checkbook, or even a pigeon dowsing a fire. The responses appear in a more or less continuous flow. The driver of an automobile emits a sequence of intricately connected behaviors that cannot occur in a random order. In fact, except for minor violations, only one sequence will achieve the goal. This sequence, in which each response is functionally connected to the prior and subsequent response, is known as **chaining** or a behavioral chain. In this chain, each response serves two purposes. It creates a condition that becomes secondary reinforcement for the preceding response and also a discriminative stimulus, or cue, for the next response in the chain.

The automobile driver reaches into her pocket and withdraws a key. Having the key in hand constitutes reinforcement for reaching into the pocket, and it serves as a discriminative stimulus for using the key to open the car door. Turning the key in the lock produces a click, which constitutes reinforcement because the door now can be opened, and it also becomes a cue to operate the door handle, the next important act in the chain. Opening the door is reinforced because the car can be entered, and it is a discriminative stimulus for climbing into the car. Entering the car is reinforced because the individual gains access to the ignition, and so forth through all the sequential behaviors in operating an automobile.

This analysis has obvious limitations, however. It might be used to explain why this sequence is emitted but not how it originated. Stepping on the gas pedal causes the car to move, the desired consequence, but how did having the key in a pocket, seeing the lock on the door, and so forth become discriminative stimuli for successive responses that did not immediately cause the car to move? For many behaviorists, the concept of chaining is useful only within a cognitive framework, emphasizing the role of thinking in the connections between links. This increasing recognition of cognitive processes is reflected in other behavioristic contexts.

In any case, chaining often occurs automatically, as small behavioral units become connected to one another, forming larger units. For example, children learn to dress themselves, recite numbers, and write the alphabet. After mastering the basic steps in each task, they no longer think about putting on socks, then shoes, then tying the shoes, but instead they simply think about getting dressed or doing arithmetic, spelling a word or, years later, writing an essay. The children's instructors, after years in the classroom and mastery of many specific tasks, approach their day in terms of even larger behavior units: setting the schedule, teaching Spanish, ordering books, and planning a health program, all connected parts of specific tasks in their morning at work.

Chaining involves the integration of small behavior units into larger ones. Shaping, in contrast, generates a gradual change in a unit of behavior, regardless of its size.

Finally, much human behavior occurs in a social context, creating the potential for mutual reinforcement. As Bertha instructed her "daughters," directing their lives, they exerted some control over her in return. She kept them obedient, offering food and shelter as consequences, and they kept her working at the orphanage, providing reinforcement through their hugs and smiles. When two or more people are interacting regularly, the situation often involves **reciprocal conditioning**, meaning that each person's behavior is reinforcing to the other, influencing that person's response.

A widely circulated cartoon depicts reciprocal conditioning, showing a rat next to a lever in a Skinner box. Speaking about the experimenter, he says to another rat: "Wow! Have I got this guy conditioned. Every time I press this lever, he gives me something to eat." But, in return, each time the rat pressed the lever, he gave the experimenter further data about operant conditioning.

Reciprocal conditioning sometimes appears suddenly between a parent and a child, especially about one year of age. By that time children have acquired likes and dislikes but remain unable to speak about them coherently. If their wishes are not met, they perhaps shriek and cry or run away.

To stop this unwanted behavior quickly, the parent may consent to the child's demands, thereby increasing the probability that the child will cry out again. Each member of the pair keeps the other responding in these ways.

Bertha's relations with the staff also proved mutually reinforcing—for the most part. She gained their cooperation. They, in turn, learned from her, earned a salary, and enjoyed the children.

Two-Factor Theory

In many instances, behavior may be influenced by both classical and operant conditioning. In classical conditioning, the learned reactions are preferences, fears, and other emotional responses. In operant learning, the reactions are spontaneous, overt behaviors. Yet the two forms of learning complement one another.

This learning, called two-factor theory, involves a sequence of classical and operant conditioning. In the **two-factor theory** of conditioning, an emotional reaction or expectancy is learned through classical conditioning, the first factor, and the problem-solving behavior for dealing with this reaction is learned through operant conditioning, the second factor. Each type of conditioning makes its own contribution to the outcome (Stasiewicz & Maisto, 1993).

The classical factor is sometimes known as **sign learning,** for the individual learns the significance of something, such as a soup kitchen or white coat, often evaluating it in positive or negative terms. The operant factor is known as **solution learning,** for the individual learns how to cope with the positive or negative event, approaching or retreating in various ways.

A student reported that during her childhood years her mother always scowled at her just before administering some punishment. Eventually, through classical conditioning, she became anxious whenever her mother scowled. One day after her mother scowled, she suddenly found herself at the sink, washing dishes. Later she realized that she avoided anxiety and possible punishment if she promptly engaged in some helpful behavior, such as washing the dishes. Through the process of operant conditioning, she began to wash dishes whenever her mother started scowling (Fernald, 1997). Sometimes she even retreated to the sink when there were no dirty dishes.

Bertha often wondered why she collected antiques. "Maybe it's because life has left me so lonely," she wrote in her journal. Two-factor conditioning perhaps occurred here too.

Again, this viewpoint would begin with classical conditioning. Bertha's affection for Viennese antiques arose through their association with happy events in her childhood, particularly mealtimes and cuddling with her father.

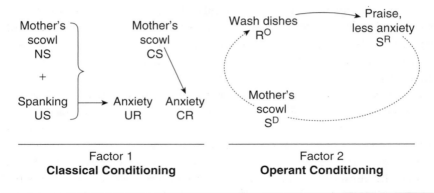

Factor 1	Factor 2
Classical Conditioning	**Operant Conditioning**

Figure 5.3   Two-Factor Theory of Conditioning. In the first factor, the mother's scowl preceded a spanking, an unconditioned stimulus (US). For the daughter, the scowl thereby became a conditioned stimulus (CS), eliciting anxiety. In the second factor, the scowl served as a discriminative stimulus (S^D) for washing the dishes. This operant response (R^O) resulted in a reinforcing stimulus (S^R), praise from her mother and diminished anxiety.

The Biedermeier cabinet may be an example. Then, through operant conditioning, she learned what to do about her affection. She purchased antiques, took great care of them, and brought them along whenever she moved to a new apartment. She could not bring her father, but with the antiques she could bring some of the feelings associated with him. Surrounded by the antiques, she felt less lonely.

Two-factor theory also applies in aversive circumstances. When children are punished physically, they experience anxiety and pain. Through classical conditioning, these negative emotional reactions extend to the people and objects associated with the punishment. Then, through operant conditioning, they try to do something about their negative feelings, as illustrated in the dish-washing behavior (Figure 5.3).

Incidentally, reward and punishment, popular everyday expressions, are less frequently used terms in operant psychology. Behaviorists instead refer to responses as being *reinforced;* they speak of organisms, people, and animals as being *rewarded.* This distinction is useful because reinforcement, by definition, depends on the outcome. Reinforcement is any event that strengthens the probability of a specific response, regardless of any intention to do so. In contrast, a reward is something that seems desirable for most people, according to social norms. But for a specific individual, it may not be reinforcing, and it does not pertain to any specific behavior.

As already noted, behaviorists speak of reinforcement in two ways, thereby gaining precision. Positive reinforcement involves the appearance of some desirable event, such as a smile or high grade. And negative reinforcement involves the disappearance of some undesirable event, such as after-school detention or a traffic ticket.

Comparable categories have been established for punishment, which weakens the probability of a response, and again, *positive* does not necessarily imply something favorable. It simply means the presence of something, just as *negative* indicates its absence. Thus, *positive punishment*, which sounds like an impossibility, involves the appearance of some undesirable event, such as a spanking or reprimand from the boss. And *negative punishment* involves the disappearance of some desirable event, such as recess or a weekly allowance. But these distinctions for punishment have not been as widely adopted as those for reinforcement, partly because so many behaviorists avoid the use of punishment altogether.

Punishment produces several undesirable outcomes, apart from humanitarian concerns. Often, it results in negative attitudes toward the punitive agent—the school, parent, principal, or other authority. It can create anxiety, uncertainty, and sometimes passivity in the punished person. Moreover, it is often ineffective, for it does not indicate the desired behavior. By providing attention for misbehavior, it may even sustain that undesirable outcome. For such reasons, behaviorists using punishment aim to do so promptly, consistently, and mildly, at the same time informing the individual about more appropriate behavior.

Well ahead of her time, Bertha prohibited physical punishment of any sort, and yet no one doubted that she ran the orphanage. She ran it completely her way, just as earlier she had controlled the nightly nursing of her father and her own brand of therapy with Josef Breuer. She expected confrontations; she even seemed to seek them. But she rarely fought with others. She simply vanquished them immediately. People who knew her, even relatives, described her as an active volcano, always on the verge of erupting, and totally unwilling to compromise even in casual conversation (Edinger, 1968).

"I think contact with adversaries," she once explained, "gives more strength and energy than contact with congenial people." So people simply avoided Bertha; she had no friends. She was too controlling, too full of fire.

Behavior Modification

Imagine that Bertha sought assistance in behavior therapy for her long-standing inability to work cooperatively with others, a difficulty dating back at least to her late-adolescent upheaval in Vienna. Behavior therapists today would not act in the manner of the gentle Josef Breuer. Instead, they would immediately consider the reinforcement principle, asking these questions: "How did this behavior arise? More importantly, what conditions sustain it?" For answers, behaviorists would study Bertha's environments.

If she had recently become self-centered and domineering, the behaviorist would look for some recent change in her current environment. Presumably this change signaled and reinforced her egocentric manner.

If, instead, this self-centered style had a long history, then the behaviorist might speculate that Bertha had never advanced beyond the self-centered stage early in life, a time when the child may gain control over her caretakers. Perhaps Bertha's parents "spoiled" her in this way in the early years, partly out of grief over the deaths of her two sisters. Even when her egocentric demands led her into difficulty later, Bertha continued to emit this behavior, presumably on the basis of partial reinforcement (Muroff, 1984). But the behaviorist would instead focus on her present behavior and current environment.

Through her long illness, Bertha gained a measure of control over her family. When she would not or could not eat, she regressed to the level of an infant, dependent on and yet demanding services from the family members. To change this response style, the behaviorist would focus on events in that particular environment.

The basic procedure would be to reinforce cooperative behaviors and to extinguish adversarial, controlling responses. Shaping would be employed, but the task would be prodigious owing to the partial reinforcement Bertha often received for competitive, controlling behaviors in everyday life.

The aim in **behavior therapy** is to remove an undesirable emotional response or behavioral problem by using the principles of classical and operant conditioning. A broader expression, **behavior modification**, has evolved to include two related methods, modeling and direct instruction aimed at changing behavior. Outside psychology, the term also refers to various non-psychological methods, such as surgery and drugs, prompting B. F. Skinner to avoid it altogether. Amid the wide-ranging practical uses of behaviorism in the workplace, school, home, or other context, behavior therapy is simply one instance of behavior modification.

A contemporary behavior therapist would treat one at a time the diverse symptoms Bertha experienced in Vienna—her fear of snakes, her eating disorder, her controlling personal style, and so forth. Unlike psychoanalysis, a symptom in behavior therapy is viewed as the problem, not as a symbol of some underlying problem. Removing the symptom removes the problem. Some symptoms are removed by classical conditioning, others through operant conditioning.

Changing Respondent Behavior

Many negative emotional responses, such as irrational fears, are acquired by classical conditioning, and they can be removed by classical counter-conditioning, which reverses the learning process. In the removal, a strong positive stimulus is paired with a weak version of the feared stimulus. The positive outweighs the negative. The fear reaction becomes an unlikely response through intentional classical conditioning.

One traditional method, known as **systematic desensitization**, proceeds in a step-by-step fashion, gradually exposing the patient to the feared stimulus, thereby making the patient less and less sensitive to it. As an aid in this process, it employs an *anxiety hierarchy,* which is an ordered list of the situations evoking tension in the patient. It is constructed by the patient and therapist together. The most-feared situations are at the top, and the least-feared are at the bottom, where the patient begins treatment. Before beginning, however, patients are trained in *deep-muscle relaxation*; they learn to relax readily in response to a signal from the therapist (Wolpe, 1961). This relaxation serves as a positive stimulus.

In treatment for her fear of black snakes, Bertha would sit in a comfortable chair, deeply relaxed; then she would imagine the item at the very bottom of her hierarchy. She might imagine a dark coiled rope looking somewhat like a black snake. If this scene prompted no anxiety, the therapist would proceed to the next item in the hierarchy, perhaps the word "snake" written on a piece of paper or a faded photo of a harmless snake. With no anxiety at this level, she next might imagine a more vivid photo of a snake, and so forth. In each instance, she would indicate an anxious state simply by pointing upward with an index finger.

Whenever a particular scene made Bertha anxious, the therapist would stop the progression and, if necessary, assist her in further relaxation or return to the next-lower item on the list. With further practice, and when she became fully relaxed once more, they would begin to move slowly up the list again, progressing in later sessions toward the entries at the top of the list, such as touching a live snake or holding a live snake.

This treatment has been effective in reducing irrational fears of all sorts, called phobias. These include fear of dentists, medical treatment, the opposite sex, schooling, and work, as well as the more traditional aversions to insects, heights, strangers, and enclosed spaces.

But many phobic people reject such treatments. They choose instead to avoid the feared object, never dealing with the irrationality of their fear. This avoidance behavior eventually becomes accepted as part of everyday living. They refuse therapy because they believe they would be confronted with the feared object—and they are right. But in systematic desensitization and similar procedures, the dosage would be carefully administered to match their tolerance.

In a more dramatic, extinction procedure called **flooding**, the therapist confronts the patient with the feared circumstance all at once, as fully as possible on the first trial. A young man afraid of anticipated loud noises avoided blown-up balloons because they might pop loudly at any moment. This fear became a social handicap, causing him to avoid birthday parties, weddings, and similar celebrations. The sound of a backfire from a car or a book dropped on the floor did not disturb him, for it had already happened. He became fearful in anticipation, and the problem dated back to his childhood. In his treatment, a pair of therapists escorted him into a room packed with 100 balloons. One therapist popped all of them as rapidly as possible while the other, as a gesture of support, stood calmly beside the tearful, visibly disturbed young man. During three such sessions, bursting more than 700 balloons altogether, the young man's response diminished steadily, and finally he tolerated the balloons with no significant fear (Houlihan, Schwartz, Miltenberger, & Heuton, 1993).

This procedure can involve a distinct risk for the person coming to therapy, for it begins with a high level of intensity of the very event that the individual fears most. If partial extinction does not occur in the first session, the person may become even more fearful, refusing all further attempts at therapy. Flooding raises the possibility of such unwanted outcomes, especially with children.

Modifying Operant Behavior

Other behavior disorders are not negative emotional responses but are more overt, voluntary reactions, such as eating problems, lack of exercise, tardiness, poor work habits, and temper tantrums. Principles of operant conditioning commonly form the basis of treatment for these problems. For each behavioral problem, therapy would begin with an analysis of the situation. To understand why Bertha did not eat, the therapist would observe her carefully before, during, and after the serving of food. What happened just before mealtime? Did she receive extra attention from family members? What happened when she refused to eat? Did someone give her a hug or make a sympathetic remark? Did someone become upset? In answering such questions, the therapist would try to discover what events signaled mealtime and what events supported, or reinforced, her resistance to food.

From the behavioristic perspective, the events that occurred immediately after she refused to eat somehow reinforced not eating. The behavior therapist would alter or eliminate these events, instructing the family members not to show any sympathy, pay any attention, or make any fuss if she refused to eat. They would be told to act normally and naturally instead, treating her no differently from any other family member who did not feel hungry at a particular meal.

At the same time, the therapist would note the objects and events that held her attention, such as music, conversation, flowers, or reading. Perhaps Bertha, at this point in her illness, spent time in conversation with visitors. That event, conversation, would have the potential to serve as reinforcement.

Then the procedure of contingency management might be implemented. In **contingency management,** a therapist and a team of people, such as family members or hospital staff, uses principles of operant conditioning in numerous ways to change the behavior of a specific individual. The behavior change occurs because the individual's entire environment, including all the people commonly in it, has been designed to bring about this change. These people provide reinforcement—in this case conversation—immediately after the desired response has been emitted.

Each day a family member or nurse would enter Bertha's room alone, only at mealtime, carrying a tray of food, the discriminative stimulus for eating. This visitor might smile at any greeting from her but would not speak until she began to eat. If she did not begin eating after a short predetermined period, perhaps one minute, the discriminative stimulus would be removed. The person would calmly pick up the tray, leave the room, and not return until the next meal.

If Bertha began to eat at a reasonable pace, the visitor would begin to converse with her. The visitor would continue the conversation in a normal fashion, listening carefully to Bertha's remarks and replying directly to them, as long as she continued eating. If she stopped eating, the visitor would cease her part in the conversation. If she soon resumed eating, the visitor would resume conversation, always in a gentle but firm manner.

Throughout this process, the family members or hospital team would keep detailed records. If Bertha ate more than on the previous day, or more promptly, then the visitor might leave some magazine or other object that she enjoyed. Gradually, through cooperation with everyone in contact with her, the criteria for the amount and rate of acceptable food intake would be raised. With this *shaping procedure,* eventually she would be required to consume in steady fashion everything on her plate in order to maintain the conversation, receive magazines, or gain some other positive outcome. If she proved resistant to meeting this final criterion, as sometimes happens with such eating disorders, a form of psychotherapy might be introduced, including cognitive behavioral therapy, described later.

If Bertha made adequate progress and then one day became resistant, a mildly aversive procedure might be employed in behavior therapy. In a gentle but firm manner, the visitor would leave the room immediately. Or the visitor might escort or wheel her into a vacant room, one without magazines or other objects that she enjoyed. In the latter procedure, called **timeout,** the undesirable behavior results in *mild* punishment through the absence of reinforcing stimuli. It becomes a form of negative punishment, for the person loses certain privileges. A timeout may last up to a half-hour or so, but even a minute or two can prove highly effective (Rachlin, 1991).

In dealing with Bertha's mute state, Breuer perhaps fostered an incidental version of shaping without any intention to do so. At first, Bertha spoke gibberish, but Breuer paid attention anyway. In later sessions, she began to utter words and short phrases. Breuer continued to listen, although she made little sense. Still later, she described tormenting hallucinations, and Breuer remained attentive. Some sessions after that, she told full tales about the onset of these hallucinations, including her visions emerging at her father's bedside, and here she captured Breuer's rapt attention.

Finally, she described her feelings about these events and people in her life. She spoke passionately, with love and anger, remorse and frustration. By consistently giving his full attention, Breuer supported this progression. He did not require steady improvements through successive approximations, but he did encourage more and more openness, more complete disclosure on her part.

If behavior therapy had been available at the time and the family members had been cooperative, a contingency management program might have been developed, not only for eating and speaking but also for other desirable behaviors, such as showing interest in the environment and interacting cooperatively with other people. If Wilhelm proved inept or uncooperative as a team member, he would have been dismissed. Then he would have been charged with some other family responsibility. The behavior therapist would not let Wilhelm simply shirk his duty. That outcome would constitute reinforcement for undesirable behavior.

Bertha's temporary improvement during therapy with Breuer has been attributed to her catharsis—the release of emotional tension over the loss of her father and related problems—but Breuer's attention became a vital factor. When she sought assurance of his presence, he held her hand. When she needed assistance in eating, he fed her. When she spoke incoherently, he listened carefully. Her steady progress kept Breuer at his unusual task, and his steady efforts slowly but surely kept her on the mend. Her words kept him listening; his attention kept her talking, working at self-discovery.

The reinforcement principle became a controlling factor. It produced reciprocal conditioning. An element of behavior therapy apparently emerged in their talking cure.

Behaviorists would show no surprise. Conditioning is expected—at work, at play, and almost anywhere else. It occurs throughout our lives in a continuous, extensive, incidental fashion, and the social environment includes innumerable opportunities for reciprocal reinforcement. But just as the sculptor shapes the clay, that clay—an inanimate object—can influence the sculptor's responses. The bent nail requires the carpenter to hammer more carefully; an error on the computer screen signals the operator to press a button; a tasty dish prompts an apprentice chef to repeat the recipe. Environmental consequences influence behavior even in the absence of other people.

Use of Observational Learning

Finally, other people can play a role in a behavior-oriented therapy that does not directly employ principles of classical or operant conditioning. It was illustrated in the therapy for the young man fearful of balloons. That therapy involved extinction, a principle of conditioning, but it also demonstrated behavior change through observational learning.

This treatment represents a less-traditional approach to behavior therapy, for it includes a significant cognitive element. In **observational learning,** an individual acquires or modifies behavior simply by noting the performance of someone capable in that situation. The person demonstrating the proper response is known as a **model,** preferably someone admired by the observer. In the balloon therapy, the tranquil second therapist served as an appropriate model of adult behavior, showing no anxiety in this context.

With children, a *peer model,* approximately the same age as the learner, may serve more effectively than a *mastery model,* who performs the task at a high level but remains socially inaccessible to the learner. For a boy or girl with a dog phobia, for example, a competent child could serve well in this role, perhaps better than a fearless adult (Bandura, 1986; Bandura, Grusec, & Menlove, 1967). Adults often do things that children are not expected or permitted to do.

The premise here is that behavior change can occur on the basis of observation alone, apart from direct reinforcement. If the model has behaved effectively and received reinforcement, then the observer has experienced *vicarious reinforcement.* The observer has been exposed to this reinforcement through the imagined participation in some else's activity, learning to remain calm, operate a certain machine, or pronounce words in a foreign language simply by observation. On a later occasion, when the opportunity arises, the observer may emit this behavior, thereby gaining the actual reinforcement rather than an imagined outcome.

Commentary and Critique

Behaviorism achieved prominence in American psychology through its elegant simplicity, clear philosophical position, and substantial research support, as well as its continuing success in numerous applied settings. In this context, B. F. Skinner was ranked first in eminence among 20th-century psychologists (Haggbloom, Warnick, Warnick, Jones, Yarbrough, Russell, et al., 2002).

Yet he and his work have been extensively criticized, especially in the public press. This resistance testifies partly to behaviorism's earlier prominence in the field, when it overshadowed rival viewpoints. In addition, Skinner's work with animals, lack of interest in human mental life, and disparaging views of human dignity and freedom created numerous opportunities for the mass media to attack his character rather than his ideas about psychology. Among psychologists, resistance has arisen over the relevance of his research for the human condition and over its inattention to the human mind.

A problem throughout psychological research, the **generalizability issue** concerns the extent to which the findings from a certain investigation can be appropriately applied in another context, apart from the original research setting. Are the results applicable elsewhere?

Skinner and colleagues conducted numerous experiments with animals because comparable research with people would have been impossible. On ethical grounds, they simply could not restrict human beings to highly controlled environments for extended periods, even apart from the prohibitive financial costs. So the generalizability question takes this broad form: To what degree are studies of lower animals in laboratories applicable to human beings in their complex, everyday environments?

Supporters point out that many investigators, using the principles of behaviorism, have performed highly successful single-participant experiments with human beings, relieving them of disorders of all sorts, ranging from problems in parenting, to bad habits at school and work, to performance enhancement in recreational activities. The evidence for individual gain from behavior therapy remains strong. Skinner's detractors reply that this research, confined to controlled environments with just one person at a time, does not make the full case. It stands at some distance from his long-range goals of making fundamental changes in our highly complex, steadily evolving culture. The problem here perhaps lies with Skinner's profound hopes for favorable social outcomes from applications of his work, generalizing from laboratory and clinical research to society at large without adequate evidence.

These hopes lay partly in a view of the human mind as infinitely malleable and therefore developed solely through learning. But research in modern biological, cognitive, and evolutionary psychology strongly suggests that the human mind, at birth, comes prepared to respond in certain "programmed" ways (Pinker, 2002). In fact, this resistance arose even in Skinner's day. Animals trained by behavioristic principles drifted instead into different behaviors, ones to which they had not been conditioned. They seemed to be restricted by inborn, instinctive tendencies (Breland & Breland, 1961).

Many psychologists and most of the general public also resist behaviorism's position on the role of mental life in behavior. A popular concept in everyday life, **mentalism** attributes human behavior to the operation of the mind. The mind exists as a separate part of reality, guiding and even energizing our behavior. Consciousness, in this view, is not completely reducible to physical phenomena. But behaviorism opposes this view. The unknown regions of the mind should not become the dominant explanation for what someone does.

A major tenet of radical behaviorism, **anti-mentalism** regards biological and other physical phenomena as the proper and eventually adequate explanation of mental activities. This idea, that all human activities can be explained on the basis of physical energy, becomes incompatible with everyday life, however. Instead, people experience mental processes as influencing their overt activity. In reading a book, attending a concert, or going to work, popular thought invokes the mind as the driving, controlling force.

Skinner renounced the mind as the locus of control for an individual's behavior. He viewed mental activities as secondary events, called *epiphenomena,* because they are incidental to more basic phenomena, such as behaviors. Moreover, they are not causal. Mental activities are the result of brain activity, but they do not influence brain activity. On this basis, they merit study only as incidental, internal behaviors, not as the causes of behavior. Radical behaviorism aims to explain human behavior without resorting to mentalism.

With ideas so contrary to popular thought, Skinner became a target for adverse reactions of all sorts. After his first daughter experienced painful mishaps in a conventional crib, and ever the inventor, he constructed a special crib for his second daughter, aimed at easing the burden of child care. This "baby tender" included mobiles, temperature controls, a transparent front, and a heavy cloth base that could be readily changed for cleanliness, all favorable innovations in the mid-20th century (Skinner, 1945). But because of Skinner's well-known experimental studies with animals in the "Skinner box," a leading magazine, *Ladies Home Journal,* introduced the new crib under the title "Baby in a Box." Then the mass media, much later, working from false assumptions, presented distortions and rumors that he imprisoned his daughter in that box, resulting in serious behavior disorders, including an alleged psychotic episode and suicide (Jordan, 1996). In fact, she lives in England today, pursuing a healthy, productive life.

Skinner's inventions extend beyond the baby tender, early teaching machines, and other labor-saving devices. His utopian fiction in *Walden Two* and philosophical treatise in *Beyond Freedom and Dignity* advocate the extensive use of behavioral technology for creating improvements throughout human society. But readers become concerned. How would someone establish this behavioral science and implement its practice? Who would take control? Many suspected Skinner of despotism, although he showed no interest in public office.

Perhaps Skinner overestimated his capacity to communicate successfully with the public. Or perhaps he underestimated the public's desire for quick and easy answers to complex questions. In any case, behaviorism is commonly misunderstood. Its basic tenets appear relatively straightforward, but its essential details are often ignored. Their useful application requires careful assessment, precise timing, steady monitoring, and patience. Without these qualities, the principles of behaviorism are unlikely to be used successfully, leading to the erroneous view that they do not work at all.

One misunderstanding concerns the use of rewards. In these demonstrations, critics establish two groups of participants who perform an *interesting* task, telling the members of one group that they will be paid or otherwise rewarded. After both groups perform the task, and after the payoff to one group, the investigators surreptitiously observe both groups again, finding that the rewarded group displays less interest in the task than does the group with no reward (Kohn, 1993). But these results do not show that rewards disrupt behavior, as the investigators suggest.

Instead, they show a misunderstanding of a behavioristic concept and misuse of a principle. Regarding the concept, the appropriate term here is *reinforcement,* which *empirically* has been found to increase the probability of a certain response in a certain individual. As indicated earlier, the proper term is not *reward,* which simply refers to anything that seems desirable to people in general. In other words, a reward is not necessarily rewarding, depending on how it is viewed by the recipient. Skinner made this distinction to avoid just such misunderstandings.

Regarding the principle, the aim in all practical applications of behaviorism is to enable *natural* reinforcers to support the desired behavior. Whenever a person performs a task well and enjoys the performance, there is absolutely no need for any contrived consequences. Supplying needless rewards often diminishes interest in the task, for the reward is then perceived as a bribe, thereby disrupting the individual's intrinsic satisfaction in that activity.

A further misunderstanding lies with the idea that behavior can be explained solely on the basis of its consequences. Antecedent conditions play a role too. The preceding stimuli exert control by signaling a time to emit the behavior, and their meaning can be understood only in terms of the individual's history of reinforcement (DeGrandpre & Buskist, 2000). By focusing only on the consequences, as in the example just cited, the public cannot comprehend the subtleties of the behaviorist position, especially the stimulus control involved in complex social environments.

Even the psychology literature contains misunderstandings. It has been stated, for example, that behaviorism rejects biological psychology as irrelevant (Eysenck, 1988). But Skinner explicitly stated that the gaps in any behavioral account must be filled by explanations from neuroscience (Skinner, 1989).

Studies of eminence in 20th-century psychology placed both B. F. Skinner and Sigmund Freud in foremost positions (Haggbloom et al., 2002). Yet Freud has been criticized because he did not do more. He developed fruitful hypotheses about the human mind but did not engage in empirical research to support his views. Skinner has been criticized because in the course of productive research on overt behavior, he did not study mental life at all. As both cases suggest, one price of prominence in behavioral studies may be the criticism that the individual did not make other advances as well.

In summary, behaviorism's contributions to modern psychology include its philosophical position, use of operational definitions, basic psychological principles, and practical applications. Moreover, the behaviorist heritage is still with us in the widespread emphasis on behavior as dependent variables throughout experimental psychology and the extensive use of conditioning techniques for investigating the physiological underpinnings of behavior (Elmes, 2000). These principles and practices are now so extensively incorporated into contemporary psychology that their origins in behaviorism have become obscured. The impact of this perspective remains firm in the field today.

Summary

Beginnings of Behaviorism

Behaviorism advanced largely through B. F. Skinner's experimental studies of learning in animals and human beings, controlled by the antecedent stimuli and also by the consequences of their behavior, called reinforcement. Skinner declared that, just as the sculptor shapes clay by pulling and pushing it in various directions, the environment shapes human and animal behavior by its consequences, colloquially known as reward and punishment.

Key Terms: **behaviorism, learning, conditioning, respondent behavior, operant behavior, reinforcement, reinforcement principle, radical behaviorism**

Classical Conditioning

As demonstrated by Ivan Pavlov, classical conditioning occurs when a previously neutral stimulus, through association with an unconditioned or automatic stimulus, thereby develops the capacity to elicit a certain emotional or physiological response. This formerly neutral stimulus is then called a conditioned stimulus. And the involuntary response, when elicited by the conditioned stimulus, is called a conditioned response. The focus in classical conditioning is on conditioned emotional responses, such as conditioned fears, happiness, and anger.

Key Terms: **unconditioned stimulus, unconditioned response, classical conditioning, conditioned stimulus, conditioned response, delayed conditioning, trace conditioning, simultaneous conditioning, stimulus generalization, discrimination, one-trial conditioning, extinction, spontaneous recovery, higher-order conditioning, biologically prepared learning**

Operant Conditioning

Operant conditioning, or operant learning, investigated and promoted by B. F. Skinner, involves the acquisition of voluntary responses according to their antecedent stimuli and consequences. Responses followed by positive consequences tend to become strengthened and elaborated; those followed by aversive or no consequences tend to become weakened. For precision, these consequences are described primarily in terms of reinforcement. In popular speech, the responses are called habits; they range from brushing one's teeth to operating a computer.

Key Terms: **operant conditioning, operant response, discriminative stimulus, reinforcing stimulus, positive reinforcement, negative reinforcement, stimulus control, continuous reinforcement, partial reinforcement, shaping, successive approximation, primary reinforcement, secondary reinforcement, chaining, reciprocal conditioning**

Two-Factor Theory

Two-factor theory brings together the processes of classical and operant conditioning. Through classical conditioning, the individual learns the significance of events in the environment. The individual learns the meaning of a harsh expression, lightning, or a hypodermic needle. This outcome is sometimes called sign learning. Through operant conditioning, the individual learns ways of responding to these environmental events. This outcome has been called solution learning. The individual learns to cope with the problem: running away, blocking the ears, or avoiding the clinic.

Key Terms: **two-factor theory, sign learning, solution learning**

Behavior Modification

Behavior therapy aims to improve a person's adjustment, not by holding a dialogue with that person but by manipulating elements in the environment. Systematic desensitization is a prominent therapy based on classical conditioning, aimed at diminishing phobias through gradual exposure to the feared stimulus, which is paired with relaxation. Contingency management is a method of therapy based on operant conditioning, aimed at developing or changing a person's habits through principles of reinforcement; it is sometimes practiced by a whole team of therapists, including hospital staff, family members, and friends.

Key Terms: **behavior therapy, behavior modification, systematic desensitization, flooding, contingency management, timeout, observational learning, model**

Commentary and Critique

Resistance to behaviorism arises over the generalizability issue—the degree to which the results of laboratory and other investigations with animals apply to human life. Another major objection concerns behaviorism's anti-mentalism, stating that physical factors alone are adequate explanations of behavior. Mental activities are the result of brain processes, not their cause. Among the public, behaviorism has been criticized for its seeming disregard for human freedom and dignity.

Key Terms: **generalizability issue, mentalism, anti-mentalism**

Critical Thinking

1. Confronted with a cloud of dust, a driver pushes on the brake, blinks his eyes, and then wipes them with a tissue. Describe these reactions in terms of respondent or operant behavior.

2. As a dinner guest, would B. F. Skinner be most compatible conversing with a biological psychologist or a psychoanalyst? Explain your reasoning.

3. "I would do almost anything to avoid hurting my father's feelings. Upon seeing me, he often tells a joke. At an early age, I learned to laugh—or at least smile—at his poor jokes. And he still tells lousy jokes . . ." Explain the conditioning process for the father and for the daughter.

6

Humanistic Psychology

175

Humanistic psychology offers an optimistic outlook on the human condition. Its popularity arises substantially from its emphasis on our inborn potential for favorable growth. If not obstructed by the environment, this capacity emerges in the choices people make for achieving fulfillment in day-to-day living. Under appropriate therapeutic conditions, it also engenders self-healing and recovery from psychological problems. In the best and worst of times, human beings possess an inborn capacity for growth and fulfillment.

After surveying the origins of humanistic psychology, this chapter turns to three characteristics of being human; then it examines selected concepts about early experience in human life; and later it addresses philosophical and practical issues. Collectively, these discussions show how humanistic psychology stands apart from mainstream psychology. It includes nomothetic interests but concentrates prominently on the individual human being, sometimes from the viewpoint of that person's experience. This focus on the individual and on subjectivity holds true in humanistic therapy as well, a discussion that appears before the closing commentary and critique of this perspective.

With these concerns, humanistic psychology presents an open approach to psychological questions, often addressing unusual case studies and elusive concepts that are difficult to operationalize. In a case study of Bertha, for example, her feelings about leadership and its accompanying loneliness would be of special interest. For such purposes, humanistic psychology employs qualitative data and interpretive analyses, especially when studying the subjective elements in human life.

After more than a decade at the orphanage, the subjective side of life suddenly changed for Bertha. She had been living only with her mother, taking full responsibility for aged Recha, providing extensive physical and emotional support. Then Recha died, and Bertha found herself totally alone. Living with no family, no partner, and no friends, all by herself on evenings, weekends, and holidays, she wrote in her journal that she felt almost like a different person.

When her father died, she experienced hallucinations, distorted thinking, and loss of body functions. Then she stayed in bed. Older and wiser when her mother died, she continued at work but fell into a different sort of depression, discouraged by other peoples' lives as well as her own (Edinger, 1968). Encountering day after day the unhealthy, unhappy, uneducated daughters of deprived women, she was deeply dismayed by these girls' dim prospects, despite her extensive efforts on their behalf. And she pondered the sad outlook for the countless thousands who would never experience the slightest benefits from her orphanage. Confronted with their plight and her own loneliness, Bertha struggled with feelings of despair.

The feeling side of life is a basic concern for human beings—men and women, young and old, wealthy and indigent. And it is a centerpiece of humanistic psychology.

Rise of Humanistic Psychology

As its name suggests, **humanistic psychology** focuses on human beings, apart from other creatures, and it does so with a distinctly optimistic outlook, emphasizing three characteristics of human uniqueness: subjectivity, individuality, and the capacity for growth. In this context, it points to human beings' substantial inner resources for self-regulation, thereby proposing an element of free will. A departure from the prior perspectives and intentionally closer to the humanities than to natural sciences, it is more philosophical, more focused on feelings, and less scientific and systematic. In other words, it is a statement about interpersonal relations and moral values in the context of human development, reminding mainstream psychology about these often ignored issues (Mandler, 1985).

In its first years, humanistic psychology raised the prospect of organizing the whole field of psychology around a more integrated conception of the person, stressing the *experiencing* individual. Further, it suggested that Western universities seek a closer dialogue between the sciences and the humanities (O'Hara & Taylor, 2000).

The early stages of this interest emerged with the clinical work of Carl Rogers (1902–1987). He emphasized the human potential for growth, as well as the feeling side of life. Later, Abraham Maslow promoted growth potential and also a framework for studying the levels of growth. With these early roots, humanistic psychologists have continued to devote extensive efforts to the practice of psychology within and outside the clinic. This focus on feelings, the individual, and fulfillment has taken precedence over the more objective, statistically oriented studies of groups of people pursued in mainstream psychology.

Rogers and Growth Potential

Rogers' parents raised their children with strong religious beliefs, which were thoroughly ingrained into their home life. So powerful was this upbringing that the children knew which behaviors were acceptable and unacceptable even without direct instruction from their parents. It had a lasting effect on Rogers' career and thus on the development of humanistic psychology.

Holding a deep conviction about the virtue of hard work, Rogers' parents moved to a farm in Illinois before he reached adolescence. This life removed their children from temptations of the city and offered opportunities for meaningful employment that were unavailable to many teenagers. Each day young Carl Rogers did chores, rising at 5:00 A.M. to milk a dozen cows. After school, he milked them again and attended to the farmyard pigs. His mind stayed awake in school but not the rest of his body. Twice-a-day milking apparently demanded too much of his arms and hands; they constantly fell "asleep" during class (Rogers, 1967).

With his schoolwork, farm chores, and religious restrictions, Rogers had no social life outside his family. But all that changed. When he went away to college and then toured foreign lands, he found himself thinking his own thoughts, taking his own stands on issues, and arriving at his own conclusions. This issue, freedom versus control, eventually pervaded his whole outlook on life, including his humanistic approach to psychology.

Decades later, as a clinical psychologist working with people in the back wards of mental hospitals, he thought about some potatoes in his boyhood cellar. Lying one winter in a pile in that dark basement, well below one small window, their growth inspired his metaphor for humanistic psychology. Despite these highly unfavorable conditions, the potatoes grew anyway, sending out spindly white sprouts, sometimes two or three feet long. They grew toward the light from that distant window, producing distorted versions of the healthy green shoots that potatoes grow in warm spring soil. These sprouts were a desperate version of an innate but, in this case, futile growth tendency. They would never realize their full potential; they would never become plants. But as an expression of the actualizing tendency, they were striving to become so, even under the most adverse conditions (Rogers, 1980).

This striving, for Rogers, showed an inborn growth process in all living organisms, a directional tendency that cannot be destroyed except by destroying the organism itself. Whether the environment is favorable or adverse, whether the entity is a worm, a potato, or a person, this life force acts in the direction of maintenance, enhancement, and reproduction. It is an automatic striving in life. Rogers broke away from psychoanalysis on this issue. Every individual, not the therapist, has the capacity to guide his or her own development.

Viewing people in those back wards, Rogers thought of their scarcely human conditions, and yet he perceived in them this directional tendency that could be trusted. In fact, the key to understanding their behavior and assisting them lay in recognizing that they were attempting to grow in the only ways they saw available at that time. Their efforts were life's desperate attempts to fulfill itself. For Rogers and his followers, a tendency toward fulfillment, most evident in human beings, exists in all living creatures, ill and healthy (Rogers, 1980). Later, in university environments, he found confirmation for this view.

Known as the **actualizing tendency,** this capacity for growth is a life force, an inborn predisposition to seek the fullest expression of one's abilities and thereby achieve meaningful goals. Barring insurmountable external obstacles, it enables an individual to realize his or her potential. This actualizing tendency appears at the core of humanistic psychology, marking this perspective as distinctly different from its immediate predecessors.

Protest of the Third Force

Occasionally called *Third Force,* humanistic psychology arose as a protest against both its immediate predecessors, psychoanalysis and behaviorism. In the 1950s, those perspectives were viewed by some psychologists as too controlling, too deterministic amid the optimism and concern for freedom arising in psychology, as well as among the public. As the first force, psychoanalysis stressed the unconscious influences in mental life that control behavior in ways we cannot comprehend. Behaviorism, the second force, emphasized that environmental factors control behavior, largely through their consequences. Opposing both positions, humanistic psychology stressed that human beings can make their own, appropriate choices in life, thereby leading meaningful lives and encountering fulfilling experiences.

As the Third Force began to expand, it included related movements and, indeed, almost anyone in American psychology who resisted the growing emphasis on large-scale statistical studies. Employing group data, those studies ignored or obscured the uniqueness of their participants. In opposition, the Third Force coalition encouraged a focus on the development of each person as a complex integration of inseparable parts. Sharing this ambitious goal, humanistic psychology has not become a highly integrated psychological perspective, especially in the manner of psychoanalysis and behaviorism, which are organized around the core concepts of unconscious mental processes and the reinforcement principle, respectively. Rather, humanistic psychology addresses numerous related, less measurable concepts: subjective experience, the actualizing tendency, congruence and incongruence, and conditions of worth.

Humanistic psychology did not displace psychoanalysis, which still has wide appeal in the public domain and stimulates research in child development and unconscious cognitive processes. With its fewer empirical findings, it did not displace behaviorism, which continues today with specialized research and specific applications in everyday life. Instead, humanistic psychology has existed on the periphery of academic psychology, flourishing with the many practical applications of its approach to therapy while at the same time retaining its comparatively loose structure.

Less directly, the humanistic movement resisted the premises in biological psychology, which reduced explanations of psychological phenomena to physiological processes. When searching outside its borders, humanistic psychology looks instead to philosophical and related literatures, which examine human experience in broader terms.

To investigate the topics of personal growth, feelings, and meanings in life, humanistic psychologists sometimes turn to **phenomenology**, studying nature according to how things seem to the observer, rather than what they may be objectively. The intention is to suspend all everyday interpretations and explanations insofar as possible, concentrating more on the mental experience and less on the observed object or event. Perceiving a flower, phenomenological observers, in their imaginations, may vary different characteristics of the flower and even different ways of visually apprehending it, striving to experience the essence of the flower or the essence of seeing the flower. More philosophical than psychological, phenomenology aims to ignore the antecedents and consequences surrounding sensation and perception. Instead, the elusive goal becomes a direct investigation of consciousness, free of preconceived notions.

This divergence in the pathways of scientific and humanistic psychology reflects a difference in the ways of knowing in the humanities and sciences. Both approaches recognize that no one can become a completely objective, detached observer; everyone necessarily functions as a participant observer. Phenomenology focuses on the individual's experience. Scientific psychology may do so too. But, more importantly, it also focuses on the ways in which specific circumstances influence that experience. In other words, mainstream psychology also studies the causality in human experience.

The humanistic research methods are largely descriptive: case studies, as well as surveys and naturalistic observation. The data are commonly qualitative, reflecting themes in peoples' speech and behavior. Topics of popular inquiry include the self, changes in awareness, and personal experience. The practical interests, usually clinical, outweigh formal research activity.

A case study of Bertha's struggle with mental illness cited a cluster of factors that produced the problem in Vienna: the childhood deaths of two sisters, the prolonged and fatal illness of her father, overcontrol by her mother, conflict with Wilhelm, and sociocultural restrictions that prevented her self-expression. It then pointed to circumstances in Frankfurt favorable to her recuperation: the extended-family support, thriving Jewish community, opportunities for charity work, and rising tide of feminism. It also noted personal factors: Bertha's will, evident in her early struggles with

Wilhelm; her capacity for writing and speaking effectively; and her wealth, which lifted a huge burden from Bertha and freed her from the drudgery of making a living. In fact, it offered the opportunity to live in luxury and, at the same time, to develop altruistic projects by using her own money as well as that of her relatives (Kimball, 2000).

As this report illustrates, humanistic psychology commonly studies the person, not people. Investigations of groups obscure the individual amid group data. Even the group average does not depict a specific individual. In fact it may not represent anyone at all in the group.

One classic case study focused on a five-year-old boy who was mute and disruptive in school. Dibs crawled around the floor, displayed violent temper tantrums, and for extended periods sat without speaking. Judging him to be mentally disturbed, his parents brought him to a humanistically oriented child therapist, and she assisted this little boy in his "search for self." In doing so, she showed respect for the growth potential in human beings; she allowed Dibs to find his own way in therapy by using toys, playing imaginary games, and speaking without fear of reprisal. After months of steady therapy, he revealed himself to be a highly intelligent child who found much greater security in the world around him (Axline, 1964). This early, detailed analysis of one little boy did much to augment interest in humanistic psychology and its therapy.

This special concern for the individual and for personal experience sets humanistic psychology apart from other perspectives. Humanistic psychologists, and also practitioners from the other viewpoints, tend toward idiographic inquiry—seeking, for example, to understand Bertha as a *particular* individual with her own special thoughts, genetic background, and personal history. Like all of us, she was different from everyone else.

During the gloomy days after her mother's death, she organized a small feminist group in Frankfurt called Care by Women. It benefited the staff, needy recipients, and presumably its founder too. This activity foreshadowed Bertha's later career in the public sector. Perhaps it was her loneliness or maybe her new freedom from family responsibilities; in any case, Bertha made a significant personal decision. She moved to a smaller apartment on Praunheimerstrasse, which brought her closer to cousin Louise Goldschmidt and into a more modest style of living. No longer would she work with the poor during the day and then return to her mother's large and lavish quarters in the evening. Maybe this "downsizing" would bring greater harmony into her life.

She brought to this apartment most of her parents' elegant furnishings and her own art objects: glassware, paintings, figurines, wood-carved clocks, and the "comforter" cabinet. They became reminders that both her parents and those earlier days were gone.

Three Human Characteristics

Each of us possesses certain inherited characteristics and, based on our personal history, certain acquired characteristics too. Moreover, we all exist in a certain time and place, different from all others in the universe. How do we express and experience our uniqueness as individual human beings? Humanistic psychology addresses this question.

In the humanistic view, all people everywhere possess three fundamental characteristics: subjectivity, individuality, and the capacity for growth (Rogers, 1951). They form the core of humanity, with the first two setting us apart from other species.

This concern with subjectivity cuts two ways, however. It creates for the humanistic approach a unique place in psychology, pointing out that behavior can be most successfully understood by adopting the viewpoint of the responding individual, not from an external viewpoint. But it also calls forth criticism, even ostracism, from some areas of scientific psychology. In adopting this approach, shared fully by no other perspective, it stands at odds with modern science, which typically insists on objectivity—the investigation of publicly repeatable, verifiable events, not private experience.

Subjectivity: The Basic Reality

The doctrine of **subjectivity** states that the study of personal, private experience is the most meaningful approach to understanding human beings. Knowing Bertha requires an understanding of her inner states, her feelings at a given moment. Human beings are sensitive creatures; they are feeling creatures. The inner dimension of human life is a crucial determinant of behavior.

Similarly, Josef Breuer, Willie, and others in Bertha's life were sensitive, feeling individuals. Breuer experienced growing feelings of affection for Bertha during their sessions together, and then he became fearful of the consequences of those feelings. Brother Willie regularly experienced feelings of anger toward his sister, on one occasion shaking her so violently that Bertha could not forget the incident. And both of Bertha's parents became anxious about their daughter when she fell into her "absences." They had good reason to worry; they remained acutely aware of the early deaths of their other daughters.

In some areas of modern psychology, the study of feelings and private experience has been regarded as a doubtful enterprise. Thus, humanistic psychologists have been viewed as contrarians in the world of science, sacrificing the precision potentially available in other research. But diverse proponents are attracted to this descriptive outlook. For them, the tradeoff is clearly worthwhile, justified by the gain in understanding a particular individual.

Humanistic interests in subjectivity appeared in a 25-year follow-up study of 10 highly creative women, selected from 400 girls attending public high schools in New York City a quarter-century earlier. As adolescents, they possessed a high potential for creativity, according to teachers' nominations and their creative products (Anastasi & Schaefer, 1969). In the follow-up study, they completed an extensive, essay-type inventory designed to assess creative processes. The results reflected their diverse backgrounds, but one characteristic emerged as ascendant for 9 of the 10 participants: the need to understand one's subjective reality. Motivated to examine their own inner worlds, these women used creativity in the arts as their pathway. As one participant explained, her own sense of a particular scene, even as a photographer, held more interest for her than the real-life story framed by her camera (Cangelosi & Schaefer, 1992).

This research, based on essays by 10 women, raises questions about the value of introspective data, the small sample of participants, and lack of a comparison group. But for humanistic psychologists, to ignore subjectivity is to ignore a basic dimension of human life.

Humanistic psychology emphasizes the individual's *experience* of external events, not the events per se or the view of some other observer. External reality of course is recognized, but it is considered of secondary importance. Humanistic psychologists stress that the reactions of all living beings are determined by the ways they interpret events, not by the objective, physical properties of those events as measured by conventional methods in the natural sciences.

Bertha's reaction to her mother's death was determined by the way *she* saw her mother, whether or not, as some claimed, her mother actually was "something of a dragon" (Jones, 1953). Bertha's sadness and lethargy can be understood only by looking through her eyes. To become more effective as a science, according to the humanistic view, psychology must develop more systematic research methods for examining and understanding personal experience.

In the dark hours of her depression, Bertha re-examined her experiences as an adult. Her twenties had been torturous years. Her thirties had been satisfying; she found a place in society. Now in her forties, she had no close ties with anyone, family or friends. She was alone—and free. Not free to do whatever she wanted but free to make her own decisions.

"The less I have to do, the more I have to be," she complained. To escape her despair, she lost herself in work, thinking less about herself, feeling less lonely and confused (Edinger, 1968).

Individuality and Self Theory

Bertha's efforts to stop thinking about herself point to the second major dimension of human uniqueness. This dimension, **individuality**, concerns the countless ways in which human beings and animals of the same species differ from one another—physically, mentally, socially, emotionally, and so forth. Each of us is different from all other people on earth. The remark of a homespun carpenter greatly impressed William James in this regard. There is only a small difference between one person and the next, he observed, but that small difference is mighty important (James, 1890).

One of James's students, Gordon Allport, a major figure in the study of personality, ventured one step further, concluding that all normal vertebrate animals on earth differ less from one another in psychological complexity and functioning than does one human being from another (Allport, 1962). On this basis, a robin and a whale differ less in psychological functioning than do a pair of human brothers, sisters, even twins, or any other human beings. This conjecture emphasizes that human psychological functioning normally occurs at a vastly higher level of complexity than that in all infra-human species (Fernald, 1995).

The result, human individuality, becomes most evident within a frame-work for studying the whole person in a broad context, one that emphasizes a narrative approach. In a self-narrative, people construct life stories about themselves, sometimes in response to certain questions, as a way of achiev-ing a clearer identity and enlarging the meaning of their lives. Based on past and imagined future events, these efforts at self-understanding also can gen-erate an increased sense of continuity and purpose. And they can serve as a framework or background for personality psychologists interested in the study of the individual (McAdams & Pals, 2006).

These persistent reflections about ourselves and our complexity occupy a central position in **self theory**, which states that all human beings have many different views of themselves—physical, social, emotional, and so forth. These views can vary markedly from situation to situation, and they exert a pronounced influence on behavior (Rogers, 1989). According to humanistic psychology, any study of human behavior that ignores self theory immedi-ately becomes flawed. William James once observed that we have as many different selves as we have people who know us well (Figure 6.1).

But of course the self itself defies simple definition. A major handbook identifies five ways in which scientists use the term and notes eight uses among philosophers. It defines the **self** as an organism's capacity for reflex-ive consciousness—to think about oneself (Leary & Tangney, 2003). In pri-mate laboratories, an animal's sense of self is sometimes tested by spraying

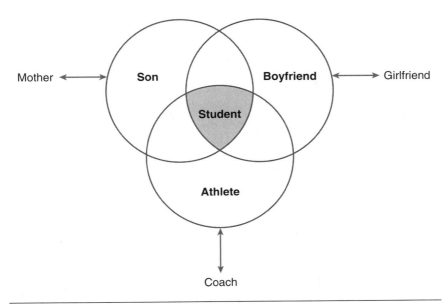

Figure 6.1   Multiple Selves and Personal Identity. A college student wrote separately to his mother, girlfriend, and coach about a dispute with a teammate, presenting himself somewhat differently in each instance. According to self theory, the "real" student is a composite of these different selves. The double-headed arrows suggest that all people construct their identities partly through multiple selves.

a bit of washable color into the hair on its head. If the animal, on observing itself in a mirror, tends to stroke or explore that body part in particular, that behavior suggests an awareness of the physical self.

The human newborn apparently has no sense of self—no sense of "me" and "not me." Through interactions with the environment, especially the parents, she begins to develop a sense of "self" and "other" and then to differentiate various parts of her self and her world. She acquires various selves and also a more global, stable sense of self, called the **self-concept**, which includes all the ideas, feelings, and perceptions recognized as *me, I,* or *myself* (Rogers, 1951). In humanistic psychology, the self-concept is considered the most useful perspective for understanding an individual (Epstein, 1973).

Psychologists commonly use rating scales and inventories to assess the self-concept and related selves. In one traditional method, the person receives a deck of 100 cards, each describing some personal characteristic such as "Has warmth," "Is moralistic," and "Keeps people at a distance." In this technique, called the Q-sort, the individual sorts all the cards according to the number required in each of nine categories. Most cards must be placed in the middle categories and only a few at the extremes, identified as the "least like" and "most like" categories (Block, 1961). The person's distribution becomes a narrative self-description, however accurate or distorted. In addition, each statement can be assigned a weighted score based on its placement in the various categories. When all scores are combined, this distribution produces an overall numerical expression of the self-concept.

In Vienna, Bertha's self-concept was that of a bright but frustrated young woman who was confused by mixed feelings toward her family, inadequate relations with the opposite sex, and pervasive gender discrimination. In Frankfurt, as an older woman in a more liberal society, her self-concept centered around her work, as it does for many adults. Responsible for the success of the whole orphanage, she viewed herself as an intelligent, decisive administrator, altruistic in spirit, and privately quite lonely—especially after the death of her mother.

At this point, she made a second fundamental decision, one that cut even more deeply into her everyday life. It represented a major change in the ways she thought about herself, and it altered her career and life plan. For years, she had heard stories of atrocities in Galicia, an eastern region of Austria. Poverty produced such desperate conditions that girls and women from the ghettos were lured or sold into prostitution. A slave market stretched from Turkey through Germany to South America. In Frankfurt, the railway served as a relay, transporting the captives to houses of prostitution all over the world.

Bertha began to think about protecting young prostitutes, as well as unmarried mothers and their babies. That goal permeated her thoughts about her own future, the self she sought to realize. Called the **ideal self**, it consists of the standards of excellence prescribed for oneself. It plays an important role in integrating and unifying the individual's behavior. In a general sense, the ideal self is the self-concept that an individual wants to attain.

The difference between the self-concept and the ideal self involves a time factor, the present and the future. The self-concept represents a person's current sense of self, the way she regards herself at that moment. The ideal self represents the person she would like to become, the way she hopes to be at some later date. Bertha imagined her future self in a new way—not as someone responsible for the care of children but as a freedom fighter, as someone standing at the front line against social injustice. One's work not only forms a major part of the self-concept; it also contributes to the development of the ideal self.

With these thoughts, and after 12 years of service, she resigned from the orphanage—but not from her calling. She sought higher ground—a home for unwed mothers. In serving soup to refugees and directing the orphanage, Bertha had broken with upper-class tradition. This new plan broke with deeper social norms. In her day, unwed mothers deserved punishment, not protection.

Speculating in the context of self theory, a gap existed between Bertha's self-concept and ideal self, which is not unusual. But that gap had recently widened. Her self-concept included a general sense of competence and well-being in the orphanage. Her ideal self had advanced to assisting disgraced women, rejected by society.

This gap between the self-concept and ideal self is known as **self-esteem**, which is an overall evaluation of oneself. A value judgment is involved, ranging from low to high. Self-esteem correlates in a limited way with the self-concept, which also can vary from negative to positive. But the self-concept is much broader, more complex, and described by such additional dimensions as stability, diversity, maturity, and especially one's roles in life. In contrast, self-esteem is described simply as a matter of degree, ranging from low to high.

Bertha clearly had higher self-esteem as director of the orphanage than as Breuer's patient in Vienna. Sheltering women from prostitution could provide another boost, as well as an opportunity for personal growth.

The Capacity for Growth

A capacity for growth is the third dimension of human uniqueness, following subjectivity and individuality. As noted already, it refers to a tendency in all living creatures to use and develop their faculties to the fullest. Most pronounced in human beings, formally known as the *actualizing tendency*, this energy is an innate impetus to achieve useful, meaningful goals. Involving the whole person, it promotes the constructive expression of all inherent capacities, if it is not blocked by external circumstances (Rogers, 1980).

This striving to realize one's full potential, Rogers declared, is the fundamental force in every living creature. It can even alleviate maladjustment. In inborn, automatic ways, it predisposes the individual toward recovery and greater satisfaction in life. It prompts people to engage in activities that are right for them as individuals. These activities yield the greatest satisfaction and productivity. But as a rule people do not advance to this level without progressing through earlier, less fulfilling stages.

Named after Abraham Maslow, who first described it, this series of stages is called **Maslow's motivational hierarchy** because it depicts a sequence of motives that guide human behavior according to a certain order. At different times in life, people find themselves at different stages of the hierarchy. But Maslow decided that most people do not reach self-actualization, the highest level (Maslow, 1970).

Our various *physiological motives*, at the bottom of this hierarchy, involve the need for food, water, oxygen, and other elements necessary for life. When these motives are not minimally satisfied, an individual becomes almost exclusively concerned with them.

The refugees arrived at the soup kitchen close to this level. But through the meals served there, the immediate threat of starvation no longer dominated their lives. On this basis, according to the theory, many advanced to the next level, where another set of motives becomes ascendant.

In the *safety motives*, an individual seeks shelter and protection from natural disasters and predators. Safety motives include freedom from harm, intentional or otherwise, and they become important after the physiological motives have been met. With certain exceptions, human beings seek safe, stable circumstances.

Together, the physiological and safety motives are sometimes called the biological motives. If they are substantially satisfied, then the individual progresses to a set of psychological motives, concerned with mental well-being, not simply physical satisfaction.

The first psychological level, the *motivation for love and belonging*, has been fostered by childhood experience, a time when human helplessness requires the support of family, friends, and others. This desire for human company also may have inborn components. In any case, human beings are notably attracted to others of their kind, so much so that the life of a recluse becomes rare and remarkable. Living as a group member, giving and receiving assistance, and enjoying personal relationships are the anticipated modes of life of most people.

But, alas, once love and belonging motives are satisfied, another level emerges. The individual experiences the *motivation for self-esteem,* defined as a person's desire for a positive evaluation of herself. For example, Bertha wants to think well of herself. How does she rate? Self-esteem is largely the difference between the self-concept and ideal self, but it also emerges from our place and accomplishments in the group. We human beings, T. S. Eliot said, "are engaged in an endless struggle to think well of ourselves."

Satisfaction of self-esteem motives, according to Maslow, does not end the progression. The individual next seeks a pair of less personal motives. The capacity for growth becomes more evident here in the *cognitive motives,* stimulating the individual to comprehend interesting experiences. The aim is to know and understand the ordinary and the novel. In contrast, the *aesthetic motives* stimulate the individual more toward artistic than scientific pursuits. The aim is to appreciate the beauty and orderliness in nature, including the complexity of the human condition.

These cognitive and aesthetic motives may reveal something about the human brain. According to evolutionary theory, the brain evolved to satisfy our biological needs for food, safety, and so forth. But in this process, it became so complex that it developed its own need to be fed. It seeks cognitive and aesthetic stimulation. Solitary confinement, sensory constancy, and other forms of stimulus deprivation are more than unpleasant. They disrupt normal human functioning and well-being.

Cognitive and aesthetic motives, toward the upper levels of the hierarchy, played a prominent role in Bertha's life, more so than for most of her acquaintances. However, she was not fully satisfied at the lower levels of love and belonging and also self-esteem. Maslow stated that the satisfaction of lower motives is usually essential for experience at the upper levels, but exceptions occur. Soldiers risk their lives for comrades, and artists endure semi-starvation to pursue lonely careers.

The capacity for growth becomes most evident at the highest level. Here the individual seeks to express her talents to the fullest, engaging in useful goals for which she is well suited. At this level, the motivation is called **self-actualization,** or the *self-actualization motive,* for the individual pursues whatever constructive activities she is best fitted to do, based on her inborn nature and personal experience. Self-actualization is the fulfillment of drives that transcend basic biological and psychological needs, extending instead to personal abilities and social concerns. Maslow believed that few people reach this level, and if they do, they are unlikely to remain there for lengthy periods. The Mother Teresas, Abraham Lincolns, and Martin Luther Kings of this world are examples of self-actualization, at least for certain periods in their lives (Maslow, 1970). Bertha remains an unlikely candidate, not just statistically but because she rarely seemed at peace with herself, even when engaged in good works.

A person need not be famous or powerful to become self-actualizing. Parents truly interested in their babies and capable of nurturing them to their highest potential can also become self-actualizing. Landscapers who enjoy their work and the fruits of their labors might become self-actualizing. Self-actualization often appears to fulfill personal needs.

During her Viennese childhood, Bertha's growth potential had been blocked, stifled by family restrictions and cultural practices. They prevented the natural expression and elaboration of her talents. In Frankfurt, things were different. Older, more settled, and without these restraints, she pursued personal goals with socially beneficial consequences. The growth tendency perhaps was manifesting itself in this movement toward social activism.

She made progress, obtaining funds from relatives and national organizations and a site in the small town of Neu-Isenburg, six miles from Frankfurt, a half-hour ride by trolley. Only a short distance in miles, Neu-Isenburg was a long way from Frankfurt politically. With its own government, it was far more liberal toward aliens of all sorts, including unwed mothers. Having obtained two acres of land on Zepplinstrasse, Bertha planned the construction of buildings that would blend into the community, enabling her children to move into the mainstream of society as easily and unobtrusively as possible. But she chose a title that made the character and goals of her new institution perfectly clear: The Home for Wayward Girls and Illegitimate Babies.

So here stood Bertha, challenging fundamental beliefs of her society. And she was recruiting others for this work.

From the humanistic viewpoint, honest work of almost any sort provides potential grounds for personal fulfillment. But this tendency toward growth can become manifest in other contexts too. External forces and internalized restrictions may inhibit its expression, but it remains an inborn potential (Rogers, 1980).

On this basis, critics raise questions about the actualizing tendency. With this inborn predisposition toward successful, satisfying experience, why are so many human beings engaged in violent struggles with one another? And why are so many living "lives of quiet desperation"? Humanistic psychologists respond that this potential has been blocked by environmental factors. Critics ask for more solid evidence of the actualizing tendency.

They also resist Maslow's hierarchy on the basis of its egocentric bias. It includes no direct mention of social responsibility. Positive psychology, described later, has been criticized on this same basis. But not Bertha, who went well beyond the usual conventions in her social activism.

The Home opened its doors during the prosperity in Germany before World War I. Prostitutes and new mothers with their babies quickly filled one building; young girls at risk for delinquency inhabited the other. The Home soon became too crowded, and its two buildings became three, the newest a shelter for young children.

Influence of Early Experience

Infancy and childhood are of course the ages of greatest dependency, at least until the last years of a long life. A person at these early stages is essentially helpless, completely dependent far longer than any member of another species. During this period, the parents and other caretakers exert an enduring influence, offering or withholding the love and attention so necessary for the child's favorable growth.

Conditions of Worth

In a biological sense, the child *requires* this loving stimulation; it is essential for optimal physical and social growth (Bowlby, 1965; Harlow & Harlow, 1966). According to self theory, this loving stimulation promotes the actualizing tendency, confirming the child's sense of self. The child understands that she is loved and accepted without reservation. All her thoughts and feelings about herself and others are worthy.

The infant seeks warmth, support, rest, and other experiences that enhance her, including walking, talking, and exploration. She rejects harsh voices, bright lights, sharp touch or pressure, and other sudden intrusions. In the **organismic valuing process**, or organismic experiencing, the individual knows her preferences and aversions and, in a general way, automatically prefers experiences that enhance the self, biologically and psychologically. The organismic valuing process therefore aids the actualizing tendency, fostering positive growth in particular ways for a particular individual.

Early in life, this process is direct and uncomplicated, based on the outcomes of the infant's experience. But gradually, as the environment becomes more complex, the child's subjective knowing about what's right for her becomes disrupted. By adolescence, she may display uncertainties of all sorts, not knowing which way to turn, even in relatively simple situations. These uncertainties delay or deter healthy choices.

How does the valuing process become disrupted? Why does it cease to function in the healthier, more direct manner evident in the early years?

Human parenting is a lengthy and difficult process, by far the longest and most complex of any species, and the human environment is indeed too complicated for any child. Inevitably, the child's behavior will threaten her own or others' welfare, and then the caretakers must place restrictions on the child. When these restrictions become necessary, communicating unconditional love becomes almost impossible. Effective caretakers indicate to the child that they accept her feelings—her impulse to behave in a certain way—but cannot permit her to endanger herself or others. Even so, offering unconditional love in daily life can be a formidable, overwhelming task. In therapy, it is considered indispensable, but that is a later story.

Instead, most parents impose conditions of worth on the child, just as they do with one another. In **conditions of worth**, love is withheld or provisional according to the values and standards of the parents or other caretakers. The child receives positive regard only when thinking and feeling in ways consistent with the parents' wishes. She no longer evaluates life in terms of her organismic valuing process. That form of experiencing is rejected or distorted and replaced by others' standards. The child thereby loses touch with her own basic, underlying feelings, a precursor to maladjustment.

Early conditions of worth for Bertha apparently included obedience to parents, denial of sexuality, resignation to having only limited schooling, acceptance of male superiority, and devotion to certain religious scriptures. Detrimental to her sense of self, they impeded her early growth. The organismic valuing process had been subverted.

By adolescence, she had developed a greater capacity to think for herself, reaching her own conclusions about religion, government, and the conditions of women. But these ways of behaving did not meet her parents' or society's expectations. She also had developed the physical capacity for female sexuality, but these experiences were restricted by her family and culture. To cope with these conditions of worth, Bertha resorted first to her private theater and then, involuntarily, to her "absences." She developed an almost complete separation between her experiences and the external conditions of her life.

Congruence and Incongruence

When a person is raised with conditions of worth—certainly the case for most people—some experiences are not incorporated into the self-concept. Even in adult life, the experiences are resisted. They are ignored as irrelevant, or because they are inconsistent with the self-concept, they are incorporated in some distorted manner. When there are only minor discrepancies between a positive self-concept and daily experience, the condition is called **congruence**, indicating that the individual experiences a harmony, a sense of integration. Everyday experience and the self-concept augment and support one another (Rogers, 1951).

When the discrepancy is large or the self-concept is negative, there is **incongruence**; an individual's self-concept remains closed to experience or the self-concept is at odds with experience. There is no significant integration. The sense of self and personal experience are incompatible (Rogers, 1951).

A key factor in congruence is the way a person perceives herself in a given situation. The doctrine of subjectivity states that behavior is governed by the phenomena of experience, not by external reality, however objectively defined. A person experiencing congruence is open to life. New experiences are integrated into the personality. In incongruence, they are denied, as happened to Bertha in Vienna and Breuer in working with her.

Initially he was open to this experience. Bertha's massive array of puzzling symptoms came as a surprise to him. Most practitioners of that day would have rejected her case in outright fashion or dismissed it through benign neglect. A few might have attempted, by providing very direct advice, to "talk her out of her symptoms." Instead, Breuer sat and listened. He did not reject this bewildering experience, saying she was a fool or a faker or bewitched. And he was not threatened initially even though he did not know how to treat her problems. For many hours, he sat and listened.

In self theory, a person open to experience, moving toward congruence, is sometimes called a **fully functioning person**—in that environment at that particular time. For the individual at that moment, there is no disharmony between the self and experience. The individual remains well aware of his own and others' feelings, thereby sustaining beneficial interpersonal relationships. The fully functioning person represents progress toward congruence—not a permanent state.

Eventually, influenced by his wife's remarks and his own feelings, Breuer experienced this therapy very differently. Falling in love with his patient did not coincide with his view of himself as a loyal and professional person; it did not match his self-concept. Breuer at that point experienced disharmony, or incongruence, and he terminated therapy abruptly. Abandoning therapy in that fashion would be considered highly unprofessional today, but a great deal more is known now about the therapeutic relationship, including countertransference, which created the incongruence for Breuer.

A person experiencing incongruence defends against the realities of that experience, denying or falsifying his feelings. If incongruence extends across several situations, it results in anxiety, and anxiety produces other adjustment disorders. At the very least, the person becomes rigid and inflexible, closed to much of life (Figure 6.2).

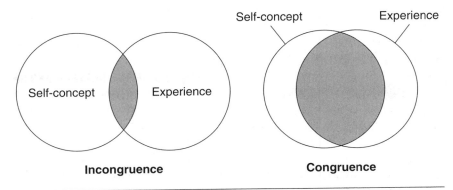

Incongruence   **Congruence**

Figure 6.2   **Incongruence and Congruence.** A student becomes tense when thinking about himself taking a math test. The circles at the left, with little overlap, illustrate the incongruence between his self-concept and that experience. After special instruction, psychotherapy, or some other growth process, congruence increases, illustrated in the largely overlapping circles at the right. His sense of self and experience in a math test are more compatible.

Back in Vienna, Bertha had reasons to think of herself as a capable, energetic young woman, and yet she experienced a dull life, finding no opportunity for the expression of these qualities. In Frankfurt, she experienced another form of incongruence—the gap between her self-concept and ideal self. Again, the greater the discrepancy, the greater is the personal discomfort. When that gap became significant, did she leave the orphanage and construct The Home, a goal at odds with prevailing social views?

Incongruence can emerge in any of these ways: through a restricted or distorted self-concept, through a poor match between the self-concept and personal experience, or through a large discrepancy between the self-concept and ideal self. Each of us, according to self theory, evaluates life on these bases.

Bertha's new work presumably reduced this incongruence. She enjoyed the challenge and sometimes seemed a long way from her troubled twenties in Vienna.

Philosophical and Practical Issues

The choices Bertha made in moving to a modest apartment, changing her career, and constructing The Home all raise a longstanding question in psychology, philosophy, and everyday life. To what extent, if any, are human beings autonomous and free, capable of making truly independent choices? Here we confront the controversy between free will and determinism. It becomes relevant because, in contrast to other perspectives, Carl Rogers and humanistic psychology have been more willing to consider this enduring philosophical issue.

Bertha's response to her career and life changes raises a second philosophical issue: her interpretation of these events and indeed of life itself. How did she think about her new freedom, her loneliness, and life's inevitable end? What meaning did they have for her? Existentialism in psychology aims at discovering the ways people search for meaning in their lives.

And finally, a practical issue arises, one with virtually no history. Soon after psychology appeared in American universities, scientists and practitioners became absorbed with studies of disturbed personal adjustment, ranging from poor school performance to serious mental illness. The field continued on this pathway until recently, when a movement in American psychology called for greater attention to the positive side of life. Psychology should pursue more studies of subjective well-being and the healthy lifestyle, certainly a vital goal. But the place of this promising movement, called positive psychology, is not yet clear in our new millennium. Its chief goals resemble those of humanistic psychology, and its approach to therapy reflects the cognitive tradition.

The Question of Free Will

Amid her depression, Bertha's change of residence became for her a diffi-cult transition, raising the perplexing question of why she ever left her mother's apartment. What prompted her to abandon the familiar and enter a new neighborhood? In a philosophical sense, this question can be consid-ered from two basic viewpoints: free will and determinism.

The doctrine of **free will** states that the causes of human behavior lie within the individual; human beings are autonomous. They have the capacity to select among several alternatives and to pursue them without any natural or super-natural constraint. They make and carry out their own decisions. There is within each person no intrinsic necessity to act one way or another. In other words, we are the agents, or authors, of our own actions.

Proponents of this view express surprise that anyone could think other-wise. They know how they feel from one day to the next; they make choices and act in certain ways. They feel successful or unsuccessful, gratified or dis-appointed at the outcome. They take personal pride in the former outcome; they feel remorseful in the latter. Subjective experience confirms for them on a daily basis a belief in free will.

The notion of free will lies embedded in the most basic fabric of our society. People are responsible for what they do. Those who behave properly receive their just rewards. How could it be otherwise? There are sanctions against people who act in illegal, immoral, or unethical ways. Without indi-vidual responsibility, society as we know it would collapse.

The opposed viewpoint, **determinism**, states that human activity is not free, not under the control of the individual, but instead is influenced by inter-nal and external forces that act on the individual. All events are determined by prior events, thereby excluding the possibility of free choice in human activity. Without this assumption of a lawfulness in nature, there would be little point in science. The current condition of the universe is the result of prior conditions and the cause of future conditions. Everything that happens reflects an inevitable, causal series of events. If scientists could identify all the influential factors, current and past, the future would be entirely predictable.

But scientists cannot do so. Psychological findings therefore become state-ments of probability, not absolutes.

In daily life and even in psychology, the free will–determinism issue presents little practical significance. Unable to identify the countless causal factors influ-encing our behavior, most of us experience the feeling of free will. In the mean-time, science proceeds on a deterministic basis, seeking to identify causal factors.

For some, this clash between personal experience in daily life and objec-tive analysis in science can be resolved by viewing the almost universal acceptance of free will as an outcome of human evolution. Individuals with that belief became better adapted to the complexities of this world, even in more primitive eras, and therefore more likely than nonbelievers to have survived and passed on this predisposition to future generations. Today, we derive some comfort, confidence, or other support from the notion that we possess a measure of free will. That experience brings some order into our otherwise bewildering environment (Rakos, 2004).

This position raises the question of how we should regard the experience of free will. Is it most usefully considered a force or a feeling? Those who view free will as a force think of the human mind as a causal mechanism in our lives. The individual behaves in a manner essentially independent of other factors. A person who resists taking someone else's money or helps someone across the street seems to experience an internal force or impetus that prevents the stealing or promotes the assistance.

From the other standpoint, free will is more properly regarded as a feeling, more like an emotion. But it is a special emotion, a feeling of doing something—different from the feeling when something is done to the individual, creating surprise or happiness or some other emotion. In this view, free will is not simply a rational thought either. Instead, the experience somehow occurs in both the mind and body, making our action more intensely experienced than a mere thought alone. On this basis, the experience of free will is an illusion, described as an "authorship emotion" (Wegner, 2002).

Among the critics of this view, one has described free will as a sensation, not an illusion. From a behavioristic viewpoint, which gives full and careful attention to the stimuli and consequences correlated with the behavior, the illusion disappears (Heyman, 2004). Another critic, from an orientation in biological psychology, accepts the concept of the illusion, which should inspire investigations of its neuronal substrates (Ito, 2004).

However it is regarded, and whatever the results of further research, espousing free will does not mean that human behavior occurs completely apart from causal factors. In the context of multiple causality, the concept of free will implies instead that the individual can operate independently of some internal and external forces.

Existentialism in Daily Life

A philosophical approach to certain dimensions of psychology, especially in Europe, existentialism commonly espouses a measure of free will. And it emphasizes the difficulties imposed on all human beings in their responsibilities for the choices they make.

A 20th-century movement encompassing several philosophical viewpoints, **existentialism** stresses each person's predicament as a self-determining doer, responsible for his or her own choices in life. But these choices are not readily understood; human beings do not possess substantial knowledge about themselves or their environment. Thus, they do not understand important factors in their choices. Moreover, human beings are governed by desires, fears, and other emotional states. They are not dispassionate observers of the world, but instead live in the very midst of that to which they must respond. For these reasons, existentialists study human "being" rather than human knowing. They aim to understand human existence in a world that focuses on a specific conventional, bewildering reality. On these bases, existentialism is a philosophical outlook more than it is an approach to psychology.

With no inborn knowledge to guide their choices, yet as agents responsible for themselves in their confusing environment, human beings become keenly aware of their vulnerability. For many people, the solution lies in conformity, a response strongly rejected by existentialists. It simply avoids the ultimate responsibility: making appropriate choices and acting with authority.

In the existential view, all people everywhere continuously create and re-create themselves through their choices. Each of us, as the only person who created our world, is the only one who can change it. No one else can do so for us (Yalom, 1980).

Whatever the individual's choices, numerous existentialists have pointed to anxiety as a fundamental human condition. Called *angst,* after the work of Soren Kierkegaard, a Danish philosopher, it refers to a collection of related feelings of dis-ease: dread, guilt, anxiety, anguish, despair, bad faith, and the like. Existential regret, for example, has been described as a profound desire to go back and make a better choice or a choice more consistent with one's beliefs and values (Lucas, 2004). In any case, angst emerges as an inevitable consequence of our uncertain universe, appearing in four basic conditions in human life.

The first condition, freedom, or the feeling of freedom, occurs with the lack of absolute structure in our lives. Even when largely restrained, most people have some alternatives. In fact, one existentialist entitled his book *Escape From Freedom,* emphasizing that human beings have difficulty dealing with the absence of absolute structure or restraint in their lives (May, 1994). Here the problem of choices returns to the fore. We must construct our own pathway through life. We are condemned to freedom or at least to feel free. We must deal with that burden.

The second condition, isolation, arises partly through this sense of freedom. Having our own individual pathways from the very beginning of life, we experience a fundamental separation from everyone else. We live in an impersonal world. As a reassurance against this feeling, we constantly seek love from one another.

And of course there is the inevitable end to all our pathways. This third condition, awareness of death and concern about what lies beyond, adds much to the angst of human life. In psychology, influential figures ranging from William James to Carl Rogers have considered the psychological implications of this awareness, noting that it can promote personal growth as well as angst (Moraglia, 2004).

Collectively, these three conditions produce a fourth concern, the central element in angst: the lack of meaning in life. With too much freedom, isolation, and the unavoidable ending, we cannot encounter any enduring meaning (Yalom, 1980). Existentialists point to our constant search for meaning among the endless decisions required in everyday life (Maddi, 2004).

Living without anyone of special significance to her, Bertha faced all these issues. Her mother's demise increased her freedom and sharply diminished the structure in her life. Bertha had already described in her journal her deeply felt sense of isolation, for which there was considerable justification. And by this time Bertha had crossed the meridian of her life. More and more she thought about that unknown day ahead when she would pass beyond all earthly understanding.

Formerly labeled "existential neurosis," this experience of meaninglessness today might be called depression. The person lives without joy or satisfaction. But amid life's uncertainties, all of us experience doubt or despair at one point or another. Existential therapists aim to assist us in coping with this prolonged meaninglessness and accompanying angst.

One of the most prominent methods, **logotherapy**, is a search for meaning, regarded as a primary force in life, not a secondary consideration. The term comes from the Greek *logos*, denoting "meaning." The therapist aims to make people more fully aware of this task of finding meaning and the significance of its outcome for their futures. It may emerge from a person's increased concern for personal relationships in the workplace or, for example, from her efforts to conserve natural resources. In any case, the only meaning of any importance would be the one that she assigns to her own life. The founder of logotherapy views this meaning not as invented or sought for itself but rather detected as a side effect in normal, everyday activities (Frankl, 1963).

Existential psychologists have used archival surveys to study the meaning in life. In one instance, they examined the views expressed in 283 quotations by 195 eminent people. Using content analysis, they sought a collective voice within this mass of information. But they found no one voice that spoke for all about the meaning of life, concluding, "The point of it all—if there is one—remains a mystery." The individual struggles alone. The human mind may even be incapable of comprehending such a monumental idea (Kinnier, Kernes, Tribbensee, & van Puymbroeck, 2003).

Further analyses generated 10 themes. The two most prominent were "Life is to be enjoyed" and "We are here to love and to help others." The least prominent themes included these views: "We must create meaning for ourselves" and "Life is absurd or a joke" (Kinnier et al., 2003).

Existentialists would concur, especially with the next-to-last of these expressions, the need to create meaning. Humanistic therapy, as emphasized later, proceeds in another direction, toward more personal growth and fulfillment. These two viewpoints share a concern for free will and the subjective side of life, but they diverge on other bases. More popular in Europe, existentialism generally confronts human limits, loneliness, and the search for meaning. Primarily an American institution, humanistic psychology addresses human development and the potential for peak experiences.

Toward a Positive Psychology

Just as existentialism stands in a long-term, somewhat distant relationship to humanistic psychology, chiefly through the questions of free will and subjective experience, positive psychology stands in a short-term, uncertain relationship, chiefly through its sudden, independent appearance in American psychology. The new millennium brought forth positive psychology in dramatic fashion, with the entire first issue of the *American Psychologist* devoted to its inauguration.

Humanistic psychologists promptly expressed satisfaction that their overall goals had received mainstream attention. In fact, **positive psychology** aimed to develop greater understanding of human happiness and to foster its presence, a goal certainly compatible with the humanistic traditional. As proponents of positive psychology pointed out, throughout the history of psychology studies of fear, anger, anxiety, and other negative emotional states far outnumber those on well-being. Positive psychology declared its purpose—to change this imbalance.

In its vigorous appearance, positive psychology gave relatively little attention to the history of humanistic psychology, which extends backward at least to William James, founder of American psychology (Froh, 2004). It includes five decades of research and practice in fostering human growth through humanistic psychology. It also includes a formal institution within the American Psychological Association (APA), the Division of Humanistic Psychology, and two former APA presidents, Carl Rogers and Abraham Maslow. The co-founder of humanistic psychology, Maslow published a book 50 years ago with a chapter entitled "Toward a Positive Psychology" (Maslow, 1954). Humanistic psychologists have expressed the hope that positive psychologists might join forces with them to extend the existing research and to fulfill one enduring goal: the development of a more holistic, less medical approach to mental illness (Greening, 2001). Such an alliance would demonstrate a positive approach to humanity, as well as to other approaches in the field of psychology (Kelley, 2004).

For positive psychology, one concern lay with the humanistic approach to psychology as a scientific endeavor. Humanistic psychology began with clear empirical support from Carl Rogers' early experimental research, but gradually the scientific emphasis became submerged amid humanistic psychology's popular appeal, spawning much "pop psychology." Aiming to bring renewed interest to the empirical study of optimism and successful self-direction, positive psychology unfurled its banner.

This research focuses on **subjective well-being,** which in popular conversation means happiness or "living the good life," typically measured on a 10-point scale ranging from *extremely unhappy* to *completely satisfied with life*. Data from random samples of many thousands of people responding to the scale present a more favorable outlook on life than philosophers and poets generally depict (Myers & Diener, 1996).

Research in different regions around the world has indicated that happiness is closely associated with at least three basic conditions in life: friends, faith, and funds. The importance of friends, including family, seems obvious. We are social creatures; we seek social support. Faith offers not only meaning and goals in life but social support as well, for most faiths are institutionally based. Finally, the importance of funds also appears obvious, but an exception occurs. Funds appear as a central factor in low-income environments, where basic human needs are threatened. In these poor regions, funds and happiness are clearly related. In affluent circumstances, with life's necessities regularly met, wealth shows a lower correlation with subjective well-being. Extremely wealthy people in the United States are only somewhat happier than people with average incomes. A major reason, of course, is that people adapt to their comfortable circumstances. Today's luxuries are tomorrow's necessities and the next day's rubbish (Myers, 2000).

These studies point to positive psychology's broad interest in subjective experience—how optimism affects health, how talent comes to fruition, what constitutes happiness and life satisfaction. The aim is not only to increase a sense of well-being but thereby to prevent the pathological outcomes that emerge from a destitute or meaningless existence. Fostering tolerance, altruism, and other evidence of good citizenship, the overall goal is to enable people and their societies to flourish (Seligman & Csikszentmihalyi, 2000).

One means of helping people to increase their level of happiness has been adapted from cognitive therapy (Ellis, 1991). The basic idea is to help people recognize and then challenge their own pessimistic thoughts. They do so in positive psychology by taking the role of some supportive person in their life, someone likely to note and resist a negative self-statement: "I'm too slow to become a keyboard operator." The person expressing this thought is charged with refuting it in the imagined manner of a critical but helpful colleague: presenting contrary factual evidence, looking for alternative viewpoints, assessing carefully all implications, and so forth (Seligman, 1991). This approach is an extension of cognitive therapy, considered in detail in the next chapter.

Another practical application appears in the form of popular books. One recent effort has produced a Happiness Model, offering advice on long-term goals. It encourages followers to regard long-term goals as means, not ends (Ben-Shahar, 2002). They become important not so much through attaining them but in having them.

This model depicts four archetypes or templates for conducting one's life: the rat race, hedonism, resignation, and happiness. Consider a man aiming to include physical exercise as a regular part of his life. Whether or not he recognizes it, his approach to both the present and future becomes a fundamental factor in his overall happiness.

The first pattern, the rat race, promises future happiness at the price of current pain. The man maintains a rigid workout schedule, seeking the most extensive aerobic and strengthening exercises in the least amount of time. He is not happy with this constant demand on his time and energy, but there should be a payoff in his later years. The second pattern, hedonism, favors the opposite pathway—immediate pleasure over future health and happiness. He exercises, but only on an irregular basis, whenever it is convenient and the urge strikes him. In resignation, the third pattern, he ignores beneficial exercise completely, foregoing a source of present and future happiness. And in the final pattern, the happiness archetype, he pursues a reasonable exercise program in a steady fashion, experiencing present enjoyment and the expectation of fulfillment in the future (Ben-Shahar, 2002).

From this standpoint, happiness is not standing on the peak of the mountain, where the wind blows hardest, and it is not wildly scrambling up the incline. Happiness lies in the experience of moving reasonably well toward a long-term goal. That distant goal fosters present happiness.

Throughout all such efforts, scientists and practitioners in psychology acknowledge the difficulties in defining happiness, well-being, self-esteem, and the good life. One widely cited definition of self-esteem, for example, depicts two dimensions: confidence in one's capacity to cope with life's basic challenges and the confidence in one's right to happiness (Branden, 1994).

These criteria appear reasonably valid, but they are not sufficiently operationalized for scientific research. And operationalizing them raises another very difficult issue, the question of values.

A half-century ago, a psychologist concluded that a value-free definition appears impossible (Smith, 1959). Emotional responses are biologically driven, but the meaning of those responses can be markedly influenced by the individual's psychological makeup. These psychological reactions, in turn, are socially derived, influenced by one's sense of self and reality, and vary across cultures. In other words, individual personal values become a significant concern in the search for universal and historical principles of well-being. Then, too, subjective well-being presumably emerges differently in different cultures, such as those in a survival mode versus those in affluent circumstances. On these bases, research on happiness and well-being must be diverse and apparently phenomenological, as well as empirical (Compton, 2001).

When their interests in human subjectivity are compared, humanistic psychology is more rational and idiographic than positive psychology—it is more concerned with the individual. It attends to case studies and the whole person, including broad concepts about the self, making data analyses interpretive and sometimes closer to philosophy than to science. Compelling evidence of reliability and verification may remain elusive. In contrast, positive psychology is more empirical and nomothetic, focused on understanding people in general. It generates large-scale surveys of specific features of groups of people, obtaining estimates of reliability through extensive statistical analyses.

An alliance between these two psychologies would prevent further fragmentation in the field and would underscore the need for further studies of human happiness. As a founder of humanistic psychology, Maslow stated decades ago that "positive psychology," or "orthopsychology," in the future would focus on healthy, fully functioning individuals, not exclusively on ill people. But this mutual interest on the part of humanistic and positive psychology occurs amid their somewhat different goals and methods, resulting in different research programs (Aanstoos, 2003). At present, positive psychology stands as a broad follow-up initiative, its capacity to bring subjective well-being into mainstream psychology yet to be determined.

Person-Centered Therapy

Despite construction of The Home, Bertha did not show the signs of happiness that might have been expected. As founder, director, and coordinator of all its activities, she often seemed too demanding, too self-centered, and too critical; perhaps she was still struggling against the excessive control exerted by her parents and society in her Vienna years.

In those troubled times, Bertha's mother had called on a general practitioner to assist her daughter, and he blindly let Bertha lead. If Bertha's mother had contacted instead a modern humanistic psychologist, that therapist would have accepted much of Breuer's makeshift pathway—but with greater understanding of the professional and ethical practices it requires. The chief humanistic therapy today reflects what the diligent, confused Breuer apparently attempted years earlier. But self-theory and modern research have brought it beyond his early efforts.

In permitting Bertha to direct her own therapy, Breuer adopted a completely unconventional approach at that time. Patients in that era were not allowed to discuss much of anything and certainly not irrational, irrelevant ideas. That wasted time. Instead, they followed the usual clinical practice; they listened to the doctor's advice. A permissive but active listener, Breuer opened the floodgates for Bertha's thoughts and feelings (Karpe, 1961).

A Growth-Inducing Environment

This capacity for facilitating open expression in a troubled person should not be regarded lightly. Only very rarely does a therapeutic release of tension appear in daily conversation. Many topics are not appropriate for such open, nonjudgmental discussion. The listeners are too concerned with their own lives and schedules to devote themselves consistently and fully to comprehending the issues of others. The conversations become too emotionally laden for the comfort of the participants. And unless a special appointment has been made for this purpose, it is never quite the right time or place for such a dialogue. For men, moreover, self-disclosure is not an easy matter (Banaji & Prentice, 1994). Women in daily conversation communicate to friends far more about their intimate thoughts and feelings than men do (Dindia & Allen, 1992). Men are less inclined to enter psychotherapy. And no psychotherapy is likely to succeed without self-disclosure and emotional responsiveness on the part of the person seeking assistance (Betz & Fitzgerald, 1993).

Thus Bertha's therapy established a new pattern in that era, the modern "talking cure." It stimulated Freud's thinking about memories and psychoanalytic therapy, and it foreshadowed person-centered therapy, the most common approach in humanistic psychology. Like today's person-centered therapist, Breuer made few if any interpretations. He did not act like a substitute parent, sympathetic friend, or even a traditional therapist. Instead he mostly listened, without interrupting (Strachey, 1955). This implicit support has become a fundamental feature in many psychotherapies today.

Including a premise of free will, **person-centered therapy** assumes that all human beings have the capacity to determine successfully their own destiny, choosing means and goals that lead to personal fulfillment. All of us, according to this viewpoint, are at the center of our own existence and therefore capable of directing our own lives, including the proper course of therapy. In fact, the person experiencing stress *must* guide the therapy; otherwise the treatment will be unsuccessful.

This capacity to guide one's own therapy arises through the actualizing tendency. In a troubled individual, it has been blocked by external or internalized barriers, and the therapist tries to release it. Hence, the three-phase premise for person-centered therapy is as follows: If the therapist can create an appropriate interpersonal environment, the capacity for growth will be released, and personal development will occur.

In Rogers' metaphor, the potatoes in that deep, dark cellar needed a growth-inducing environment. They needed rich soil and sunlight.

With all human beings, an appropriate interpersonal environment is the crucial factor, and here three characteristics of the therapist's response play an essential role: empathy, genuineness, and unconditional positive regard. Collectively, they communicate a warm, nonjudgmental atmosphere in which the therapist thinks with, rather than about, the person. Then the person seeking help begins to adopt a more positive view of herself, caring for herself as a person. Her potential becomes released, and she begins to respond in ways appropriate to herself (Rogers, 1971).

Someone with **empathy** understands the state of mind of someone else. The empathetic person knows how another person feels—but does not feel that way too or to the same extent. Breuer seemed to have empathy for Bertha; he understood and accepted her turmoil without feeling upset himself. Sympathy is a state of experiencing someone else's feeling, usually an unpleasant feeling. Sympathy may disrupt efforts at understanding, particularly when the feelings are strong.

The reports Breuer published and sent to the hospital provide little direct information about **genuineness**, which means acting in an open, honest fashion, without pomp or pretense. Sometimes called *authenticity,* genuineness is based on honesty and sincerity, which Breuer demonstrated in those early sessions, openly acknowledging the death of Bertha's father, revealing his intention to use force in her hospitalization, and explaining the purposes and procedures of his therapeutic efforts. In any ethical treatment, it is assumed that a therapist's integrity and authenticity enhance open expression by the person seeking help, promoting change and constructive growth (Rogers, 1980).

The third characteristic is an attitude toward people. In this growth-inducing environment, there can be no conditions of worth, no reservations on the part of the therapist. Even in Bertha's most trying times, Breuer never dismissed her or any of her symptoms as unworthy of his attention. Instead, he showed a no-strings-attached regard for her as an individual, regardless of her behavior. When a therapist, caretaker, or any other person communicates love and acceptance without reservation, this attitude is known as **unconditional positive regard**. It is a fundamental belief in the dignity of any person, troubled or otherwise. When a therapist demonstrates this warmth and caring, people know they are accepted regardless of their thoughts and feelings. The acceptance is obvious and constant (Zimring, 1990).

In describing the therapeutic environment in these ways, Carl Rogers opposed earlier approaches to psychotherapy, which were modeled more on theoretical conceptions and specific techniques, less on the person-therapist relationship. In traditional psychoanalysis, for example, the analyst seeks a degree of neutrality, maintaining a separation from the person. In the person-centered approach, the therapist aims instead for greater warmth in the relationship. Rogers' focus on empathy, genuineness, and unconditional positive regard played a major role in developing a concern for the therapeutic alliance. But favorable outcomes are most promising only when the therapist shows a natural inclination toward these characteristics, together with extensive practice and self-monitoring during therapy.

In person-centered therapy, an individual can use this acceptance to examine her own experiencing. Under no pressure from others, she guides the course of therapy according to her needs and discoveries about herself. As she becomes aware of her own experiencing, she becomes responsive again to directional trends in the organismic valuing process. In this way, she fosters the basic force in her life, the actualizing tendency.

From the person-centered viewpoint, Bertha's condition improved during her therapy with Breuer because she found herself in an open, growth-inducing environment. Breuer approached her not in a paternalistic or protective way, but apparently with empathy, maybe genuineness, and initially an effort at unconditional positive regard. Each session offered Bertha a catharsis, a release of emotional tension.

In modern person-centered therapy, Bertha would begin by discussing with her therapist all sorts of "safe" topics—making laces, doing housework, and horseback riding—with no mention of gender roles or sexuality. Her anger over the favoritism shown to Wilhelm was not understood as a cultural issue, and she did not perceive it that way at the time. Her complete absence of sexual responsiveness was not even regarded as a problem, or it was viewed as a topic to be avoided.

Gradually, in this special interpersonal environment, the actualizing tendency—the capacity for more complete development—would be released.

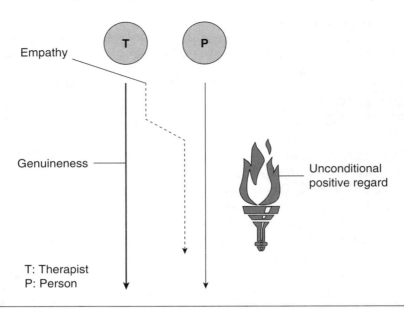

Figure 6.3   Person-Centered Therapy. The therapist aims for three characteristics that cannot become effective when assumed naively or superficially. Empathy, depicted by the dashed arrow, involves "walking" in the other person's footsteps, understanding that person from her viewpoint. In the counseling relationship, genuineness, represented by the straight, solid, downward arrow, means that the therapist is authentic and trustworthy, not a phony or defended person. In unconditional positive regard, the therapist shows unwavering, nonjudgmental loyalty, warmth, and acceptance, symbolized by the lighted torch.

Bertha then would begin to address some of her frustrations, beginning with those close to her awareness, such as parental overprotection and religious restrictions. Later she would consider less accessible, more difficult issues, such as the imbalance in gender roles. Eventually, she would examine psychological obstacles still further from normal consciousness, the personal and social conditions that prevented her from achieving a normal sexual adjustment (Noshpitz, 1984).

In her sessions with Breuer, over many months, she spoke at length about her father, idealizing him in displays of affection and compassion. She mentioned her brother only in one or two incidents. And she spoke of her mother not at all. These disparities and omissions in Bertha's discourse suggest that she was unable to engage in self-discovery in Breuer's therapeutic environment (Figure 6.3)

Facilitating Self-Exploration

In modern person-centered therapy, Bertha would more readily confront the sources of incongruence in her life. Her experience with menstrual periods and other evidence of physical development regularly informed her that she was a sexually mature woman. Yet her sexual interests and expression remained at a preadolescent stage. Similarly, her daily experience informed her that she was an intelligent, capable woman. Yet her parents restricted her to dull, trivial work, especially in comparison with Wilhelm. Incongruence in both spheres, sexual and intellectual, lowered her self-esteem and stunted her personal development.

To encourage self-exploration, the person-centered therapist responds in ways that reflect acceptance of the person seeking assistance. Holding up a metaphorical mirror, the therapist enables people in therapy to see themselves more accurately. Some of these ways of responding include active listening, restatement, clarification, and silence.

These ways have been successfully used by person-centered therapists around the world (Motschnig & Nykl, 2003). But they cannot become effective when applied in a mechanical or rote fashion. They cannot serve as how-to techniques. They are attitudes and feelings as well, requiring extensive experience and a clear commitment by the therapist, who must have a deep belief in the person seeking therapy and in the helping relationship as often more important than medication (Fisher, 2003).

In *active listening*, the therapist shows attention by emitting almost inaudible vocalizations at just the right moments. These sounds are not words with semantic meaning; they are nonintrusive signs of thoughtful interest, such as "mmmhm" and "ummmhmmm." Through their timing and consistency, together with eye contact and facial expression, they would convey to Bertha, "I am with you."

In *restatement of content*, the therapist goes one step further, rephrasing the person's thoughts in similar words. This response shows active listening *and* understanding. The content of the remark is reflected, not just attentiveness.

Still another response goes beyond restatement. In the *clarification of feelings*, the therapist tries to assist the person in sorting out her thoughts and feelings, which are commonly scrambled, mixed with one another. Here the therapist repeats the person's verbal expressions but uses different words, aiming to discover whether he and the person in therapy have correctly identified her various feelings. If so, they have opened a pathway for dealing with them. Here, still holding up a mirror, the therapist may gently remark on the patient's tone of voice, gestures, or posture, or the therapist may demonstrate these reactions, simply showing the patient how she is behaving. The therapist makes no interpretation.

The response of *silence* makes a strong, unambiguous statement. It shows full acceptance of the person and the therapeutic process. There is no need to fill silences; they are not awkward; they are time for reflection. The person is left with her own thoughts, free to express them whenever and however she wishes.

Within these ways of responding and a growth-inducing interpersonal relationship, the actualizing tendency is released and control "goes inside"—the person takes charge of her own life. She identifies areas of incongruence, explores them, and achieves some resolution (Rogers, 1951, 1961).

In this setting, Bertha eventually would reconsider the loss of her father, injustices by her mother, and comparisons with Wilhelm. In time, evidence of interest in peers would emerge, including thoughts of sexuality. These outcomes would confirm a feeling of progress, leading to further understanding, further relief, and perhaps even increased accord with her mother and the often tyrannical Wilhelm. But Breuer lacked this background and understanding of person-centered therapy. He listened attentively and held up the metaphorical mirror for a while, helping Bertha to look at herself (Tolpin, 2000). With his abrupt departure, she never finished her task.

But Breuer deserves special credit for his tolerance. He did not muddy the waters, intruding into Bertha's self-exploration. The merits of his achievement, he wrote, lay in his recognition of the scientifically important case that chance had left to him and in his unwillingness to disrupt the facts and progress of that case with preconceived opinions (Hirschmüller, 1989).

In this dedication, Breuer vaguely sensed the importance of the patient-therapist relationship, regarded today as a critical element in any form of therapy. For a positive outcome, especially in humanistic therapy, the patient must believe that the therapist truly understands her and cares about her welfare, and the therapist must merit these attributions, a condition called the **therapeutic alliance**. For many practitioners, this alliance may be more important than the method of treatment.

Today the significance of a successful therapeutic alliance is better understood, and Breuer brought it to scientific attention. In fact, he suggested that this early evidence for the interpersonal nature of the therapeutic process, brought forth in Anna O.'s surprising transference reaction to him, stood as his most important contribution to the world (Freud, 1925a).

Bertha formed such an alliance, which made Breuer's sudden departure all the more disruptive. Had she continued with this therapy, and had Breuer been more knowledgeable about it, eventually she might have seen herself differently—as a young woman rightfully resisting any role that depicted her as an extension of her mother, substitute for her sisters, foil for her brother, or submissive spouse to someone with perhaps less intelligence. She might have accepted herself as a person seeking self-expression, dealing with unrecognized sexuality, and desiring her own way of life.

Apparently Breuer created a promising interpersonal environment for this therapy, which did not reach a long-term conclusion. When his affection for his patient became incompatible with his standards of professional behavior, he ceased treatment. He did not allow Bertha any opportunity to object, to continue for a while, or even to plan for its termination. For this sudden cessation of therapy, Breuer would find himself today liable in another malpractice suit.

But his society did not recognize this ethical issue. So Josef Breuer should be remembered instead for his sustained effort at enhancing health and effectiveness in human beings, even those seemingly without significant adjustment problems. This goal underscores the optimistic outlook in humanistic psychology. Human beings can control their own lives. They are determining, as well as determined. Every human being has the potential to achieve fulfillment.

Commentary and Critique

One broad limitation in all psychological inquiry occurs with the dilemma considered earlier: investigating the parts or the whole, seeking precision or fullness. Study of the parts, known as reductionism, appeared earlier in the discussion of biological psychology. Here in humanistic psychology we turn to the study of the whole. Any commentary on psychological perspectives must consider the ways in which they respond to this issue.

Reductionism, the common, highly productive pathway in modern science, is not universal in psychology. Many investigators believe that complex phenomena can never be adequately explained in terms of their basic elements. Reductionism sets narrow boundaries, limiting the concern with multiple factors. The premise in **holism** is that an organic entity, especially a human being, is different from the sum of its parts; it can be understood only as a totality. The parts interact; they gain something from their interdependence— or they lose something. The concern lies with their *relationships*. Hence, they must be studied together, as a *unified* whole, which is a special concern in humanistic inquiry.

The narrative of Bertha illustrates this concern. It presents her life in the context of culture, a vital consideration because personality never develops free from culture. Told partly by Bertha and partly by her biographers, this narrative expresses her experiences in upper-class Vienna and working-class

Frankfurt, providing a broad, holistic view not so readily possible outside a storytelling mode (McAdams & Pals, 2006).

The term *holism,* incidentally, sometimes appears with another first letter, as *wholism.* The latter spelling more readily communicates the idea of a whole or complete entity, as opposed to a *hole,* but it is less commonly used.

One hears the term most often these days in the context of holistic health, meaning that the body, the mind, and their parts function as inseparable units, each influencing the well-being of one another. Thus, treatment for some disorders must focus on their integration within the whole person.

Consider a simpler example. In a large pile of bricks, the relationships are random. One brick can be broken, displaced, or even removed without altering the whole pile in any significant way. A soap bubble is a different matter. The "parts" are integrated. A pinprick in one area produces a drastic change in the whole bubble (Wertheimer, 1972). In a metaphorical sense, every investigator must decide whether to approach a certain phenomenon as a pile of bricks or more like a bubble. Reductionistic and holistic goals can seldom be pursued simultaneously.

Reductionism places the highest priority on precision and control, which are matters of degree. Holism suggests an absolute condition—that all possible elements can be included, which simply does not occur in psychological research. An investigation of depression might aim to include afflicted persons, their families, home life, sleep habits, nutrition, exercise, friendships, childhood experiences, and work settings. But examining all these and other elements in detail, all seemingly relevant to depression, becomes prohibitive, even in a single case study. For this reason, psychologists sometimes refer to a single investigation of comparatively large units of behavior as *nonreductionism.*

In this context, two types of wholes should be acknowledged. An aggregate or additive whole is simply the sum of its parts, as in a random pile of bricks or bisected rectangle. In a functional or organic whole, involving special relationships among its parts, their sum may not be equal to the whole. An individual's personality is not simply the sum of certain traits. The traits combine in various ways. Individuals with similar traits can be different indeed, depending on how their traits interact.

Characteristics of a functional or organic whole not evident in its elementary properties are called **emergent properties**. They appear only in the *union* of the parts, and they are not necessarily predictable from a knowledge of them.

As a functional whole, a Dickens novel employs words available to any speaker of English, but the relationships among them produce emergent properties—the power of his prose. A successful painting gains something special from the combination of colors, shapes, sizes, and so forth. One sometimes hears this expression: The whole is greater than the sum of its parts. But that outcome may fail to appear; the functional whole also may be less than the sum of its parts. A team of highly promising individuals may perform below its expected level because of disruptive relationships among its members. The family, society's basic social unit, fosters favorable psychological development depending on the relationships among parents, siblings, aunts and uncles, and other people in that unit. More accurately, an organic whole may be *different* from the sum of its parts, whether that whole is a brain, a person, or a culture. Humanistic psychology takes a marked interest in expressions of holism.

Most organic entities are regarded today as interactive systems, and one major research aim is to gain further understanding of them as systems—their parts in relation to one another. Without this concern in psychology, many investigations of mental life, behavior, and their disorders would fall to biology, chemistry, physics, and other basic sciences. Emergent properties would be ignored; the concept of mind as mind would disappear from science (Wertheimer, 1972). And the concept of self as self would disappear from psychology, or it would be described in terms of submicroscopic particles of energy and matter. The fundamental challenge therefore lies in integrating a hierarchy of findings from different levels of inquiry (Pinker, 2002).

In the study of people, psychology inevitably becomes concerned with organic wholes. And more than the other perspectives, humanistic psychology reflects holistic aims, involving the most inaccessible realms of human experience. Currently, these free-ranging explorations become possible only at the cost of precision in measurement.

Diminished precision leads to a potential **problem of reliability,** meaning a concern with the accuracy and consistency of measurement. Would a different investigator obtain different scores? Would the same investigator obtain the same scores on a different occasion? Compared with the instruments and techniques employed in experimental and survey research, those used in case studies and observational methods are comparatively unstructured, making the collection and analysis of data less statistical, more thematic, thereby increasing the chances for investigator bias. Especially in a single case study, the numerical data do not permit use of advanced statistical methods for assessing reliability.

Among the perspectives, psychoanalysis and humanistic psychology also have been most susceptible to the falsification problem, partly because of their reliance on the traditional case study. In an applied setting, the case study can offer useful solutions to everyday problems. In a research setting, it can incorporate extensive psychological knowledge and respect for the rules of science, producing helpful data and suggesting productive hypotheses. But it remains an interpretive statement. Without substantial controls, it cannot be shown to be false.

Humanistic psychology often accepts such tradeoffs, emphasizing that the field is a human science, requiring research methods different from those of the natural sciences. Psychology, in this view, should not be limited to objective observations in highly controlled settings. This stance elicits obvious resistance from mainstream psychology. So the nonreductionism in humanistic and psychoanalytic psychology pushes these perspectives to the edge of modern science. Some would say they lie beyond its borders.

The problem of precision appears in still another context, recognized earlier. The foundations of humanistic psychology include several **nonoperationalized concepts,** offering little or no consensus on how they can or should be measured. These entities include the actualizing tendency, conditions of worth, organismic valuing process, incongruence, and the self, among others. According to critics, they are too vague to be measured and tested adequately.

The organismic valuing process, for example, plays a vital role in the self-concept. But it remains difficult to assess. It seems virtually impossible to know when a person, especially a preverbal child, is choosing activities that enhance one's self. Conditions of worth suffer the same problem. They remain unclear because the organismic valuing process cannot be clearly conceived. Useful in theory, such concepts need to be readily measurable in research.

Nevertheless, early in the emergence of humanistic psychology, Carl Rogers and his colleagues conducted the first experimental, nonreductionistic studies of personal growth gained through psychotherapy. Using several inventories and rating scales, they studied intensively 52 people ranging in age from the twenties to forties, whom they divided into an experimental or therapy group and a control or waiting group. The motivation to enter therapy can be influential in therapy outcomes; therefore, they assigned to the control group only people who had requested therapy but agreed to remain on a "wait list." Moreover, half the people in therapy served as their own control group, waiting a certain interval before entering therapy, thereby providing a comparison in their mental health for two periods, before and after therapy. Rogers thereby implemented several procedures for control in an era when even competent practitioners considered therapy too intuitive and intangible to be studied by objectively controlled methods. In fact, many therapists strongly opposed any attempt to assess the outcomes of psychotherapy (Gordon, Grummon, Rogers, & Seeman, 1954).

Electronic recording instruments had just become available, and Rogers used them extensively, obtaining permission to tape each session anonymously and thereby collecting the first large set of data on therapeutic dialogues. These tapes enabled the psychologists to evaluate their therapeutic procedures, to present evidence of the growth process, and thereby to provide support for the person-centered approach to therapy (Rogers & Dymond, 1954).

Expanding this work to include group therapy, Rogers and his colleagues focused on the ways members gave, received, and exchanged emotional support with one another, as well as the ways they redefined themselves after the group meetings. These findings raised awareness about subjective experience, as well as the growth process. Gradually, the person-centered approach became prominent in therapy facilities around the country—business, schools, hospitals, the military, and elsewhere. The humanistic perspective thereby made its mark in psychology—through psychotherapy, rather than extensive basic research.

Summary

Rise of Humanistic Psychology

Promoted by Carl Rogers, humanistic psychology achieved a prominent position, partly through its optimistic outlook. Compared to other psychological perspectives, it places less emphasis on science and more on human subjectivity, individuality, and the capacity for growth. For Rogers, potatoes in a cold, dark cellar became a metaphor for humanistic psychology. Their response in this adverse environment demonstrated an inherent tendency toward growth, called the actualizing tendency.

Key Terms: **humanistic psychology, actualizing tendency, phenomenology**

Three Human Characteristics

The starting point for humanistic psychology is human subjectivity—the private experience of the individual, not the objective world as defined by popular consensus. Human individuality, the second dimension of human uniqueness, appears in many forms, including our capacity for self-awareness, which results in the self-concept, ideal self, self-esteem, and other views of oneself. Humanistic psychology's optimism occurs largely through its emphasis on a third human characteristic—the actualizing tendency, an inborn impetus in any living organism toward the fullest possible development.

Key Terms: **subjectivity, individuality, self theory, self, self-concept, ideal self, self-esteem, Maslow's motivational hierarchy, self-actualization**

Influence of Early Experience

A temporary state, congruence occurs when an individual's views of the self and personal experience are compatible with one another. Incongruence reflects a poor self-concept. It also reflects a poor match between the self-concept and personal experience or between the self-concept and the ideal self. The roots of incongruence are laid early in life, whenever conditions of worth stifle the organismic valuing process, disrupting the child's contact with her most basic feelings about herself.

Key Terms: **organismic valuing process, conditions of worth, congruence, incongruence, fully functioning person**

Philosophical and Practical Issues

In psychology, the humanistic view of free will assumes that human beings have the capacity to make choices appropriate to their own lives, thereby achieving personal growth. Existentialism also makes the assumption of self-determination but with greater attention to the problems of freedom, isolation, death, and finding meaning in life. Positive psychology emphasizes the study of subjective well-being; its emergence raises a practical issue about its relationship to humanistic psychology and cognitive therapy.

Key Terms: **free will, determinism, existentialism, logotherapy, positive psychology, subjective well-being**

Person-Centered Therapy

Person-centered therapy relies on the capacity of the individual to solve her own problems. With empathy, genuineness, and unconditional positive regard, the therapist creates a nonthreatening environment that releases this capacity, allowing the individual to explore her own thoughts and feelings in whatever ways seem appropriate. The therapist supports these explorations through active listening, restatement of content, clarification of feelings, and silence, figuratively holding up a mirror for the person to view herself.

Key Terms: **person-centered therapy, empathy, genuineness, unconditional positive regard, therapeutic alliance**

Commentary and Critique

More than the other perspectives, humanistic psychology tends toward holism, aimed at awareness, personal growth, fulfillment, and other broad dimensions of human life. This goal has the potential for examining emergent properties, but measurements thereby become less precise, producing uncertain reliability. Several important but nonoperationalized concepts also raise the issue of precision in research.

Key Terms: **holism, emergent properties, problem of reliability, nonoperationalized concepts**

Critical Thinking

1. Consider Carl Rogers' *conditions of worth,* B. F. Skinner's *reinforcement history,* and Sigmund Freud's *early experience.* Describe how these concepts are similar. Then indicate some differences, according to the perspectives in which they appear.

2. Modify Maslow's motivational hierarchy to include a concern for social issues. Be specific. Indicate where and how you would include another stage or modification of a pre-existing stage.

3. An adolescent experiences a school phobia. Explain a fundamental way in which a humanistic psychologist and behaviorist would view the problem differently. Do more than describe each treatment; focus also on the origins of the problem.

7

Cognitive Psychology

Cognitive psychology examines the ways people manage the flow of information in their minds. In a general sense, it studies perception, the intake of information; memory, the storage and retrieval of information; and thinking, the diverse uses of this information in reasoning, language, and other mental activities.

Contemplation about human mental activities has occurred from the earliest stages of human history, but the forerunners of modern cognitive psychology appear in the late 19th century. After describing these diverse foundations, but before presenting cognitive therapy and the final commentary, this chapter considers successively our current knowledge about perception, then memory, and finally thinking.

In this context, imagine young Bertha's memories and thoughts on hearing these words in the streets of Vienna: "Hochere Tochter! Hochere Tochter!" Dressed in expensive clothing and jewelry, idle much of the day, she and others of her age and upper-class background became the targets of discreet ridicule. The lower classes jeered them as society's parasites, each a lazy and overindulged "High Daughter." But these leisurely, high-born young women were not at fault. In fact, they were victims.

They were prevented from acquiring further education and careers outside the home; instead, their parents bestowed on them luxuries designed to gain attractive offers of marriage. They viewed their daughters as opportunities for conspicuous consumption. Families gained their reputation by squandering their resources on superfluous goals and extended idleness.

But how did these young women think about themselves? How did they process this information about their unusual social position?

Some overlooked the exploitation, enjoying their leisurely status. They accepted their golden handcuffs with ease and grace; they did not acknowledge or even recognize the cultural restrictions. Others viewed the problem as a family injustice. They overtly resisted this sexual discrimination at the cost of pain and hardship, as well as family discomfort. Still others regarded themselves at fault, or at least they experienced the problem internally. They developed various illnesses, mental or physical—nervousness, backaches, fears, weaknesses, and sensory disorders (Kaplan, 1984).

In her youth, Bertha fell into the third category. Surrounded by wealth, she lay in a gilded cage, sick and unhappy, prohibited from meaningful work despite her special talents. In Frankfurt, she began to understand herself differently, shedding her golden handcuffs by assisting orphans, prostitutes, and finally unwed mothers. Then one day a magazine moved her further toward the second category. Articles and editorials in *The Woman* caught

Bertha's attention. They increased her knowledge, strengthened her understanding, and stimulated her resistance to a problem broader than her own: the plight of women throughout society.

Foundations of Cognitive Psychology

In modern psychology, knowledge and understanding are known as *cognition*. Thus **cognitive psychology** deals with knowing, understanding, and all other mental processes—including perception, memory, thinking, and numerous components of these major processes yet to be identified. Like the biological perspective, cognitive psychology is an extensive enterprise, a loose confederation of diverse interests so broad that it may seem more like a diverse subfield than a single systematic perspective in contemporary psychology. With the human mind as its subject of inquiry, cognitive psychology faces an immense challenge.

Expressed in simpler terms that emphasize this breadth, modern cognitive psychology seeks to discover how knowledge is represented in the human mind (Mandler, 1985). Strictly speaking, cognitive psychologists study mental processes only, without concern for their biological background. They believe they can investigate the software, which is human cognitive ability, without substantial knowledge of how it would be implemented in the hardware, the human brain (Byrnes & Fox, 1998; Neisser, 1967). In a word, the focus is largely on consciousness—with practical applications in social behavior, school achievement, job performance, and other mental activities (Sternberg & Dennis, 1997).

Cognitive psychology stands in marked contrast to radical behaviorism, which concentrates on overt actions. The cognitive approach aims to discover what goes on inside the "black box," as the human mind has been called because of its mysterious, seemingly inaccessible state. Also in contrast to behaviorism, cognitive psychology stimulates theory-building, for mental processes cannot be observed directly. It generates ideas about the way human knowledge is represented in the mind and about the processes that shape and transform these representations, making them useful mental mechanisms (Mandler, 1985).

With these aims, cognitive psychology has become an open, dynamic approach to psychology, emerging without any particular individual becoming the overall leader. It developed instead under the influence of several prominent figures. With its broad mandate and the accelerated development of new equipment, it continues to change rapidly from its earlier roots, which are lengthy, tangled, and diverse.

Efforts in Gestalt Psychology

Like biological psychology, the cognitive perspective developed early roots in Wundt's laboratory, in experiments aiming to explore the human mind or, more exactly, its basic contents. But early cognitive psychology lacked adequate instruments and techniques for measuring mental life. Its method of introspection failed because participants' reports of their experiences and feelings could not be studied in a consistent, accurate manner. Psychology at that time simply could not look inward in any reliable fashion.

Soon a more empirical approach came forth. Called **gestalt psychology,** for the German word *gestalt* means whole or configuration, it emphasized the study of unified patterns or wholes, especially of natural organizations, focusing on perception and the role of insight in thinking. In Berlin and elsewhere, the gestaltists insisted that complex phenomena can never be adequately explained in terms of their basic elements. The parts interact. The organic or functional whole may be something more or less than the sum of its parts—or something different altogether.

In an early demonstration, two stationary lights blinked on and off, one after the other, at a constant interval. If the lights were close together and the interval brief, the viewer saw both of the lights blinking at the same time. If their positions were far apart and the interval lengthy, the viewer saw one light and then the other, each in a different location. But with an appropriate distance and interval, the apparatus created the illusion that just one light appeared, moving from the first to the second location. There was no movement of any sort, as the reader well knows from observing modern neon signs. The stationary whole included an emergent property: the illusion of movement.

Gestalt psychologists found this illusion so compelling, yet so simple, that they named it after a single letter of the Greek alphabet, the *phi phenomenon.* For them, such demonstrations made a convincing statement about the study of cognitive phenomena. Examining the whole person, the whole mind, became more important than examining characteristic parts in a more precise but isolated fashion. Information about the parts is of course essential and inevitable because attention must become focused, but the overall phenomenon requires a more holistic approach.

Nevertheless, gestalt psychology failed to achieve its promise. The problems here lay outside the laboratory. The Nazi regime of the 1930s disrupted its work, prompting Max Wertheimer, Wolfgang Kohler, and other leaders to emigrate to the United States, where their investigations contributed to our understanding of learning, thinking, perception, and problem solving. American colleagues extended the fundamental gestalt ideas on wholes and patterns to studies in motivation, social psychology, and organizational psychology, focusing on the place of individuals within the group. But in America gestalt psychology faced stiff opposition from the rising tide of behaviorism, which soon gained ascendancy in the field. Gestalt psychology offered an early research platform for cognitive studies, but it did not come to full fruition.

Piaget's Cognitive Studies

Amid these interrupted efforts in early cognitive psychology, an exception appears in the early, steady work of a Swiss psychologist, Jean Piaget (1896–1980). For 30 years, he produced major findings in relative obscurity, often studying his own children in everyday settings, rather than research participants in a laboratory. His equipment, crude by today's standards, showed his ingenuity. He preferred informal, flexible methods, chiefly naturalistic observation and the interview. Partly for these reasons, he is not fully representative of modern cognitive psychology. Moreover, he limited his studies to **cognitive development**, the typical changes in mental abilities during the life span, as people grow older. Cognitive development is just one of several domains in the subfield of *developmental psychology*, which also examines changes in physical, sexual, emotional, and social development throughout the life cycle.

Piaget's promise in science first appeared with his description of a rare albino sparrow. He was pleased with this publication early in his career—at age 11. Further articles and his work with mollusks in his hometown of Neuchatel, Switzerland, brought him the opportunity to serve as curator of mollusks in a Geneva museum. But he declined the opportunity, deciding to finish high school instead. Then his godfather, thinking Piaget too young to be so specialized, stimulated the youth's philosophical interests, which, along with science, lasted the rest of his life (Singer & Revenson, 1978).

Completing graduate studies in biology and seeking work that would include philosophy, Piaget turned to cognitive psychology. He planned a 5-year study of the development of thought in children—but continued with it for more than 40. He called this work genetic epistemology, for it examined the origin, or genesis, of knowledge (Boden, 1979).

Family events also influenced Piaget's career, particularly the birth of Jacqueline, his first child, followed by Lucienne and then Laurent. Observing their behavior stimulated his interest in the complex mental processes that develop in human beings even before they can understand or use language. He watched his infants trying to find lost toys and throwing things onto the floor. At later ages, he assembled their toys in various ways and then posed questions about them. Still later, he inquired about the moon, being naughty, dreams, and more abstract concepts, all with the aim of understanding how children's knowledge evolves (Piaget, 1952a).

In this extensive effort, Piaget's coworker, Valentine Chatenay, deserves special credit. As Piaget's wife, the children they studied were her children too. She not only supplied the participants; she also made observations and collected data. Their research program, which began almost as a summer job for Piaget, blossomed into a collaborative marital effort and a lengthy career for him.

Her husband is best remembered for identifying four stages in cognitive development, leading to the conclusion that a young child's understanding of the world is not just inferior to that of an adult. It is fundamentally different.

From birth to 18 months or older, Piaget discovered, children do not think in the usual adult sense at all. With no substantial capacity for recall, the infant simply senses its environment and reacts to it, prompting Piaget to call this first phase of cognitive development the *sensorimotor period*. When his daughter Jacqueline was a few months old, Piaget showed her a rattle, and she cooed and squirmed with pleasure. But after she watched him cover it with a blanket, she showed no disappointment at all. She did not even look for the toy. Apparently the rattle had vanished from her thoughts (Piaget, 1954).

Around the time of the second year, the child does look for the toy. Memory is developing more rapidly. The child begins to gain images for thinking about things not immediately present—but cannot use these symbols in flexible ways. This stage is called *preoperational thought* because the child often cannot think logically about these objects, especially about the operations that might be performed on them. From an adult viewpoint, these childish mistakes are amusing. For psychologists, they depict the most intriguing of the four Piagetian stages.

A traditional test requires the child to explain what happens when certain operations are performed on certain objects. Two identical, tall beakers are filled with colored water. After the child agrees that the beakers contain equal amounts, and while the child is watching, the contents of one beaker are poured into a third empty beaker, which is low and wide. Then the child is asked: "Now which one has more, this beaker or this one—or do they have the same amount?" The psychologist points to the second tall, thin beaker, filled with water, and to the third beaker, low and flat, filled with an equal amount of water. Attending to the height of the tall column of water, the preoperational child chooses that beaker. This child reasons in terms of the dominant stimulus, not the operations involved, thereby demonstrating *preoperational thought* (Piaget, 1954).

By age six or seven years, or even earlier, depending on the specific features of the task, the child becomes surprised by the question, answering, "They're just the same!" This capacity to think logically and solve problems that are physically present is called *concrete operations.* The child can reason success-fully, knowing that the quantity of liquid has not changed, just its shape.

A hypothetical situation is a different matter, requiring *formal operations,* the capacity for abstract thinking. Around 11 years of age, the individual *may* begin to reason logically, even in situations that are not concrete. The child may then be able to imagine the possibilities in a hypothetical situation. Emerging into the teen years, some adolescents begin to form and test hypotheses about government, philosophy, business, and other aspects of daily life solely by reasoning, solving problems entirely in abstract terms (Piaget, 1950, 1952b).

These early efforts by Piaget spawned thousands of investigators in the 20th century. Consistent with science, they have revised or advanced his groundbreaking work, showing that his little Jacqueline and other children knew far more about the world than her father suspected, as noted later.

The Cognitive Revolution

With Piaget studying cognitive development on one side of the Atlantic, American revolutionaries began to appear on the other, separately at first, individually resisting behaviorism, which largely ignored the human mind. These scattered dissidents wanted to bring mental life back into mainstream psychology.

In fact, modern cognitive psychology did not arise as a protest against humanistic psychology, a more immediate predecessor, emerging in the 1950s. Lacking a strong empirical base, humanistic psychology never gained ascen-dancy in scientific psychology, although it established its own special, more holistic position in the field. Wryly speaking, psychology lost its mind with behaviorism—but then regained it with the protest of cognitive psychology.

Intrusions into the behavioristic rule had begun earlier in small ways, even within the stimulus-response (S-R) expression of traditional behaviorism. To emphasize that an organism intervened between the stimulus and response, the expression sometimes became modified: S-O-R. An organism mediated the stimulus, converting it into a response. Eventually, these mediating activ-ities gained the attention of diverse scientists in disparate locations, produc-ing the growth of cognitive psychology.

Among these psychologists, Jerome Bruner maintained a strong interest in perception, stressing that what one perceives is a function not only of the primary stimulation, as studied in behavioristic laboratories, but also of the observers' values, needs, and other expectations. In other words, the individual's personal orientation could not be ignored. Bruner waggishly called this viewpoint the "New Look" in perception because it brought a fresh approach to the study of visual responsiveness. It did so by pointing to the importance of the O, the organism's mental readiness, between the S and R.

In contrast, George Miller came from a background in mathematical psychology, information theory, and speech perception. Eventually this versatility brought him to the study of consciousness and how we store information in the mind. Without memory, human beings would be totally helpless. We would not know what to do about anything. Miller's subsequent research, assigning a finite, numerically defined capacity to immediate human memory, aroused considerable interest among psychologists, many of whom were not yet committed to bringing the mind back into psychology. Miller's work brought hope, a challenge, and a peek inside the black box.

The study of business organizations and their executives initially led Herbert Simon to investigations of human thinking, especially decision making and problem solving. Later, he viewed the human mind as a symbol-manipulating system or, as a colleague expressed it, an information-processing system. But even with this language, Simon and his colleagues lacked the technology to conduct productive studies of thinking. Seeking precision, they noticed that early computers were not just "number crunchers." They too were symbol manipulators, possessing the potential for manipulating all kinds of information. That realization brought forth the idea of *computer simulation,* using the computer to depict human information processing and using the computer languages as descriptions of those "thought processes" (Simon, 1980).

These, then, were three early major strands in the re-emergence of cognitive psychology: perception, memory, and computer simulation of human thought. But the field still lacked a name. Another psychologist, Ulrich Neisser, supplied that with the title of his new book a decade later, *Cognitive Psychology* (1967), the first text in the field. It played a basic role in outlining this perspective, organizing current knowledge, and presenting the computer as a metaphor for thinking about human information processing.

Enormously aided by improved electronic equipment, the cognitive psychology movement gathered momentum, eventually including linguists, engineers, anthropologists, and many others representing diverse interests. Thus, as cognitive psychology gained more adherents, it did not develop the coherence of a highly systematic perspective. It became a loose alliance of diverse psychologists and others sharing an interest in the mysterious phenomenon known as the human mind. Informally called the "cognitive revolution," that expression perhaps overstates the case, for the cognitive perspective was not new according to Wundtian and Piagetian standards, and it has not been embraced by the entire field (Greenwood, 1999). But since the 1970s it has remained a prominent force, calling attention to the tremendous complexity of information processing in our everyday lives.

In psychology, **information processing** refers to the representation of the world within an individual—the symbolic activities that constitute the flow of knowledge between an individual and the environment (Mandler, 1985). The most popular general concept in cognitive psychology, it serves as a broad reference to diverse mental processes, all related to intelligence.

In fact, the concept of information processing overlaps with **intelligence,** broadly defined as the capacity to adapt to new situations and to learn from experience. In psychology, intelligence is a much older term, associated in the early years with psychometric testing—the measurement of mental ability, focusing on amount. The goal, then and now, lies in measuring how much intelligence an individual possesses, comparing people in this respect, and comparing differences in mental functions within one individual. This aim still plays a useful role in society.

But the information-processing viewpoint has become more prominent in recent decades. It focuses not on how much intelligence a person possesses but on how intelligence operates, stressing the relationships among our mental functions in managing various types of information and the ways they produce our understanding of the world. From this viewpoint, differences in intelligence are viewed as differences in information processing.

One dimension of information processing, *speed of processing,* appears regularly in daily life. When told a telephone number, for example, some people repeat it quickly; others need more time and more "tellings." Fast learners generally are more capable than slower learners, just as older children are mentally quicker than younger ones (Miller & Vernon, 1997). Characterized by biographers as quick-witted, sharp-tongued, and always ready with a retort, Bertha may have possessed considerable speed in information processing, at least in the verbal realm.

The second dimension, *knowledge available for processing,* includes all information retrievable from long-term memory. The greater an individual's expertise in some area, the greater is that person's ability to acquire and store new knowledge in that same area. In discussions about law, Wilhelm would appear more intelligent than Bertha because he had developed a more extensive background in the law, increasing his storage capacity and his capacity for perceiving and using new information about legal matters. Wilhelm also had more and better schooling. But in the context of feminism, the tables would be turned.

A third dimension, using *strategies for processing new information,* also is influenced by age and experience. Adults confronted with a simple memory task would use mnemonic devices not even imagined by children. Of course schooling plays a role; mathematics, for example, offers numerous strategies for estimating time, distance, and mass, and these estimates can increase the speed of processing.

Thus, intelligence depicts the human mind in rather static fashion; information processing stresses mental activities. But the basic dimensions of information processing—speed, knowledge, and strategies—certainly describe intelligence too, including its measurement.

Current Models of the Mind

Recently, cognitive psychology has been influenced by still another view of the mind emerging from philosophy and appearing in biological and evolutionary psychology. This view stands in opposition to the work conducted by many prior investigators who considered the human mind as a unitary whole with continuously merging functions. But the idea of the mind as a general-purpose mechanism, operating in a fully unified fashion, now appears to be an oversimplification.

Piaget's conclusion about broad, universal shifts from one cognitive stage to another, for example, still remains generally useful, highlighting the fascinating stage of preoperational thought. But subsequent research shows that these shifts are not as broad or uniform as Piaget suggested. Instead, the child's cognitive development seems to emerge within more specific and separate domains of knowledge (Carey, 1990). And the cognitive activities of adults also reflect more specific, independent mental processes than previously thought.

Today, many contemporary psychologists no longer accept an all-purpose model of the human mind. For them, our mind is not a **general-purpose problem solver**, a unitary whole with enormous flexibility, engaging in the solution of diverse problems in all kinds of situations. They point out that the potential problems and settings are virtually infinite and potential outcomes too improbable (Tooby & Cosmides, 1992). This view of the mind as a single, awesomely flexible system is certainly popular with the public. But many cognitive psychologists today regard the human mind instead as a collection of distinct subsystems or modules, each called a **domain-specific problem solver**, each highly specialized to respond to a specific type of information in *particular* situations. For this reason, these subsystems, which are relatively independent of one another, are sometimes called *content-specific problem solvers*. The human mind may include some general-purpose subsystem, but overall it appears to be made up of a large number of idiosyncratic cognitive mechanisms that communicate with one another in a restricted fashion (Fodor, 1983).

Evidence for domain-specific cognitive modules appears in daily life. Someone observing a visual illusion remains subject to the misperception, even after it has been explained. Part of the mind, one cognitive module, continues to experience the illusion. Another part knows the truth. But that knowledge does not cause the illusion to disappear. The visual mind and the knowing mind function independently. In certain cases of brain injury, called blindsight, a patient claims to be completely blind in one section of the visual field and yet, without awareness, can make discriminations in that area. Case studies and laboratory manipulations of visual experiences have become popular means of demonstrating that conscious experience is not necessarily continuous with brain activities. We may not even be aware of much complex processing in the brain (Roser & Gazzaniga, 2004).

Incidentally, not all domain-specific modules are innate. Reading, for example, is acquired during a person's lifetime, and once learned, the reading response becomes impossible to suppress. We cannot avoid reading any known word we look at carefully. Moreover, these acquired modules need not be completely domain specific, and they may not even be hard-wired in specific brain areas. In fact, a specific psychological module does not necessarily emerge from a corresponding neural module. There may be no essential connections between cognitive and neural modularity (Flombaum, Santos, & Hauser, 2002).

The domain-specific problem solver probably is not a homogeneous mechanism but instead an assembly of numerous subsystems that, in aggregate fashion, can best account for our seemingly unlimited capacity for adaptation. These cognitive systems are content specific and substantially separate from one another (Fodor, 1983). As noted later, human mental life is sometimes described today as using **parallel distributive processing** because different sources of information about any one stimulus event—its color, sound, movement, and other features—are processed simultaneously in different brain areas. Thus, disparate pieces of information are manipulated in parallel, meaning at the same time, and in distributive fashion, meaning in diverse regions of the brain. Then these separate bits of information are integrated, creating everyday experience.

Thus, cognitive psychology seeks to understand the mind's design and arrangement of its parts, focusing on its functional organization. Biological psychology aims to understand the integration of the complexly organized brain structures or parts. The former is more mental, the latter more physical, and the integration of the two approaches currently indeterminable. As research continues, these different pathways of investigation should become increasingly interconnected.

One indispensable component of this integrated cognitive design would be a specification about how we store memories. Other components would involve how we integrate sensation and perception, how unconscious thought influences problem solving, and so forth. The complexity of human mental life suggests that we should view the whole domain in the plural, as cognitive structures or architectures (Estes, 1991).

In contrast to Piaget, modern cognitive psychologists have developed a strong commitment to formal experimental methods, made possible by electronic apparatus for presenting precisely controlled stimuli and recording highly specific responses. In this context, a modern computer serves as the model or metaphor for cognitive psychology. The parallel lies not with the electrical wiring and other hardware, which are comparable to brain anatomy, but with the computer program, the software, which is comparable in restricted ways to human mental processes.

The computer receives information through data entry; the human mind obtains information through the process of perception. In the computer, this information is stored by pressing the "save" key, or it is stored automatically. Psychologists and other scientists are still in the very early stages of discovering how information is stored in human memory. Finally, programs enable the computer to manipulate the incoming information, compare it with previously stored information, and use both sources of data to emit a response, thereby solving problems. In the human mind, this manipulation of incoming and stored information is called thinking.

In summary, the computer and human mind share three basic processes: the input of information—perception; its storage—memory; and its use—thinking. The concept of information processing expresses these shared functions, referring to the ways human beings obtain, retain, and use information. But these processes are interactive, each influencing the others. Their borders are arbitrary, roughly marking different phases of cognition.

The computer model has clearly advanced cognitive psychology. But inevitably it includes limitations. Most important, the human mind makes meanings. It has an extraordinary capacity for doing so, whereas the computer remains inept in making its own meanings. The human mind *interprets* information. It searches constantly for the significance and implications of events in daily life, just as Bertha's mind did in studying various articles in *The Woman*. The human mind creates its own explanations, thereby deepening and broadening itself in unpredictable ways.

Reading *The Woman* gave Bertha a new view of women's place in the world and what she might do about it. It literally expanded her mind. In addition, it championed an English editor of momentous importance for her. Mary Wollstonecraft, born exactly 100 years before Bertha, almost single-handedly began the modern English-language feminist movement in the Western world.

Both women possessed a strong will, enjoyed writing, challenged injustice, and struggled with gender bias throughout society. As the saying goes, they also came from opposite ends of the rope, especially with respect to social status. Mary came from the lower class, Bertha from the upper.

Owing to her sexual behavior, giving birth outside wedlock, and perhaps because of her feminism, the public regarded Mary Wollstonecraft as a corrupt woman. But the poet William Blake, a personal friend, remembered Mary differently, as a gifted, sensitive human being. In a touching eulogy, he lamented the public perception and saluted her memory, thinking of her as a lonely pioneer.

Sensation and Perception

These cognitive activities—perception, memory, and thinking—are ways of knowing about the world and are hardly separable from one another. But perception stands at the beginning of the cognitive sequence. It is sometimes called the gateway to knowledge, the portal of the mind.

The processes of organizing and interpreting incoming sensory information are collectively called **perception**. Through perception, we learn about ourselves and our surroundings, using contributions from two sources: the present environment and past experience. On this basis, psychologists make a distinction between sensation, which comes first, and then perception; they have overlapping meanings. In **sensation**, a person becomes aware of present stimulation; sensation provides raw, unorganized information about the immediate environment, directly from the sense organs. A person experiences, for example, loud and whispered tones and shadows and lights through receptors in the ears and eyes. In perception, she combines this incoming sensory information with past experience, making an interpretation. She realizes that some friends have just arrived for her surprise birthday party.

When sensation and perception are compared with one another, sensation is more biological, closer to the neural activities of our sense organs. Perception is more cognitive, closer to the mental processes in the human mind. But perception requires sensation in the first place, and sensory information, by itself, makes little sense until it is associated with previously acquired information, stored as memories, expectations, and the like.

In advancing the cognitive viewpoint in the mid-20th century, Jerome Bruner noted that studies of perception commonly took place in a darkened laboratory with a participant carefully instructed about accuracy. Yet experiences in anthropology and sociology led him to appreciate the extent to which personal, social, and cultural factors could influence perception. Perceptual experience emerges from external and internal sources; the physical properties of wavelengths and psychological expectancies both influence the observer.

The ignored internal factors became Bruner's concern. In the "New Look" in perception, he examined all sorts of influences on the perceiving organism, including stress, mood, and language. Observers, he pointed out, mold their perceptions in accordance with personal expectancies.

At the outset of this research, he confronted people with incongruous stimuli, at odds with daily experience and quite different from the usual laboratory tasks. Using a tachistoscope for rapid exposure of visual images, he asked 28 college students individually to report everything about each of five briefly exposed images of playing cards. Some cards were normal; others were deviant, with the color of the suit reversed. When first confronted with a red two of spades, for example, some participants responded with a disruptive comment: "I'll be damned if I know . . ." But the major reactions, "two of spades" or "two of hearts," provided overwhelming evidence that perception is greatly determined by the observer's expectations.

In another instance, Bruner asked children from affluent and deprived backgrounds to manipulate an adjustable circle of light until it matched the sizes of various coins, ranging from pennies to half-dollars. As predicted, the children overestimated the size of the more valuable coins and underestimated the size of less valuable coins. And economically deprived children showed more value distortion than did the children from wealthy families (Bruner & Goodman, 1947). The children also showed greater distortion between a quarter and a nickel than between like-sized metal disks. Thus, even in the estimate of magnitude, presumably a simple matter of physical size, personal values confound judgment. This emphasis on personal and social needs and values became the cornerstone of the New Look, leading to more cognitively oriented studies of perception.

In other words, visual perception depends partly on what is in front of our eyes—the stimulus—and partly on what is behind our eyes—our memories and expectations about what we will see in the first place (Fernald, 1997). It emerges from both sources simultaneously.

Using current terms for these two sets of influences on perception, **bottom-up processing** starts with what is "out there," noting the available features of a stimulus, such as its shape, brightness, and movement. In the visual realm, the responding neural cells are called **feature detectors** because they react only to a single, highly specific characteristic of a stimulus—an oval line, a particular hue, a certain angle. Countless visual features are recorded in this fashion, although little is known as yet about how they are combined. In perceiving Bertha Pappenheim, feature detectors would yield information on the arch of her eyebrow, the shadow across her face, and the shape of her mouth, all of which are part of the overall impression.

In **top-down processing**, perception begins with what is already "in there," stored in memory, based on prior experience. It reflects the expectations an individual brings to a perceptual experience. In perceiving Bertha for the first time, some of this stored information would convey knowledge about people in general. Called a **schema**, this knowledge represents typical details about a particular stimulus or concept, specifying the usual conditions. In perception, it offers an overall framework or background of experience, including several integrated concepts; this framework is useful for perceiving something. A schema about people would include considerable information about the usual size and shape of their physical features, typical and atypical nonverbal behaviors, common range of vocalizations, and so forth. Schemas are efficient ways for the brain to store information. Top-down processing takes advantage of what the perceiver already knows about people, thereby facilitating the incorporation of bottom-up information about a particular individual. Other stored information would be more personal or temporary, as in William Blake's view of Mary Wollstonecraft as a friend and lonely pioneer.

Bottom-up processing starts with the stimulus, top-down with the perceiver. Our capacity for quick, accurate perception of complex events depends on both approaches (Figure 7.1).

As noted earlier, human beings automatically engage in parallel distributive processing. They manipulate different pieces of information at the *same* time in different regions of the brain. In a flash, the human being can recognize a friend's voice, note that he is no longer wearing a beard, and resist the odor of his cigar. This experience involves bottom-up and top-down processing. Moreover, the separate bits of sensory information, detected by primarily

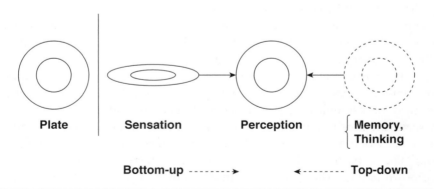

Figure 7.1   Information Processing in Perception. The solid circles and oval represent a plate, the dashed circles a plate in memory. That plate is round, but from an angle the sensation is an oval retinal image. And yet, with the contributions of memory and thinking, the plate is correctly perceived as circular. The combined influences of bottom-up and top-down processing create a perception that matches the object, despite the limited sensory impression.

inborn domain-specific cognitive mechanisms, are transmitted by different nerve pathways and reach different areas of the brain, where they are processed simultaneously. The sensory systems operate for the most part independently, but the sights, sounds, and odors of the same scene are relevant to one another, encoded as different aspects of the same experience. In short, separate but parallel processing permits human beings to perceive different dimensions of the same object without confusion among them (LeDoux, 2002).

Studies of word recognition support an *interactive model* of perception, combining up and down processes. They show that people recognize a given letter more readily when it is part of a word than when it is included in a nonword. The top-down context supplied by the word aids bottom-up processing of the letter. But how can word recognition facilitate recognition of the letter? Without letter recognition, the word would not have been perceived in the first place. This phenomenon, called the word-superiority effect, has prompted research and debate, and various explanations have been proposed (Balota & Cortese, 2000). The most common view is that neither bottom-up nor top-down processing need be complete before the other can commence. Various subprocesses could be operating simultaneously, provided that their outputs are continuously available to the other concurrent processes.

In summary, human information processing takes advantage of its multiple pathways. As more and more feature detectors become activated, the perceiver increasingly anticipates a certain outcome, and this anticipation facilitates the perception of further details. These processes are interactive, almost instantaneous, and occur automatically.

The great advantage of top-down processing lies in the efficiency it brings to bottom-up contributions. The perceiver need not start anew in each encounter with a person, object, or event. But a great disadvantage occurs whenever the perceiver has an incorrect expectation, producing a disruptive set.

Colloquially called a "mind set," a **set** is a readiness to respond in a certain way regardless of the stimulation. It is a tendency to perceive a *certain* something or to perceive it in a *certain* fashion. The public was predisposed to perceive Mary Wollstonecraft in an unfavorable light. William Blake showed a readiness to perceive her differently. For anyone, it is almost impossible to approach a familiar scene from an entirely neutral standpoint.

Mary and Bertha shared a mental set about family life. One a promiscuous pauper, the other a celibate princess, they both viewed family life with intense dissatisfaction, especially the preferential treatment accorded boys. Mary twice became pregnant outside marriage; Bertha never became pregnant and never married at all. Both experienced unhappiness to the point of depression.

Mary's book, *A Vindication of the Rights of Women*, became the opening salvo in the modern feminist movement. Impressed by this book, Bertha translated it into German, paying for its publication herself. That work launched her career as a feminist and, eventually, as the leader of the women's movement in Germany (Kaplan, 1984).

Processes in Memory

Bertha's fervor for feminism, like Mary's, arose initially from childhood experiences of favoritism toward her brother. Those early scenes, etched firmly into her memory, decades later played a major role in her dedication to "the cause." She also recalled her high-daughter imprisonment in Vienna. In Frankfurt, those memories persisted, even while the environment helped her move constructively toward overt resistance.

This capacity for reviving prior experience, called **memory**, is not a single faculty. Among its many forms, the most fundamental include recall and recognition. In *recall,* a prior experience is reproduced without cues. Try to recall the face of your kindergarten teacher. In *recognition,* the details are available. From among several faces, can you select the face of your kindergarten teacher? A much easier memory task, recognition simply shows awareness of prior experience.

People use the term *memory* as a catch-all expression, but specialists in this area usually employ a modifier. Not a separate, unitary mechanism, memory involves diverse mental processes and all sorts of brain organs operating in different ways. Just which ones become involved and how they interact depend on the context evoking the memory (Mandler, 1985).

This position of course raises a fundamental question about the structure of memory. Do human beings possess a single, flexible memory system that includes different ways of processing different kinds of information? Or do they possess several separate memory systems, each designed to respond to different memory tasks? Either way, the concern lies with the cognitive design of memory, not the neural design of the brain (Balota & Cortese, 2000; Estes, 1991).

For decades, psychologists have studied this design in terms of three stages: sensory memory, short-term memory, and long-term memory. But the first stage is not explicitly cognitive, for the incoming information has not yet reached the central nervous system.

Sensory and Short-Term Memory

For just a moment after experiencing any event, the peripheral nervous system contains a brief impression of that event. In this first stage of memory, known as reception, or **sensory memory**, the fleeting residual information from the senses remains in the sensory system; it has not faded away or been transferred to the central nervous system. Sometimes you can hear a remark made an instant earlier, although you were not conscious of that remark when it was uttered. This auditory residue is a form of sensory memory, called *echoic memory,* for it is "still in your ears." Similarly, you can still feel a fly on your cheek for a moment after it has flown away, which is another sensory memory, *haptic memory,* referring to the sense of touch. The image of an exploding firework remains in your visual experience for an instant after the display—*iconic memory.* All these experiences show that some trace of the sensory input remains, very briefly, after the experience has been terminated.

This unprocessed information will disappear without some prompt effort to retain it. For retention, it must pass to the second stage. Originally known as **short-term memory**, the second stage may continue up to 30 seconds following the event, during which the new information is being prepared for storage or it is being ignored. If not processed, it will be lost. In other words, short-term memory can serve as an organizing and loading platform for long-term memory storage.

A major advance in revealing the architecture of human memory, specifically short-term memory, occurred partly by chance. George Miller reluctantly presented his tentative research findings in a public setting, consoling himself by giving them a whimsical title, "The Magical Number Seven, Plus or Minus Two" (Miller, 1956). He impishly explained that he had been persecuted by this number for seven years, assaulted by it in the mass media, and bedeviled in his research. It assumed various disguises, sometimes a little larger, sometimes slightly smaller, but it never changed beyond recognition. Some design lay behind this number, he mused.

In research on perception and memory, Miller had noticed a common element: The maximum amount of information managed in a task at any one time was approximately seven items, whether the task involved the loudness of tones, intensities of taste, or brightness of visual displays. Using different tests, he found this same average limit of seven in the span of immediate memory. On these bases, it seemed that human beings have some rather specific limitations for the management of new information, built into them through learning or the structure of the nervous system. This suggestion of a fixed capacity for processing or retaining information gave many psychologists what they needed—a substantial platform for further study. The human mind had fixed, short-term limits for perceiving or remembering new information, usually around seven items but sometimes ranging from five to nine (Miller, 1956).

The concept of short-term memory has become popular among the public, but people seriously misunderstand it. They think it means the ability to remember events that occurred just a few minutes, hours, or even days earlier.

But after any of those intervals, the experiences are stored in long-term memory, or they have never been remembered at all. During short-term memory—which lasts only a matter of seconds—information is being converted to long-term memory, or it disappears from awareness.

Miller's report still stands as a classic, but current investigators view its central message as most closely related to the principle of grouping, or "chunking," considered as a means of increasing the short-term storage capacity. In fact, Miller was somewhat tentative about setting the specific limits as seven items, apparently doing so partly through coincidence, partly through a light-hearted effort to generate interest. Today, speculations about other fixed limits have drawn mixed reactions (Avons, Ward, & Russo, 2000; Bachelder, 2000; Cowan, 2000).

Is the storage, whatever its magnitude, a capacity-limited system, meaning that it only has space for a specific number of chunks of information? Or is it time-limited, meaning that it can remain available only for a certain interval while the individual rehearses new information? Or is it both? And what is a "chunk" of information? Neither Miller nor current investigators have provided a satisfactory answer to these questions (Beaman, 2000). The issue remains unsettled, although this research has clearly advanced our understanding of the organization of human memory.

With short-term memory increasingly understood as a prelude to storage, many psychologists began speaking instead of working memory, emphasizing not the brief interval but the numerous cognitive activities in progress. Some investigators use these terms interchangeably. Still others think of short-term memory as one of the components, or activities, of working memory. From the latter viewpoint, **working memory** serves both functions: as a system for holding and manipulating newly acquired information prior to its use and also for preparing that information for long-term storage (Baddeley, 1992). This viewpoint emphasizes that much of memory is an active process, not a passive state. In many respects, working memory is *conscious thought*—the time and place for doing mental work. To become conscious, information must come from perception or memory. In either case, it occupies the mind at that moment. Although working memory can apprehend only a very limited amount of information at any one time, in the course of a day it records, temporarily, the immense amounts of information that become our daily consciousness.

Laboratory studies have confirmed that the limits in working memory are not determined solely by the amount of information but also by the ways we process it. Ask someone to read aloud slowly to you the following sequence of seven single-digit numbers. Afterward, try to repeat it: 7 2 9 3 4 8 1. Then use the same procedures with a list of seven random two-digit numbers. For most people the first list poses a challenge. The second presents an impossible task. What is the reason?

Our span for short-term or working memory depends not only on the number of items or chunks but also on the time it takes for rehearsal, that is, for saying to ourselves at least once the list we just heard. We can remember more single-digit than double-digit numbers because we can say more of them in a limited period. And we have a longer span when we say the numbers quickly rather than slowly. Various studies have demonstrated that our short-term capacity for repeating the list is limited to the amount of material we can repeat to ourselves in approximately two or three seconds. If rehearsal takes longer, the first part of the list will have faded from working memory before we can rehearse the end of the list. A similar limitation occurs in the visual realm (Baddeley, 1992; Baddeley, Thompson, & Buchanan, 1975).

In processing relatively simple information, working memory may use rote memory or rehearsal. More complex information requires more elaborate **encoding**, a term that emphasizes that the new experience must be thought about or transformed in some special way to be well remembered. This more textured encoding process involves at least three dimensions: organization, chunking, and cueing.

In *organization*, new information is arranged or rearranged in some systematic, sensible manner. Consider the following seven words: *dog, buy, couple, floor, store, walk, groceries*. One obvious way to enhance recall is to organize them into a story about a couple who walks to a store with their dog to buy groceries that spill on the floor. Consider another series: *drink, festive, bar, cool, eating, ah, goodbyes*. This memory task offers a story too. It also offers an alphabetical organization in which each word is a letter longer than its predecessor. The learner thereby knows the first letter and length of each word, which serve as alternative memory aids (Fernald, 1997). These examples are contrived, but they illustrate the need and value of imposing some meaningful organization on the material to be learned.

In laboratory research on organization, some participants are asked to remember long lists of words using *free recall*, meaning any convenient order. Others must remember the same lists using *serial recall*, which requires memorization in a particular sequence. Comparisons between the two groups show a surprising result. Serial recall, a seemingly more difficult task, produces better memory. The reason appears to lie with the minimal but *specific* organization required by serial learning (Earhard, 1967).

A second dimension of encoding concerns the amount of material to be memorized. If the prior lists were three or four times their current length, they would constitute a formidable task, exceeding the capacity of working memory. In *chunking*, items that are similar in some way are grouped together, producing fewer categories than the number of items in the full list. Then the chunks can be recalled one at a time, each including its own items, providing their number is appropriately limited. Otherwise, more chunks are required. For example, the prior lists include fourteen items altogether. They can be recalled by thinking of them in two chunks or groups, each with seven items or in two chunks with two subgroups each, none containing more than four or five items. In this way, all chunks become manageable.

In a third encoding dimension, called *cueing*, the learner finds or prepares some stimulus that serves as a signal or reminder for retrieving the stored memories. At one time or another, all of us have been at a loss for cues. We exclaim: "Oh, I know that! I just can't recall it right now." The memory has no ready means for evoking it.

Retrieval cues involve stimuli relevant to any of the senses. One well-known example appears in Marcel Proust's passage about memories associated with a particular pastry. Even decades later, its odor and taste served as powerful cues for evoking vivid childhood memories of this early treat.

In other instances, the retrieval is even more automatic. An emotional experience produces a flashbulb memory, so called because the details are so completely etched in memory. Even without sensory cues, the memory is readily produced—though not necessarily with greater accuracy (Schmolck, Buffalo, & Squire, 2000). At the height of their father's illness, Wilhelm shook Bertha vigorously because she was eavesdropping at the sickroom door. That sudden experience apparently produced a flashbulb memory for Bertha; she could not forget the details of Wilhelm's anger, her fear, and even what she was wearing at that time.

Simple repetition of the details, called *rehearsal*, also serves to extend the span of working memory. It is not considered encoding because the new information is simply repeated and practiced, without arranging it into some meaningful organization, creating chunks, or establishing retrieval cues. One of the most prominent reasons for so-called poor memory is the absence of careful encoding or rehearsal.

Memories in Long-Term Storage

Like perception, information comes into working memory from two directions: sensory memory and memory in long-term storage. In **long-term memory**, which has no known limit for capacity, information is maintained for indefinite intervals ranging up to the individual's full lifetime. Sometimes simply called *storage*, long-term memory is not an intermediate or processing stage. The information has been deposited in the memory system. It is memory in the usual sense of bygone experiences stored somewhere in the system. We are not conscious of long-term memory until seeking access to it. In contrast, working memory is a conscious process.

The question of different memory systems and processes emerges prominently in the study of long-term memory. Contemporary psychology has identified several varieties, and they differ from one another in the ways they are retrieved, as well as their content. Two conspicuous pairs have been labeled accordingly: explicit and implicit memory.

Explicit memory reflects our usual manner of thinking about how we retrieve a memory. When we search our memory storage, making a definite, controlled effort to retrieve an earlier experience, the outcome is called **explicit memory**. The retrieval process may be slow, sometimes halting and laborious. "Let's see. Where did I leave the key to the front door?" Other memories occur without any direct attempt at remembering. In **implicit memory**, we respond automatically and quickly, even without awareness of attempting retrieval. With a key in hand, you insert it into the lock without asking yourself: "Let's see now. What do I do with this object?" An implicit memory enters consciousness suddenly, just as Bertha, without intent, remembered Wilhelm shaking her at their father's door. In other words, explicit and implicit memory differ in the intent and effort expended in retrieving the stored experience.

Explicit memory is often viewed in two categories, specific and general. The former, called *episodic memory*, involves events—specific personal experiences, such as the weather yesterday, an embarrassing moment in biology class, your first kiss with an unrelated adult. You remember particular episodes. In contrast, memory for general facts and broad realms of information, not attached to any particular time or place or event, is called *semantic memory*. It is more diffuse, less tied to a specific context. Its extensive range includes the meanings of words, shapes of common objects, ways of nature, and so forth. Thus, episodic and semantic, the specific and general, are the two main categories of explicit memory.

Implicit memory includes conditioned responses, primed memories, and motor memories. As described earlier, a *conditioned response* arises through associative learning, the pairing of stimuli and responses. A *primed memory* occurs when some prior stimulus prompts or improves recall. For example, observing an old photo of someone not seen for many years increases the chances of recognizing that person in a crowd some days later. And finally, a *motor memory* is a physical behavior or sequence of behaviors performed automatically, without any substantial conscious effort, such as riding a bicycle, making a cup of coffee, and remembering how to access e-mail. Many motor skills are also known as *kinesthetic memory*, for they are based on movements of muscles and other body parts. Most people, years after their last time on a bicycle, ride successfully without directions or reminders about pedaling, braking, steering, and balancing. But we certainly do forget some skills, such as how to operate an old computer or execute a certain dance step learned years earlier. All these differences—within implicit memory, among the types of explicit memory, and between explicit and implicit memory—suggest that long-term memory is not a single, unitary capacity (Figure 7.2).

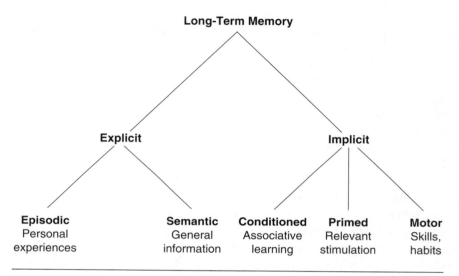

Figure 7.2   Types of Long-Term Memory. These different memories are distinguished by the kinds of information involved and the most responsive areas of the brain. Generally speaking, explicit memories are located toward the front of the brain, implicit memories toward the back. Conditioned memories refer chiefly to classical conditioning; primed memories involve cues that prompt retrieval.

Little is known about the limits of the long-term memory system, and investigators are just beginning to discover the most relevant brain areas. These include the cerebral cortex for association among memories, the hippocampus for the formation of new memories, and the cerebellum for the storage of well-practiced habits, especially the coordination of body movements.

An earlier description reported the case of H. M. who, in the 1950s, had his hippocampal regions removed to relieve epileptic seizures. The surgery ended the seizures but left this young man unable to create new, explicit memories. Living a confused life, he still possesses normal awareness of immediate stimulation but remains unable to recall events that have occurred even just a few moments earlier. One time a psychologist tested him for heat sensitivity by placing on H.M.'s forearms disks that were gradually heated to increasing temperatures. He tolerated unexpectedly high temperatures, and the psychologist pointed out the slightly discolored circles they left on the skin of anyone taking this test. But moments afterward, before the circles had faded away, H. M. walked to the nurses' station and asked why he had circles on his arms. Later, he ate a full meal and when a staff member offered him a second meal shortly thereafter, he consumed that meal as well (Hebben, 2005). Clearly, he had no memory of the test experience or his recent meals. Even the bodily conditions were insufficient to stimulate recall.

In several sessions some years ago, H. M. attempted to master a novel drawing task that required the use of a mirror and screen. Before every practice session, he declared that he had never encountered the task previously, which showed a deficiency in explicit memory. He could not remember the prior practice episode. On each occasion, the investigator had to explain the instructions and apparatus anew. But it is noteworthy that, apparently without searching his memory, H. M. performed with increasingly greater competence in each successive session, demonstrating implicit memory (Milner, 1965).

On these bases, forgetting becomes a complex issue. Should H. M. be charged with forgetting when he cannot retain something in the first place? Does forgetting occur as a result of defective working memory? Should someone be called forgetful after failing to attend to the original event?

Information that cannot be retrieved is said to involve **forgetting**. However, the failure may not be attributable to inadequate memory. People sometimes decide that they have a faulty memory for something when in fact that experience has never been fully encoded, or incorporated, in the first place.

It has been speculated instead that memories in storage gradually fade away, a view of forgetting called **decay theory**. The unused memory perhaps deteriorates through the continuous metabolic action of the nervous system, wearing away the memory trace. Yet the role of decay alone has not been demonstrated, chiefly because it is impossible to rule out other influences on forgetting.

According to **interference theory**, memories are lost because they are disrupted by other memories. The warehouse gets too full; memories interfere with one another. In one type, called *proactive interference*, earlier memories disrupt the storage or retrieval of later memories. Information previously in the warehouse somehow prevents access to more recent information. In another type, called *retroactive interference*, later memories disrupt the storage or retrieval of earlier memories. New information in the warehouse has been piled onto the old, apparently blocking access to that prior information. Extensive evidence supports both types of interference, which may involve failures in retaining or retrieving (Anderson & Neely, 1996).

One way to cope with retroactive interference is to avoid activity immediately after acquiring new information. After studying for an examination, rest and relaxation, and especially a good night's sleep, are the best prescription. In other words, do not engage in highly stimulating activities and certainly do not study for another exam. Retention following sleep is better than retention after the waking state (Dempster, 1988; Jenkins & Dallenbach, 1924).

Still another view of forgetting arises in psychoanalytic theory. In repression, also known as **motivated forgetting**, the memories allegedly remain in long-term storage, but the person does not want to be aware of them, which reflects a problem in retrieving. The necessary cues, no longer available, presumably become activated only in certain moments of therapy or other unusual circumstances.

Then, too, forgetting may occur through **inadequate retrieval cues**. Again, the memory remains in long-term storage, but there is no resistance to recall, as in motivated forgetting. Instead, the memory has not been sufficiently integrated into the vast network of associated concepts by which it might be recovered. Moreover, the immediate external cues are also insufficient. The problem here may be poor recording in the original circumstances.

When a memory cannot be retrieved, returning to the circumstances directly or vicariously may produce adequate cues. Visiting the original setting again can enhance recall, known as *context-dependent memory*. Also, adopting the mental or physical state one was experiencing when the events took place, even without returning to the scene, may improve recall, known as *state-dependent memory* (Bower, 1981; Godden & Baddeley, 1975). For Bertha, returning to Vienna, falling into another depression, or any other repetition of the original circumstances presumably would aid recall of those earlier days.

Modern psychology emphasizes memory as an active process, especially in encoding and retrieval. Human beings do not file away memories in some complete and static fashion, later to be automatically evoked in perfect detail by the proper cue. Under such conditions, our storage and retrieval systems would be clearly overloaded. Memories, instead, are fragments of past experience. We reconstruct them from bits and pieces. We assemble our memories, and the requisite mental processes can create distortions and even false memories.

Bertha's reconstructions brought forth early memories of her parents' preference for Wilhelm, her father's restrictions on her social life, and the scenes at his bedside. Some of these memories were distorted; others were incomplete. But the roots of her feminism lay in these recollections, suddenly given a focus through Mary Wollstonecraft's book.

Prompted to write her own feminist literature, Bertha produced a three-act play called *Women's Rights*. Her language left no doubt about her views.

Women deserved the opportunity to earn a reasonable wage, maintain property, and enter into legal contracts, all of which they were denied (Pappenheim, 1899). Her thinking was logical and dramatic, and she announced it with conviction.

Thinking and its accompaniments, especially language, constitute a major element of human cognition. They are the primary means for the transmission and evolution of culture.

Thought and Language

While Bruner and Miller continued their studies of perception and memory, Herb Simon had been thinking about thinking. He and Al Newell planned to teach something to a computer, using the instructions to the machine as a crude model of human thinking. For this new venture, chess seemed too complicated, so they chose instead to teach the machine to discover proofs in Newton's *Principia Mathematica*. They began with theorem 2.15, and when Simon wrote a long-hand proof in sufficient detail that it could be programmed into the computer, he celebrated that moment as the birthday of problem solving by computer, calling this program the *Logic Theorist* (Simon, 1980).

Later, combining the Logic Theorist with other programs, Simon and his colleagues developed the *General Problem Solver,* a more versatile program that considered each problem in terms of a current state and goal. For someone traveling from a certain place in one city to a certain place in another, for example, the place of origin represented the current state and the next immediate destination represented the goal or subgoal. The number of miles between the two points represented the difference between them. By considering the distance and options, the computer could decide at each current state whether to walk, ride a train, or take an airplane. For traveling from Boston to San Francisco, a distance longer than 500 miles, the computer would dictate taking an airplane. But first, for the 15 miles to Logan Airport, it would recommend the train. And to reach the train station, less than a mile from home, it would suggest walking. Using this means-end analysis repeatedly, performed at each stage on the basis of solutions at prior stages, the General Problem Solver eliminated the difference between the current state and next goal, eventually solving the problem (Fernald & Fernald, 1985).

After the success of the General Problem Solver, Simon and his colleagues programmed the psychological foundations for thinking, called the *Elementary Perceiver and Memorizer.* It provided the basis for a theory about rote verbal learning, thinking, and problem solving in human beings.

Components in Thinking

A general term for the representation and manipulation of information, **thinking** includes almost the full span of mental activities. It ranges from fantasy to high-level problem solving. Rarely used without a modifier, it includes *analytical thinking,* which is separating a whole into its basic components, and *synthetic thinking,* which proceeds in the opposite direction, developing a whole from diverse parts. It includes *convergent thinking,* aimed at discovering a central idea or single answer to a problem, and *divergent thinking,* which produces several different answers to the same problem (Sternberg, 2000). Except for immediate sensation, thinking depends on memory.

But what do we manipulate in thinking? To a large extent we manipulate concepts. A **concept** designates a category or a general idea about something; it considers a group of objects or events as equivalent in some respect, for they possess a common property. Many words express concepts. The word *book* expresses a concept; it refers to sheets of printed pages bound together. A textbook, novel, and biography are subclasses of a book; each of them also represents a concept. Thinking is based on concepts that, in turn, are acquired through thinking.

The words *Principia Mathematica,* meaning Newton's book, refer to that particular object; therefore, they are not a concept. The words *Logic Theorist* do not designate a concept, for they too refer to a particular object, event, person, place, or other specific instance.

In effective thought, concepts must be organized in some meaningful fashion, often expressed in a *proposition,* which is a statement or declaration. Thinking in the **propositional mode** uses words and makes a statement; it proposes or asserts something in words. As symbols, these words typically do not resemble their referents; they do not appear like whatever they represent.

In contrast, *images* have the appearance of their referents. A visual image of a book looks like a book; an auditory image of a song sounds like that song, and so forth for gustatory, kinesthetic, and other sensory modalities. Even without immediate sensory experience, some images may be quite vivid. Thus, thinking in the **imaginal mode** involves the mental manipulation of physical likenesses of some things that were previously experienced. Mental images can express concepts, and as reflections of previous experience, they play a vital role in memory.

These two modes, propositional and imaginal, are viewed as independent but connected systems for expressing concepts and representing and processing other information (Katz, 2000). Relying on words and perceptual experience, they appear throughout human cognition (Figure 7.3).

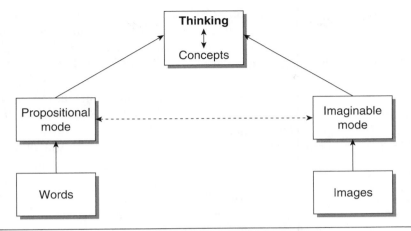

Figure 7.3   Components in Human Thinking. The solid, two-headed arrow indicates that human beings think with concepts and develop concepts by thinking. Words and images express concepts, embedded in the propositional and imaginable modes. The dashed, two-headed arrow shows that the relationship between these parallel modes remains unclear, awaiting further research.

Approaches to Problem Solving

When computers are employed for the type of thinking called problem solving, such as assisting in medical diagnosis, this use is called **artificial intelligence.** The aim is not to enable computers to perform in a human-like manner but simply to produce efficient solutions to human problems.

As noted in the work of Herb Simon, psychologists and others also use computers to study the problem-solving process, a procedure called **computer simulation** or computer modeling. The computer and its programs are constructed to represent elements of human thinking, including the relationships of parts to one another and to the whole. This simulation occurs without any effort to represent brain physiology or anatomy. In other words, computer simulation requires investigators to develop hypotheses about human thinking, and it provides opportunities for testing of those hypotheses.

As the pioneering effort in computer simulation, the *Logic Theorist* eventually produced proofs for three-fourths of the theorems in *Principia Mathematica.* Most importantly it did so without considering every possible alternative at each step. An exhaustive search of that sort, using an algorithm, would have required more than a hundred years (Newell, Shaw, & Simon, 1958).

An explicit set of directions for solving a specific problem, an **algorithm** is completely unambiguous—a finite number of steps indicating *exactly* what to do at any point. It provides a guaranteed solution, whether the problem involves calculating the average salary of social workers, making a cake, or setting up high-tech electronic equipment. An algorithm for the salaries might begin as follows: (1) Place all the numbers in a column, one below another, except for the first number. (2) Justify all the numbers against a right-hand margin. (3) Draw a horizontal line below those numbers. (4) Call the digits in the extreme right column the current column. (5) Add all digits in the current column. (6) If the sum is less than 10, record that sum below the line under the current column. (7) If the sum is greater than 10, record the . . . (Carberry, Khalil, Leathrum, & Levy, 1979).

Computers in artificial intelligence commonly employ algorithms to check spelling, complete a memory search, and play certain games. But to solve some problems they may require tremendous amounts of time. Experts calculate, for example, that the many possible moves in a chess game would take the fastest computer decades to consider. Algorithms are most useful with a limited number of alternatives.

Human beings use algorithms in some situations. A man searching for a lost earring may walk back and forth in the grass, from end to end, each trip just beyond the unexplored edge of the prior one. Providing he looks carefully and has lost the earring in that grass, he is employing an algorithmic-type strategy, assuring a successful solution to the problem. But instructions for everyday tasks are not prepared as algorithms; human beings typically think in faster ways.

These faster ways are called heuristics. A **heuristic** is a speculative guide, rule of thumb, or shortcut for solving a problem, often increasing efficiency but providing no guaranteed solution. It offers an approach likely to yield a prompt solution, as opposed to a tedious search of all possibilities. The crowning achievement of the *Logic Theorist* was its successful use of heuristics, providing the proofs in a much shorter time.

In daily life, people commonly begin with some readily available heuristic, the most convenient strategy. Or they use the most promising strategy. The man who lost an earring would not start a systematic search at one edge of a yard. He would look immediately in the place where he thinks he lost it. Then he might search in the shortest grass or places near the walkway. Without heuristics, human beings would take forever accomplishing the tasks in daily living. Instead, they become *selective*, using all sorts of heuristics, ranging from working with probabilities to establishing subgoals for complex problems.

Investigators have studied heuristics in all sorts of problem solving. They have focused on the constraints in problem solving, valid and invalid conclusions, gains and losses in group decision making, and unsuccessful heuristics

(Holyoak & Spellman, 1993; Kerr & Tindale, 2004). In virtually all such studies, two forms of thinking appear: inductive and deductive reasoning. And they are readily evident throughout daily life.

For example, to promote her new book, *Women's Rights,* Bertha remained undecided how to acknowledge her authorship. In reaching a decision, she probably used both these forms of reasoning. People everywhere use them in rapid, mixed ways without even thinking about them. In many respects, they represent Piaget's formal operations, for they involve abstract thinking.

The process of **inductive reasoning** proceeds from particular facts to a general conclusion that may explain something about those facts. But it does not yield a logically certain conclusion. It produces one or several well-founded, fairly probable conclusions (Sternberg, 2000).

In Bertha's time, almost all books were authored by men. Men had more credibility as authors. At this early stage of feminist thought, a feminist book by a female author would seem self-serving. Using these facts, Bertha could never be certain which choice would be best: publishing her work anonymously, employing a pseudonym, or using her own name. Through inductive reasoning, she could only generate possibilities and choose among them. Eventually, she decided to use a pseudonym.

In selecting a particular pseudonym, a deductive approach would prove useful. The process of **deductive reasoning** begins with some general statements or premises and tests a specific instance. If the premises are sound and the thinking is logical, deductive reasoning leads to a valid, specific conclusion. It shows whether a certain decision is warranted, based on the premises. If the premises are wrong, the conclusion may be logically valid, but it will be incorrect (Sternberg, 2000).

Bertha wanted subtle evidence that the book was her work. The pseudonym should give her disguised credit. Thus, a deductive approach might take this form:

A good pseudonym will suggest my name.

P. Berthold suggests my name.

Hence, *P. Berthold* will be a good pseudonym.

This pseudonym uses Bertha's initials in reverse order, giving her subtle credit. This sequence is sometimes called a *syllogism,* a formal type of reasoning in which a specific instance is deduced from two or more premises. People in daily life do not construct formal syllogisms—a practice left largely to logicians—but they regularly employ deductive reasoning in this way, however attenuated.

A good pseudonym would also suggest male authorship. Further deductive reasoning might proceed along these lines:

A good pseudonym will seem like a man's name.

P. Berthold seems like a man's name.

Hence, *P. Berthold* will be a good pseudonym.

Berthold is a masculine version of her first name, suggesting male authorship. Whatever her reasoning, Bertha chose this pseudonym.

In daily life, people employ combinations of inductive and deductive reasoning easily and regularly without thinking about their thinking. But they also make mistakes.

Errors in inductive reasoning occur because people do not check the facts carefully. Instead, they search for facts that bolster their beliefs about the best solution. This tendency to seek support for our beliefs and to ignore contrary evidence is so widespread, even among scientists, that it is called the *confirmation bias.* Well aware of this bias, Charles Darwin made a point of jotting down immediately any observation that failed to confirm his views. Observations endorsing them needed no special attention.

Errors in deductive reasoning occur on a different basis. Bertha strongly believed that social workers should be underpaid. The lower salary would remind them that they were pursuing a calling—like physicians, ministers, and educators—rather than holding a job. She reasoned this way:

High salaries do not attract altruistic people.

Good social workers must be altruistic.

Hence, good social workers will not be attracted by high salaries.

But the conclusion does not follow. Both premises are incorrect. They are stated too broadly, which is often the error in deductive reasoning. High salaries may attract *some* altruistic people. And *some* good social workers may not be altruistic. Many physicians, educators, and others today show these exceptions.

In fact, Bertha herself proved an exception. Her daily life as a social worker displayed bedrock altruism; her evenings offered privilege and gentility in the style of Old Vienna.

Language: Symbols of Thought

In earlier days, Bertha captured Breuer's interest through her storytelling, aptly calling it "chimney sweeping"—cleaning the dark places in her life.

In her darkest hours, she coined an expression that Breuer found most compelling, one still widely used to refer to all forms of psychotherapy today: "the talking cure." Offering enrichment sessions for children from The Home, she honored her little visitors with a special title, "Tuesday Guests." Throughout her career, she used language skillfully, and language of course aids problem solving.

At a more basic level, language aids thought. These two processes develop and function together. For some psychologists, they are inseparable. In fact, language is sometimes described as overt thought. A true **language** is a system for manipulating symbols of thought, providing an infinite number of meanings and messages, punctuated in written and oral form with stylistic devices.

The basic elements of language are three: phonemes, morphemes, and syntax. A **phoneme** is the smallest functional unit of sound in a language. English has 26 letters, but the pronunciation of some of them, together with certain pairs of letters, produces 40 basic sound units in our language. Composed of one or more phonemes, a **morpheme** is the smallest unit of meaning in a language. The work *speak* is a morpheme. The word *speaking* includes two morphemes—the verb and the gerundive *ing*, which acquires its meaning in conjunction with the verb. And finally, **syntax** is the set of rules for organizing various units—words, clauses, sentences—within a language.

Infants know nothing of morphemes and syntax, and they hear phonemes as a stream of unintelligible sounds. How do they break up this speech? How do they begin to make use of it?

This question in fact became a pivotal point in support of emerging cognitive psychology. Linguists viewed grammar, syntax, and other language structures as too complex to be acquired solely through reinforcement. Especially when applied infrequently and irregularly, reinforcement cannot produce the exquisite capacity for language demonstrated by normal people. A major confrontation with behaviorism occurred when Noam Chomsky, a linguist, reviewed B. F. Skinner's book, *Verbal Behavior* (1957), written from the viewpoint of nurture, describing how language is used. Chomsky's review, from the standpoint of nature, described how language is acquired (Chomsky, 1959). Pointing to the indisputable contributions of the organism, he and other linguists thereby earned themselves a solid place in the cognitive revolution.

These contributions become manifest in the phenomenal speed with which very young children master language, the major instrument for human communication. They do so readily because at birth they are "wired" for acquiring the rules for using phonemes and morphemes and for creating appropriate syntax. Observing the similarity of languages throughout the world, even in nonessential ways, linguists speculated about a universal grammar, an inborn tendency for language acquisition that enables the enormous flexibility of our thought and expression (Chomsky, 1959).

In addition to the speed of language learning, behaviorism also did not account well for the child's steady progress and predictable errors in language mastery. Abundant evidence has shown that all normal children proceed through essentially the same stages in the acquisition of language, progressing from cooing and babbling in infancy to word recognition and naming by the end of the first year. During the second year, words appear in combinations, accompanied by typical errors. Later still, sentences progress from simple to complex. Eventually, the child uses basically correct syntax and considerably longer sentences, though improvements continue for years (Fernald, 1997).

Between the ages of two and six years, most children increase their vocabularies by approximately 10 words per day, reaching more than 10,000 words, and this process continues at a slower rate well into adulthood. The larger vocabulary offers much greater potential for expressing thoughts. But does language shape our thinking?

An early study of the Inuit, living constantly in snow, indicated that they had many more words for snow than did people living in the upper Mississippi Valley and that Aztecs, in their hot climate, used only one word to speak of ice and snow (Whorf, 1956). This particular research has been called into question, but it brought forth the hypothesis of **linguistic relativity**, stating that language determines thought. Later studies of the Dani, in New Guinea, showed that they had only two words for colors, one representing warm colors and the other cold colors. But when tested for color recognition and color matching, they performed as well as speakers of English, who use almost a dozen basic words for different colors (Rosch, 1973). The hypothesis holds only to a limited degree; it is stated too strongly (Pullum, 1991).

Language does not determine thought, although it certainly shapes and influences it. This influence is readily evident when you learn new words, such as *gestalt* and *morpheme,* enabling you to think about things differently or more precisely. Studies have shown, for example, that people would rather pay taxes to "halt rising crime" than for "law enforcement," although the funds go to the same places. And they are more favorably inclined toward "assistance to the poor" than toward "welfare" (Rasinski, 1989). The descriptive phrases have more appeal than the labels. People also prefer to support an endeavor with an 80% chance of success rather than one with a 20% chance of failure (Kahneman & Tversky, 1984). From the commercial world to social activism, people invent euphemistic expressions to induce favorable thoughts about their enterprises. A simple example appears in the abortion issue: "Pro Choice" and "Pro Life."

In Bertha's day, the influence of language on thought became readily evident in the "woman question," as the feminist movement was sometimes called. Moreover, all women were believed best suited for careers in the "maternal professions," such as teaching and nursing. That language would offend both genders today. Language indeed influences thought, as testified by our efforts to degender English.

The expression "high daughters" ridiculed the upper-class young women in Bertha's Vienna. She knew of this derision, just as she knew about the "maternal professions," career pathways that seemed far beyond her capabilities during her early illness. At that time, her prospects for a satisfying home life appeared dismal too, based on her sharp opposition to marriage and conventional family life.

Had she stayed in Vienna, she might have remained sick and distressed much of her life, plagued by a spectrum of disorders. If she then came to cognitive therapy, especially after the humanistic approach, she would have been in for a rude surprise.

The Cognitive Therapies

The major humanistic and cognitive therapies are distinctly different; in fact, they are opposed, for they begin with very different assumptions. In the humanistic, person-centered approach, therapists assume that patients know best, and they follow the patients' lead. In cognitive therapy, therapists assume that they, the experts, know best and request the patient to follow their instructions explicitly.

At the time of her father's illness, Bertha wore golden handcuffs. Her resentment of this status and the demands of her nightly nursing drove her into bed. She broke down, exhausted by too much work, the lack of career opportunities, and constant worry. But despite her effort, a modern cognitive therapist would have challenged her, perhaps even criticized her for her predicament. She brought it on herself through irrational thinking.

Research in cognitive psychology has focused mostly on memory, but cognitive therapy emphasizes thinking. In fact, cognitive therapy has relatively little to do with memory or perception, and its concern with thinking lies largely in faulty reasoning. Cognitive therapy owes almost nothing to research in cognitive psychology. It arose out of practical concerns for a quick, inexpensive treatment.

The therapist plays a dominant role in **cognitive therapy**, which assists people with personal problems by helping them change their ideas about themselves and the world. In this respect, most cognitive therapy stands in sharp contrast to person-centered therapy. The cognitive therapist, with greater experience than the patient in dealing with adjustment problems, takes charge of the sessions. The person-centered therapist allows the person in therapy to determine its course.

With its focus on conscious thought, cognitive therapy also stands in contrast to psychoanalysis. Cognitive therapy makes the assumption that adjustment problems begin with irrational thinking, which eventually leads to emotional disorder. Psychoanalysis reasons the other way around. Emotional disorder causes irrational thinking.

On these bases, treatment sessions in cognitive therapy proceed differently from those in person-centered therapy and psychoanalysis. The therapist is more active, changing the patient's conscious thought through instruction, persuasion, guidance, and homework assignments. The process is somewhat like traditional education or medical practice in Breuer's time. The therapist gives advice and the patient listens. Breuer, working the other way around, was an exception to that rule.

At the outset of cognitive therapy, Bertha might discuss "safe" topics, such as riding horseback and collecting antiques. But the cognitive therapist would not hesitate to identify instances of irrational thought and direct her attention to them. If she skirted certain topics, the therapist would call attention to them too, asking about her mother, her sex life, and gender issues, which are far easier to consider today than in Bertha's era. The emphasis would focus largely on clarification of thought and less on clarification of feelings—as in person-centered therapy.

One concern surely would be the nursing stint she undertook for her sick father. Vienna in that day, perhaps the most sophisticated city in Europe, boasted advanced medical practices and a corps of medical personnel available for in-home care. If the family employed a nightly caretaker, which was a normal practice for affluent families, Bertha could have been uniquely helpful by entertaining and supporting her father during the day (Noshpitz, 1984). Instead, she nursed all night, while he slept, and then slept herself during his waking hours.

Why did Bertha wear herself out so needlessly? Why did she take on this burdensome task at all? Why did she not cherish her father's waking moments? The cognitive therapist would ask such questions and seek rational answers.

Cognitive therapists assume that they, not their patients, are the best people to guide the therapeutic process. They ask questions and then offer advice just like lawyers, financiers, physicians, and other consultants.

Rational-Emotive Therapy

One cognitive approach, *rational-emotive behavior therapy*, states that emotional problems can be alleviated by identifying the irrational thoughts behind them, correcting these thoughts, and then practicing the new ways of thinking. In this method, traditionally known as **rational-emotive therapy**, the therapist offers advice in a very direct fashion, contradicting and even attacking the patient's irrational ideas, seeking the rigorous application of the rules of logic. The therapist becomes an instructor, challenging and encouraging the patient to develop straight thinking in everyday life (Ellis, 1999).

Sooner or later, the therapist teaches the patient the ABCs of better living. The **ABC technique** requires the patient to focus on three elements: *A*, the activating event; *C*, the consequences; and especially *B*, the patient's belief about the activating event. When *B*, the belief, includes irrational thinking, it produces *C*, the undesirable emotional consequences (Ellis, 1991).

In discussing Bertha's role in her father's illness, the rational-emotive therapist would ask her about *B*, her silent sentence. She might resist, claiming she said nothing to herself. But the therapist would insist, pointing out that she told herself something when her father became ill—something to the effect that she alone should be the nighttime caretaker. Only she would be adequate to the task. Or she told herself a different irrational thought—that she would be an irresponsible, ungrateful daughter if she did not take on this responsibility. In any case, Bertha said something to herself that eventually contributed significantly to her emotional disorder. The critical factor, according to the ABC technique, was *B*—whatever she believed and told herself about her father's illness. Without *B*, then *C* would not have occurred.

Bertha's father fell ill, the activating event, *A*. Bertha suffered dire emotional consequences, *C*. But she did so because of her belief, *B*. She told herself something like, "I must nurse him nightly." "Only I can do it." "It would be terrible for me to ignore this responsibility." Those beliefs were irrational.

Irrational thinking contributed to another problem for Bertha. Again, a silent sentence lay at its roots.

At age 21, she had passed through puberty, a major transition in the life cycle, giving her a new body with its sexual characteristics. Physically, she possessed a feminine identity, but psychologically she showed no such signs (Noshpitz, 1984). She had not accepted her adult sexuality. The rational-emotive therapist would inquire directly about this failure. What did she say to herself about sex? What was *B*, Bertha's belief?

"Nice girls do not have sexual fantasies." "Sex is bad." "I should not be thinking about sex." Irrational statements of this sort certainly would have delayed the social and emotional dimensions of her sexual development, contributing to adjustment disorders. The rational-emotive therapist would vigorously attack this illogical thinking and supply missing information.

In positive psychology, incidentally, a person simply seeking greater fulfillment in life presumably has no therapist. Therefore, instead of imagining what her therapist might say, she imagines someone she knows well making frank but friendly comments about her maladaptive thoughts. In this way, she moves herself through the traditional stages: *A* representing the activating event or adversity, *B* the belief, and *C* the consequences. Then, in *D*, she engages in disputation, disagreeing with her own irrational beliefs as vigorously as possible. Finally, *E*, for energization, draws her attention to the increased energy she feels after successful disputation. In this ABCDE way, a person may change her dejection into more cheerful ways (Seligman, 2002).

Therapy for Depression

In a more collaborative approach, **cognitive therapy for depression**, the therapist acts less as a critic and more as a colleague and collaborator, helping people discover the negative things they say about themselves, their world, and their future. In particular, the focus is on their negative views of themselves (Beck, 1991).

The therapist provides this assistance by using the Socratic method, a question-and-answer dialogue, which moves gradually toward a new understanding, one step at a time. Guided by the therapist, the patient makes her own discoveries about her susceptibility to the major modes of maladaptive thinking. In these **categories of maladaptive thinking**, people tend to distort information about themselves and their world through selective attention, overgeneralizing, and polarized thinking.

In the first category, selective attention, the depressed person thinks only about the negative aspects of her life. She ignores the positive, disconfirming factors—the confirmation bias again. In the second category, overgeneralizing, she extends negative thinking beyond reasonable limits. She applies some small negative detail to all or most of her life, making it overly important. And in polarized thinking, the third category, she interprets events only in terms of extremes. A mildly negative event becomes an awful event, a ghastly outcome. In all three instances, the individual overreacts to a negative circumstance (Beck, 1991).

The illness of Bertha's father certainly was a negative event, and she became depressed, unable to eat, talk, or even leave her bed. In cognitive therapy for depression, she would be encouraged to understand that she was overreacting even to this catastrophe. To combat her selective attention, the therapist would ask her to enumerate any favorable circumstances in her life. There were many. The family lived in a most comfortable home. Her father had the very best care. They could afford round-the-clock nursing. Friends offered support. To discourage overgeneralizing, the therapist might help her realize that her father's illness did not extend to all phases of her life—to riding horseback, dancing, collecting antiques, and so forth. And the therapist would try to dissuade her from polarized thinking by encouraging her to look between the extremes, noting that her father was not in great pain and that they had shared many good times.

Examining maladaptive thinking in these ways, the patient is often surprised by the extent of her negative statements and by the lack of substantial support for them. The patient finds herself engaged in self-pity.

Then, too, Bertha had recently passed through adolescence, often a turbulent stage marking the transition from childhood to maturity. She found herself with a different body, new thoughts, and unexpected feelings. Such changes can contribute to an *identity crisis,* in which adolescents and young adults experience uncertainty and confusion about their places in society. The capacity for abstract thought reaches a new level in adolescence, evident in rebellious ideas about parents and schools, religion and society, politics and business. New causes are sought, new goals adopted. At the same time, the young adult has a special potential to be inspired and fulfilled (Noshpitz, 1984).

Despite her youthful potential, lively and talented Bertha found no outlet. Her irrational thinking was partly a developmental problem, reflecting identity issues. It was also a cultural problem; she resisted the golden handcuffs. And it was a family problem. After the deaths of her sisters, she had become a replacement child, clearly overprotected by her family (Bloch, 1984).

But in one important respect, her thinking was not irrational at all. Her thoughts on gender discrimination were well in advance of her culture, at least by today's standards. The effective cognitive therapist would not try to dissuade her from these viewpoints. Rather, he would assist her in living productively within these social constraints, constructively resisting and changing some while temporarily accepting others.

In doing so, he would use a procedure shared by rational-emotive and cognitive therapy for depression. Rational-emotive therapy becomes direct and demanding; cognitive therapy for depression offers a gentler exploration of irrational thought. But both therapies encourage reframing, also called *cognitive restructuring.* In **reframing**, the individual thinks about her circumstances differently, viewing them in a more positive, constructive manner. Both therapies imply that human beings control their own destiny through reason and judgment, and both require the patient to practice reframing in homework assignments—learning to detect silent sentences, avoid self-critical statements, and foster rational thought.

Bertha never experienced any form of cognitive therapy, but eventually she reframed her problem anyway, thinking about it differently. She perceived gender discrimination not as her prison but as her challenge. With this outlook and her struggles for reform, she found her calling.

According to cognitive therapy, Josef Breuer did not terminate the sessions too soon. Rather, he went about them the wrong way. If he had entered more directly and focused more precisely on Bertha's thinking, he could have helped her eliminate her irrationality about family responsibilities and nursing obligations. At the same time, he could have helped her understand that her ideas about gender discrimination were reasonable and rational and that, in this respect, she was living in an irrational society.

Advocating rationalism for alleviating disruptive behavior, cognitive therapy succeeds partly through empiricism. The therapist confronts people with factual evidence that contradicts their disruptive beliefs. Those in therapy encounter this evidence directly, through various homework assignments, and indirectly, in conversations with the therapist. In this way, they are helped to discover, test, and alter their maladaptive cognitive styles.

Commentary and Critique

Among all the perspectives, people view cognitive psychology as the most open and least restrictive. Protesting behaviorism's focus on topics outside the mind, it gathered supporters with all sorts of backgrounds in psychology, including those who resisted behaviorism and those who simply wanted to study the mind in one way or another. Many were prominent and creative in their goals, but no single, unifying leadership emerged. The revolutionary "army" was too scattered, the research interests too disparate.

During the early years, the bonds among the primary figures were strongest. Some leading experts—Bruner, Miller, and Simon, for example—united for a time. But after the revolution, cognitive psychologists tended to go their separate ways.

For this reason, cognitive psychology has not yet promoted a highly integrative **central concept**, meaning some specific thought, idea, or notion essential and unique to a given perspective, providing a special focus for research. Information processing, the most widely cited core concept, is virtually synonymous with cognitive psychology. Broadly inclusive, information processing does not stimulate research in a particular direction; it does not create a focus comparable to unconscious motivation in psychoanalysis, the reinforcement principle in behaviorism, or the modularity doctrine in biological psychology. In fact, information processing carries much the same meaning as "the mind," referring in a general way to all mental activities—an enormous sweep of topics in psychology. Increased focus may be forthcoming, perhaps through combined efforts with other perspectives, especially biological and evolutionary psychology. But a huge advantage of this less restrictive approach lies in the latitude it offers for the many interdisciplinary studies, which presumably will become even more vigorous in the future.

Moreover, cognitive psychology did gain focus when it adopted the **computer metaphor**, depicting the ways people process information. In a metaphor, one object or event suggests a similarity with another; knowing the former assists in understanding the latter. The computer model represented a substantial gain over the earlier flow charts, which used arrows and geometric figures to diagram the speculated flow of information in our mental life. Again, the parallel lies not with the computer hardware and anatomy of the brain but with the software and human information processing. But even so, critics call attention to the limits of the computer model. The human mind does not operate just like a computer. It responds more slowly and makes errors. With proper input, the computer responds rapidly and correctly. The human mind responds emotionally, which contributes to its errors; the computer has no feelings at all. In addition to these issues of speed and accuracy, both in favor of the computer, two major difficulties remain with the computer model.

First and foremost, the computer passively awaits input from the outside world. It does not actively seek information. In contrast, the human mind is a vigilant system, almost constantly gathering information about the world, about itself, and about the body it inhabits (Mandler, 1985). It aims to understand the objects and events impinging on its sensory apparatus, thereby enlarging its own capacities.

Second, the computer model largely ignores meaning-making—a cardinal capacity of the human mind, an outgrowth of its vigilance. Episodes of meaning-making constantly infuse daily life—through street talk, myths, magic, media, and countless other verbal and nonverbal ways (Donald, 1997; Pasqual-Leone, 1997).

In adopting the computer model, focusing on how we process information, cognitive psychology gained precision—and moved toward a mechanical reductionism. It examined narrower questions with increased controls. Had it elected instead to study how human beings make meanings, something the computer cannot do, cognitive psychology might have become broader, less reductionistic, and more relevant to everyday life (Bruner, 1990). But thereby it would have forfeited precision, a considerable loss.

An early leader in cognitive psychology, Jerome Bruner in particular has noted the limitations of the computer model for investigating the ways people construct meanings in their lives. Emphasizing systematic, logical thinking in the laboratory, the computer model often overlooks our freer, more imaginative, more personal, and more emotional ways of knowing our world. As co-founder of the first laboratory of cognitive psychology, Bruner believes that human beings make their lives meaningful largely through storytelling.

We tell stories in school, while waiting for the bus, beside the water fountain, in the kitchen, everywhere in daily life. The human mind is a pattern-making, pattern-recognizing system. We develop many of these patterns by telling stories. Accordingly, a narrative metaphor might prove lucrative for cognitive psychology, bringing culture further into this research (Bruner, 1990).

In this context, a sustained criticism of cognitive psychology concerns the relatively little attention it devotes to the complex emotional factors in human thinking. These factors play a major role in cultural experience and in our self-narratives. Respected research has revealed the human mind as more emotional and less rational than typically viewed in lay and even psychological thought (LeDoux, 2002; Tversky & Kahneman, 1974).

Extensive use of laboratory experiments in the study of information processing has prompted the related problem of external validity. This issue is also loosely called generalizability, and indeed the two terms are almost synonymous. But generalization is often used in a nonspecific fashion, simply questioning whether certain research results apply in the everyday world.

With a more specific meaning, **external validity** assesses the extent to which the results from a specific investigation correctly reveal relationships among variables in some particular real-life setting, outside the research context. It does so by focusing on elements of the research design: the participants, setting, manipulations, observations, and so forth. For example, are laboratory findings obtained with a particular sample of college students applicable to certain college students elsewhere or to participants of other ages in other settings? Laboratory research in cognitive psychology confronts this question, as it does in the other perspectives as well.

Laboratory studies on memory, for example, employ students in controlled settings sometimes responding to unusual tasks that have no obvious meaning in their everyday lives. Does such research shed light on the cognitive capacities required of human beings in their highly complex daily environments, further complicated by diverse emotional factors? The issue of external validity becomes a special concern in laboratory studies.

Cognitive psychologists have accomplished important research with diverse methods, including naturalistic observation, case studies, and the survey. But the balance favors laboratory experiments, which can provide information not otherwise obtainable.

For example, using electronic laboratory equipment unavailable to Piaget, modern investigators have studied mental activities in infants too young even to reach successfully for an object. Rather than hiding a toy in the living room, they present the infant with detailed visual scenes, measure the infant's eye movements, and detect minute patterns of bodily activity. They examine the baby's eyes as a window into its mind, asking the speechless infant: "Can you make any sense out of this scene?"

In one series of experiments, 24 four-month-old infants observed a rolling ball on several occasions. After losing interest in this image, they were shown two follow-up scenes. In one, the ball rolled into a barrier and stopped. In the other, it somehow rolled through the barrier. Measures of gaze showed that the infants studied the impossible event significantly longer than the natural one, supporting the view that the perceptual experience of infants is more coherent than Piaget concluded (Spelke, Breinlinger, Macomber, & Jacobson, 1992).

Speaking broadly, these follow-up studies suggest that Piaget underestimated the capacity of infants in the sensorimotor stage and of children in preoperational thought. At the other end of the sequence, he overestimated adult progress into formal operations. Much of the former error lay with his homespun methods. Much of the latter occurred because he studied only Europeans, and culture clearly influences cognitive development.

As early investigators, Piaget and Freud have much in common. The work of both men is widely recognized and more susceptible than usual to investigator effects, owing to their informal research methods. Moreover, Piaget's stages, like those of Freud, are not as universal as he suggested, and the transitions from one to another now appear more gradual than he indicated. However, both men enormously influenced modern psychology. Freud brought child rearing and irrational thinking into greater focus; Piaget brought educational practices and the development of normal human thought into the spotlight (Rotman, 1977).

With these roots, psychology has returned to the study of the mind—not through introspection, as in earlier days, but through inference. For this reason, and with remarkably improved equipment, it has also turned toward brain and computer science.

Cognitive psychology today stretches from studies of imitation in birds and numerical ability in dolphins to the latest developments in human brain imaging. In fact, all the processes that take place between the input of some stimulus and the output of an organism's response can be included in the domain of cognitive psychology (Neisser, 2000). With these broad boundaries, it becomes difficult to say what is and is not part of contemporary cognitive psychology. It exists as a systematic perspective more in name than in fact and is perhaps more appropriately considered a large subfield today. Its major recent advances lie in our increased understanding of human memory in particular, as well as advances in perception, thinking, and use of language. Further progress can be expected with the steady development of ever-more sophisticated research methods, electronic instruments, and interdisciplinary investigations.

Summary

Foundations of Cognitive Psychology

Modern cognitive psychology emerged in the mid-20th century through investigations in language, computer science, and memory. The earlier work of Jean Piaget focused on children, using mostly observations and interviews. Modern cognitive psychology adopted the computer as a metaphor because the software, in restricted ways, is similar to human mental activities, involving three stages of information processing: input, storage, and output.

Key Terms: **cognitive psychology, gestalt psychology, cognitive development, information processing, intelligence, general-purpose problem solver, domain-specific problem solver, parallel distributive processing**

Sensation and Perception

Through sensation we become aware of stimulation, but perception includes the processes of recognizing, organizing, and interpreting this incoming information. The outcome of perception, some form of understanding, is influenced by the specific features of the stimulus, through bottom-up processing, and the schema or expectations held by the perceiver, through top-down processing. Both types of information are managed rapidly and simultaneously in the brain, a circumstance called parallel distributive processing.

Key Terms: **perception, sensation, bottom-up processing, feature detectors, top-down processing, schema, set**

Processes in Memory

Memory is an active process; human beings typically search for the elements or parts of their memories and reconstruct them. Memories are acquired in three stages: sensory, working, and long-term memory. Sensory memory, composed of fleeting, unprocessed information, promptly disappears without some effort at retention. Working memory prepares incoming information for storage; it involves rehearsal or more elaborate encoding through organization, chunking, and cueing. Long-term memory, which exists in several forms, involves storage for indefinite periods. Retrieval from this storage usually requires special encoding and cueing.

Key Terms: **memory, sensory memory, short-term memory, working memory, encoding, long-term memory, explicit memory, implicit memory, forgetting, decay theory, interference theory, motivated forgetting, inadequate retrieval cues**

Thought and Language

Among adults, reasoning commonly occurs in two forms, inductive and deductive, used jointly. Inductive errors occur because people overlook contradictory evidence; deductive errors arise from incorrect premises. Language aids thought, and the average child gains language rapidly, progressing through a universal, predictable sequence, showing that the process is significantly innate. Language does not determine thought, but it can be highly influential in adult thinking.

Key Terms: **thinking, concept, propositional mode, imaginal mode, artificial intelligence, computer simulation, algorithm, heuristic, inductive reasoning, deductive reasoning, language, phoneme, morpheme, syntax, linguistic relativity**

The Cognitive Therapies

The cognitive therapist aims to educate or indoctrinate the patient in more useful ways of thinking. The major premise is that most patients make themselves unhappy through their irrational thoughts. Rational-emotive therapy employs the ABC technique, emphasizing A, the activating event; C, the consequences; and B, the patient's irrational belief. Less confrontational, cognitive therapy for depression encourages the patient to examine maladaptive thinking in terms of three categories: selective attention, overgeneralizing, and polarized thinking.

Key Terms: **cognitive therapy, rational-emotive therapy, ABC technique, cognitive therapy for depression, categories of maladaptive thinking, reframing**

Commentary and Critique

Cognitive psychology does not have the coherence generally associated with a systematic perspective, partly because of the great breadth of its central concept, information processing. The mechanistic reductionism in its computer model has led cognitive psychology away from a more open, narrative approach, often viewed as the way people create meanings in their lives. A problem with external validity arises partly because much cognitive research takes place in laboratory settings with college students performing novel tasks.

Key Terms: **central concept, computer metaphor, external validity**

Critical Thinking

1. Suppose cognitive psychology had adopted a narrative metaphor. Describe how research on cognition might have developed differently. Focus on likely research topics or goals and also on research design, both experimental and observational.

2. After a successful high-school career, an adolescent believes he cannot manage his new job as a store clerk. Make a case for cognitive therapy in this instance.

3. On a long bus trip, would Jean Piaget prefer to ride with a behaviorist or a biological psychologist? Give reasons for your viewpoint.

8

Evolutionary Psychology

Roots of Evolutionary Psychology

Evolution of Sexual Behavior

Adaptations in Parenting

Dispositions in Group Living

Promoting Behavioral Change
  Assessing Therapy Effectiveness
  A Catalogue of Hypotheses

Commentary and Critique

E volutionary psychology states that the newborn human mind is not a clean slate awaiting its contents. It is an adapted mind, containing specific fears, preferences, and behavioral tendencies inherited from our ancestors, especially those eons earlier.

The human mind of course is not completely shaped at birth; life experiences contribute enormously. But evolutionary psychology examines the presumably evolved mechanisms present in all of us at the outset of our lives, arising from our common genetic background as *Homo sapiens*.

Following an introduction on the roots of evolutionary psychology, this chapter describes these evolved mechanisms in a developmental sequence, beginning with human sexual behavior. Then it turns to adaptations in parenting, including pregnancy and child care, and finally to dispositions in group living, ranging from language acquisition to our inclination toward aggression. With no therapy available for our evolved makeup, the chapter ends with a general discussion on promoting behavioral change, followed by the customary commentary and critique.

According to evolutionary theory, these mental mechanisms evolved gradually in the course of human history, as our ancestors struggled for survival. Among our ancestors, those most adapted to the environment survived and typically reproduced, passing on their genetic makeup to their offspring. In this way, the characteristics most associated with mastery of these two tasks—individual survival and sexual reproduction—tended to be transmitted and augmented in successive generations. Reproductive men tended to be attracted to certain features in women, and reproductive women in turn tended to favor certain qualities in men.

In the sexual realm, Bertha was an exception. She showed no overt attraction to anyone and, in fact, no interest in closeness or intimacy. Even when working with others, she lived a lonely, loveless life. Her sexual behavior instead provides an important reminder that inherited predispositions of all sorts are always subject to modification by environmental factors. Both components are always present and influential in complex ways.

Then one day Bertha embarked on a mission that included human sexuality and a tour of forbidden places—but no sexual behavior on her part. In her fifties, she planned further combat, this time against the "world's oldest profession."

She would battle the corrupt businessmen and civic leaders who profited from the international traffic in women (Kimball, 2000). She would also meet the prostitutes at their places of work. Her itinerary would include houses of prostitution in Budapest, Jerusalem, Moscow, Warsaw, and several other cities.

Bertha possessed a background for this challenge. Working daily with former prostitutes, she understood their deprivations, especially their need for education. And these personal contacts gave her a strong sense of purpose. She viewed herself as the enemy of an underworld empire, threatening its financial gains.

Roots of Evolutionary Psychology

Selling, bartering, and otherwise contracting for sexuality have occurred throughout human history. In fact, the challenge of negotiating for sexual activity exists for all sexually reproducing species, and our ancestors evolved various solutions to it. As a new perspective, emerging prominently in the late 1990s, evolutionary psychology aims to understand our evolved solutions to these and other adaptive tasks.

Specifically, **evolutionary psychology** studies the design of the human mind, focusing on the psychological mechanisms evolved by human beings in solving the two adaptive tasks most fundamental to our species: individual survival and sexual reproduction. It seeks to identify the ways in which human beings, in solving these problems, have acquired certain longstanding fears, preferences, and other behavioral tendencies (Buss, 1995a).

Evolutionary theory has a long past. The idea that human beings are descended from animal ancestors dates back to early Greek philosophers. They suggested that one species could change into another, that human beings descended from fish, and that differences among species could either decrease or increase. By the 19th century, Jean-Baptiste Lamarck proposed a detailed theory of evolution, illustrating the ancestry of human and animal descendants, but he stressed the inheritance of *acquired* characteristics. Giraffes acquired their long necks by constantly reaching for leaves high in the trees. The results of this stretching somehow were passed from one generation to the next. But with no plausible conjecture about how an organism's repetitive behaviors might be transmitted to another generation, the Lamarckian view lost much of its credibility.

The Darwinian Influence

Also in the 19th century, Erasmus Darwin anticipated the modern concept of evolution. But scientists, philosophers, and the general public credit instead his grandson, Charles Darwin (1809–1882). The younger Darwin's massive contributions were both empirical and rational. He collected an extensive array of facts, and then he developed a far more complete, more carefully constructed theory of evolution. In this theory, incidentally, human beings are not viewed as descended from apes. Rather, the two species have common ancestors.

As a youth, Darwin collected specimens, and one day he discovered not one but two rare beetles, catching one in each hand. Then he spied still another, awaiting capture if he acted quickly. Fearful that it might escape, Darwin thrust one of the pair into his mouth. That creature emitted a bitter fluid that burned Darwin's tongue, causing him to spit out his prisoner and, alas, to lose the opportunity to capture even two members of the trio (Darwin, 1876).

That episode illustrates that Darwin pursued his own goals in tenacious fashion, but not those of his father, who insisted he attend Edinburgh University in preparation for a medical career. But Charles experienced an aversion to medicine, especially to witnessing surgery performed without anesthesia. Transferring to Cambridge University for training in the ministry, he showed little interest there too, finally completing an undistinguished academic program. But he greatly enjoyed informal contact with faculty members in the sciences, especially botany. After his graduation, one of them recommended him for unpaid work aboard H.M.S. Beagle, a vessel assigned to sail around the world to survey South American coastlines, Pacific islands, and other places. As an unpaid naturalist, Darwin's job was to study rock formations, plants, and animals. For five years and 40,000 miles, he gathered facts and collected specimens.

On his return, he decided that the information he had so meticulously gathered might "throw some light" on that mystery of mysteries—the origin of species. For several years, he catalogued his specimens, and then he continued to contemplate the significance of this work, writing occasional articles on related subjects and standing for hours in his garden puzzled by some plant, insect, or experience aboard the Beagle. He also ruminated on the possible repercussions of his conclusions for social, religious, and even political thought. Altogether, he pondered his findings for 23 years before publishing them—almost too late to earn credit for their originality.

When finally published, his work was favorably received by some, vigorously protested by others. The critics resisted any suggestion that human beings possessed an animal ancestry, pointing instead to divine origins. Ill and tired, Darwin suffered in silence. As a scholar and man of great integrity, he simply could not ignore the conclusion forced on him by the facts of his voyage.

Two events prompted him to publish the book: his failing health and the arrival of a rival manuscript. When Alfred Wallace expressed ideas remarkably similar to his own, Darwin, in three more years, published his epochal work, *The Origin of Species* (1859). It appeared just 20 years before the founding of scientific psychology.

Among Darwin's evidence, studies of emotion carried considerable weight. Observing animals, human infants, and adults in different cultures, he noted the continuity in emotional expression. People bare their teeth in rage, though this reaction serves no physical purpose in most adult combat. In animals, it prepares an organism's most powerful weapon. Also, it may frighten the adversary. Thus, he viewed human emotional expressions as carryovers from our animal ancestry.

For Darwin, the mind, like the body, evolved through natural selection. In this process of **natural selection**, poorly adapted organisms perish; unable to escape predators and outdo others of their own species, they produce fewer offspring and therefore pass on fewer or no genes. The better adapted survive and reproduce, transmitting their more favorable heredity to their descendants, resulting in the "survival of the fittest," a phrase not suggested by Darwin. "Reproduction of the fittest" would be more to the point. In any case, selection of the fittest results in the adaptation of each species to its surroundings. According to this principle, any slight variation in a species, if useful for survival, is preserved by natural selection.

Variation within the species plays a vital role. Without random variations, there would be no evolution. Random variation provides the differences essential for natural selection, bringing about inheritable changes that may prove adaptive in later generations (Figure 8.1).

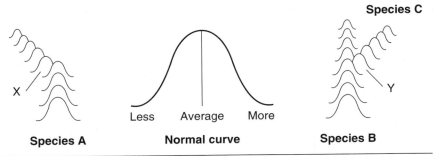

Figure 8.1   Evolutionary Changes in Species' Characteristics. The large normal curve shows the usual distribution of a human trait. The smaller curves show the trait in successive generations. In species A, a slight variation appeared in era X, useful in the preservation of this species. Subsequent generations showed successive shifts toward this variation. In species B, a favorable variation appeared at Y, eventually producing species C, a related but different species (Futuyma, 1983).

In his book, Darwin described nature as a continuous series of struggles among all living creatures for their niches in the environment. The lion, with its teeth and claws, is equipped with knives and, with its thick mane, a shield as well. The parasite is equipped with legs and claws by which it clings to the hair on the lion's body. Lions do battle with one another and with other species, just as parasites struggle for their place in nature.

A battleground serves as the metaphor for evolutionary psychology. All individuals become warriors on three fronts: competing against the forces of nature, their predators, and others of their own species. In these battles, Darwin suggested, we can console ourselves knowing that those who adapt best to a specific environmental niche will survive and multiply, passing their inherited characteristics to the next generation (Darwin, 1859). In fact, in making his observations and developing his theory, Darwin knew nothing about the transmission process. He had no idea how living creatures pass on their inherited characteristics. He simply observed that they did so. The physical mechanism for this process had not yet been discovered.

Genetic Transmission

Today we understand that all our biological inheritance passes from generation to generation through many thousands of submicroscopic structures called **genes**, which guide the expression of most physical and certain behavioral characteristics. The word *guide* appears appropriate, rather than *control* or *direct,* for today the expression of genes seems less rigid and automatic than once thought. All genes exist in an environmental context, and that context can augment or diminish any genetic predisposition.

Incidentally, the erroneous notion that genes inevitably and unavoidably control behavior is known as **genetic determinism**. Instead, genes always operate within an environment, and that environmental input influences the behavioral outcome. Legions of experimental studies with selectively bred animals and quasi-experimental studies with human beings underscore this point. Genes never act alone, which is the fallacy of genetic determinism. Human behavior occurs through a particular genetic background and environmental influences that mediate those inborn dispositions.

Evolutionary psychology must be understood in this same way. It is not a form of genetic determinism. It studies interactions. It examines behavioral outcomes of our genetic adaptations as triggered by specific stimuli in the modern environment.

Within this environment, all human genes operate in pairs, and sometimes one member is dominant. The characteristic carried by the *dominant gene* becomes manifest whenever it is present, though its expression may vary, depending on diverse factors. A *recessive gene* becomes influential only when paired with another recessive gene.

A few human characteristics, such as eye color and certain diseases, become expressed through a single pair of genes. But most characteristics are more complexly determined. In these outcomes a *polygenic trait* emerges, influenced by multiple pairs of genes acting with various degrees of expression but without dominance, making the outcomes less predictable. The full genetic makeup of an individual, called the *genome* and estimated to include thousands of genes, can only be inferred.

In any species, some genes increase the chances of survival and reproduction; others diminish these prospects or play no significant role. Insofar as these differences in genes are transmitted from one generation to another, they give rise to evolution through their interplay with the environment, which is constantly changing. From the Ice Age to the Electronic Age, the environment has been altered by forces of nature and changes induced by human and other beings. Without these environmental changes, all living creatures theoretically would evolve to a maximum adaptation in their particular niches.

Genetic differences occur on two bases. First, at conception each individual receives a random assortment of countless genes from the two parents. Thus, all individuals except identical twins differ in their genetic backgrounds. These differences emerge from a tiny but vital portion of the genes passed on to us by our particular parents, each with his or her own genetic background, providing us with our own unique genetic makeup. Second, a sudden alteration, called *mutation*, sometimes occurs within a gene, producing the potential for a characteristic in the offspring not found in the parents. These intermittent deviations in gene replication are usually disruptive or inconsequential, but some are useful. With the massive number of genes possessed by each parent and the potential combinations in the union of the mother and father, together with the capacity of genes to mutate, the possibilities for diversity among human beings are almost unfathomable.

In more fundamental ways, however, human beings also have a common genetic background. With an overwhelming preponderance of common genes, we all share the numerous physical and behavioral characteristics that make us human beings, just as members of other species possess common characteristics.

Evolutionary theory states that the genes underlying these common characteristics have been selected by features of the environment over millions and millions of years. After countless generations exposed to natural selection, the most adaptive traits in a particular environment become prominent; the less-adaptive traits tend to die out and disappear. According to evolutionary biology, the human thumb, lumbar curve, and other physical structures emerged through this selective process.

For Darwin, the human mind also underwent adaptation, producing evolved tendencies in human behavior. He closed his book with this prediction: Psychology some day would be based on the idea that human mental capacities have been acquired by gradual adaptation (Darwin, 1859).

Mechanisms and Instincts

The fundamental premise of evolutionary psychology is that human mental characteristics also have been shaped by the process of natural selection over the eons of hunter-gatherer existence. Recorded human history is the product of a few thousand years. In contrast, our Pleistocene ancestors lived as hunter-gatherers for two million years, and their ancestors spent several hundred million years in a forager existence of one sort or another (Cosmides, Tooby, & Barkow, 1992). Compared with those indefinitely lengthy periods in human prehistory, our agrarian ancestors lived just yesterday, and the Industrial Age happened but an instant ago. Speculation about the nature of these long-evolved traits, together with empirical research to test these hypotheses, are the province of evolutionary psychology.

Especially since the 1990s, the evolutionary approach has gained increasing prominence in psychology, much of it through the energetic efforts of Leda Cosmides, John Tooby, and others, especially David Buss. With grades too low for college, Buss gained admission by a lottery and promptly developed interests in evolution and psychology, earning national recognition for his promise as a young scientist (Distinguished Scientific Awards, 1989). These and other modern pioneers have established a perspective that Darwin envisioned but did not pursue. Articulating the theory of evolution became enough for his lifetime.

As emphasized throughout this chapter, evolutionary psychology does not investigate the theory of evolution, which is impossible to confirm. Instead, starting with the idea of evolution, it develops specific hypotheses about human beings and then tests them for empirical support.

Often these studies begin with some common behavioral characteristic, such as the tendency of pregnant women to experience sickness or the tendency of people everywhere to speak a language. Then evolutionary psychologists speculate on the ways in which this behavior solved a problem of survival or reproduction in much earlier human history. Afterward, through widely diverse methods, especially the survey, they investigate this tendency in different cultures. The aim is to discover whether this behavior occurs throughout these societies. If so, it probably is not a culturally acquired trait but rather a product of human inheritance, and it is interpreted from the standpoint of evolutionary theory (Buss, 1999).

Many behaviors occur only in some cultures. Alcoholism, arranged marriages, and alimony are not universal. They stimulate little research among evolutionary psychologists. Traffic in women flourished in Alexandria, Buenos Aires, and Constantinople—places of interest to Bertha—but moral and legal conditions prohibited it elsewhere. On this basis, evolutionary psychologists would not study *enforced* prostitution as an adaptive phenomenon. However, in one form or another prostitution occurs in every carefully studied society around the world, and men become virtually the sole consumers of this practice. It emerges as an outcome of two related factors: the male desire for short-term sex, which has a long evolutionary history, and the female need or choice to provide sexual services for economic gain (Buss, 1999). Thus, the male desire for short-term sex has become a topic of research in evolutionary psychology.

Also called adaptationists, evolutionary psychologists aim to understand the *adapted* human mind—how the contemporary human mind has been designed by natural selection to solve the highly specific problems of survival and reproduction confronted by our hunter-gatherer ancestors. This effort to determine what the mind was shaped to do then, and how it operates today, is the basis of the evolutionary approach.

Evolutionary psychologists therefore take a controversial position. They resist the *tabula rasa* view that the contents of the contemporary human mind arise solely from the world outside the individual, through experiences in the environment, guided by just one or a few basic tendencies such as intelligence and learning. As in cognitive psychology, they do not regard the mind as a general-purpose computer that uses global intelligence to solve a wide array of problems. Instead, they view the human mind as designed through natural selection to respond in particular ways to specific circumstances. In this view, the human mind is a complex network of functionally specific computer programs (Cosmides & Tooby, 1992).

Each of these highly specialized programs is regarded as an evolved mechanism. In general terms, an **evolved psychological mechanism** is an inherited set of processes within the individual that responds to specific information about a recurrent problem of survival or reproduction and initiates a response to that problem. It becomes activated whenever the individual is confronted with events similar to those that signaled the problem in prehistoric life. In other words, an evolved psychological mechanism emerged gradually in human ancestors as a solution to some specific problem of individual survival or reproduction. It responds only to a narrow stimulus or piece of information informing the organism about that adaptive problem. Through decision rules, that input is transformed into an output that may be behavioral, physiological, or merely cognitive, directed toward a solution to that problem (Buss, 1999).

Now consider a simpler definition. As the central concept in evolutionary psychology, an *evolved psychological mechanism* often takes the form of a fear, preference, or behavioral tendency. It does not inevitably solve an adaptive problem in the current environment, but it tended to do so in the environment in which it evolved (Buss, 1999).

At this point, the reader may wonder how an evolved psychological mechanism differs from an instinct, a concept with a long and checkered history in psychology. Eventually **instinct** became defined as a relatively *complex, unlearned* behavior pattern occurring in *all* members or same-gender members of a species. On this basis, most modern psychologists regard human behavior as too flexible and too variable across cultures to be considered instinctive, although debate continues on several points, especially language. In any case, the concept of instinct does not explain much. It simply states that a certain behavior is somehow automatic.

The concept survives in everyday speech, nevertheless. People speak of someone as possessing an instinct for public speaking. Sports announcers describe certain athletes as having "good instincts." But if performance in sports and public speaking were instinctive, *all* of us could perform at a high level without any training or practice. Clearly, *learning* is required, as well as good reflexes in cases of physical abilities.

One major difference between an evolved psychological mechanism and an instinct lies with the variability in response. The fears, preferences, and behavioral tendencies in evolved psychological mechanisms are less predictable and more open to diversity than instinctive behavior. Their genetic background is more "tentatively wired," and the resulting behavior is only *relatively* fixed. An instinct is more *fully* fixed, its genetic background "firmly wired."

A man's interest in a potential mate is triggered partly by a woman's appearance, including her waist-to-hips ratio. According to extensive cross-cultural surveys, men of different ages and diverse backgrounds almost universally find a waist-to-hip ratio of 0.70 most attractive. Larger and smaller ratios are less appealing (Singh & Young, 1995). This triggered preference is the essence of this evolved psychological mechanism, for the man's subsequent behavior is not highly predictable. It may range from a fleeting thought about the woman's posture to a prompt bid for a close encounter.

Among fish, the male, three-spined stickleback also responds to the shape of the female's body. If she exhibits a swollen abdomen, showing that she is about to lay eggs, the male immediately constructs a nest and commences an elaborate mating dance, swimming rapidly in circles, then back and forth, all in highly specific patterns, by which he induces her to enter the nest and lay her eggs (Tinbergen, 1953). All normal male sticklebacks emit this same intricate mating dance in response to the shape of the female's body.

In other words, male sticklebacks possess an instinct, an inborn, firmly fixed reaction to the female's swollen belly. The concept of instinct implies inevitability and complexity. Adult human males are not so universally and explicitly responsive, even to the most compelling female abdomen. They possess an evolved psychological mechanism—a behavioral tendency, far less predictable as a pattern of reactions. The concept implies only a broad tendency or predisposition. There may be no overt reaction at all.

Women are different from men in this respect. They show a mild preference for a 0.90 ratio in men, with the waist and hips almost the same size. Compared to men, this preference is even more variable and the woman's overt response even less predictable (Singh, 1995).

Specificity in Adaptation

From the perspective of evolutionary psychology, modern human beings are living, inexact fossils. They carry with them ancient tendencies for all sorts of reactions shaped by natural selection over the millennia. Still present today as part of "human nature," these reactions are evoked by cues for the earlier adaptive problems—a wayward mate, poisonous food, loss of status, invasions of territory, and many others. As remnants from life long ago, they can be maladaptive today. They give us, in some respects, a cave dweller's brain in a modern skull. But of course all current brain processes are not necessarily an outcome of evolution.

In addition, each broad adaptive problem—survival and reproduction—includes specific subproblems, resulting in numerous evolved psychological mechanisms. The subproblems in the survival realm include obtaining food, managing in harsh climates, avoiding parasites, cooperating with others, acquiring a language, and becoming a competent worker, among others. In the reproductive realm, the chief subproblems include attracting a mate, preventing the mate from another alliance, achieving conception, avoiding poisonous foods during pregnancy, escaping from dangerous situations, and recognizing emotional expressions in infants and children and responding appropriately to them. But all subproblems involve a host of even more specific tasks. Attracting a mate, for instance, typically entails the following actions: acquiring the resources or characteristics anticipated by a potential mate, negotiating social institutions, competing with members of one's own sex for potential mates, forming a successful alliance, appeasing—or at least not alienating—the potential mate's family and friends, successfully courting the mate, and engaging in other forms of alliance (Buss, 1991).

Many widespread human fears, preferences, and behavioral tendencies are viewed as responses to these specific problems, that is, as evolved psychological mechanisms. In the survival realm, human beings show more fear of snakes, insects, and high places than of automobiles and electrical appliances, which in contemporary civilization are far more dangerous. They show a strong taste preference for foods high in fats and sugar, a mechanism perhaps designed to increase caloric intake in the active life of hunter-gatherer societies but causing health problems in today's more sedentary world. Human beings show a greater ability to solve social-contract problems than other problems of equal difficulty, a possible adaptation to avoid exploitation in social exchange. And they show the universal acquisition of language, an evolved psychological mechanism that has greatly furthered human evolution, providing a means of cooperation within and across generations.

In the reproductive realm, modern men show greater preference for youth and beauty in their mates than do women, perhaps an adaptation to the younger female's reproductive promise. In turn, women traditionally have shown greater preference for experience and economic resources in the mate, a possible adaptation for the provision of offspring (Buss, 1995b).

These preferences, like all other evolved psychological mechanisms, do not require an intent to pass on one's genes. An individual of course may have this aim on occasion. But people sometimes misunderstand evolutionary psychology in this way. If people possessed only the goal of passing on their genes—to maximize their genetic reproduction—they would behave differently. Men would not visit houses of prostitution, and they would refrain from masturbation, lining up instead to make donations at sperm banks. And women might make their times of heightened fertility known more publicly (Buss, 1995a).

For the continuation of our species, people do not need to be motivated to replicate their genes. Instead, through natural selection, modern men and women have become especially responsive to cues *most likely to result* in reproduction anyway, just as they have become responsive to environmental cues triggering a wide variety of other behavioral dispositions, such as fears of snakes and darkness, taste preferences for fat and sugar, and the tendency to acquire language. The growing list of these adaptations extends from recognizing objects and judging distance to evading predators and avoiding disease. It includes, among many others, developing friendships, deterring aggression, and bargaining successfully (Cosmides & Tooby, 1992).

Moreover, common sense and mathematical calculations do not support the traditional view of the human mind as an all-purpose, general-capacity system. Rather, they indicate that a potentially infinite number of conclusions could be drawn from the facts of most circumstances in everyday life, and an infinitely accommodating "blank slate" simply could not function effectively. The human mind-brain mechanism must be designed to reach only a limited number of conclusions about a particular constellation of facts. Biological psychology points to specific adaptations throughout the animal kingdom. Different species show sharp, innate differences in drives, habits, and abilities, ranging from food preparation to celestial navigation. Cognitive psychology suggests that human beings are specifically prepared for the comprehension of language, recognition of faces, perception of color, analysis of physical space, and other ways to interpret the world (Hirschfeld & Gelman, 1994; Pinker, 2002). According to evolutionary psychology, many specific fears, preferences, and behavioral tendencies in modern life have been shaped by the demands of individual survival and reproduction in ancestral cultures.

In this view, the human mind is a series of modular mechanisms. The concept of *modularity* here, broadly consistent with the doctrine in biological psychology, emphasizes restrictions in information processing. The content or information available to one module does not necessarily become available to other modules in that same system. Cognitive neuroscientists are just beginning to understand how biological modularity mediates and constrains specific cognitive activities (Flombaum, Santos, & Hauser, 2002).

This view that the human mind is divided into modular domains has aroused extensive debate within and outside evolutionary psychology. After all, we generally experience a unified self. How could this confederation of independent entities be possible?

Answers to that question await further research in psychology and related sciences. At this point, evolutionary psychologists simply assume that the modern human mind gradually evolved over the millennia of human history. It emerged through steady inheritance from countless ancestors who solved *specific* problems of survival and reproduction. The outcomes of their success appear today as evolved fears, preferences, and behavioral tendencies.

Afraid of snakes, fond of Viennese pastries, and fluent in four languages, Bertha showed some of these fears, preferences, and behavioral tendencies. Like the rest of us, she also showed some exceptions, notably with regard to sexuality. In all such instances, evolutionary psychology recognizes the reciprocal roles of heredity and environment in producing individual differences. For everyone, including Bertha, the result is an interplay between these influences.

In the sexual realm, Bertha apparently became an exception through environmental influences. Her success in mating had been seriously impeded by her early illness, which prevented socialization and sexual development at a crucial stage. Later, her domineering, self-centered personality disrupted prospects for reciprocal alliances, successful courting, and so forth. Her deepest involvement with human sexuality occurred in her expedition to the brothels.

Arriving in Budapest, she met with a tall Hungarian in clerical clothes. She explained her mission and he replied, "I am not interested in this matter."

Reminded that he served as chairman for the Society for the Protection of Children, he responded: "Yes, but only children up to 12 or 13 years. Older ones are not my business." So ended Bertha's effort in Hungary, her first attempt to overthrow forced prostitution in Eastern Europe.

At a consulate in Greece, she raised the problem again and received a hasty disclaimer. "What do you want? The poor sell their children like chickens!"

On a Saturday night, she entered a house of prostitution in Salonika. There she met the women at their work. Later that night, she wrote about Jolanthe, one of these women. "The most beautiful one I saw here, maybe the most beautiful Jewish woman I ever saw, perhaps the most beautiful alive, I found today in a brothel." Bertha pondered her discovery. "I can understand that a man will risk all for such a woman," she mused (Pappenheim, 1924).

Evolution of Sexual Behavior

Human sexuality marks the starting point for a discussion of various evolved psychological mechanisms because reproduction marks the beginning of the life cycle. Without reproduction we would not exist. Without a fear of snakes, tendency toward language, or preference for sweets, we still might exist, though in modified form.

But there is a drawback to this focus on human sexuality. The chief criticisms of evolutionary psychology relate to the findings and interpretations of mate preferences and mating patterns. They have been viewed as counterproductive to the pursuit of gender equality. At this point, the reader is encouraged to follow the data and theories of evolutionary psychology, the focus of this chapter. As usual, the chapter closes with commentary and criticism of this approach to psychology.

Preferences in Mate Selection

From the standpoint of evolutionary psychology, Bertha was quite correct. Men would be attracted to Jolanthe's beauty. Other things being equal, they prefer beautiful women.

Why does that happen? How does this preference arise?

Consider a society without mating preferences. Through random pairing, males who mated with infertile females would not become anyone's ancestors. Those who mated with females high in fertility would produce progeny, passing on their genes, including their preference for female characteristics associated with fertility. As this selective process continued for millions of years, even with very slight genetic variations among individual members, males would acquire a tendency for mating with fertile, rather than infertile, females. Without any intent or motivation in men, this tendency would be passed on as an evolutionary adaptation—an evolved psychological mechanism.

Through these reproductive adaptations, men and women have developed mate preferences. The concept of **mate preferences** refers to the characteristics desired in a partner, and these preferences are based largely on the gender roles in the reproductive process, which are quite different for men and women. With millions of sperm readily available, a reproductive man must find and engage a woman who is fertile—a characteristic difficult to assess. As a rule, the younger the mature woman, the greater is her potential for reproduction. But just as fertility is uncertain, age is not readily determined either. There are, however, reliable cues for age. A woman with smooth skin, glossy hair, shiny teeth, and a light, sprightly style is probably young and therefore likely to be fertile. Similarly, a woman with physical symmetry shows a sign of health and therefore likely fertility. Over the eons of evolution, men attracted to these fertility cues produced more offspring than men attracted to women without such cues. They thereby passed on this preference for these physical characteristics in a mate (Buss, 1999).

In Hungary, Greece, and elsewhere, Bertha found these characteristics among the prostitutes. The male preferences in mate selection were reflected in the brothels.

The woman's investment in reproduction is indeed different from that of a man. With a limited number of eggs, available only at certain times, and the extensive demands of gestation, birth, nurturance, and especially child rearing, women must find a mate with an ability and willingness to furnish the necessary resources for successful parenting. These include, among others, food, shelter, time, territory, and protection. Mates with such resources provide a selective advantage for the woman and her progeny. On this basis, status and possessions, power and territory, and so forth should emerge as female preferences in a mate. However, human beings often mate at relatively early ages, before a man's resources are fully acquired. For this reason, females too should use predictive cues, such as intelligence and industry (Buss, 1999). A man who is bright and hardworking is likely to acquire resources. Hence, these qualities have emerged as female preferences in mate selection.

These evolved preferences do not guide the selection process completely. They make a contribution as an inborn tendency or disposition. As evident in social psychology, other factors, conscious and otherwise, contribute to this complex process. Especially important are the extent to which potential partners are alike in fundamental ways, such as intelligence, interests, values, and in many societies, the extent to which they know one another (Botwin, Buss, & Shackelford, 1997; Homans, 1961). These two factors, similarity and familiarity, can distinctly moderate the tendency among men and women to seek mates high in attractiveness and resources, respectively.

Variations in these tendencies, produced by individual genetic differences and environmental factors, are of no special interest in evolutionary psychology. But they are not inconsequential. Without variations among individuals, there would be no grist for the mill producing the survival of the fittest.

Environmental factors may even produce group differences. For example, social-role theory suggests that as women in developed societies gain increased economic advantages, their preferences in mates may be shifting away from supportive males and toward attractive men as desirable partners (Eagly & Wood, 1999).

Whatever their preferences, members of the same sex vie with one another for mating opportunities. Men compete with men in intelligence, industry, and so forth, just as women compete with women in various ways. For the losers in these battles within the sexes, the result is not death of the individual but rather few or no offspring (Darwin, 1859).

These mating preferences do not necessarily operate at a conscious level. There are, of course, "gold-digging" women, consciously aiming to tap a man's resources. Presumably, they are also impelled by their evolutionary history, directing their preferences toward male traits consistently associated with the resources, willingness, and ability to engage in the labor-intensive activity of successful parenting (Ellis, 1992). Similarly, men divorce older wives and marry younger women, sometimes called "trophy wives." The label suggests that the men have been winners in some sort of contest, and their high-value mates are the prize. Again, men may consciously engage in this behavior, seeking a young and beautiful wife as a status symbol. But this conscious effort does not rule out for them, or for males throughout the world, a universal interest in such women as a function of a lengthy, selective evolutionary history.

Common Mating Patterns

In addition to mate preferences, this same evolutionary history has shaped the **mating patterns** of men and women, meaning their overall approach to sexual encounters during their lifetime. And different patterns have emerged. The ancestral man who experienced high reproductive success mated not only with one fertile woman but with many fertile women. Compared to monogamous men, he was far more likely to produce dependents. In this process, continued over millions and millions of years, males evolved a predisposition for sexual variety; they developed a tendency, or pattern, for mating with several partners (Symonds, 1979).

A woman who achieved reproductive success found a man capable of investing in the high costs of rearing offspring and willing to make that investment. Gaining continuous access to these resources became a primary benefit for the woman. On these bases, women evolved a reproductive pattern of sustained mating with a single partner.

Under these conditions, evolution has shaped men to a more **polygamous** disposition, oriented to sexual encounters with multiple partners. And it has shaped women to more **monogamous** relationships, the practice of mating with the same partner. These different outcomes evolved from the fundamental asymmetry between the sexes at minimum levels of parental investment. Such levels are much lower for men and much higher for women, leaving men less restrained by the consequences of the reproductive act. In other words, men have more interest in casual sex, as popular knowledge attests. Evolutionary psychology aims to understand the origins of this difference in evolutionary history, rather than in current social roles, which certainly are influential.

Impregnation by an ancestral man would require nine months of gestation on the woman's part but no further investment by him. During this same interval he might engage in numerous copulations with other women, resulting in several pregnancies. She in turn would experience only one birth. Thus, for men, compared with women, short-term mating resulted in a far greater number of offspring. Carried on through millions of generations, this inclination toward polygamy and short-term mating would become an evolved psychological mechanism in men.

Substantial support for this view comes from the presence of prostitution and extramarital affairs in modern life. Both provide evidence that men, more than women, seek short-term mating patterns. The consumers of prostitution are essentially all men. Participation by women remains negligible. The famous Kinsey Reports brought forth the first substantial scientific data, showing that 70% of men went to a prostitute at one time or another. The frequencies for women who did so were too miniscule for further consideration (Kinsey, Pomeroy, & Gebhard, 1953; Kinsey, Pomeroy, & Martin, 1948).

The Kinsey Reports also showed wide gender differences among those who participated in extramarital affairs, with men engaged at nearly twice the rate of women. Once again, these findings have been supported by subsequent surveys. But social-role theory enters here too. With fewer behavioral restrictions for women today, the gender difference in extramarital affairs has decreased, though it still remains substantial (Janus & Janus, 1993).

The difference between these two forms of short-term mating accounts at least in part for the stability of prostitution and changes in extramarital affairs. The former is only a sexual encounter; the latter includes some element of love or romance, as well.

Moreover, casual sex involves far greater costs for women than for men. These costs include a higher risk of sexually transmitted disease, unwanted pregnancy, and loss of value as a long-term mate. Prostitution carries all these risks, including contact with other unstable activities.

This polygamous tendency in men worldwide of course promotes prostitution. After her meetings in Hungary and Greece, Bertha realized the extent of prostitution, appearing literally around the globe. The women most susceptible to recruitment were young, impoverished, and ignorant about sex. Their pregnancies became burdensome for all. Unwed mothers could not care for themselves, much less for their unplanned babies.

Adaptations in Parenting

Pregnancy, too, has been shaped by natural selection, according to evolutionary psychology. In particular, the early weeks reflect an adaptation over the millions of years in hunter-gatherer societies.

Pregnancy Sickness

Modern women in the 2nd to 10th week of pregnancy experience nausea, vomiting, and food aversions, incorrectly called morning sickness. This condition varies among different women but appears in virtually all societies. It is not limited to the morning and strictly speaking is not a sickness. Early in the pregnancy, avoiding certain foods and vomiting others are healthy responses, nevertheless known as **pregnancy sickness**. These aversive reactions, created by hormonal changes in pregnant women, shield the unborn baby from **teratogens**, poisonous and other substances that produce birth defects (Profet, 1992).

From the viewpoint of evolutionary psychology, food aversions evolved as an adaptation of our hunter-gatherer ancestors, who foraged for anything edible. Through a broad diet of nutritious and harmful foods over millions of years, aversions to poisonous foods became an evolved psychological mechanism, protecting the pregnant woman from malnutrition that would harm her unborn baby. Several studies have demonstrated that the *absence* of nausea and vomiting is associated with higher neonatal abnormality and mortality (Brandes, 1967; Tierson, Olsen, & Hook, 1986). In other words, pregnant women who vomit tend to experience fewer miscarriages, stillbirths, and related problems (Klebanoff, Koslowe, Kaslow, & Rhoads, 1985).

The timing of this sickness matches the development of the **embryo**, the prenatal period from the second week through the second month, during which the baby's neural organs, in particular, begin sustained growth. The embryonic period is thereby the most important of the entire pregnancy for the healthy, prenatal development of human organs. Expressed differently, it is the stage of maximum susceptibility to teratogens.

Plants are consumed by numerous predators, including insects, animals, and other plants. To defend themselves, they have evolved diverse chemical substances as weapons against attack. These toxins, or poisons, appear even in apples, bananas, cherries, and other common elements of human diets. However, coffee, tea, cocoa, and vegetables contain unusually high concentrations of toxins for human beings, and they are the foods women find most aversive early in the pregnancy.

Then too, the sense of smell becomes more acute during the first weeks of pregnancy. At this stage, pregnant women are repulsed by odors previously found satisfying. In particular, pungent and bitter odors arouse an aversive reaction, causing rejection of all highly spiced foods and many vegetables. This change in olfactory sensitivity favors bland foods, which contain lower concentrations of toxins, thereby diminishing the potential for toxicity during the embryonic period. In fact, many pregnant women experience food cravings as well. The aversions may be due to changes in the sense of smell, the cravings to an impaired capacity for taste. Both responses appear to play a protective role for the embryo (Dickens & Trethowan, 1971).

In addition to their role in pregnancy, most innate food aversions have emerged as protections against toxicity throughout the life of the individual. Pregnancy sickness is an extra, early, short-term defense against embryonic birth defects. During the period of the **fetus**, beginning at the third month and lasting through the remainder of the pregnancy, this nausea disappears; then prenatal neural developments require a substantial increase in maternal nutrition (Profet, 1992).

Infant-Directed Speech

After the birth, the mother begins responding to the neonate, and once again evolution appears to shape the process. The new mother speaks to the baby long before the infant develops even the rudiments of language. Moreover, she speaks in a very distinct manner. Through highly specific, almost musical patterns of pitch, range, and intonation, known as **infant-directed speech**, the caretaker communicates her feelings and controls the infant. The baby cannot understand language but has the maturity for feelings. It becomes aroused, approved, prohibited, and comforted by the mother's speech, which uses modifications informally called *motherese* (Fernald, 1992).

Adults usually speak to one another in a quick, choppy fashion. Caretakers speak to their infants more slowly and with more emphases.

To arouse the infant and catch its attention, the mother uses a wide range of pitch. Then she ends these vocalizations with a sharp rise in the last syllable: "Can you get it?" To express approval, she again employs a wide range of pitch, but she ends with a falling tone: "That's a good bo-oy." The mother is communicating her positive feelings and, at the same time, rewarding the baby.

For prohibition, infant-directed speech takes on a very different character. The caretaker employs a low pitch with little variation. The smooth, musical quality for catching attention and showing approval does not appear. Instead, the sounds are shorter, more intense, more abrupt: "No. No!" Staccato sounds serve as unconditioned stimuli; no learning is required. The infant responds to the noise completely apart from its linguistic features.

As with prohibition, infant-directed speech communicates comfort in a low pitch with little variation. However, the sounds are longer and softer, less intense: "Mmmmm. Oh, Honey." Like prohibition speech, the sounds that induce comfort appear to be unconditioned stimuli. The infant's response is automatic. Low-frequency, continuous white-noise sounds also function effectively for soothing a distressed infant. In white noise, the intensity is constant, as in the common quieting sound, "Shhhh."

In simple terms, infant-directed speech employs exaggerated intonation. Used consistently in cultures throughout Africa, America, Asia, Europe, and other parts of the world, it appears as an evolved adaptation of mothers' attempts to communicate with their prelinguistic infants. The baby's limited perceptual abilities require this responsiveness by the mother. These patterned modifications serve to regulate the infants' attention, communicate feelings, and increase the potential for speech perception and comprehension. They form an early basis for infants' experiences about themselves and those who care for them (Fernald, 1992).

One cross-cultural study of both parents compared infant-directed speech with adult-directed speech in English, French, German, Italian, and Japanese. Similar modifications from adult speech appeared in all languages, supporting the evolutionary predictions. They even occurred with men, although at a lower level, perhaps owing partly to infants' lesser interest in men's voices. The American mothers, speaking English, showed the most pronounced modifications, thereby illustrating cultural differences as well (Fernald, Taeschner, Dunn, Papousek, de Boyson-Bardies, & Fukui, 1989).

Virtually universal in women, infant-directed speech improves with experience. The caretaker makes adjustments according to the baby's response, eventually speaking "advanced motherese." Without babies in her own home, Bertha missed the intensive child care that fosters this further development. An element of learning is involved in infant-directed speech.

Throughout her adult life, Bertha also missed a sustained relationship with an adult partner. And the two conditions appear related, both perhaps with roots in her Vienna days. Her work with residents and staff of The Home thereby played a major role in her personal life. But despite these associations, she remained without friends and even without regular companions (Edinger, 1968).

Alone on the ship sailing to Egypt, she sought social support. When her cabin neighbor discovered she was not married, he pointed out that it was still not too late. If she colored her hair, she might look 30. Bertha ignored the entreaty. Her birth certificate showed she was 52.

After that man left the ship, Bertha wrote, "There's nothing to report except that it's the worst day of my trip. It pours!"

In Alexandria, a police officer escorted her to several brothels. In one, she and her guide sat at a large table with three girls, all of whom were wearing colorful shawls and similar necklaces, made up of strings of tiny beads and coins. Two of the girls were 16 and 17 years old. They spoke freely, but the third prostitute remained silent. Later, she pointed at Bertha and remarked, "She shall be blessed, and her family also, for no such woman has ever thus spoken to us."

In a visit to Lodz, then part of Russia, Bertha described her mission to a German woman who was highly respected in feminist and other circles. She readily understood Bertha's concern. Then she heard Bertha's goal: to diminish or destroy the slave trade.

She stared with raised eyebrows. "A swallow wants to drain the sea?" she asked incredulously.

Arriving in Warsaw, still alone, Bertha began again to doubt her mission and herself: "I am not necessary. For nothing and to no one." She sorely missed conversation, companionship, even the most minimal social life.

Dispositions in Group Living

Human beings are fundamentally social creatures. Responsiveness to others is perhaps the most obvious aspect of human existence. Evolutionary psychologists speculate that the human tendency toward social behavior evolved through the advantages it offered in the struggle for survival. By working together for millions of years, people gained increased success in building shelters, finding food, caring for the young, and defending against attack.

In other words, to behave adaptively our remote ancestors needed to acquire a capacity for responding not only to their physical world but also to their social environment. As members of social groups, those most suited to survival were those who developed mental mechanisms for **social exchange**, a broad term referring to all sorts of behaviors for solving problems in a social context—dealing with other people, their relationships, emotions, motivations, interactions, and other conditions of social life. This capacity for social exchange is also known as cooperation, reciprocation, and reciprocal altruism (Cosmides & Tooby, 1992).

For several reasons, skill in social exchange appears to be a long-term adaptation. If it were a recent social invention, there would be evidence of some point of origin, and there is none. In addition, there is no substantial evidence that it has been spread by contact among different peoples. Social exchange is not sparse or absent in some cultures and complex in others. It appears in highly elaborated patterns in all cultures. Moreover, social exchange is not unique to human society. Social exchange occurs among chimpanzees, our nearest relatives, and among baboons, suggesting that it appeared at least as early as our common ancestors, several million years ago (Cosmides & Tooby, 1992). Major social tasks include using language, transmitting and interpreting facial expressions, and detecting cheating in a social contract.

Acquisition of Language

With the acquisition of language, the ultimate mechanism in social exchange, humanoids could assist one another in the nuances of these tasks. And language plays a central role in the most intimate social behavior—finding and maintaining a mate. There are, of course, competing explanations about how human beings acquired language.

From an evolutionary perspective, human language began with grunts and gestures, gradually increasing in complexity until, over the millennia, it reached its current intricate stage. A result of natural selection, learning language today is not like learning to play the piano or to balance a checkbook. Through natural selection, human beings have become genetically *predisposed* to learn language; it unfolds almost automatically, as another evolved psychological mechanism. Vocabulary, specific rules, and stylistic devices of course must be learned, but people are born with the basic structure in mind, a so-called universal grammar. Common to every normal person, this **universal grammar** is an innate understanding of how language works—an inborn comprehension of the fundamental components of language and their relation-ships (Chomsky, 1957, 1972).

Signs of this universal grammar appear in speech. All the world's many hundreds of languages are alike in important but non-essential ways. For example, they employ just a few of the many sounds human beings might use in speaking. Infants can make many sounds found among animals, including birds, but they do not use them as adults. There is no logical neces-sity for this narrow range of sounds in existing languages, and cultural dif-ferences would work against it. This uniformity appears to be a function of an inborn tendency, a common biological inheritance around the world.

In addition, no primitive language exists today. And there is no significant evidence that cultures are learning or developing their languages in basic ways. In complexity of structure, the languages of aborigines are comparable to those of the modern industrialized world. This condition might reflect the absence of written reports from much earlier times, but even the available records, some from 5,000 years ago, do not indicate any increase in complexity. The earliest reconstructible stage for families of languages includes all the complexities and capacities of Bertha's modern German, French, Italian, and English.

The speed, sequence, and universality of language learning add impressive evidence to the concept of a universal grammar. Children sometimes acquire 5 to 10 new words per day, and they learn in the same sequence, as noted earlier, moving in a few years from cooing and babbling to complex con-structions, along the way making similar, predictable errors in grammar and syntax (Miller & Gildea, 1987).

In forming questions, and without being told, the child learns that the *wh* words—*when, what, why, where*—come first in the sentence. And the child already knows that nouns precede verbs. Hence, in some languages, children ask: "Where the ball is?" Later, they reverse the sequence with *wh* words. As the quintessential human skill, mastery occurs in a stable, reliable pattern (Brown, 1973).

Severely retarded persons, unable to acquire many basic skills, typically acquire language ability, although at a slower rate. In fact, children can understand language before they can comprehend many other social codes in their community—manners, customs, bartering, and reciprocity. These forms of social exchange are the fabric of society. They bind citizens together. Like the capacity for language, mastery is essential for survival in one's group. On all these and other bases, human beings appear predisposed to learning lan-guage, an evolved psychological mechanism.

Shared Emotional Expressions

The ability to express and recognize emotional states emerged as another mechanism of social exchange. Predecessors with this capacity possessed an adaptive advantage. They were more likely than others to identify desirable mates, anticipate attack, appeal successfully for assistance, and the like.

Darwin described the emergence of emotional expression through natural selection. Prior to fighting, certain animals thrust the head forward, assume a firm stance, bare the teeth, and gaze intently at the opponent. These postures and gestures, the first stages of attack, provide an advantage for the aggressor; they prepare fighting weapons. Moreover, if these preparatory behaviors suffice to subdue the opponent, the victory is accomplished without bloodshed. For the opponent, anticipation of the attack becomes crucial to defense and counterattack, and submissive behaviors sometimes prevent the physical encounter. Natural selection favors the expression and recognition of emotional signals (Darwin, 1859).

On the same bases, human beings have evolved the capacity to send and receive nonverbal signals about their emotions. These **facial expressions in emotion** are consistent patterns of movements and positions of the face associated with certain feelings: happiness, sadness, anger, fear, surprise, and disgust. Concentrated around the eyes and mouth, these movements and positions also appear in the forehead, nose, and even the chin. As still another evolved psychological mechanism, human beings reliably depict their feelings, wearing them not on their sleeves but on their faces.

Contemporary research has examined these six emotional states—happiness, sadness, anger, fear, surprise, and disgust—in human beings. Obtaining many pictures of various people in these circumstances, investigators measured the position of each part of the face and its degree of displacement from the normal or relaxed state. Using these findings, they produced composite or "typical" photos for each state. Also, they asked actors to assume the various positions and again took photographs. Then they presented these photos to people in Argentina, Japan, Chile, Brazil, and the United States.

Asked to assign one of the six feelings to each photo, observers in all cultures attributed the same feelings to the same facial expressions, matching the original situations. Additional studies with eight different cultures provided the same result. Even preliterate people in the remote highlands of New Guinea responded the same way as people from other cultures—with one exception. They made no distinction between the expressions for surprise and fear (Ekman, 1992; Ekman & Friesen, 1975). These results suggest a universality in sending and interpreting these emotional expressions.

Other expressions vary from culture to culture. Scratching the cheeks may show indecision in the United States; in some Asian societies it is a sign of happiness. Clapping the hands, evidence of joy here, indicates worry or disappointment in certain Asian groups. Europeans show displeasure by whistling, a sign of approbation in this country (Fernald, 1997). All these expressions are learned, transmitted by elders in the culture. They are not universal, not evolved psychological mechanisms.

Human facial expressions are also accompanied by gestures and postures that vary markedly from one person and moment to another. Angry people may clench their fists, turn their head aside, or assume a stiff posture, and yet these same behaviors may accompany fear, sadness, or some other emotional state. In other words, their behavior shows the way they are coping with an emotion. Within the limits of the six basic emotional states, their facial expressions reveal what they are feeling, recognized universally, even by "foreigners."

Making Social Contracts

Another form of social exchange, useful in almost any group, is skill in making social contracts—dealing with others on a cost-benefit basis. In a **social contract**, one individual, at some personal cost, becomes entitled to a benefit from another individual or group. The concern lies with the cost-benefit outcome. A well-formed social contract becomes mutually advantageous; each party gains a benefit that outweighs the cost.

In the evolutionary metaphor, people negotiating social contracts wage wily, subtle battles. Rather than attacking one another physically or fighting over limited supplies, the warriors compete in an exchange of property or services. Throughout history, human beings have made endless exchanges of all sorts, ranging from food and shelter to child care and combat assistance. Those who possessed special skill in making such bargains maintained an adaptive advantage. They obtained more food and mates and produced more descendants. Predecessors who lacked this skill negotiated unsuccessfully. They became less likely to survive and reproduce.

On this basis, the reasoning of modern human beings about social contracts should be superior to their reasoning about problems without a social contract. Indeed, people today do solve problems about violations of social contracts more readily and successfully than they solve comparable problems on other topics. Moreover, the possibility of a payoff, by itself, is not the critical factor. The superior reasoning occurs even when there is just the potential for a violation (Cosmides & Tooby, 1992). The critical issue seems to be a rule about potential costs, benefits, and wrongdoing, apart from the specific contents of the problem.

This capacity to detect violations, sometimes called a *cheater-detection mechanism,* does not imply that people are invariably successful in detecting cheating—far from it. It indicates that, other things being equal, most people are more successful in detecting cheating in a social contract than in solving other problems with the *same* structure but without a social contract, such as conventional nonsocial situations, abstract problems, or nonsense conditions. Human beings are not notably adept at solving logical problems, but they do better than usual when cheater detection becomes involved (Figure 8.2).

A number of investigations support this viewpoint, demonstrating that the outcome is independent of one's familiarity with the topic. But the evidence is not yet complete or distinctly convergent (Evans & Chang, 1998). The hypothesis about cheater detection in social contracts awaits further support.

Human beings enter social contracts regularly. They satisfy many of them automatically by shaking hands, making a purchase, or obeying a rule. It is impossible to imagine human society without such contracts. They exist in fundamental ways within and across cultures.

Shortly after her arrival in yet another culture, Bertha shook hands and entered into an unwritten social contract with Countess Barbara, her

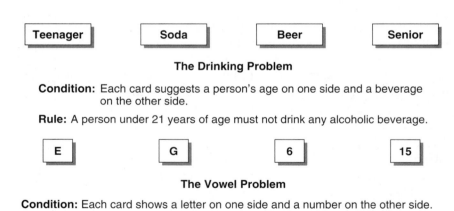

| Teenager | Soda | Beer | Senior |

The Drinking Problem

Condition: Each card suggests a person's age on one side and a beverage on the other side.

Rule: A person under 21 years of age must not drink any alcoholic beverage.

| E | G | 6 | 15 |

The Vowel Problem

Condition: Each card shows a letter on one side and a number on the other side.

Rule: A card with a vowel on one side must have an even number on the other side.

Figure 8.2   Detecting Violation of a Social Contract. Which cards must be turned over to detect a rule violation? Most people respond successfully to the drinking problem, turning the first and third cards, and unsuccessfully to the vowel problem, again turning the first and third cards. Card 15, not 6, may violate the vowel rule. That rule does not state that a card with an even number must have a vowel. Similarly, the drinking rule does not state that anyone over age 21 must drink alcohol.

hostess in Moscow. In return for a tour of the poor sections of the city, she would inform the Countess about social activism in Germany.

This social contract, or *sharing* of information, appeared beneficial to both. The cost to each, explaining one's culture, was relatively low and the benefit high because a first-hand description of that foreign land was otherwise a scarce commodity. When resources are scarce, sharing is one method of redistribution, thereby diminishing deprivation. Lack of food, even for a few days, makes individual survival impossible. Sharing in times of feast lessens the potential for times of famine. According to evolutionary psychology, the tendency to engage in social contracts evolved because it usually results in mutual benefits, though of course there are exceptions.

Mutual benefits occurred for Bertha and Barbara, and apparently neither cheated. But their contract bore more costs than either expected. They promptly found themselves ideologically opposed.

Both women were headstrong, and they possessed very different ideas about prostitution. The Countess repeatedly declared she had "no sympathy" for prostitutes. Bertha expressed deep compassion. They argued vehemently and finally dropped the subject—a tacit agreement that made the rest of their time together tolerable.

The Countess supervised a government institution for the homeless. For their nighttime expedition, her part of the contract, she invited Bertha to come with strong nerves and a short skirt. Bertha accepted, wearing a skirt above the ankles. It would not drag on the floor and thereby collect vermin.

"I need not tell you what I saw," Bertha reported to her subscribers. Then she gave some details anyway. "I almost suffocated when I saw drunken men and women, heard their yells and laughter . . . saw the basement where the bodies of those killed in all-night fights were dumped." The amateurs, not the professional prostitutes, posed the most serious threats to themselves and others.

Finally, at 11:00 P.M., Bertha thanked the Countess for a most illuminating experience. The Countess replied that she was pleased to be useful.

"My thanks were sincere," Bertha later declared, "though I knew that, conventionally and politely, I shook hands with an enemy."

Returning to Frankfurt following 15 months of travel, Bertha organized national and international committees to combat slavery-induced prostitution. Later, she decided that she had failed in this compelling mission, noting that she had brought few people into the cause. This outcome became one of the few substantial disappointments in her working life. But she gained one small habit. During board meetings later, she occupied herself by stringing together tiny beads and coins, making necklaces like those she had admired on the three young prostitutes in Alexandria (Freeman, 1972).

Inclination Toward Aggression

The different inherited dispositions of men and women toward sexual behavior and parental investment appear to be natural outcomes of their different biological structures. These biological differences also have profound implications for gender differences in aggression. They result in different tendencies toward within-gender rivalry and the type of aggression, physical or verbal.

Throughout the world men, more than women, resort to **physical aggression,** which includes any form of bodily assault, from simply pushing and shoving to homicide (Archer, 1994; Wrangham & Peterson, 1996). Women, more than men, engage in **verbal aggression,** which is any form of attack on another person by using language, ranging from insults to hostile gossip and slander. The latter behaviors can be potent indeed, sometimes causing more damage than a physical attack. In both cases, these forms of aggression are more likely to occur *within* than between genders (Buss, 1999).

Early research focused on the environmental factors stimulating physical aggression: the presence of weapons, observations of aggressive people, and frustrating circumstances. For example, observing television violence contributes to aggression in children (Eron, 1982; Hoberman, 1990). But the presence of physical aggression down through history and across societies suggests some inherited predisposition, and here evolutionary psychologists have collected data and proposed explanations.

In urban life, men have committed over 80% of the homicides, and their victims have been at least 80% males. In a large number of societies, male-male homicides exceed female-female homicides by a ratio of 30:1 (Daly & Wilson, 1988). Observed with such little variation throughout the world, this pattern has prompted questions about the reasons for this gender difference, and the chief hypotheses once again turn to the difference in reproductive roles. Men today respond aggressively in instances of direct sexual competition because throughout evolutionary history those who reacted in this way were more likely to reproduce and thus to contribute to the genetic inheritance of men. All men are exposed to **paternity uncertainty,** meaning the possibility that they are not the father of their partner's child. For this reason, some jealously guard their mate and fight with potential rivals. Women may not know who fathered their baby, but they do know that they are the mother.

On these bases it is not surprising to find gender differences in response to a partner's infidelity. A man exposed to infidelity risks the expenditure of energy and resources for another man's genes. A woman risks losing those resources, perhaps diverted to another woman. Thus, evolutionary psychologists predicted that male mating jealousy should be directed to cues of *sexual* infidelity, and female jealousy should arise from cues of *emotional* infidelity.

Several investigations have examined these hypotheses by measuring psychological and physiological responses, and replications have appeared in other cultures. In one instance, 256 college students in the United States imagined a scenario in which their partner had engaged in passionate sexual intercourse with someone else or had become deeply attached emotionally to that person. Then they indicated which type of involvement they would find more distressing. The results clearly supported the predictions and earlier findings. Follow-up studies investigated which types of infidelity they would be more likely to forgive and which would more likely prompt them to break up with their partner. Again, the results confirmed the prediction (Shackelford, Buss, & Bennett, 2002). These findings become vital in the context of male sexual jealousy, the most prominent cause of spouse battering around the world (Daly & Wilson, 1988).

In addition to sexual rivalries, other conditions fostered aggression in the long sweep of history. Aggressive people gained and stockpiled resources, defended against attack, negotiated for higher status in the social hierarchy, and also deterred their mates from infidelity. These specific contexts suggest that aggression today is not a blind instinct or totally unpredictable human tendency. It appears instead as an evolved psychological mechanism, closely tied to specific situations that are similar to those encountered by progenitors who responded aggressively and thereby gained adaptive advantages (Buss, 1999).

Aggression in women, typically verbal, usually occurs toward other women, labeling them as promiscuous or unattractive. Here too, sexual rivalry apparently plays a fundamental role in human aggression. Both remarks depict the slandered person as sexually undesirable (Campbell, 1993). Women also engage in physical aggression, but compared to men they are less prone to this behavior and less violent.

Again, environmental factors can sharply modify inherited tendencies. Studies of 20th-century college students show a decrease in verbal and physical aggression over a 10-year period. Questionnaire data were collected from 603 students in 1986, 414 students in 1992, and 571 students in 1996; all of these students were between 18 and 24 years old, and all were engaged in a dating relationship. For both men and women, self-report scores showed that physical and verbal aggression had diminished for each successive time period. Perhaps more significant, the reports also showed a decrease in the partner's aggressive reactions over the decades. Expressed differently, in recent years fewer men and women indicated that they were in a mutually violent relationship. And finally, an increased percentage of women described themselves as perpetrators of violence, rather than victims, a finding consistent with other research on dating couples (Billingham, Bland, & Leary, 1999).

Whether these results will be confirmed by future studies and whether they partly reflect changing social roles have yet to be determined. From a sociocultural context, it may be useful to recognize more fully that women also become aggressive and that a more egalitarian approach may be helpful to both genders.

Throughout her life, Bertha tended to resort to verbal aggression. Even 12 years after her battle of the brothels, she expressed anger over her almost complete failure. But she channeled her feelings in a productive fashion, writing a book entitled *Sisyphus Work,* describing her efforts as like those of the Greek mythical character compelled eternally to pushing a boulder toward the top of a hill, always losing his grasp, and watching it roll down again. In fact, the analogy is imperfect. Bertha never approached the top of the hill, and she discontinued her efforts after that one sustained attempt.

Promoting Behavioral Change

In dealing with her anger and disappointment, Bertha would find no assistance in evolutionary therapy. There is none. Evolutionary psychology offers no therapy for depression, frustration, or any other human reaction. Human beings can make changes in their lifestyles and environments, but they cannot change their evolutionary history.

Evolutionary psychology also does not study the ways one person is different from another. It has little interest in individual differences. It focuses exclusively on shared characteristics, aiming to understand humanity, not particular human beings. For this reason, too, there is no therapy in evolutionary psychology.

The absence of an evolutionary therapy leaves a space here to consider a vital issue for all psychological therapy. What are the outcomes? To what extent is therapy helpful? These questions present a challenge for scientists and practitioners, and several have undertaken the difficult task of finding answers.

Assessing Therapy Effectiveness

Modern therapies in psychology offer a range of choices. In choosing a therapy, one chooses a particular technique or focus. Biomedical therapy alters the nervous system; psychoanalysis explores unconscious motivation; the goal in behavior therapy is to modify overt behaviors; humanistic psychology aims to generate self-understanding and perhaps release the actualizing tendency; and cognitive therapy corrects irrational, depressive, self-deprecating thinking.

At the outset, it should be noted that all therapies certainly are not effective with everyone—far from it. In fact, much research in psychology has been devoted to discovering which therapies are most useful for which people experiencing what kinds of problems. No medicine, diet, exercise, or work situation is beneficial to all, and therapy for adjustment problems is no exception. The old expression applies: "Different strokes for different folks" (Lipsey & Wilson, 1993; Luborsky, Singer, & Luborsky, 1975).

Assessing the effectiveness of a therapy becomes a difficult task. First, it must be demonstrated that the therapy is superior to no therapy at all, for symptoms sometimes disappear without any formal treatment, an outcome called **spontaneous remission**. To demonstrate that a particular therapy is more effective than spontaneous remission, at least two groups of subjects are necessary, one receiving the therapy, the other without it.

Then another problem arises. The no-treatment group cannot be randomly selected from the general population. People seeking therapy are motivated to change, and motivation plays a vital role in therapy outcomes. The treatment and no-treatment groups must be similar in motivation. For this reason, studies of therapy effectiveness often assign to the no-treatment group people on waiting lists, seeking to enter therapy. They too are motivated to change.

And a further problem emerges. The no-treatment groups needs some sort of treatment in order to assess the placebo effect. A *placebo* is any event without therapeutic properties that the recipient nevertheless views as a treatment; it might be a conversation, group meeting, pill, shock, or séance, presumably offering therapeutic value. Thus, the **placebo effect** includes any improvement in therapy arising solely from a person's expectations about the value of the placebo treatment, which is assumed to be the real therapy. Especially with a new treatment, when hopes are high, the placebo effect may be as important as the therapy itself.

Thus, at least three groups are needed: a no-treatment group, called the control group; a no-therapeutic treatment group, called the placebo group; and the treatment group, known as the experimental group. If the placebo and control groups perform similarly, there is no placebo effect. If the placebo and experimental groups perform similarly, there is no therapy effect. The therapy serves no better than a placebo.

But here again, the answer is not simple. Including a placebo group enables the investigator to determine the influence of expectancy alone, apart from any treatment. But in the case of insight therapies, or talking cures, social interaction is part of the therapy. If the placebo involves social interaction, then it rules out the effect of social interaction in the therapy group. And yet, the personal-social dimension is widely acknowledged as a major ingredient in talking therapies (Elkin, Shea, Watkins, Imber, Sotsky, Collins, et al., 1989; Wilkins, 1986).

Finally, all sorts of other factors can influence therapy outcomes: characteristics of the person in therapy, the type of personal problem, type of therapy, qualities of the therapist, length of therapy, occurrence of other factors in the person's life, the criteria for reaching a decision, when they are applied, and so forth in seemingly endless numbers. Nevertheless, after 60 years of research, producing hundreds of studies involving thousands of people, the overall answer is that therapy does help. People who complete therapy show more gains in adjustment than comparable persons who do not enter therapy (Bentler, 1991; Lipsey & Wilson, 1993).

The findings of course vary from one investigation to another, depending on the many factors just enumerated. But the overall results show that 70 to 75% of the people in therapy achieve a more favorable outcome than those who sought or needed therapy but did not receive it (Grissom, 1996; Smith & Glass, 1977). Another early review revealed that approximately 80% of all investigations of therapy yielded basically positive results (Luborsky, Singer, & Luborsky, 1975).

Ultimately, successful outcomes in therapy depend on an interaction among three factors: the therapist, method, and person in therapy. As a rule, therapy is most promising when the person offering therapy is experienced; the person seeking help is relatively young and intelligent; and both parties truly believe in the specific therapeutic method. Overall, the essential ingredient for a positive outcome is a *therapeutic alliance,* meaning a relationship in which both parties make a deep commitment to the goals of therapy and to one another (Grotstein, 1990; Smith & Thompson, 1993).

But evolutionary psychology has no therapy; human beings cannot modify their genetic history. They can, however, find assistance in the management of some personal and social problems. These possibilities arise because evolution does not impose a *genetic determinism,* wherein behavior is completely controlled by the genes. Rather, evolution produces a disposition or tendency that sometimes can be modified by social and cultural factors.

A Catalogue of Hypotheses

Without a therapy, evolutionary psychology can still assist people with inherited fears, preferences, and behavioral tendencies. Appropriate information should enable them to increase their understanding of themselves and to adopt healthier, more productive views on life. In this regard, a systematic *catalogue of evolutionary hypotheses,* especially those with empirical support, could become a useful instructional device (Gray, 1996). It could describe each hypothesis, its rationale, evidence for and against it, and recommendations for further reading. The successful consumer would seek further information directly from peer-reviewed journals or indirectly through materials based on these sources. These materials would provide readers with second-hand reports about original research, broadening their outlook on their own and others' lives.

Most women in their first pregnancy, for example, remain cautious and a bit uncertain, seeking information on the birth process. When confronted with daily nausea, the expectant mother should find comfort and consolation from a reliable catalogue of information explaining that the greater her sickness, the greater are her child's chances of freedom from birth defects.

This catalogue could promote other benefits derived from understanding pregnancy sickness. Pregnant women experiencing only mild sickness may decide to avoid high levels of dietary toxins anyway, as a cautionary measure. Those who experience severe sickness may consider its advantages and disadvantages before consuming medications to alleviate this condition. And women who have smoked or suffered other impairment of the sense of smell might take extra precautions in their diet (Profet, 1992).

Information about child-directed speech should be helpful for new parents. When managing the highly sensitive infant, voice modulations can communicate approval, prohibition, and comfort, as well as call for the baby's attention. By the same token, a harsh or loud tone, directed anywhere within the baby's earshot, can be disruptive. Despite its lack of language, the baby is listening.

The somewhat older child may protest against going to bed alone, especially in darkness. Parents are sometimes surprised at this reaction in their child, particularly if they have taken precautions against any frightening circumstance. From an evolutionary view, the child's fear is quite normal. In hunter-gatherer life, predators were a constant threat, particularly when they could not be seen. With few animal predators in modern life, the child's problem may be alleviated by telling her that such fears were reasonable when wild animals roamed freely. Now dangerous animals are far away or in cages. Special lighting, music, and the proximity of adults may prevent the child from feeling abandoned in the dark (Gray, 1996).

For parents, information on male-female differences in sex roles and relationships can be helpful with a significant social problem: men's physical violence, especially against the women in their lives. In all parts of the globe, husbands beat their wives, despite cultural and individual differences. This violence often emerges from sexual jealousy. Wives less frequently beat their spouses. From an evolutionary viewpoint, male jealousy and violence evolved as an adaptive response. A cuckolded man could spend his precious resources raising his rival's children. His jealous behavior played an important reproductive role. It ensured his paternity of the children born to his wife, whom he then supported (Wilson & Daly, 1993). Understood in this context, male violence certainly is not condoned or irremediable. But this evolutionary perspective may help citizens deal more effectively with this problem.

Violence toward children also has been viewed from an evolutionary perspective. A serious social problem, the incidence of child abuse varies with the genetic backgrounds of the parents. Child abuse is almost 40 times higher in families with stepchildren than in families in which the children are the biological offspring of the parents. Again, the interpretation centers around the evolved predisposition for expenditures of resources in behalf of one's own progeny (Buss, 1995a).

These irrational fears and forms of violence point again to the three fronts in Darwin's battleground metaphor. Human beings have made substantial progress against the forces of nature, developing weather forecasts about impending severe storms and constructing special shelters, clothing, and instruments for living in the coldest climates, highest altitudes, and deepest parts of the ocean. Also, human beings have conquered most of their predators, confining them largely to areas beyond human civilization. But we have not made comparable progress in living with one another. In the long run, our struggles among ourselves, especially over possession of nature's resources, may represent the most monumental challenge to our survival.

A catalogue of findings from evolutionary psychology could help us become more responsive to the dangers we create for ourselves, including the destruction we impose on our polluted and deteriorating environment. These reports could become a valuable part of public education and would be especially informative because many modern environments are so entirely different from those of the incomparably longer Pleistocene era.

Commentary and Critique

A partial list of these inferred psychological mechanisms shows their diversity: patterns of specific fears in infants, including stranger anxiety and darkness discomfort; adult phobias about harmless spiders, snakes, and other non-dangerous creatures; specific food preferences among children and adults, especially for fats and sugars; patterns of language acquisition in children, including its remarkable rate, invariant sequence, and predictable errors across cultures; the potential abuse of children, many times higher for preschoolers with adoptive as opposed to biological parents; morning sickness in pregnancy, occurring in embryonic development and in reference to fairly specific food categories; and adults' landscape preferences, favoring relatively open spaces as opposed to mountains or heavily wooded regions (Buss, 1999).

But these examples overlook a fundamental issue: gender differences. Human beings are men and women. To understand humanity, we need to know what women are like, as women, and men, as men.

In accepting this challenge, evolutionary psychology enters an arena fraught with controversy. The study of gender differences raises a special concern, as does the study of gender similarities. In almost any form, investigations of gender evoke criticism.

Research in evolutionary psychology has identified numerous gender differences as evolved psychological mechanisms: differences in risk-taking behavior, far greater for young males than females; differences in memory, with women superior in spatial-location and men in spatial-rotation capacity; differences in mate preferences, with men responding to reproduction potential and women to cues to a man's potential investment of resources; differences in mating patterns, with men more polygamous and women more monogamous; differences in sexual jealousy, greater for men than women; differences in interest in babies, with women far more involved than men; differences in sexual fantasy, with men engaging in it more frequently and more explicitly; and a host of other differences (Buss, 1995b, 1999).

In the investigation of gender differences, one major issue concerns gender equality, an expression used in social, political, and economic spheres denoting equal rights and opportunities. This goal is laudable, and yet the term "gender equality" may contribute to misunderstanding and confusion. Men generally possess greater size and strength than women. In turn, women possess the capacity to give birth and breast-feed babies. The first difference is quantitative and variable, the second qualitative and fixed. On this basis, equality becomes impossible. The concept of gender parity might serve better, denoting functional equivalence in value without implying the impossible structural equality. Commonly used in expressing status or amount in different markets, parity acknowledges the obvious inequalities in physical capacities and thereby assists all of us in advancing toward the overriding goal— greater respect for the similarities *and* differences between the genders.

In any case, a useful behavioral science should enable people of both genders to gain increased understanding of themselves and their cultures. The usual obstacles in pursuing this goal are not only the accuracy of the scientific findings but also the way they may be interpreted and exploited in the media and elsewhere. Amid these difficulties, the politics of gender on one hand and the science of gender on the other create **ideological issues**, matters of controversy or debate between parties with different ideas and concerns about human life and cultural influences. Beginning with different assumptions, the science and politics of gender each demonstrate a way of thinking about human behavior, each with its own interests, assumptions, and goals.

A second major issue concerns the interpretation of the findings. In contrast to the evolutionary viewpoint, **social-role theory** states that men and women become psychologically different because their roles in society demand different adjustments. Gender differences are not necessarily the result of inherited differences but rather of unequal opportunities in society. They arise from the gender-typical ways men and women are expected to act—women more than men emitting communal behaviors, men more than women emitting agentic behaviors (Eagly & Wood, 1999). These behaviors emerge from the women's typical homemaker role, at least with infants, and the men's typical role as resource provider, at least in the family's early years.

Prominent gender differences appear in response to partner infidelity, as noted already. But there is no reason to believe that male sexual jealousy and female emotional jealousy arise solely on the basis of biological factors. Cross-cultural investigations with German and Dutch participants have demonstrated the same jealousy patterns identified in the United States. However, the differences were smaller in both European cultures, and these cultures approach sexuality and extramarital relationships with more openness and acceptance than generally occurs in the United States. Thus, the appearance of the predicted gender differences supports the evolutionary view. The fact that these differences were smaller than anticipated shows the impact of environmental factors (Buunk, Angleitener, Oubaid, & Buss, 1996).

Grandparents' differential investments in their grandchildren also illustrate the potential for different contributions by gender. Substantial research has demonstrated that when choosing among all four grandparents, the grandchildren typically identify the maternal grandmother as making the greatest contribution to their welfare, evident in the warmth of relationships, provision of resources, time spent together, and the like. Almost invariably, the paternal grandfather receives the lowest ranking, and the maternal grandfather and paternal grandmother stand in intermediate positions (Euler & Weitzel, 1996). The low position of the father's father involves two instances of paternity uncertainty; the high rank of the mother's mother involves no uncertainty. Each of the two remaining grandparents experiences one instance of uncertainty. All these outcomes were predictable according to paternity uncertainty. As genetic relatedness becomes doubtful, investment in relatives diminishes—a primary tenet of evolutionary psychology.

And, again, social-role theory can point to environmental factors. Women are typically trained in child care, and many find it gratifying. This inclination should not suddenly disappear on becoming a grandparent. Around the world, grandmothers contribute greatly to the raising of their grandchildren. Here too, evolutionary theory and social-role theory are not necessarily incompatible.

Many social-role theorists accept the concept of an evolved organism. And evolutionary psychologists have long discarded the false **nature-nurture issue,** which stated the problem in an oversimplified fashion, investigating inborn versus acquired factors. All living organisms have a heredity, and all exist in some environment. For years, later investigators focused on identifying the special contributions of each. But today we speak of the **heredity-environment interaction**, referring to their combined, catalytic influences, recognizing that each is directly influential and also indirectly influential through its capacity to modify the other (Figure 8.3).

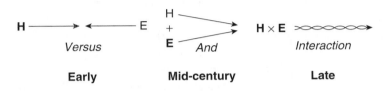

Figure 8.3   The Heredity-Environment Research Question. Early in the 20th century, research focused on heredity versus environment, often emphasizing hereditary factors in human development. By mid-century, the debate changed to heredity and environment, shifting greater attention to environmental influences. Before the end of the century, the concern lay with the heredity-environment interaction, the ways in which each component influences the other, a major interest today (Wahlsten, 2000).

In other words, evolutionary psychology and social-role theory recognize both sets of influences. But they do so from different starting points. Evolutionary psychology begins with our lengthy primeval history, which produced genetically different psychological mechanisms in men and women. Social-role theory begins with our current social environment, which poses different opportunities and creates different restrictions for men and women. A bat, cat, rat, and human beings all have different natures, and all require specific types of environmental stimulation to develop and function properly (Buss, 1995a). Evolved psychological mechanisms are mediated by specific features of the environment, co-producing evolution through genetic and social processes (Buss, 1995b; Eagly & Wood, 1999).

But within the social-role viewpoint, differences have arisen over the extent of gender differences revealed in research—prompted partly by divergent views within the feminist movement. Taking a minimalist position, some observers favor or seek findings of no or small differences, weakening evidence for gender stereotypes (Eagly, 1995). Others, from a maximalist position, favor large gender differences, especially in language, conversational style, and nonverbal behavior. The latter are inevitably magnified in the mass media, which are always in search of differences, debate, and drama (Hyde & Plant, 1995). In fact, survey research has demonstrated that the perceived gender differences, whatever their true size, do not do women a disservice. As demonstrated by well-respected female investigators, the stereotypes attributed to women in the United States overall are more positive than those attributed to men (Eagly, 1995; Eagly, Mladinic, & Otto, 1991).

Evolutionary psychologists would respond that the psychological mechanisms in men, evolved over the millennia since life in the Stone Age, impel them toward physical battles and sexual promiscuity, traits not well tolerated in our different civilization. Evolved psychological mechanisms in women concern monogamy, pregnancy, communication with children, and their nurturance. These characteristics are far more respected in contemporary society.

Both these gender-related behaviors are associated with biochemical underpinnings. Prevalent in women, especially in the stages of childbirth, oxytocin also has implications for bonding. Regularly prevalent in men, testosterone is recognized as influential in aggression. These substances appear in both genders—but in very different amounts.

Turning to nonideological objections, critics state that evolutionary psychology engages in **post hoc reasoning,** the error of assuming that an event following another event was caused by that prior event. They point out the inability of evolutionary psychology to demonstrate that evolution caused any particular evolved mechanism, regarding post hoc reasoning as "storytelling." A causal relationship may be present, but it is not verified merely by the sequence of events.

The elephant's trunk, a duck's mode of swimming with webbed feet, and human facial expressions in emotion could not have been predicted as evolutionary outcomes, for there are countless ways to solve any adaptive problem (Buss, 1996a, 1996b). Without interests in child care and investment in children, men might have evolved as less brave than women, accomplishing the task of survival by fleeing from dangers rather than risking their lives in fighting (Cornell, 1997). On such bases, it can only be speculated that evolution has been the responsible agent.

Evolutionary psychologists reply that they only assume evolution was the causal factor. This assumption stimulates hypotheses about human and animal behaviors as adaptive responses, serving as a springboard for investigations. The studies of gender differences in response to partner infidelity, for example, arose on this basis. But evolutionary theory exerted no influence on the research design or the merit of the research results.

Critics also state that evolutionary psychology encounters the falsification issue. Evolutionary theory cannot be shown to be wrong. It cannot return to earlier eons to examine directly the pressures and outcomes of natural selection. It is no more falsifiable than other views of our origins. But, again, supporters state that evolutionary psychology has no direct need to test the theory, and it makes no attempt to do so.

They also reply that evolution, even as a theory today, is widely accepted within and outside academic circles. Among scientists, nearly universal support often substitutes for falsifiability. Moreover, the falsifiability criterion does not apply to high-level assumptions in science, especially those with overwhelming acceptance. It applies instead to low-level empirical predictions. Nevertheless, the debate continues over the extent to which evolutionary psychology is a justifiable science.

Critics object on still another point—the idea of human mental life as composed of an inherited set of *specific* mental mechanisms. And they resist the idea that the multiplicity of these mechanisms accounts for the seeming versatility of human thought. Instead, the public regards the human mind as a general problem solver, capable of adapting to an almost endless variety of challenges. They explain human behavior with numerous broad concepts, such as learning, reasoning, remembering, problem solving, and the like, operating in unconfined fashion across a sweeping range of tasks.

Finally, some psychologists resist on more particular bases. They ask for more precise definitions of evolved psychological mechanisms. And what is the speculation on their number? If our mental apparatus has become modularized into separate components, how do we experience an integrated mind? And how are these mental mechanisms mapped onto the modular brain? Answers to such questions of course await further research.

Summary

Roots of Evolutionary Psychology

Evolutionary psychology proposes that natural selection has shaped human psychological structures, resulting in certain adaptive fears, preferences, and behavioral tendencies called evolved psychological mechanisms. In this context, a battleground becomes the metaphor for evolutionary psychology. Each individual battles against predators, the natural elements, and members of its own species. The most successful survive and transmit their genetic backgrounds to offspring.

Key Terms: **evolutionary psychology, natural selection, genes, genetic determinism, evolved psychological mechanism, instinct**

Evolution of Sexual Behavior

Through random pairings over the millennia, males have evolved a preference for fertile mates, females a preference for mates who can provide resources for raising offspring. Through their unequal levels of investment in children, the mating patterns of men have emerged as more polygamous and those of women as more monogamous.

Key Terms: **mate preferences, mating patterns, polygamous, monogamous**

Adaptations in Parenting

Pregnancy sickness appears to be an evolved psychological mechanism that protects the embryo against birth defects. Nausea and food aversions cause the pregnant woman to reject substances likely to be toxic for the developing embryo. Another evolved mechanism, infant-directed speech, enables the new mother to communicate with her linguistically undeveloped child. She uses exaggerated rhythms and tones to catch attention, express approval, indicate prohibition, and communicate comfort.

Key Terms: **pregnancy sickness, teratogens, embryo, fetus, infant-directed speech**

Dispositions in Group Living

The human capacity for language is viewed as an evolved psychological mechanism for reasons relating to the speed of learning, universality of language, and predictable errors in grammar and syntax. The capacity to recognize and transmit emotional expressions also appears to be an evolved psychological mechanism, offering advantages in obtaining a mate, anticipating attack, and so forth. Similarly, skill in making social contracts appears to be an evolved mechanism, providing an adaptive advantage in gaining property and detecting cheaters.

Key Terms: **social exchange, universal grammar, facial expressions in emotion, social contract, physical aggression, verbal aggression, paternity uncertainty**

Promoting Behavioral Change

Evaluating the effectiveness of any therapy often requires at least three groups of subjects: a control group, a placebo group, and a treatment group. Successful therapy outcomes usually depend on an interaction among the therapist, method, and person in therapy. Evolutionary psychology offers no therapy, but it can make its hypotheses and findings available to the public. These results are not confined to problems of adjustment; they also provide information on how to make everyday life more effective and fulfilling.

Key Terms: **spontaneous remission, placebo effect**

Commentary and Critique

Evolutionary psychology stimulates debate about ideological issues. Social-role theory states that the different adjustments of men and women are influenced by the expectations of the society in which they live. Other critics point out that evolutionary theory is not falsifiable and that the mind is a general-purpose problem solver. Evolutionary psychologists reply that the theory has stimulated many useful, testable hypotheses.

Key Terms: **ideological issues, social-role theory, nature-nurture issue, heredity-environment interaction, post hoc reasoning**

Critical Thinking

1. Assume that natural variation in earlier eons produced a genetic predisposition toward a highly mobile, swan-like neck in one or a few human beings. Describe the conditions under which that neck might have become prominent in people today. Describe the conditions under which it might have disappeared.

2. As a member of a consulting team, how would Charles Darwin feel in partnership with a behaviorist? Describe the intellectual reasons for congeniality or discord.

3. Consider the instinct for nest-building in rabbits and the evolved psychological mechanisms for mate preferences in human beings. Using these examples, explain how the concepts of instincts and evolved psychological mechanisms are similar and different.

Sociocultural Foundations

S ocial and cultural viewpoints, which are distinct from one another, both emphasize that virtually all human behavior takes place in a human context. Other people, past and present, inevitably influence our daily activities and experience. We are inescapably social creatures, so much so that we find it extremely difficult to live apart from others of our kind. Rightfully or not, we regard a hermit as a strange person, and solitary confinement remains one of our cruelest psychological punishments.

This chapter begins by noting the importance of social and cultural interactions and traditions in our lives. Afterward, it turns to the social domain separately and then to the cultural domain. Each, with its own aims and assumptions, pursues the same overall goal: to understand the ways people influence one another.

The Inevitable Human Influence

In this sociocultural milieu, we think about ourselves and other people almost constantly. Even when absent, other human beings become influential in our experience.

And so it was for Bertha at dawn on a dark November day in postwar Germany. She traveled a difficult pathway over roots and leaves and puddles, pelted by cold rain and snow. But her thoughts turned to Raymond Poincaré, the French premier whose troops ruled Germany in the aftermath of World War I. She held him largely responsible for her current troubles. He should plod that nasty pathway himself before dawn, she mused. Then he would know the hardships the Germans suffered (Pappenheim, 1923).

In fact, Bertha traveled with a teenage assistant and a baby in a rickety carriage. That little trio moved in a silent partnership. Bertha pulled, her helper pushed, and baby Emmy enjoyed the bumpy ride. In those early hours, Bertha's speechless companions, so distant in age and experience, provided a meager social setting.

The cultural setting also provided little comfort. Under French military rule, Germany had lost much of its native character. The Great War resulted in poverty, inflation ran rampant, and yet there was nothing to buy. Age 64, living under foreign dominance in her devastated country, Bertha plodded along, a weary, practically penniless senior citizen.

She was headed to Crumstadt to rescue little Irmchen Weingart, one of her adopted children. The foster father, Mr. Gruenbaum, had beaten his wife two days earlier. That home would not be right for any child. Bertha had alerted the Gruenbaum family to prepare for Irmchen's departure (Pappenheim, 1923). She had placed several foster children in this French-occupied village 20 miles south of Neu-Isenburg. It was time for another inspection of adoptive homes.

Baby Emmy was headed in a different direction. To make her mission more efficient, Bertha was taking the baby to Frankfurt, the first stage of Emmy's trip to Holland, where foster parents awaited her.

Interactions and Traditions

This tendency to live and work in groups underlies the domains of social and cultural psychology, considered subfields owing to their great breadth and flexible paths of inquiry. Social psychology stands as a major subfield, and cultural psychology has become increasingly broad and prominent in recent years.

In restricted ways, social and cultural viewpoints appear in virtually all the perspectives—the family triangle in psychoanalysis, reinforcement principle in behaviorism, conditions of worth in humanistic psychology, influences on perception and thinking in cognitive psychology, and social exchange in the evolutionary perspective. Even biological psychology becomes responsive to sociocultural influences, for its mechanisms mature in a sociocultural context; they are shaped partly by environmental factors, especially in the early years. These mechanisms underlie all human behavior and experience, whether in a human context or otherwise. In fact, the biological perspective, at one end of the continuum, and the sociocultural, at the other, represent the outer borders of mainstream psychology, yet they have fundamental connections too.

In particular, **social psychology** examines the ways in which human behavior is influenced by the actual or imagined presence of other human beings. It approaches behavior as inevitably shaped by views of oneself in the context of others. The research methods are often experimental, for social psychologists have developed laboratory analogs of social situations in everyday life. Using role playing and videos, they examine with precision human interactions in almost all imaginable contexts: altruism, cooperation, competition, interpersonal attractions, leadership, pecking orders, roles and status, and numerous other situations.

This longstanding subfield has become so extensive that at times it seems like a separate discipline. Wherever people interact, there are opportunities for social psychologists.

Cultural psychology also lacks the coherence of the more systematic perspectives. Sometimes incorrectly known as cross-cultural and global community psychology, the broad domain of **cultural psychology** examines the ways a society's practices and products influence human behavior—through its laws, customs, language, religions, politics, and other institutions. It does so chiefly through descriptive research methods, far more common here than in social psychology. In particular, cultural psychology emphasizes participant naturalistic observation and case studies of individuals, groups, and institutions. In these ways, it examines shared activities and also shared meanings—the whole constellation of ideas and standards of behavior that define a particular community (Greenfield et al., 2003). In doing so, it looks to the past and future, as well as the present.

The impact of culture begins even before birth and extends into all significant spheres of human life—from the foods we eat to the ways we educate children, from the religions we adopt to the games we find amusing. A moment's thought suggests the tremendous influence of culture in Bertha Pappenheim's life. A social dimension is commonly present in all these contexts too. But the cultural spheres affect our thoughts and actions in profound, often unrecognized ways.

These influences can operate in unexpected directions too. Bertha's tolerant, supportive attitudes toward prostitutes and unwed mothers were completely unconventional in her day. Her sharp prejudices against women wearing makeup and fashionable clothes were inconsistent with her impeccable upper-class manners and grace, readily evident and widely admired. When smoking was considered improper for women, she adopted the practice. When it became acceptable, she abandoned the habit (Dresner, 1954).

In her leadership of The Home, she displayed a style well known to social psychologists. A so-called *task specialist,* she focused exclusively on identifying the problem, finding a solution, and implementing it, regardless of the cost to others (Bales, 1958; Hogan, Curphy, & Hogan, 1994). She expected and demanded immediate obedience, not only from the staff but also from the children. She set high standards and strictly maintained them.

In contrast, Bertha took no pains to become a *social specialist,* someone who focused on group cohesion and morale, gaining productivity through teamwork. She totally overlooked the benefits of satisfying personal and social relationships. Instead, she approached her colleagues and children by wielding her authority.

Studies of Obedience

The most controversial research of the 20th century concerned obedience to authority. Stanley Milgram's dramatic findings in the United States stimulated investigators in other countries to repeat this research, prompting considerable interest in social and cultural psychology, as well as among the public. Disturbed by the Nazi leadership and war atrocities around the world, Milgram focused this research in the 1960s on obedience to a malevolent authority.

And it involved a pair of major deceptions. First, Milgram made no mention of obedience. He told each of the many volunteers in this research that the investigation concerned the influence of punishment on learning. Working alone as a "teacher," each volunteer was instructed to administer an electric shock whenever a learner made a mistake. Moreover, each teacher was under orders to increase the shock by 15 volts after each mistake. In **obedience**, the conditions are not negotiable; an individual responds to a request or demand. Under these conditions, the individual is expected to follow orders. The social situation demanded that the teachers respond as instructed.

Before beginning this procedure, Milgram administered to each teacher a sample shock of 45 volts in order to help him understand the conditions for the learner. Strapped to a chair in another room, the learner made errors. As the teacher administered increasingly stronger shocks, the learner complained, screamed, and finally stopped answering. Unknown to the teacher, the electrical apparatus was rigged; the learner never received any punishment at all. That was the second deception. His yelling and screaming came from a prerecorded audiotape.

Various groups of people had predicted that no teacher would administer more than 300 volts, and certainly nobody would punish the helpless man with 450 volts, the maximum shock available. Yet 60% of all teachers applied the maximum shock. They followed all of the orders (Milgram, 1974).

Because of its deception, this study has been widely criticized. One dissident declared that Milgram himself had engaged in immoral behavior, deceiving the participants and demanding that they perform a disagreeable, apparently injurious task. According to this view, the research findings and their alleged importance did not justify the discomfort of the participants during the experiment. Moreover, several participants experienced self-doubt afterward (Baumrind, 1964). Milgram answered these criticisms carefully, but the issues implicit in this important investigation prompted psychologists to develop more extensive ethical standards for research.

Owing to its totally unexpected outcome, so different from common sense, this study has become a classic in social psychology, now called **Milgram's obedience research**. It shows the power of the social situation, which may override personal dispositions. In an extensive survey, experts in psychology identified this research as the most significant single investigation in the 20th century (Boneau, 1990). It reminds us that all human beings live their lives in a context of social constraints and prescriptions.

The totality of this social context is known as culture. Broadly speaking, *culture* is a system of shared meanings that goes beyond the interpersonal; its norms and expectations about ways of living influence our conceptions of reality. Culture provides a pervasive, influential framework for human development, shaping that development by its economic, political, religious, and other products of human life. It transmits to its members the nature of human experience and standards of behavior (Miller, 1999). From this viewpoint, a human society is not simply essential to the formation of psychological processes; it becomes a powerful selective force in setting the specific patterns of those processes.

In this context, one wonders about obedience elsewhere. How would people from other cultures perform as Milgram's "teachers"? Would they show similar levels of obedience to a malevolent authority?

The overall answer is affirmative. Among two dozen studies in eight countries, the median level of obedience was 65%, the same as found in Milgram's first study in the United States. The level ranged from approximately 30 to 90%, owing to changes in the procedure and different participants, as well as cultural influences. Of the eight countries, six were Western; the other two were South Africa and Jordan (Blass, 2000).

Most of these studies were conducted three decades ago, and it might be argued that times have changed and people today would not be so obedient to a malevolent authority. But this viewpoint lacks empirical support. Ethical concerns have prevented more recent replications of Milgram's research. One review of the many earlier investigations showed no relationship between the date of the study and the amount of obedience. It also showed no significant difference in obedience between men and women (Blass, 2000).

A degree of obedience is, of course, essential to the functioning of any society. But circumstances arise when disobedience may be the proper course of action.

In Germany, an investigator assigned people to serve as teachers in one of three conditions. In the first, 46 participants followed the original Milgram procedure. In the second, with 25 participants, each teacher observed an accomplice of the experimenter posing as a teacher and refusing to continue to administer shocks after 45 volts, thereby demonstrating marked disobedience. In the third, with 30 participants, the experimenter gave each teacher the usual instructions and then clearly tolerated disobedience, saying, "It's up to you to decide if and how much to punish the learner."

In the exact repetition of the Milgram procedure, 85% of the first group continued all the way to 450 volts. When participants in the third group were offered an opportunity to disobey, only 7% of them continued to the strongest shock. But the disobedient accomplice in the second group failed to deter most of the teachers, and 52% administered the maximum shock available. Overall the German participants were more obedient than those in the United States. Cultural forces also shape behavior, within and outside the laboratory. When asked after the experiment what they thought happened to the learner, many believed that he might have died or fallen unconscious (Mantell, 1971).

Looking back on all this research, Milgram decided that the social context and prescriptions led to the unexpectedly high level of obedience to malevolent authority. He concluded that comparable social conditions pre-cipitated the Nazi rise to power. And he believed that similar conditions could arise elsewhere in the world. Certainly the studies in Western cultures support this conclusion (Blass, 2000).

In fact, the social unrest in Germany after World War I played a critical role in the rise of Nazi rule. Food had become scarce. Money became worthless. The French controlled communication. These frustrations laid the groundwork for Adolph Hitler.

Postwar travel had become almost impossible, especially in bad weather. For her journey to Crumstadt, Bertha could not find a taxi, and the French had closed the railway. So she guided her charges along their muddy route. When they reached the automobile waiting at the end of the pathway, the driver ordered Emmy to be placed in the car first. Then he told the helper to enter. Afterward, he turned to Bertha.

"Granny, with a few hops you'll get in too!"

In Frankfurt, Emmy departed for her new life in the Netherlands, still in the care of Bertha's helper. And Bertha caught a train for Eberstadt, her first stop en route to Crumstadt. She traveled in a cold, fourth-class car. Steam heat did not reach that section of the train. She gazed at the sullen faces of the passengers. "If one looks and listens in a fourth-class car," she noted, "one will understand conditions in Germany—tired, worn, angry faces."

A pale, sickly passenger, sitting next to Bertha, learned about the latest price of bread. She jumped up and yelled desperately. Then others began to complain. A man grumbled that the young folk, able to earn money, were unwilling to help. A woman protested that many young people smoked cig-arettes and wore sheer stockings. A couple of men suggested that farmers were hiding their crops, feeding them to animals, and selling the livestock only for dollars.

Nearly all the Eberstadt passengers traveled with subdued expressions. In low tones, they voiced their frustrations to one another.

Social Psychology

Bertha's journey to Crumstadt illustrates two basic topics in social psy-chology. The first, social cognition, concerns our judgments of people. How do we make decisions about them? How do we decide what they are like? The second, social influence, concerns the ways we modify one another's behavior. How do we alter the behavior of other people? Sometimes our efforts are direct and blatant; on other occasions, they are more subtle.

Forming Impressions of People

In the first of these topics, **social cognition,** people obtain and interpret information about themselves, other people, and their relationships, and they then reach conclusions. The interest lies in the ways people form impressions about social life, not how they react overtly. What do we think about the driver at the end of the footpath in Neu-Isenburg? He ordered Bertha to wait; then when everybody else had entered the taxi, he ordered her to enter by taking "a few hops." A complete stranger, he also called her "Granny." And what do we think about the sickly woman on the Eberstadt train? She suddenly jumped up and yelled about the price of bread. How do we view her? And how do we view the other passengers?

On the basis of her sudden, desperate yelling, an observer might decide that she is a nervous, tense person, prone to emotional outbursts. If so, the observer would be attributing her behavior to internal conditions, events inside her. An attribution is an explanation about the causes of a person's behavior. This explanation would be called a **personal attribution,** or *internal attribution,* because the behavior is assigned to traits or dispositions within the individual. The sickly woman behaved in a frightened, distraught manner because she is that way.

From another viewpoint, an observer might decide that she acted this way because of the poverty and destruction in her homeland, an explanation attributing her behavior to external conditions, events in the outer environment. This explanation would be a **situational attribution,** or *external attribution,* because the causes of the behavior have been assigned to the circumstances, not to the person.

Which explanation seems most appropriate? We do not know, of course, but we do know how observers typically assign causes, especially in ambiguous instances. In judging the behavior of other people, observers generally place too much weight on personal characteristics and too little on the situation, a tendency so pervasive that it is called the *personal attribution bias.* This tendency to overlook environmental influences arises because people usually do not have the time, inclination, or opportunity to make an investigation of the potential situational factors. Instead, they take a short cut, simply ascribing the behavior to factors within the individual (Gilbert, 1989; Gilbert & Malone, 1995). This inclination is so prominent and fundamental in social cognition that it also has been known as the **fundamental attribution error.**

But in the case of the sickly woman, we become somewhat less susceptible to the fundamental attribution error because the other passengers complain too. There was a consensus among them, suggesting that the situation also contributed to her behavior. In all probability, both sets of factors were involved. In explaining someone else's behavior, the appearance of the fundamental attribution error depends partly on the behavior of other people in that situation.

Especially when the circumstances seem otherwise normal, observers tend to make a personal attribution about unusual behavior. A taxi driver encounters a dignified, elderly woman, and yet he calls her "Granny." He shows less respect for his prospective passenger than we might anticipate, and we make a personal attribution about him, perhaps that he is somewhat insensitive or obtuse.

What happens when people instead view *their own* behavior? How do they explain themselves? Knowing the details of their own circumstances, they tend to make situational attributions, particularly when their behavior has been inappropriate. They explain that the situation called for that behavior (Overholser & Moll, 1990). But there are exceptions. In instances of notable success, they may ascribe their behavior to personal characteristics. The later reaction is part of a broad **self-serving bias**, the inclination for people to view themselves in more favorable ways than others view them. These attribution errors are common, though not universal (Gilbert, 1989; McArthur, 1972).

We can summarize these findings readily. People tend to assign their own behavior to the situation; they explain that they acted according to the circumstances. People tend to attribute others' behavior to personal characteristics. They decide that others act in certain ways because they are that way (Nisbett, Caputo, Legant, & Marecek, 1973).

On the Eberstadt train, most of the passengers reacted in the same way, and we make a situational attribution. The circumstances in Germany caused their sullen expressions. Yet one woman stood out among the others, suggesting a personal attribution. But maybe in this instance we make the fundamental attribution error, explaining her behavior without knowing further details of her situation.

Modifying Others' Behavior

Arriving in Eberstadt, Bertha changed trains for Pfungstadt, her final train stop. That journey provides a clear illustration of social influence, a second basic topic in social psychology. It does not deal directly with how human beings explain their own and others' behavior. Social influence focuses instead on how people alter the behavior of others.

On the Pfungstadt train, Bertha rode in fear of the passengers' anti-Semitic remarks, which she heard as she entered the fourth-class car. The only seats lined the outer edges of the car with their backs to the walls, leaving an empty space in the center. A red-haired Galician Jew sat on the floor with his packages around him, taunted by loud, hostile outbursts.

"What did we pay for potatoes in peacetime?" cried his chief tormentor. "Three marks for 100 pounds," the group hollered almost as a chorus.

"What did we pay for material for aprons?" the man called again, well aware that the Jew was a tailor, owing to the yardstick extending from the top of his high boots. "Eighty pfennigs," yelled the spectators.

"And this dirty Jew asked today 100 pounds of potatoes for one meter of material for aprons!"

The group roared its disapproval.

"He is even worse than a Jew," called out a woman. "You should be strung up," she yelled to him. "All of them should be strung up," she called to the crowd. "A stone around their neck, dumped into a river."

Laughter followed. Bertha shivered at the dark humor behind this scene. The passengers were arousing one another. With a drop of alcohol, they might quickly become an ugly mob (Pappenheim, 1923).

Conditions such as these caught the attention of early social psychologists, raising the question of **social influence**, which is concerned with the ways people modify one another's behavior. How do we influence each other, purposefully or otherwise? At the purposeful end of the continuum, people make demands of others, who are expected to show *obedience,* as noted already. The conditions are not negotiable. But no one asked the Pfungstadt passengers to act aggressively or to behave more peacefully. Their behavior was not prompted by obedience.

At a lower level of social influence, **compliance** involves direct pressure to behave in a certain manner, but no individual has full authority over another; no one can request obedience. Instead, the interpersonal relationship involves persuasion or negotiation. A classic example occurs when an automobile salesperson employs various techniques to persuade a prospective buyer to make a purchase. In the foot-in-the-door technique, the salesperson begins by seeking a small degree of compliance, asking the prospective buyer simply to sit in the car and then just take it for a test drive. People who agree to a small request, or several small requests, are more likely to agree later to a larger one, such as buying the car (Wagener & Laird, 1980). In the door-in-the-face technique, the tactic is much the opposite, for the salesperson requests an unusually high degree of compliance, perhaps suggesting that the buyer pay cash for a very expensive, deluxe model immediately, before the price changes. The strategy here is that the prospective buyer will refuse but, not wanting to be a complete contrarian, may then become more receptive to a much smaller request, such as purchasing a standard model under a gradual payment plan (Cialdini, 1993).

At the lowest level of social influence, there is no effort to induce anyone to behave in any particular fashion. In **conformity**, an individual behaves in a certain way without any direct pressure to do so, reacting spontaneously to the presence of others. The social influence can be completely unintentional. In most groups, the members display some degree of agreement in interests, abilities, language, dress, or other characteristics, and those who join the group experience implicit pressure toward conformity. In any group, there are unstated expectations about behavior that most members do not want to violate. Examples of such groups range from adolescent gangs and athletic teams to people on advisory boards.

A subtle form of conformity appears apart from the similarity in dress, manners, and other relatively superficial characteristics of a group. In fact, its focus is not on group membership but instead on group behavior. It can occur even in an incidental group, in which the members do not know one another and have no recognizable common bond except as human beings.

Early investigations of social influence revealed this phenomenon, called **social facilitation**, meaning that the presence of other people increases or intensifies an individual's behavior. On the train to Pfungstadt, one passenger spoke, then another, and another. They aroused themselves without any call for obedience or compliance. The group presence became a force, perhaps inducing some sort of conformity. The Eberstadt passengers also incited one another, though in a lesser way.

Social facilitation appears regularly even among animals. Rats and fish eat more in groups than when eating alone (Harlow, 1932; Strobel, 1972; Welty, 1934). Ants increase their nest-building activities when in the company of other ants (Chen, 1938). These studies of animals are legion.

Among human beings, the more people at the table, the more food each individual consumes. This outcome occurs on weekends and also on weekdays, when gatherings are less festive (de Castro, 1991). In all sorts of situations, the presence of others augments the activity of a group member—whether eating, drinking, digging, fighting, or complaining (Zajonc, 1965).

But further studies eventually revealed another outcome. People learning mazes and memorizing nonsense syllables did not perform better in a group (Pessin, 1933; Pessin & Husband, 1933). People completing math problems and manipulating unfamiliar garments in a group setting performed at an even lower level than when engaged in these activities alone (Littlepage, Morris, & Poole, 1991; Markus, 1978). How might these contradictory findings be explained?

A moment's reflection shows that the tasks associated with these different outcomes are quite different too. Eating and digging are relatively simple, well-practiced habits. Memorizing nonsense syllables and completing math problems are more complex, less familiar tasks. Investigators hypothesized that the difficulty of the task played a role in social facilitation. Then they tested this hypothesis in diverse settings.

In one instance, four investigators played the role of an audience, observing college students playing pool in everyday life. Keeping unobtrusive records, they identified above-average and below-average pairs of competitors. Then, as a group, they approached each of the tables closely enough to make the players aware of them as an audience—without interfering with the play. There they silently counted the total number of shots and the number of successful shots in the next 24 attempts. They found that the success of above-average players increased from 71 to 80% in the presence of an audience. In contrast the success of below-average players decreased from 36 to 25% when they were being observed (Michaels, Blommel, Brocato, Linkous, & Rowe, 1982).

The explanation appears to lie with the person's level of arousal and the difficulty of the task. Performing in front of others, even with a small and inattentive audience, raises one's level of arousal. This increased activation enhances individual performance when the task is simple or well practiced. It disrupts performance when the task is difficult or unfamiliar (Zanjonc, 1965). In the latter instance, the outcome is called **social interference**, indicating a diminished performance in the mere presence of others.

But science is an endless process. Again, one investigation answers some questions and raises others. And so it has been for research on social influence. Yet another factor becomes influential, illustrating an old adage about the answer to any complex question: "That depends on several factors."

The additional factor in this case is the size of the group. When it is large, and completion of the task requires extensive effort, the individual's performance often diminishes. In **social loafing**, people in a group exert less effort and perform at a lower level than when by themselves, providing that their individual contributions are unlikely to be noticed (Hardy & Latane, 1986). In other words, when the individual is one among many performing an arduous task, social loafing may occur. When the individual is one among few, social facilitation and social interference are likely outcomes, depending on the person's level of arousal and the difficulty of the task.

Owing to social interference and social loafing, which impair performance, all such studies sometimes are known collectively by a more general term, *social contagion,* which does not imply any increased or decreased performance. It simply means people are influenced by the mere presence of other people. But the traditional term, social facilitation, continues in widespread use.

These diverse studies of incidental groups give only the merest hint of the breadth and depth of social influence. One can just imagine the far greater influences of more intimate, longer-lasting groups, such as those in families, clubs, school, work, and political organizations.

The incidental group on the Pfungstadt train was small; the passengers could observe one another; and they engaged in a simple activity: complaining. They complained about other people and about the devastated economy. Their individual complaints incited one another, an instance of social facilitation. Suddenly the whole group became volatile, shouting aggressively and threatening physical violence.

Grateful to leave that scene and to complete the second leg of her journey, Bertha alighted at Pfungstadt, mentally and physically fatigued. She looked around for Mr. Bergen, the schoolteacher who was to take her to Crumstadt in a car. Except for a cold breeze, the place was deserted—no Mr. Bergen and no car.

She tried the telephone at the station. It did not work. She walked to the Blum General Store. It was closed. Then she discovered from a neighbor that the French would not permit anyone to meet her at the Pfungstadt station. She should take the mail coach. Teacher Bergen would meet her at Crumstadt.

Bertha walked to a tavern to wait for the coach. There she encountered again the red-haired tailor, sitting by himself. He spoke to no one, looked at no one, and soon departed. Afterward, a beer-drinking patron made loud, hostile remarks like those on the train. Again, the young man was accused of exploiting Germany's poverty, a prejudice spreading rapidly from Munich and Bavaria, the early seat of Nazi activities.

After she left the tavern, Bertha doubted her courage. "Did I remain silent out of cowardice when I twice experienced vulgar talk?" Then she consoled herself—the tormenters never would have been convinced in a few minutes.

Prejudice and Stereotypes

Blaming the young tailor for Germany's postwar poverty of course is preposterous, but prejudice toward people from certain religious, racial, political, and other identifiable groups has contributed immeasurably to worldwide human misery. As a form of social cognition, a **prejudice** is an emotional reaction, usually a negative judgment about someone, something, or some group of people, made without objective evidence. The instance has been *prejudged,* prior to adequate inquiry. The Pfungstadt passengers showed a prejudice against the tailor without knowing him at all, apparently because of his Jewish background.

When prejudice arises simply because someone or something is a member of a particular group or class, this oversimplified reaction is called a stereotype. Based on a rigid set of beliefs, positive or negative, a **stereotype** exaggerates differences among groups and overlooks differences among individuals in the same group. Shortly after World War I, the Nazis promoted the stereotype of Jewish citizens as shrewd and mercenary, just as stereotypes about other national and religious groups emerged or faded elsewhere. At this time, young Americans apparently showed a self-serving bias, stereotyping themselves as industrious and intelligent (Karlins, Coffman, & Walters, 1969).

Like other forms of social cognition, a stereotype saves effort and energy. Quite apart from whatever motives may be involved, it gives a prompt, easy answer to questions about people we do not know well, answers that range from reasonably accurate to partly correct to absolutely false. In forming first impressions some stereotypes may even be more useful than brief, direct observations of behavior (Gage, 1952). Think about adolescents, used-car dealers, and research scientists. Some characteristics within these groups are not widely shared with individuals in the other groups.

But stereotypes can be harmful too. Their accuracy often remains indeterminate; they certainly do not apply to all members of any large group; and, most critical of all, they may be negative.

Sitting around the tailor in that cold fourth-class car, the passengers took no interest in him as an individual. Instead, they viewed him in a negative, stereotyped fashion, as a member of an undesirable group. They ridiculed his speech, his possessions, and his religion. Then they made him a scapegoat. In irrational fashion, they held him responsible for creating the poverty in postwar Germany. This term, *scapegoat*, emerged centuries ago when people sacrificed a goat in order to escape or avoid misfortunes. In modern terms, a **scapegoat** is some innocent human being or group made to bear the burden of others. People not responsible for certain problems are nevertheless blamed for them.

Prejudices and stereotypes, forms of social cognition, often precede scapegoating, a form of social influence placing an individual or group in cruel, unjustified circumstances. Through social facilitation, conformity, and other types of social influences, other people may join the scapegoating process. As Milgram emphasized, human beings are regularly caught in a web of social and cultural constraints.

The incidents Bertha witnessed on her trip to Crumstadt illustrate a basic tendency in human societies around the globe and down through history. People take the viewpoint of their own group as the appropriate outlook on the world. This tendency is called *ethnocentrism* when it places one's own group as superior to any other, especially those that have different customs and standards. Other cultures are regarded as odd, immoral, or "lower" because they do not share the standards of one's own group. At a simple, innocuous level, ethnocentrism appears in food and dress preferences, which vary in systematic ways across all cultures. In its most dangerous form, it can result in the savagery displayed throughout ancient and modern civilizations, illustrated on the broadest scale by the Nazi regime of the 20th century. Even today, subtle and unobtrusive measures of apparent egalitarianism suggest that the high ideals of groups of people are often accompanied by less-than-ideal practices (Devos & Banaji, 2005).

Thus the Jewish tailor became the target of displaced aggression. There he sat on the Pfungstadt train, abused with insults and threatened with physical violence by otherwise presumably normal citizens.

When the mail coach finally arrived at Pfungstadt, a half-hour late, it proved to be an open potato cart, pulled only by a hungry-looking nag. The horse moved slowly. Darkness fell. An icy wind blew half-frozen rain across their path. Bertha wore an old military coat, so thick and heavy that it did not hug her body. "We were freezing," she reported.

Two hours later, she climbed from the cart in Crumstadt, introduced herself to Mr. Bergen, then paid her fare. It was 15 billion marks.

In their home, the Bergens escorted Bertha to a couch, took out their best china, and served noodle soup. Turli, their foster child, born to an unwed mother, began life at The Home in Neu-Isenburg. He happily unwrapped Bertha's gift. Later she spent the night on the couch. In the morning, Ms. Bergen appeared with ersatz coffee, jam, and homemade bread. She proudly offered her guest a small pat of butter and a bit of milk, which Bertha kindly refused. Little Turli, observing carefully, asked what holiday they were celebrating.

"I felt quite strange when the child was told that *I* was the holiday," Bertha confessed. "I made thousands of good resolutions for my entire life to be worthy of this word" (Pappenheim, 1923).

Little Turli's innocent question revealed self-doubts in Bertha. Without taking any satisfaction from the compliment, which she certainly deserved, she decided that she had not yet earned it. How could *she* be worthy? It also revealed the influence of culture. The little boy, in a postwar society, knew only a poor neighborhood, a rural environment quite different from Bertha's upper-class Vienna and Frankfurt. These cultural differences contributed to his naiveté and to her embarrassment.

Psychology and Culture

In studies of these influences, cultural psychology focuses on the conventions in a society or group, investigating the ways in which political, economic, religious, and other institutions give meaning to human experience and standards of conduct (Miller, 1999). From this viewpoint, culture becomes a powerful force in setting the patterns of our knowledge and behavior. But the influences go in the other direction too. Our psychological processes affect our culture (Lehman, Chiu, & Schaller, 2004). Culture and the human mind mold one another (Markus & Kitayama, 1991).

Cultural psychology concentrates on the influences in both directions. Cross-cultural psychology is another matter, as noted later. It compares cultures, studying their similarities and differences.

As a body of behavioral and cognitive norms shared by some groups and not others, **culture** enables its members to achieve individual and group goals. According to the evolutionary perspective, culture emerged through its adaptive advantages. Living alone exposes an individual to excessive dangers. The cooperation in culture fosters success in survival and reproduction. According to a more existential view, culture arose as a shield against the anxiety associated with our knowledge of our own mortality. It provides a collection of rules and values for acceptance in a human community. From still another standpoint, culture may have arisen as an unplanned byproduct of everyday social interaction (Lehman, Chiu, & Schaller, 2004). However it originated, culture provides a context for human development.

Goals in Cultural Studies

Cultural psychology is not an integrated systematic school of thought in the same way as most of the perspectives discussed earlier. And it does not represent any new or radical break with mainstream traditions. In fact, it has been described as an interdisciplinary extension of general psychology (Valsiner, 2000). It is a point of view relevant to all approaches in psychology, urging a renewed commitment to the cultural dimensions of the environment (Miller, 1999).

Even in Wundt's work, laboratory and cultural psychology received more or less equal attention. The former served to investigate the basic mechanisms of the mind, the latter to understand how these workings are modified by the realities of culture (Blumenthal, 1975).

During the 20th century, especially with the domination of behaviorism, the cultural dimension fell to a secondary status, and attempts to reintroduce it into mainstream psychology have encountered considerable inertia. The proverbial fish fail to appreciate the significance of water in their lives, for it is always around them. Similarly, human beings underestimate the power of culture until they encounter one distinctly different from their own (Cole, 1996). Before regarding any findings as universal, mainstream psychology needs to demonstrate their generalizability.

In the last decade of the 20th century, psychologists in the United States began to recognize more fully that human psychological processes are inherently structured by culture, as well as by the brain. Cultural foundations began to emerge as the other bookend in the psychology curriculum, balanced against the old standby, biological bases of behavior (Berry, 2000).

The "cognitive revolution" played a mixed role in this resurgence, both fostering and inhibiting the cultural viewpoint. At its outset, some leaders turned away from the biological bases of behavior, as well as away from the anti-mentalism of behaviorism, moving toward the external, cultural influences shaping our mental life. That tendency became a positive force. At the same time, the computer metaphor came into prominence, encouraging the view of the human mind as a general-purpose mechanism because the computer could solve so many problems. But, in fact, the computer could do so only if human beings very carefully instructed it in the solution of each separate problem. Thus, the cognitive revolution in general and the computer metaphor in particular did not approach the human mind as a domain-specific, context-driven mechanism, one inevitably bound to its cultural and historical origins. The particular culture became overlooked in the search for general patterns. The mind is content-oriented, especially after a lengthy exposure to a particular culture. It is constructed and altered by the processes of obtaining meanings and resources in that culture (Schweder, 1990).

Compared with investigations in mainstream psychology, research in cultural psychology today is often more naturalistic and holistic, concerned with lifestyles, themes, patterns, and emergent properties. Using descriptive methods, investigators observe and participate in a particular culture, studying individuals and groups in their everyday settings. Mainstream psychology, in turn, employs more experimental methods and laboratory settings, focusing on narrower units of behavior. From the cultural viewpoint, one solution to this divergence might incorporate into scientific psychology some of the more interpretive approaches of the humanities (Cole, 1996; Schweder, 1990). But a basic tension exists between the methods and goals of mainstream and cultural psychology (Lehman et al., 2004).

Cultural psychology seeks to understand how culture produces universal behaviors beyond language, gestures, emotional reactions, and other obvious commonalities. A **universal behavior,** or shared practice, occurs among all individuals in a given category, broadly or narrowly defined. How does culture produce these characteristic behaviors, despite inevitable variations among cultural environments?

Cultural psychology also seeks to understand how a unique cultural practice arises. It aims to discover why some responses and experiences become culture-bound, or **culture-specific behavior**, occurring only in a particular form or particular culture. How does culture produce this behavior, which does not appear elsewhere?

With its many complex and simultaneously influential variables, achieving the goals of cultural psychology appears challenging indeed, perhaps even unrealistic at this stage. But these concerns with universal and culture-specific behavior are not incompatible. In fact, they are almost inseparable. Cultural psychology cannot expect to encounter universal behavior without the study of many cultures, just as it cannot expect to examine culture-specific behavior without the study of many cultures (Bond & Smith, 1996). A common goal remains: to discover how general and specific cultural patterns arise and function.

The criteria for the measurement of cultural patterns are another issue. They may involve cultural values. From what viewpoint should someone judge human roles, rituals, religions, myths, morals, mores, and other practices? Their assessment raises a common concern, expressed in the context of cultural relativism.

According to **cultural relativism**, our most fundamental human concepts cannot have an absolute or universal meaning. Each culture is unique; no culture can be evaluated by the standards of any other culture. Virtue, honesty, beauty, and work are regarded differently in different cultures. Principles derived from one have a particular meaning in that culture; they cannot be applied elsewhere.

But this view also has its critics. According to **cultural absolutism**, some standards and methods of psychological measurement can be broadly applied across cultures. There are, for example, widespread restrictions against relatively rare practices, such as sacrifice, serious body mutilation, and genocide. But the importance of culture is diminished here, and in a broader context the issue remains. To what extent can there be universal standards for the scientific study of human beings? All such investigations must take into account the potential for different meanings in different cultures (Berry, 2000).

Individualism and Collectivism

Exposure to cultural differences occurred several times during Bertha Pappenheim's life. Raised in artistic Vienna, she worked in commercial Frankfurt. Socializing with the upper class, she cared for the lower class. She knew peacetime Europe and wartime Europe. Psychologists interested in culture often make comparisons between and among such settings.

These studies reveal two markedly different patterns. People in the major cities of northern Europe and North America display a noticeable orientation toward personal interests, pursuing their own goals. In East Asia and other parts of the world, an orientation toward group or community goals becomes more prominent. This cultural difference is referred to in numerous ways, commonly as individualism versus collectivism or independence versus interdependence. These two orientations, although not universal, are indeed pervasive, representing contrasting approaches to the vexing social questions of individual autonomy and group allegiance. From a relativistic standpoint, each has its merits and constraints.

In a so-called **individualistic society**, members regard personal goals as more important than group goals. They emphasize self-enhancement, explaining behavior in terms of the person and pointing to personality traits. The orientation is toward individuation and independence. In a **collectivist society**, members often place a higher value on group goals than on personal goals. They are more inclined to explain behavior in terms of the situation, that is, on the basis of social expectations, constraints, and roles. The orientation is toward membership and interdependence (Greenfield et al., 2003; Markus & Kitayama, 1991).

In one extensive study, investigators developed three different measures of these independence-interdependence orientations. European-American and Asian-American participants were placed in groups ranging in size from 27 to 52 members, approximately equal in gender distribution, and comprising 205 participants altogether. They viewed 35 abstract geometric figures, each composed of 9 subfigures, and ranked their favorite among the subfigures. Sometimes eight of the subfigures were alike and one was unique, such as a diamond intermixed with eight triangles. Sometimes an abstract figure contained two, three, or four subfigures that differed from the rest, rather than just one. The aim of this first task was to assess individual preferences for conformity or uniqueness in an abstract context.

On a different task, participants were asked to choose as a gift one pen from a set of five, each pen orange or light green in color. Presented as a random set from a large supply, any color split for the five pens was always 4:1 or 3:2. The aim of this task was to assess an individual's choice for conformity or uniqueness in a social context.

On both tasks—preferences among abstract figures and choices of material goods—the results confirmed cultural differences. With the abstract figures, Americans exceeded the Asians by approximately 2 to 1 in preferring the unique subfigures. On the choice of pen, 74% of the Americans chose the more uncommon item, as opposed to only 24% of the Asians.

The third measure required no participants. It involved a study of the themes in 157 Korean and 136 American magazine advertisements, all full-page ads extracted from four comparable categories of magazines published in the same month in both countries. The aim here was to discover whether the cultural preferences and choices made by individuals were represented at a collective level in the national media. Three themes were chosen to represent conformity: collective values, group harmony, and following a trend. Four formed the uniqueness category: choice, freedom, uniqueness, and resistance to collective values. Native coders made these judgments for the ads in their national magazines, and the results were again consistent with prior findings. Among the Korean ads, 95% employed conformity themes, as opposed to 65% in the American magazines. In contrast, uniqueness themes appeared in 89% of the American ads and only 49% of the Korean ads (Kim & Markus, 1999).

Note that both orientations can be labeled favorably or unfavorably. Individualism can be regarded as uniqueness or deviance, collectivism as harmony or conformity. From this standpoint, assertiveness, highly valued in the United States, may be viewed as a lack of cultivation or respect in certain Asian societies (Kim & Markus, 1999).

A simpler study provides still further evidence. Large samples of students at Japanese and American universities supplied written answers to a series of questions in this form: "What proportion of students in this university have higher intellectual abilities than yourself?" Other questions asked about memory, athletic ability, sympathy, and similar characteristics. American students reported that, on average, only 30% of their peers exceeded them on the various traits and abilities, suggesting that they lived at the fictional Lake Wobegon, "where all the children are above average." The Japanese students estimated that about 50% possessed more of a certain ability or trait, which of course is the logical outcome for any representative sample of students evaluating themselves in an objective fashion (Markus & Kitayama, 1991).

Overall, the differences between these two orientations can be summarized in three variables: traditional styles of thinking, sense of life satisfaction, and mode of social involvement. In general terms, tradition among European North Americans emphasizes linear, logical, analytical thinking; tradition among East Asians fosters more holistic, relational, inferential thinking. With regard to life satisfaction, personal feelings and sense of self are more important to European North Americans; interpersonal relationships are more important for East Asians. And finally, in social activities, European North Americans more often project their views onto other group members; East Asians are more inclined to recognize or accept the viewpoint of another group member (Lehman, Chiu, & Schaller, 2004).

All people everywhere face the conflicting demands posed by individual expression versus loyalty to the group (Marjoriebanks, 1997). At the international level, these orientations sometimes become loosely known as the West and the Rest, respectively. The individual becomes the fundamental unit in the former, the family or community in the latter, which may include African, Latin American, and other cultures (Hermanns & Kempen, 1998). Extensive empirical research supports the distinction between independent and interdependent orientations.

But this dichotomy, like most others, oversimplifies the issue, ignoring the fact that families and cultures exist on a continuum. No culture is completely egocentric or sociocentric. All social groups possess common and distinctive features (Hermanns & Kempen, 1998).

Resistance to the independence-interdependence research has been confined largely to survey investigations that compare national samples of college students. Objections have been raised about the cultural insensitivity of the questionnaires, evident in the failure to consider socioeconomic status and level of education as cultural influences. Also, the use of national labels overlooks subcultural differences (Greenfield et al., 2003). China, for example, with several times the land mass of the United States, has a high potential for subcultural differences. Populations in the coastal regions show characteristics different from those of people living in distant inland areas, and both groups show differences from regions undergoing cultural transitions. Similar regional differences occur in the United States. Rapid cultural change also blurs this independence-interdependence distinction. Young adults from collectivist orientations converge toward individualism when compared with their parents, especially following immigration to the United States (McCrae et al., 1998). Moreover, as Asian countries have undergone economic development, mothers have entered the workforce outside the home and childrearing changes have occurred in an individualistic direction (Greenfield et al., 2003).

One study examined the extent to which the individualistic-collectivistic orientations of young adults could be attributed to the orientations of their parents. The investigators surveyed 320 families in Australia, all with Anglo, Greek, or Italian backgrounds. Collecting data from these families on two occasions, when the offspring were 11 and 21 years old, they found Anglo parents most individualistic and Greek parents the most collectivistic. In all three groups, the scores for the offspring as young adults converged toward the individualistic orientation when compared with the scores of their parents (Marjoriebanks, 1997).

Without question, the cultural viewpoint offers a special perspective on human life, stressing economic, religious, political, educational, and moral convictions. All of these standards and expectations leave their mark. Friendships with classmates, for example, might have diminished Bertha's early personal problems, but educational and religious restrictions deprived her of the necessary opportunities. And discrimination against women blocked her later career aspirations. These cultural realities, encountered during her formative years, perhaps became the personal issues driving her later life.

That night, still ruminating on Turli's question, Bertha had an odd idea for dealing with the deprivation in her postwar culture. Out of the old newspapers in her briefcase, she would make herself some warm clothing. The next morning, she fashioned herself a vest and wore it under her dress. It crinkled a bit when she moved.

"My stuffing did not protect my lower limbs," she noted.

After a walk across town, the critical moment arrived. She knocked, and Mr. Gruenbaum answered the door. Then Irmchen appeared with a cheese sandwich and cardboard box containing her few possessions. She promptly announced that she would never return. That spirit pleased Bertha.

The whole business turned out to be much easier than expected. For the return trip to the Pfungstadt station, they sat in a small open carriage, which drove off in a great hurry. After almost an hour in the cold, they arrived— 10 minutes too late for the noon train. But the newspaper vest showed its merit, shielding Bertha from the frigid weather.

Suddenly she thought again about this underwear. The French prohibited newspapers in the occupied zone. Suppose they noticed the slight rustle in Bertha's movements. Would they order her to undress? No one would believe that she wore the forbidden newsprint just to keep warm.

Waiting for the next train, Irmchen chattered incessantly, predicting that Bertha would die soon because her hair was so old. She asked if each child at The Home had a bed. Satisfied with the answers, she turned to questions about Bertha, her husband, and marriage. To change the subject, Bertha resorted to changing Irmchen's underwear. That kept both of them occupied.

"A cookie helped me out of this difficult situation," Bertha added later (Pappenheim, 1923).

Bertha's discomfort with the child's questions testifies partly to her sexual inexperience. She avoided discussions of sex with everyone. It also testifies to her culture and times. In that era and place, more closed than our society today, people did not discuss sexual matters in public. Acceptable and even admired in some contexts today, open expressions of sexuality were regarded as vulgar and wrong in Bertha's era. We must consider her behavior in the context of her culture, not ours.

Cross-Cultural Comparisons

With comparatively few absolute standards for judging culture and its behaviors, *cultural psychology* includes a range of research methods. Some are scientific in the traditional sense. Others are more informal and spontaneous, adapted to the immediate circumstances. The primary goal is to study the ways culture and psychological characteristics influence one another. The concern lies with understanding psychological processes.

In contrast, **cross-cultural psychology**, using largely empirical methods, examines cultural similarities and differences, such as those evident between individualistic and collectivist societies. Those findings came largely from cross-cultural studies, which also make comparisons within a particular society, noting similarities and differences among subcultures or between them and the dominant culture.

Cultural psychology and cross-cultural psychology are alike in seeking to understand human behavior in the context of human environments. But cultural psychology seeks basic explanations of human behavior by focusing on the acculturation *process*, the ways culture influences behavior and experience. Cross-cultural psychology focuses more on the *outcomes*, making comparisons among cultures (Valsiner, 2000). The two approaches overlap, but the terms are not synonymous.

In fact, cross-cultural psychology has been described as a subdiscipline in mainstream psychology aimed at determining the generalizability of its findings on human mental life (Schweder, 1990). Thus, this chapter closes with several cross-cultural comparisons in basic realms of human functioning: perception, thinking, personality, and maladjustment.

With perception as the gateway to knowledge, early cross-cultural studies began with this question: Would people from markedly different cultural settings view a relatively simple stimulus differently?

One group of investigators developed the "carpentered-world hypothesis," stating that people living in traditional Western buildings, regularly exposed to the rectangular shapes of walls, doors, tables, and the like, become especially prone to visual illusions involving right angles. They tested this hypothesis in cross-cultural studies. Observing straight lines of different lengths meeting at different angles, residents of the United States, living in a carpentered culture, were distinctly susceptible to a rectangular illusion of distance. The Zulus of southeast Africa, who live in circular huts, keep their cattle in circular corrals, and engage in religious ceremonies oriented to the circle, were notably less susceptible (Herskovits, Campbell, & Segall, 1969). Similarly, people living in cultures with open vistas are more susceptible to a

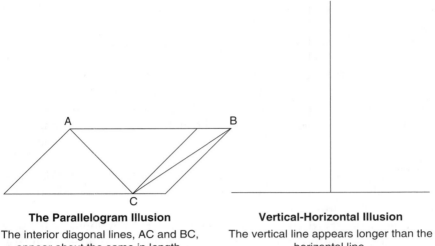

The Parallelogram Illusion

The interior diagonal lines, AC and BC, appear about the same in length.

Vertical-Horizontal Illusion

The vertical line appears longer than the horizontal line.

Figure 9.1   Culture and Illusions of Distance. Susceptibility to some illusions varies with experience. In the image on the left, if the parallelogram were a table top viewed obliquely from above, AC would represent a greater distance across the surface than would BC. In the image on the right, if the vertical and horizontal lines extended across the earth's surface, the vertical line, receding into the distance, would encompass a greater length than the horizontal line, extending across the horizon.

simple illusion of vertical and horizontal distance than are people living in densely vegetated environments that prevent broad vistas (Figure 9.1).

Studying more than a dozen cultures, the investigators found susceptibility to these illusions in all of them, showing the role of biological factors. But the large differences between some cultural groups when observing a few straight lines clearly indicate the role of culture as a mediating factor. If a difference occurs when perceiving a simple stimulus, one can only imagine the cultural differences implicit in the more abstract dimensions of human civilization, such as ethics, religion, government, and interpersonal relations.

Cross-cultural research on thinking has focused on how culture shapes children's thought, especially in the context of Piaget's theory of cognitive development. One investigation considered rational thinking, called "concrete operations," in children from 6 to 14 years of age living in one of three rural cultures: Dorset Eskimos on the tip of Baffin Island, Australian Aborigines in the Northern Territories, and Ebrie Africans on the Ivory Coast. With children of various age levels from all three cultures, the total sample involved 190 children, equally divided between males and females. The tasks involved explanations of changes in quantity, weight, and volume when these conditions were manipulated in various ways.

One hypothesis stated that the African children, living in a sedentary culture of agricultural production and high food accumulation, would understand the conservation of quantity, weight, and volume at an earlier age than the Eskimo and Aboriginal children, living in cultures with low food accumulation, reliance on hunting, and nomadic tendencies. The findings offered partial support for this hypothesis, especially in children at the older ages. One possible explanation lay with differences in Western values in the different school environments.

In any case, the overall results showed that the development of early logical thought was not uniform among the groups. The differences in level of thinking may reflect the adaptive value of knowing about quantity, weight, and volume in specific cultural, ecological settings (Dasen, 1975).

Cross-cultural research on personality addresses one of the broadest concepts in psychology. The term **personality** refers to a person's characteristic and unique ways of responding to the world over an extended period. With this emphasis on typical and unusual behavior, it includes the full array of a person's abilities, interests, personal relationships, and almost all other psychological characteristics. In a sense, personality describes the whole person as known by others.

In the most prominent cross-cultural studies, investigators have reported the similarities in personality makeup to be greater than the differences. Rather than regarding personality as solely culture-specific, they emphasize a universal personality *structure,* referring to the building blocks of personality. From this standpoint, five central traits may provide a reasonably comprehensive framework for depicting the personality of any individual, regardless of culture. Called the **Big Five traits**, they are agreeableness, conscientiousness, extraversion, neuroticism, and openness to experience (Costa & McCrae, 1992; Norman, 1963). In nonalphabetical order, they produce an acronym: OCEAN.

Each central trait represents a continuum from one extreme to the other. In a broad sense, openness to experience refers to behavior that is inquisitive, spontaneous, and artistic versus rigid, close-minded, and unimaginative. Conscientiousness implies a tendency to be orderly and respectful as opposed to impulsive and unconventional. With regard to extraversion, some people are extremely outgoing, others are remarkably introverted, and most are somewhere between the two extremes. Agreeableness reflects the fact that some people are consistently good-natured, a few are downright nasty, and most are in the middle. The neuroticism factor ranges from emotional stability to chronic agitation. Bertha, like the rest of us, would show some constancy in her particular positions on these traits and some variation from one situation to another.

Moreover, each central factor or trait includes subtraits with different shades of meaning, specific manifestations of the central trait. Worried, poised, impatient, temperamental, comfortable—all are variations of neuroticism. The central trait with the widest divergence in subtraits is openness to experience, also called culture. On this trait, Bertha might show considerable variation.

The Big Five traits emerge through nomothetic research on personality. Extensive cross-cultural studies indicated the presence of these five factors in many large groups of people. Now this set of traits can be used in idiographic research, assessing the personality profile of a particular person. On a rating scale for these five variables, Bertha, for example, might reveal relatively high scores on conscientiousness and extraversion, a low score on agreeableness, and intermediate scores on neuroticism and openness to experience.

Not all cross-cultural studies have supported the Big Five traits. Sometimes only four factors appear consistently, and sometimes seven describe personality more adequately, as in a Spanish sample (Benet-Martinez, 1999). One confounding factor is education. Another is the cultural distance between the groups, which has not been extensive in such studies. People from nonliterate cultures, compared with those from highly literate communities, have different standards of living, types of families, religions, and other characteristics (Triandis & Suh, 2002).

Nevertheless, each of the Big Five traits, collectively called the Five Factor Model, offers survival advantages in a human culture and may have become universal on that basis. Even as adaptive traits, of course they carry somewhat different meanings in different cultures, but the overall structure of personality may be more universal than previously understood (McCrae et al., 1998).

Personality, of course, does not emerge solely from isolated traits. People with similar standing on central and even subtraits may have different personalities owing to situational influences, developmental changes, and especially interactions among these traits. The human environment inevitably plays an influential role, shaping culture-specific dimensions of personality.

And personality sometimes goes awry. Cross-cultural research therefore includes **psychopathology**, the study of mental abnormality or maladjustment, although the boundaries between normal and abnormal often remain elusive

(Lilienfeld, 2000). They depend on the specific situation, era, and culture, as well as the individual's age, gender, and even outlook on life. Many reactions acceptable in children, for example, are not acceptable among adults. Bertha's construction of The Home for Wayward Girls and Illegitimate Babies, tolerable in semi-rural Germany early in the 20th century, would have been regarded very differently in downtown Vienna a century earlier.

In this context, two broad criteria sometimes define psychological maladjustment: personal discomfort and socially disruptive behavior. All normal adults have experienced discomfort at one time or another, and intentionally or otherwise, they have disrupted the lives of others in some way. Thus, the frequency and intensity of these occasions must be considered in any instance of an alleged adjustment disorder.

Among them, schizophrenia is a serious condition, observed in one form or another in cultures around the globe. A condition of special interest in abnormal psychology, *schizophrenia* involves extreme withdrawal from reality, including loss of mental and emotional control. A form of psychosis, it has become a prime research target, owing not only to its severity and widespread incidence but also to its puzzling, often idiosyncratic symptoms.

Some investigators focus on a core of schizophrenic symptoms existing across cultures. Others study cultural differences; they aim to understand the unique expression of this disorder in one culture or another. Identifying cultural similarities and differences eventually may prove helpful in understanding the fundamental components of this disorder. In any case, different approaches have provided tentative evidence that schizophrenia in developing countries has a more favorable prognosis than in developed countries (Lopez & Guarnaccia, 2000). If this finding is supported, does the explanation lie with differences in the schizophrenic condition, the community response, or both? These kinds of questions frame cross-cultural research in psychopathology.

Schizophrenia also tends to be viewed differently depending on the individualism-collectivism orientation of a particular culture. People in the former cultures, regarding the self as independent and separate from others, generally view schizophrenia as a personal issue. For those in a collectivist culture, with stronger family and interpersonal ties, it becomes more of a community issue (Lopez & Guarnaccia, 2000).

Culture-specific syndromes of mental illness occur in all parts of the world. In *taijin kyofusho,* a distinctive Japanese phobia, an individual becomes fearful that his or her body parts or functions are offensive to others through their appearance, odor, or movement. The Spanish expression *mal de ojo* means "evil eye," suggesting that an individual, usually a child, has fallen under some sort of spell, inducing diarrhea, vomiting, fitful sleep, and crying without apparent provocation. Chinese and other East Asian societies recognize *koro*, a disorder of sudden, intense anxiety about the penis, or vulva and nipples, receding into the body and causing death. These diverse disorders, pervasive in certain cultures, merely suggest the array of culture-bound syndromes for which there are seldom clear equivalents in the United States (American Psychiatric Association, 1994).

In summary, any culture creates much of the reality perceived by its citizens. People are sociocultural creatures, enmeshed in local customs, constraints, and conformities. These influences penetrate deeply into the ways in which they view themselves and others. They leave an indelible mark, especially early in life.

Vienna left its mark on young Bertha. Frankfurt did later. The hardships in postwar Germany did likewise. As the saying goes, "You can take the person out of the culture, but you can never take the culture out of the person."

Sitting in that cold Pfungstadt tavern, alone with her thoughts except for squirming little Irmchen, Bertha remained only too aware that her prewar culture had vanished. She now knew poverty too well.

Suddenly she decided that she and her little waif had stayed too long in that chilly place. With Irmchen wearing new underpants, and Bertha wearing a newspaper vest, they returned to the railroad station, which they found even colder. The train finally arrived, barely heated, and brought them to Eberstadt; then they changed trains to their final destination, the Frankfurt station.

Back in her unheated apartment, Bertha could not go to sleep. "I heard the clock strike twelve, and one, then two," she later wrote in her journal. "I could not get warm, nor fall asleep, until a good cry gave me some release from my tension" (Pappenheim, 1923). Bertha's two-day mission had ended in complete success. Perhaps she cried in relief, for that achievement required considerable stamina and prudence in her devastated country.

Perhaps she wept for another reason. Despite Irmchen, Turli, and the hundreds of other adoptees and their families whom Bertha had assisted, she lived a lonely life. When work was over, she always went home—alone. Her tears perhaps expressed her sense of isolation, her lack of intimacy and close personal support in our inescapably social world.

Culture promotes and sustains our ways of behaving and experiencing our social milieu, so much so that our responses to our own culture seem natural and universal. Many of them we do not question. Much research has revealed the potency of culture in forming our perceptions, thoughts, feelings, and overt reactions. No social response occurs apart from a culture of some sort.

Summary

The Inevitable Human Influence

Human beings live with one another amid the practices and products of other human beings. The sociocultural viewpoint examines both dimensions: the interpersonal relationships in our social lives and the shared customs, laws, and artifacts in our cultural lives. A prominent study of obedience to malevolent authority showed that human behavior can be markedly influenced by social and cultural factors.

Key Terms: **social psychology, cultural psychology, obedience, Milgram's obedience research**

Social Psychology

Social psychology examines the ways in which people understand and modify one another's behavior, called social cognition and social influence, respectively. In social cognition, attribution theory explains that people tend to view other people's behavior as a function of internal characteristics, a personal attribution. They are more likely to view their own behavior as called forth by the circumstances, a situational attribution. Studies of prejudice and stereotyping have shown how scapegoating can occur, commonly arising through the belief that one's own group is superior to others.

Key Terms: **social cognition, personal attribution, situational attribution, fundamental attribution error, self-serving bias, social influence, compliance, conformity, social facilitation, social interference, social loafing, prejudice, stereotype, scapegoat**

Psychology and Culture

Culture exerts a pronounced influence on human behavior and experience, sometimes resulting in universal behaviors, those that appear in most cultures, and sometimes producing culture-specific behaviors, those found only in one or a few cultures. In an individualistic culture, personal achievement and self-enhancement are primary; in a collectivist culture, group goals become ascendant. Human beings everywhere experience cultural influences on perception, thinking, personality, adjustment reactions, and all other mutable characteristics.

Key Terms: **culture, universal behavior, culture-specific behavior, cultural relativism, cultural absolutism, individualistic society, collectivist society, cross-cultural psychology, personality, Big Five traits, psychopathology**

Critical Thinking

1. The cost effectiveness of Milgram's obedience research has been debated for 40 years—the gain in knowledge versus the anguish and self-doubt endured by participants. Explain your view today, acknowledging the changes in ethical standards.

2. A tourist in a foreign land mistakenly assumes that a customs officer's friendly gesture is the sign of a nasty disposition. Explain how the fundamental attribution error might be involved. Also explain how ethnocentrism may play a role.

3. Consider research in cultural and cross-cultural psychology with regard to their potential for promoting world peace. Focusing on their different research goals, make an argument for each approach, including an example in each instance.

10

Psychology in Perspective

The various perspectives approach psychology differently, each with special assets and limitations. From one standpoint, they reflect a hybrid vigor, bringing a healthy diversity into a field still in adolescence, not yet with a clear identity. From the opposite standpoint, they highlight the fragmentation in the field already exacerbated by psychology's enormous breadth, ranging from biological to cultural studies, including a full spectrum of intervening topics.

This closing chapter considers the six perspectives together, rather than separately, providing comparisons among them. It addresses them first with regard to the multiple bases of aggressive behavior. Then it turns to the commonalities and differences among the perspectives in research and practice. Finally, it presents each perspective's view of human nature and closes with comments on the future of psychology as a science.

Loosely considered, human nature and science share certain features, for science is a human endeavor. Contrary to much thought, it is not a completely impersonal, omnipotent force, functioning apart from the human condition. Science includes checks and balances not regularly encountered in everyday life, but of course it is not impervious to internal, personal influences. Scientists are human beings, possessing wisdom and biases, creativity and failings. In a general way, they show human qualities not so different from those of Bertha and Breuer and all others. Our brain is a thinking brain and also an emotional brain.

Then, too, the people who manage the funds for scientific research are also human beings, each with personal preferences, fears, rivalries, and so forth, favoring some research programs, necessarily ignoring or rejecting others. Human hopes and foibles exist in all spheres of human life, including the management of human institutions.

In managing The Home for many years, Bertha showed obvious human skills and frailties, including sometimes painful discrimination, favoring some children and not others—until she grew too old and tired for this full-time work. Then in her mid-seventies, she confronted the uncertain prospects of old age, including her increasing ailments. "Who can make long plans with a bad gallbladder?" she complained. But she made them anyway.

She decided to return to Vienna one last time. There she visited old friends and familiar places and divested herself of her cherished laces, donating them to the Capital Museum for Arts and Crafts. She browsed among the book stalls and rummage stores of her childhood and then met with Wilhelm, prepared for a confrontation.

Bertha typically did not think about her own verbal aggression. Yet she regularly inflicted wounds on others. At The Home, she fired staff members callously, calling them unfit to care for themselves—their own bodies, minds, and homes. At board meetings, she openly rebuked members not only for their ideas but even for their personal grooming. Whenever a donor to The Home presented a gift of doubtful value, she "thanked" the contributor with a rather stern note (Edinger, 1968; Freeman, 1972).

This verbal aggression yielded gains for Bertha on many fronts—but it gained her no friendships. Apparently unaware of its consequences, she often wondered why she was so lonely. According to relatives and colleagues, she never showed any concern about her scathing remarks, though deeply troubled by aggression in others (Edinger, 1968).

"I've often thought that if there's nothing to love," she said on another occasion, "to hate something is a good substitute" (Edinger, 1968).

Verbal or physical, expressed individually or in a group, aggression remains a serious problem for humanity. Most perspectives investigate this issue, and their diverse approaches focus on a number of contributing factors within and outside the individual.

Multiple Bases of Behavior

At the outset, some definitions are in order. In brief terms, **aggression** is behavior directed toward another individual for the purpose of causing harm. The aggressor believes that the behavior will cause harm and that the potential victim would be or is motivated to avoid it. A high level of aggression, called *violence,* is aimed at causing extreme harm.

At any level, aggression can be hostile or instrumental. Thus, *hostile* aggression involves impulsive behavior, driven by unplanned anger and the goal of harming a victim. Also called *reactive* aggression, it occurs as a response to some perceived transgression. In contrast, *instrumental* aggression involves pursuit of some other goal, apart from harming another individual, who becomes a victim as a byproduct of the action. This aggression serves as a means or an instrument for attaining that goal. In other words, both types involve an intention to harm, but they differ in the ultimate purpose, serving primarily to induce harm or to gain some profit (Anderson & Bushman, 2002). These definitions can apply to *physical aggression,* involving bodily injury, and *verbal aggression,* occurring through hostile words, both of which can produce mental, emotional, and other psychological harm.

The Search for Causes

When it comes to physical aggression, the chief hypotheses in biological psychology concern *testosterone,* a sex hormone produced primarily in males but found in both sexes. This chemical substance influences motivation and emotion by acting on various brain areas, including the hypothalamus. The hypothalamus, in turn, influences the endocrine system and therefore the secretion of testosterone. Studies of diverse species have shown that male animals injected with testosterone attack others they would normally ignore or even avoid, and females injected with testosterone become increasingly aggressive. Aggression in boys rises with the onset of testosterone secretion at puberty, and violent men have elevated levels of testosterone (Archer, 1996; Mazur & Booth, 1999). Throughout experimental and clinical studies with animals and people, testosterone emerges as an influential factor in aggression.

The implication of testosterone makes it tempting to say, "There is the cause—*the* reason for aggression, especially in men." But viewing testosterone as the only factor grossly oversimplifies the issue. It prompts a reminder. The **fallacy of the single cause** wrongly attributes a certain condition or outcome to one and only one factor. Every scientific hypothesis has limits. The testosterone explanation alone becomes overzealous, attributing complex personal and social behavior to a single physiological mechanism, a specific hormone. Low levels of serotonin, for example, also increase aggression. Testosterone appears to be an important contributing factor, but it fluctuates with variations in several factors, including competition and dominance. In fact, testosterone may serve primarily to increase aggression once the behavior has commenced (Virgin & Sapolsky, 1997). And testosterone provides little explanation for the sometimes severe aggression on the part of women against members of their family.

Traditional psychoanalysis hypothesizes that human aggression is an inborn impulse or instinct, automatically driving us toward destructive acts. An element of the id, it functions as a counterpart to the impulse for life and love. But modern psychoanalysis takes a more moderate view, regarding aggression as an innate tendency, its expression dependent on external factors (Marmor & Gorney, 1999). It can become markedly augmented by childhood conflict and other difficult early experiences, such as parental favoritism, family tragedy, and cultural patterns. Through repression, the aggressive impulses become hidden, but they do not disappear. They emerge in disguised forms, called unconscious motivation.

In one common disguise, called *displaced aggression,* the hostility is directed toward some object or individual, not the true, original source of the problem. The individual behaves aggressively instead toward other people and events—criticizing his bosses, gossiping about colleagues, attacking the government, scapegoating minorities, and the like. The hostile feelings become expressed in these diverse ways, but their earlier, underlying causes may remain hidden.

Freud also stressed the harm in verbal aggression. Words, he said, are powerful instruments, the means by which people communicate their feelings and influence one another. They can promote unspeakable good, and they can inflict terrible wounds (Freud, 1927).

For behaviorists, the environment contains the keys to aggression. The basic concept is the reinforcement principle. Behaviors followed by positive consequences tend to be repeated; those that result in no consequence or negative consequences tend to be discarded. On this basis, people become aggressive because they gain certain outcomes (Catania, 1998). Aggressive political campaigns yield advances in the public domain; combative business practices increase profits; doubtful lawsuits produce preposterous fortunes. On the playing field, in the classroom, at work, and even in religious endeavors, the aggressive pursuit of self-interests often results in personal gain, although it can yield socially beneficial outcomes too.

In observational learning, a viewpoint that includes elements of behaviorism and cognitive psychology, children become aggressive partly through modeling the aggressive behavior of parents, other elders, public figures, and television characters. Especially when parents aggressively punish aggression or seem to gain some favorable outcome for their aggression, the child is likely to imitate the parent later (Bandura, 1986).

With its positive outlook, the humanistic approach devotes comparatively greater attention to the origins of aggression than to its mode of expression, concentrating on two potential sources. First, it points to environmental factors, blocking opportunities for self-actualization. This disruption begins with conditions of worth in childhood, leaving the individual likely to engage in antisocial behavior. The second source operates in the other direction, suppressing aggression, and it arises with another central concept in humanistic psychology: empathy. People who understand the distress of someone treated aggressively are less likely to engage in aggression themselves because of their empathetic response to the victim's pain. Research has also shown that low maternal empathy is linked to child abuse (Eisenberg, 2000).

In its traditional form, cognitive psychology focuses not so much on everyday social issues but instead on specific mental activities: visual perception, working memory, inductive and deductive thinking, and so forth. The basic concern lies with how human beings process information, not how they acquire meanings. Nevertheless, research in this perspective includes cognitive studies of the aggressive personality and the role of disciplinary measures in child rearing. The basic rationale states that people develop their own rules about how the social world works and how to respond, and these interpretations guide their behavior (Anderson, 2000). From the viewpoint of social cognition, investigators have also examined the inferences people make about others' aggressiveness (Eron, 2000).

From the evolutionary perspective, aggressive behavior evolved through natural selection, owing to its obvious advantages in survival and reproduction. As noted already, both of these adaptive tasks require aggressive responses: hunting for food, protecting territorial rights, obtaining access to mates, and building shelter (Buss, 1999; Darwin, 1859). In one form or another, aggression occurs in all human societies, and, unlike many animal species, human beings have no innate inhibiting mechanism, such as the submissive response in certain animals, which brings the attack to an end. Men are more physically violent than women, and breeding experiments with animals have shown clear genetic bases for aggression (Maxon, 1998; McGuffin & Thapar, 1998; Rowe, Almeida, & Jacobson, 1999).

Among early Native Americans, their mode of dress characterized different orientations toward aggression. The Zuni wore long, flowing robes, appropriate for their pastoral existence. Warlike instead, Comanches dressed for battle, even in everyday life (Linton, 1949). These differences in dress and behavior in earlier, more isolated societies suggest that culture can mold human beings in peaceful or aggressive ways, perhaps even apart from their biological needs.

No perspective or investigation can examine all sides of a question with all sorts of participants and all available methods. Each contributes in its own, restricted way, or it does not address the topic at all (Figure 10.1).

This circumstance raises a vital question. How can several different perspectives contribute useful findings to the same question? The answer lies with the complexity of human behavior. Each perspective considers a different aspect of the behavior. Collectively, they prompt a reminder about the fallacy of the single cause. Psychologists today speak instead about **multiple causality**, meaning that any complex human reaction is influenced by several factors within and outside the individual. Their number and relationships presumably are finite and orderly. Thus, they are potentially discoverable, but the task remains challenging indeed.

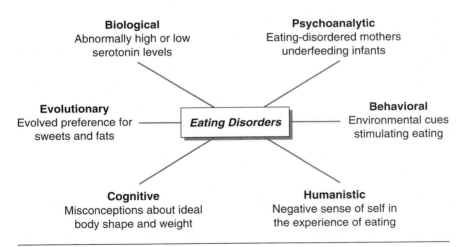

Figure 10.1   Multiple Bases of Behavior. Diverse causes underlie most human behavior, including eating disorders. Severe eating disorders often appear in adolescence, although signs of potential problems may become evident years earlier, especially low self-esteem, concerns about body image, and unsuccessful dieting (Agras, 2000).

This concept, multiple causality, remains implicit throughout psychology. One justification for presenting psychology in six perspectives lies with the multiple basis of behavior. Along with empiricism and rationalism, multiple causality represents a recurrent theme in the field today.

Convergent Evidence

When answering any research question, a degree of uncertainty always remains. Even the various perspectives together fail to give a full and complete answer. For this reason, psychologists look for convergent evidence, which shows the predominant outcome in a large number of investigations. Individually, each research finding may count for little, but in **convergent evidence** many different investigations, each somewhat flawed, point to the same general conclusion. In other words, convergent evidence shows the consensus among many studies.

Today's conclusions about the hazards of smoking required a half-century of diverse investigations. Early naturalistic observations and surveys suggested a relationship between smoking and cancer. But rebuttals claimed that people who smoked were susceptible to disease. Or they were in ill health anyway and perhaps already had cancer. Then, in clinical settings, case studies showed a higher-than-normal rate of lung cancer among smokers. But the tobacco industry rejected these findings as isolated instances. The clinical evidence was sporadic, not sufficiently scientific and systematic. Then experiments with animals demonstrated a causal outcome; rats given access to a device for "smoking" developed higher rates of cancer than those without this experience. But even these results were not conclusive. They simply showed that rats should not smoke cigarettes. And so it went, on and on, including quasi-experimental studies with human beings, each study adding to the accumulation of findings. Eventually, convergent evidence demonstrated that smoking constitutes a health risk (Viscusi, 1992).

Any judgment about the weight of the evidence of course can still be subjective. For this reason, psychologists often perform a meta-analysis, which literally means an analysis of the analyses—that is, a study of the existing studies. This technique does not involve collecting new data. Instead a **meta-analysis** reveals the thrust of the overall evidence by examining investigations already completed, using statistical techniques for assessing their significance with respect to sample size, method, results, and so forth. In short, a meta-analysis offers a reasonably objective approach for reaching an overall conclusion about the evidence from numerous investigations.

Since the 1970s, psychologists have studied the influences of aggression in the media. Although no one study by itself makes a convincing case, the overall evidence is convergent, as shown in meta-analyses. Media violence is associated with aggression in the viewers (Murray, 2000). In one extensive experimental study, for example, participants were assigned randomly to view violent programs or programs with other content, and the results showed that aggression in the media significantly increased aggressive behavior in the members of the audience (Wood, Wong, & Cachere, 1991). Evidence of this sort, persuasive for psychologists, has not yet created among the public any momentous demand for diminished aggression in the media.

One reason is that all such findings reflect probabilities. They are not categorical proof of something. In fact, psychologists rarely use the word *prove*. They speak instead about findings that offer *support* or *some support* or *no support* for one hypothesis or another. Or they speak about findings that confirm or fail to confirm a particular hypothesis.

Investigations show that aggression is associated with poverty. But most poor persons are not aggressive, and some people from affluent circumstances, like Bertha, show aggressive behavior. In other words, psychological research yields **probabilistic findings**, indicating the likelihood that one factor is associated with another or causes another. Physical abuse often causes aggression in children; delinquency is commonly associated with sexual abuse; and antisocial behavior may be increased by exposure to community violence (Margolin & Gordis, 2000). These outcomes are likely. In the philosophical view known as *probabilism*, certainty is impossible. Always, there is some doubt, but the probability may be sufficient for making practical decisions. A scientific finding reveals a trend or tendency.

Experiments have shown that after receiving injections of testosterone, animals rise in the dominance hierarchy of their colonies. And after the disappearance of the dominant member, the animals remaining near the top of the hierarchy experience an increase in testosterone. In these animals, biological and environmental factors *combine* to contribute to aggression. There is a reciprocity between them (Cacioppo, Bernstein, & Crites, 1996).

The same conditions hold for human beings. A person's inherited potential may be fostered in one environment and suppressed in another. Or it may lie fallow. In a rough sense, heredity sets a variable limit on an individual's potential as a warrior, writer, or welfare worker, and environment shapes that potential in various ways.

Several perspectives point out that potential aggression can be molded into socially acceptable or even admired ways, depending on the environment. Freud speculated extensively about aggression in the context of defense mechanisms, a concept that has received support (Cramer, 1997). In one mechanism, called *sublimation,* aggressive impulses are not openly directed toward adversaries or even innocent people but instead toward social conditions that make life difficult for others. In this struggle, the individual gains social approval, or at least tolerance, and at the same time finds at least a partial release for aggressive energy. Bertha's major crusades in life can be viewed in this way.

Freud also speculated about humor, especially in jokes, describing how they can serve as an outlet for latent aggressive tendencies. Near the end of her life, Bertha used humor in this way, writing five witty obituaries for herself, each pretending to take the viewpoint of some group she had opposed: white-slave merchants, anti-feminists, persons opposing aid to prostitutes, well-paid social workers, and Zionist members of her religion. Calling herself "an old and active enemy" of all these people, she concluded each piece with a sarcastic refrain: "What a pity!" (Edinger, 1968; Hirschmüller, 1989). With these fictitious death notices, she pushed back at the opposition.

Shortly thereafter, her gallbladder became infected, and she placed herself in the hands of a surgeon. "I was in such pain in Ischl," she wrote to The Home, "that I submitted to the claws of Aesculapius" (Edinger, 1968). She received rough treatment from the Greek god of medicine and healing. Then she incurred further illness.

Not long after that trip to Ischl, her condition became critical, left her bedridden, and then proved fatal. At her request, no one delivered a eulogy at the funeral. But Martin Buber, the Austrian philosopher, commemorated her life and career later in a memorial service, noting her vigorous and independent dedication to serving humanity.

Like his contemporaries at that service, he held a very different view of Bertha than the one we have today. Knowing her early illness and family history, and her later tendencies toward verbally aggressive leadership, we view her here in more complex terms, specifically through the different perspectives. They add to our understanding of her textured life, just as that life and work provide a human setting for discussion of these perspectives.

The Perspectives Revisited

These diverse perspectives create a vitality in modern psychology. As the prior discussions show, each makes its own contribution toward our understanding of a particular topic, such as human aggression. Here the focus changes, turning instead to direct comparisons among them and examining their similarities and differences in research and practice.

Orientations in Research

The perspectives are alike in a few basic ways: All of them pursue the study of behavior. All have assets, and all have deficits. And none can investigate the full spectrum of human behavior. Moreover, all run the risk of investigator effects, and all face the challenge of generalizing their findings to various contexts.

Beyond these fairly superficial similarities, what more can be said? Here we come full circle, returning to the research goals, methods, and data analyses described at the outset of this book. Now, with a background in all six perspectives, each can be viewed as inclined toward one or another research orientation, despite their differences in central concepts and theoretical viewpoints.

A moment's reflection shows that most research psychologists pursue nomothetic goals, aiming to establish universal principles of human behavior, which are applicable to people in general or to certain categories of people. To identify these principles, especially cause-and-effect relationships, they study groups of people and employ experimental methods, the most rigorous among all approaches to scientific inquiry. For group findings, they also use the survey. And to interpret the findings, they use statistical analyses, essential for creating precise measurements and understanding relationships among variables. This *nomothetic-experimental-statistical orientation* to research reflects the longstanding model of the natural sciences, evident in biology, physics, and related fields.

Biological psychology and cognitive psychology, with its computer metaphor, have this research orientation. They tend to investigate groups of people, often in controlled experimental settings, and focus on some narrowly defined component of a basic psychological process. Although they do so from different starting points—the body and the mind—they give the highest priority to precision, achieved through experimental methods and statistical analyses. In all phases of research, reliability of measurement remains a fundamental concern. Data analyses typically include descriptive and inferential statistics.

But these perspectives reflect differences as well. Biological psychology sometimes advances through research in exceptional case studies, such as H. M.'s inability to create new memories owing to destruction of the hippocampal areas and Phineas Gage's loss of emotional control following damage to the frontal brain regions. And cognitive psychology, as a complement to its experimental studies, commonly employs methods of naturalistic observation. These studies, focusing on perception, memory, and thinking in everyday environments, are often more relevant but less controlled than the usual laboratory studies.

Behaviorism and evolutionary psychology also reflect a nomothetic-experimental-statistical orientation—but in less traditional ways. Behaviorism seeks universal principles, employs experimental methods, and uses some statistical analyses. But rather than investigating groups of people, it also employs a single-participant experimental design, studying one individual at a time. These experimental studies focus on a narrow range of behaviors in highly controlled environments, making possible individual comparisons and generalizations among them, analyzed largely through descriptive statistics. In these ways, behaviorism has revealed a number of widely recognized universal laws of behavior, ranging from the fundamental principle of reinforcement to many related principles.

Less experimental than the other perspectives, evolutionary psychology fits less clearly in this cluster. Clearly nomothetic, it collects data from large numbers of people, employs inferential statistics, and uses experimental procedures. But in contrast to the other perspectives in this cluster, it places greater reliance on a descriptive method, the survey—using questionnaires, interviews, self-reports, and public records to seek findings consistent across groups and cultures. It also employs naturalistic observation throughout diverse societies, collecting data without the usual controls employed in laboratory settings. Nevertheless, its emphasis on nomothesis, group data, and statistical analyses makes evolutionary psychology a potential entry in this cluster.

But psychology is a complicated enterprise. One cluster cannot accommodate all perspectives. Especially in applied psychology, investigators pursue idiographic goals, aiming to understand a particular individual, event, institution, or other specific instance. To do so, they typically use descriptive research methods, often the traditional case study or naturalistic observation. And the data analyses are commonly thematic, ignoring extensive statistical interventions. This *idiographic-descriptive-thematic orientation* is guided by a research protocol, a flexible research plan permitting deviations based on unexpected events in the course of the research.

Traditional psychoanalysis and humanistic psychology reflect this orientation. Founded on case studies, psychoanalysis takes a special interest in the unique ways different individuals express and disguise their innermost concerns. With special interest in subjectivity and the self, humanistic psychology also relies heavily on the case study for flexibility in data collection and analyses, supplemented by observational methods and the survey as well. The complexity of any individual human being requires this broad, flexible approach, especially in the areas of personality and clinical psychology (Ozer, 2000).

Both perspectives sometimes forego opportunities for increased precision in favor of the greater breadth and improvisation essential in the study of particular instances. In this context, the traditional case study stands in marked contrast to the single-participant experiment. It takes place in a less controlled setting with less precise measurements, almost inevitably yielding a less rigorous conclusion. In these ways, traditional psychoanalysis and humanistic psychology may proceed beyond the borders of modern science and mainstream psychology. Contemporary research on psychoanalytic concepts is a different matter, employing carefully controlled experimental methods (Westen, 1998).

On these bases, the six perspectives fall into a pair of clusters. Those in the cluster of four—biological, cognitive, and evolutionary psychology, along with behaviorism—maintain a **quantitative orientation**, studying a large number of participants in a restricted, well-defined way, obtaining a narrow band of information about people in general. As basic research, they aim to discover precise relationships between two or a few well-defined variables. Often oriented toward the laboratory, they typically pursue nomothetic goals, use experimental or survey methods, and employ statistical analyses. In the fashion of the natural sciences, they search for universals.

Proceeding in almost the opposite direction, traditional psychoanalysis and humanistic psychology maintain a more **qualitative orientation**, investigating a particular instance—pointing to the distinguishing attributes of some person, event, small group, or institution. They aim to present the fullest description feasible of its essential nature. More often associated with questions outside the laboratory, they tend to pursue idiographic goals, use descriptive methods—especially participant observation and case studies—and employ thematic analyses, sometimes supported by basic statistics. In a flexible fashion, they become more involved with everyday life and holistic concerns.

In ordinary language, the quantitative orientation places a primary emphasis on precision; the qualitative orientation gives greater priority to fullness and relevance. Both orientations would like precision as well as fullness and relevance if they could have them, but all research requires such choices. This necessity marks a major issue and schism in the scientific study of behavior, dating back even to William James's pioneering efforts in psychology.

The quantitative orientation is primarily deductive, proceeding from a hypothesis to the collection of data; this research approach is widely used in modern psychology. Called *hypothesis testing,* the investigator aims to discover whether a certain theory or hypothesis will be supported by the data collected in a particular investigation. This research is often conceived in three steps: forming a hypothesis, testing the hypothesis, and verifying the results. But these idealized steps do not reflect the less orderly nature of much research.

The qualitative orientation is more flexible and often inductive, proceeding in the opposite direction—from data collection to the construction of hypotheses or theories. The aim is to develop concepts and theories from the data. Sometimes loosely known as *exploratory research,* especially in naturalistic observation, investigators may examine some behavior or event with no clear hypothesis in mind (Chiesa, 1994). And the investigation may include an intuitive, subjective dimension, along with more objective procedures.

In summary, the quantitative perspectives commonly address science-oriented questions with the highest possible precision in measurement and statistical analyses. The qualitative perspectives tend to focus on more human-oriented questions in the broader context of everyday experience. The data from both approaches require interpretations, though with greater structure in quantitative analyses and greater flexibility in qualitative analyses. In fact, throughout the research process—planning the project, collecting data, analyzing the data, and writing the report—the stages of quantitative inquiry are more fixed and specific, those in qualitative inquiry more variable.

No one research orientation always serves best. Ideally, as science advances, the objective, reductionistic, numerical procedures in the quantitative orientation can be complemented by the subjective, more holistic, interpretive procedures in qualitative research (Runyan, 1984). Together, they offer a range of research options.

Eclecticism in Practice

In its short history, psychology has evolved in numerous ways, readily evident in its different perspectives. Often emerging as protests against the status quo, these perspectives have also arisen as a way to establish their own workable boundaries within this vast discipline. Thereby, they have modified and advanced the field.

These perspectives are now less distinct from one another than they were decades ago—when they were known as systems of psychology. Improved research methods have increased psychological knowledge and stimulated them to become broader and more flexible. There are now many varieties of biological psychologists, psychoanalysts, behaviorists, and so forth, and many of them simply call themselves psychologists. Nevertheless, readers pondering these different schools of thought sometimes expect an assessment, some measure of their overall merit.

From the standpoint of *dualistic thinking,* all knowledge is either right or wrong, or it falls into two other categories: known or unknown. In any case, this incorrect notion of absolutes states that there is only one right answer, one best perspective (Perry, 1970). But most dualistic thinking eventually becomes eroded by the complexities of our environment.

Even superficial scrutiny shows that human knowledge is incomplete. Even the experts sometimes disagree. In *multiplistic thinking,* an element of doubt enters, producing three categories: right, wrong, and uncertain. Ultimate truths cannot be known; therefore, no perspective is better than any other. It makes no difference which is adopted.

But some answers *are* better than others, depending on the context. According to **contextual thinking,** all knowledge must be understood and evaluated with reference to a specific situation or circumstance. In an instance of aggression, the behaviorist considers reinforcement history. In the same or another instance, biological psychology examines brain activity. The observer decides on the usefulness of a particular perspective in a particular context (Perry, 1970).

The special comfort Bertha experienced with the dark Biedermeier cabinet seems best understood from the viewpoint of behaviorism. No other perspective offers an equally compelling explanation for her strongly favorable reaction to that piece of furniture, apparently attributable in a large measure to classical conditioning. Its aesthetic qualities and Bertha's knowledge of its history may have played a role too, as suggested in cognitive psychology. But the behavioristic perspective in particular points to Bertha's emotional reaction.

With regard to her avoidance of snakes, preference for sweets, language acquisition, and recognition of facial expressions of emotion, the evolutionary perspective offers a promising interpretation. Evolved psychological mechanisms may underlie all these behaviors. In lesser ways, other perspectives may be relevant too, as emphasized in the concept of multiple causality.

Contextual thinking is also called *relativistic thinking,* for a decision is reached in relation to a particular situation. Our world is one of contingent knowledge and divergent values (Perry, 1970). Each perspective contributes in its own way, broadly or narrowly, in one setting or another. No one perspective serves best in all circumstances.

Contextual thinking, together with the increasingly permeable boundaries among these perspectives, has promoted in applied psychology a tendency toward eclecticism, which means being selective. In **eclecticism**, a person selects whatever perspectives, or whatever features of one or another perspective, seem most useful in a given circumstance. A natural outgrowth of contextual thinking, eclecticism has become increasingly prominent in certain realms of applied psychology, notably psychotherapy. A flexible, pragmatic spirit pervades this approach, which is not bound to any single viewpoint.

In research, many psychologists continue to work within one or another perspective, maintaining a systematic emphasis on a particular set of concepts, such as modularity doctrine or the reinforcement principle. They become experts in that approach, conducting their investigations with the highly specialized knowledge essential in modern research. Alert to useful developments, they may use behavioristic models for research in biological psychology, for example, or employ evolutionary theory in studying cognitive concepts. But investigators typically remain within a given sphere.

In practice, many psychologists today become eclectic by design, offering an array of techniques in psychotherapy, thereby better meeting individual needs in a particular instance. They aim to transcend the limitations of one school of thought. Broadly based, **multimodal therapy** combines methods from the different perspectives, though without necessarily developing a fully integrated practice (Wachtel, 2000). Behavior therapy, psychoanalysis, and cognitive therapy may be used with different people experiencing different adjustment problems or, less likely, with one person at different stages of the therapeutic process. The goal is to take advantage of the different strengths of the various perspectives. But eclecticism, in turn, requires the sacrifice of greater expertise in a particular approach.

One notable combination of methods today occurs in **cognitive behavior therapy**, which includes a cognitive element focused on conscious thought and a behavioral element directed to less mindful habits. The assumption is that both conditions contribute to adjustment disorders and therefore both must be considered in therapy (Brewin, 1996). Cognitive behavior therapy aims in both directions: to diminish irrational thinking and to reinforce desirable ways of behaving. On this basis, it incorporates from behavior therapy the reinforcement principle and such techniques as contingency management, observational learning, and systematic desensitization. From cognitive therapy, it includes methods for reducing irrational or inappropriate thinking, such as the ABC technique, categories of maladaptive thought, and reframing. With this concern for changing behavior *and* thinking, cognitive behavior therapy has achieved widespread popularity. Also, it includes diverse forms of homework, such as keeping a journal of thoughts and behaviors; it focuses on ways of testing beliefs; and it identifies reinforcement contingencies (Kendall, Krain, & Henin, 2000).

Consulting psychology requires considerable eclecticism, for it encounters a variety of problems in many spheres of everyday life: education, medicine, law, business, and other contexts. To become most effective, consulting psychologists must employ an array of methods for reaching useful decisions about people and situations, thereby resolving a wide variety of psychological problems. Each problem must be examined in a flexible manner, each for its own complex content and unique characteristics.

This book depicts an eclectic outlook. Each perspective appears in a different phase of Bertha's life, one well suited to illustrate its particular concepts and merits: the biological perspective through her treatment for neurological problems in a Swiss hospital; psychoanalysis amid her relapses, fantasies, and growing interest in storytelling; behaviorism in her entry into the world of work at the orphanage; humanistic psychology through the fulfillment she experienced with The Home in Neu-Isenburg; the cognitive perspective in her dedication to the feminist cause; and evolutionary psychology amid the issues raised in her unsuccessful journey to the brothels.

But Bertha never knew that her last journey to Vienna also proved to be a failure. She returned one final time for something more than books and laces and a meeting with Wilhelm. She made extensive efforts to destroy all remaining evidence of her psychological disorder experienced 55 years earlier, cautioning members of her extended family against speaking about that part of her life.

It came to light anyway. Years later, on a trip to Vienna, one of Freud's biographers discovered Anna O.'s true identity—common knowledge among her relatives. Then he revealed it to the world as a footnote in his three-volume work on Freud, which was widely read at the time (Jones, 1953). He did so, he said, to honor Bertha's achievement. Through her self-styled therapy with Breuer, she became the real discoverer of the cathartic method of psychotherapy. Her name deserved commemoration.

Protesting vigorously, the Pappenheim family regarded the gain as irrelevant, the cost as momentous. A Homberger cousin tried to rescue Bertha, or at least to save the family reputation, writing an open letter of protest (Guttmann, 2001).

But Bertha only added to her modern reputation when she failed to cover the traces of her earlier illness. With our remarkably different attitudes today, she becomes all the more admirable for her impressive response to mental disorder.

Psychology in the Making

Since the dark days of Anna O., psychology has expanded enormously, including the emergence of its systematic perspectives. Its national associations in the United States, not even in existence when Bertha arrived in Frankfurt, have grown to include more than 100,000 members. These associations include more than 50 specializations, each adhering to its own concepts and goals, methods and assumptions, jargons and journals. Today many hundreds of psychology research journals publish new issues on a regular basis.

Unfinished Business

Despite this vigorous growth, psychology's overall goals remain—to gain greater understanding of human behavior and experience and to improve the human condition. In fact, the permanence of these goals prompted William James to describe them as psychology's "unfinished business." Further work always remains. New research findings extend, challenge, or supplant the old, as the cycle repeats itself again and again.

Research proceeds at an irregular pace, and discoveries vary widely in importance. This unpredictable progress readily appears in research on a popular topic: "human nature." The difficulty in measuring this concept, and even defining it, contributes to this unfinished business.

Consider these examples. Someone parks a car illegally. Someone else assists an adult with a baby. Children want to dress like their friends. People loosely describe such acts as human nature. But they cannot be human nature, for they are not characteristic throughout our species. Not everyone engages in these behaviors.

Strictly speaking, *nature* refers only to the natural world, including the laws and principles guiding our universe. From this standpoint, **human nature** refers to the psychological and behavioral characteristics and tendencies in people that distinguish them from animals and that remain when the influences of nurture have been discounted. But that definition is so broad that the term has no firm usage in psychology. Implicitly, it means "without nurture," excluding the endless behavioral tendencies acquired during our lifetimes.

But that condition is impossible because nurture begins even before birth. During any human pregnancy, nature is modified by the woman's ingestion of substances, exposure to emotional circumstances, regularity of exercise and sleep, and other events. But ignoring these influences—exceedingly difficult to measure—what are the natural tendencies of newborn human beings? An age-old question arises: Are human beings by nature basically good or basically evil? It has challenged philosophers and lay persons throughout human history.

Investigators in psychology's first laboratory studied biological and cognitive psychology without making extensive speculations about human nature. Each perspective today maintains its special interest in the human body or the human mind, respectively. Both biological and cognitive psychology point to characteristics deemed uniquely human. But in this process, neither has reached any fundamental, widely recognized philosophical position about the essential, innate tendencies of human beings.

The other perspectives have taken stronger, distinctly different positions. Psychoanalysis, humanistic psychology, behaviorism, and evolutionary psychology leave little doubt about their views.

Traditional psychoanalysis describes human nature in pessimistic, negative terms. People are not gentle creatures waiting to be loved, Freud declared. They are endowed instead with a powerful element of aggressiveness, waiting to exploit a neighbor in the workplace, to take advantage of a person sexually, to gain someone else's possessions, even to humiliate another individual. After listening to his patients describe their lives, Freud challenged his readers to dispute this conclusion.

Socialization, he continued, restricts our satisfactions in life. It imposes such sacrifices on human aggression and sexuality that people cannot be happy. Unconscious motivation to emit these behaviors remains constantly at odds with the social order. Nothing is so contrary to human nature as the commandment to love thy neighbor as thyself (Freud, 1930). The mutual hostility of human beings constantly threatens their civilization with disintegration.

Experiences in everyday life, and especially World War I, prompted Freud to hold this view. Since his day, with warfare around the globe, many people have adopted this troubled outlook. Broad and vaguely articulated, it may be part of the answer—but no final statement.

Humanistic psychology takes the opposite stance, viewing human nature as basically positive. Rogers' concept of the actualizing tendency underlies this optimistic outlook. This capacity for growth, inherent in all living creatures, promotes fulfillment of one's potential, providing it is not obstructed by external forces (Rogers, 1951).

During his career, Rogers envisioned people with this potential living successfully in a rapidly evolving culture, adapting to its changes, experiencing personal growth and the satisfying use of their abilities. He foresaw them as open to new experiences, both external and within themselves; desiring a wholeness in life, expressed in the integration of thoughts, feelings, and physical energy; acutely aware that life is always changing; and caring for others in a nonjudgmental way (Rogers, 1980). He also urged that we assist people in communicating more successfully with one another, especially in nonverbal ways (Rogers & Russell, 2002).

Human beings cherish the natural world, according to Rogers. They must form an alliance with it, rather than aim to conquer it, a view now shared by many in our global economy.

Needless to say, the traditional psychoanalyst and humanistic psychologist would not make promising dinner partners. They are poles apart in their views of human nature.

And it is not true, as sometimes alleged, that radical behaviorism takes no position on human nature. It too adopts a clear stance: There is no such thing as human nature—until the environment becomes influential. Resisting both prior perspectives, Skinner declares in *Walden Two* no faith at all in human nature. He has nothing to do with ideas of innate goodness and evil. His faith lies instead with our capacity to create and change human behavior (Skinner, 1948).

Applications of behaviorism have produced impressive techniques for behavior modification in everyday life, including remarkable assistance for people with presumably inborn, intractable personal problems. But these achievements do not demonstrate that human beings have no human nature—no substantial innate behavioral tendencies.

The psychoanalytic, humanistic, and behavioristic perspectives stand at odds with one another. In further juxtaposition, evolutionary psychology resists all of them, including behaviorism's blank slate. It states that human nature is not bad, not good, and not completely absent.

From the evolutionary perspective, we possess at birth an assembly of inborn, independent psychological predispositions, and they are components of our human nature. These evolved psychological mechanisms are activated by specific circumstances in everyday life and related to problems of survival and reproduction in ancestral eras. In modern society, some are negative, others positive. The so-called negative mechanisms arouse fear, anger, jealousy, and related emotions. In bygone millennia, they promoted successful responses to dangerous situations and engendered competition among human beings (Buss, 2000).

The more positive evolved mechanisms, including mate and food preferences, kinship patterns, and social exchange, contributed to happiness. Natural selection has designed in human beings certain landscape preferences, for example, favoring patterns of good weather and signs of the harvest, resisting dense forests and completely open plains. For living spaces, human beings consistently prefer savanna-like landscapes over other natural and even human-made environments (Buss, 1995a, 2000).

According to the evolutionary perspective, at least a portion of human nature appears in these highly evolved psychological mechanisms, positive and negative. Human nature includes the many ways in which natural selection, over the eons of human prehistory, designed us for survival and reproduction.

In summary, these four perspectives show successively different responses to the question of human nature, appearing almost completely independent of one another. And yet each may contain an element of truth. It is noteworthy too that the earlier, more philosophical perspectives—psychoanalysis, humanistic psychology, and behaviorism—all take firm categorical positions. Among the later, more topical perspectives, evolutionary psychology approaches human nature in pluralistic fashion, including a mixture of inborn "programs." And modern biological and cognitive psychology, if forced to a position, would move toward evolutionary psychology, reflecting the interest in mind-brain systems and subsystems.

The question of human nature puzzled the ancient Greek philosophers, stimulated interest through the Renaissance, rose again during the Enlightenment, and poses a substantial challenge in our own era of science. For example, one piece of this unfinished business concerns the ways in which the subsystems in our mind-brain apparatus are sufficiently malleable to result in learning completely novel adult tasks. At the same time, they must be sufficiently fixed to learn human language, understand facial expressions, comprehend physical space, and acquire at a very early age countless other dimensions of a human culture (Pinker, 2002). Continued inquiry into the nature of human nature appears essential for humankind. Knowledge and assumptions about our nature underlie all debate about human values, human society, and the optimal conditions for human development (Leahey, 2000).

Pathways and Prospects

This book began with observations about the breadth of modern psychology and the life of Anna O. Then it turned to the six perspectives, one by one, encountering in that process various stages in Bertha's career. Here, following a brief testimony to her work, it presents issues in contemporary psychology and conclusions about psychology's future directions.

Broad public acclaim came to Bertha decades after her death. In 1954, her adopted country issued a series of commemorative postage stamps called Helpers of Humanity. On one of them, the German government honored her life and work: Bertha Pappenheim, Pioneer Social Worker.

Modern psychology also remembers her in a special way—as the spirited but deeply troubled Anna O., who led Breuer to the "talking cure." She thereby became a pioneer in psychotherapy too.

Looking backward on someone's life is one matter. Looking ahead, forecasting psychology's pathways and prospects, becomes more challenging, especially in a field with distinct growing pains, inevitable in any rapidly developing human enterprise. Psychology's growing pains have appeared in three major contexts: the gap between psychology's two cultures—research and practice, its overlapping borders with other disciplines, and its current trajectory of intermittent new perspectives. In these respects, youthful psychology faces an uncertain future, especially in comparison with the more established natural sciences.

Almost since its inception, psychology has experienced the challenge of maintaining two identities: a scientific stance in research and a professional posture in everyday life. In fact, only a few decades after the founding of its original national organization, the American Psychological Association (APA), the practicing membership also formed its own group, the American Association of Applied Psychology. After a brief period, the applied psychologists reverted to the original APA group, but 50 years later another split occurred, this time initiated by the research psychologists. Many of them joined the Association for Psychological Science (APS), as it is called today, devoted strictly to the advancement of psychological science at the national and international levels, encouraging cooperation among all scientists in fields of psychology (Hakel & Herring, 2000). Many psychologists today are members of both organizations. But these rifts, initiated by each group, testify to the ideological and practical differences between them.

The scientists view the field from a deterministic, generally reductionistic standpoint, emphasizing objectivity in the study of psychological phenomena.

Practitioners, especially those in human services, often work in a more holistic, interpretive fashion, recognizing subjectivity as the fundamental human experience (Kimble, 1984). The competent practitioner employs scientific thinking and scientific instruments, but the analysis of data becomes a more judgmental, interpretive task. The practitioner can build a case for one conclusion or another but, without sufficient controls, cannot rule out alternative explanations.

This breach between scientific and practical goals is not confined to psychology. It appears throughout human inquiry. But it is unusual to find both goals so vigorously pursued in the same discipline. In coming decades, the term *psychologist* may continue to understate the differences between these spheres.

A separate but related challenge appears in psychology's overlapping borders with other disciplines. Spread in so many directions, the field may cease to remain a single endeavor and instead become gradually absorbed into those related fields. Biological psychology may merge into departments of neuroscience or medicine, cognitive psychology into computer or cognitive science. Psychoanalysis, with its massive conceptual framework for idiographic studies, may continue to flourish in departments of humanities (Scott, 1991). The trend toward interdisciplinary approaches may include humanistic psychology in philosophical studies and behaviorism in schools of education, business, nursing, and other professional enterprises, perhaps affiliated with a practice-oriented social psychology. And evolutionary psychology may develop a closer alliance with departments of organismic and evolutionary biology.

Many of psychology's major advancements have occurred at these boundaries. In the long view, it matters little whether they are credited to psychology or to interdisciplinary approaches (Hilgard, 1988).

But psychology's remarkable early growth suggests that it will not become dispersed into these related disciplines. Instead, absorption may take place in the opposite direction. Other disciplines in behavioral science may look to psychology for leadership and innovation, especially as it acquires increasingly sophisticated research methods and instruments. Some of these related disciplines may become part of an even broader field of psychology.

And, finally, apart from the two cultures and related disciplines, there is the question about psychology's overall pathway. Lacking a paradigm, will the field continue its past pattern, producing another new perspective in the next generation or so? For many psychologists, this trend is a healthy, expected condition in an emerging field. Systems of thought develop without a paradigm, and the behavioral sciences currently may be suited to this status.

Perhaps, instead, two or three perspectives may become increasingly allied, as suggested in the recent exchanges among biological, cognitive, and evolutionary psychology. Pushing research frontiers toward mind-brain-behavior relations, they have taken a stand against popular opinion and the older perspectives—psychoanalysis, behaviorism, and humanistic psychology. This trend suggests that modern psychology is moving away from systematic, philosophically based perspectives toward more open-ended, research-oriented subfields. The history of any science reveals such trends, reflecting the successive changes in questions the field has addressed (Kagan, 2006).

Implicitly or explicitly, the earlier perspectives regard the mind-brain mechanism as a general problem solver. Psychoanalysis views the mind largely in terms of levels of awareness, without any prominent attention to its specialized functions. Behaviorism, with no substantial interest in human mental life, approaches learning as an almost infinitely flexible process guiding the acquisition of behavior. And humanistic psychology, focusing on subjective experience, devotes almost no attention to the architecture of the human mind.

The newer approaches view mind-brain-behavior relations in terms of special systems or functions. A *system* is a set of relationships among parts concerned with the same larger function, forming a single whole. In **systems analysis,** scientists aim at understanding a system, a complex yet *unitary* function, in terms of the relations among its parts or subsystems. Of course the relevant parts in psychology are not pieces of hardware or software, as in systems analysis with computers. In a group of people, they are the individuals. In one individual, they are that person's organs, the larger parts including smaller parts as further components or subsystems. In the biological sphere, the cells are basic parts; aggregates of cells form tissues; tissue collections become organs; organs, in turn, form components or systems in the individual—digestive, skeletal, endocrine, and others. In the social realm, systems appear in families, commercial institutions, religious groups, and countless other organizations of individuals (Rapoport, 1968).

Modern biological psychologists, using the latest equipment, view the brain according to modularity doctrine. Our brain operates through the interaction of distinct units, systems, or modules, each functioning in an independent but coordinated fashion with other brain systems. In cognitive psychology, investigators speak of the mind as composed of domain-specific, or content-specific, problem-solvers, processing at the same time the different features of a particular scene—such as color, size, and shape—and doing so in distributed fashion, meaning in different brain regions. These parallel but separate systems produce integrated information, although it is not yet clear how they do so or how they are mapped onto specific brain modules. And in the evolutionary approach, evolved psychological mechanisms are viewed as innate dispositions to respond in specific ways to narrow bands of information related to survival and reproduction. According to these perspectives, the human mind is not one all-purpose, problem-solving device—an outlook also consistent with a systems approach.

From this standpoint, understanding how we experience integrated information becomes a substantial research challenge. Investigators today informally speak of this integrative communication as "cross talk," meaning the inferred but as yet unknown ways in which the systems and subsystems send messages to one another.

These modern perspectives—biological, cognitive, and evolutionary psychology—share a more textured, pluralistic view of mind-brain mechanisms, partly because the necessary instrumentation has become available to reveal it. Loosely united through the concept of evolution, they may become more closely connected as a single, overarching model, integrating some of psychology's perspectives and linking the field with other life sciences (Buss, 1999).

If such an integration occurs, it may alter the protest-and-replace pattern evident among prior perspectives, perhaps marking instead movement toward a paradigm, accompanied by substantial challenges. Biologically based inquiry would need to be integrated with studies of individual and group behavior. Emerging from cognitive and biological psychology as well as evolutionary influences, cognitive neuroscience, for example, aims to discover how the brain creates the mind (Kosslyn & Koenig, 1992). But its contribution to our knowledge of human behavior demands greater understanding of the complex relationships among findings from various levels of research, reductionistic and holistic, across the broad spectrum. According to some scholars, cognitive neuroscience is not part of psychology but instead is a reductionistic, interdisciplinary field, whereas the study of behavior remains at the center of mainstream psychology (Tagler, 2000).

Psychology instead may be suited to a pre-paradigmatic stage. Its focus on human behavior, and especially the human brain, greatly complicates scientific study, resulting in divergent views about the proper course of the field. In fact, communities of social scientists addressing behavioral questions show more and larger disagreements about legitimate scientific questions than do communities of natural scientists addressing the purely physical world (Kuhn, 1970). The fact that none of the behavioral or social sciences has achieved paradigmatic status suggests a fundamental difference from the natural sciences.

At this point, it is not clear whether psychology should even be viewed in the context of the so-called stages of science: pre-paradigmatic, paradigmatic, revolt, and then a new paradigm. Moreover, a basic tension exists within psychology, reflecting the contrasting worldviews of the natural and social sciences, the former more objective and rationalist, the latter more subjectivist and relativist. Both conditions reveal unsettled issues in contemporary psychology, characterized today by an emphasis on specialization, apparently at the cost of integration in inquiry (Driver-Linn, 2003; Kashdan & Steger, 2004).

If psychology does develop a paradigm, that model may not follow the pattern of the natural sciences, which implies that all causal forces operate upward from lower-level phenomena. It may give way to a model in which we study ourselves from a more *reciprocal* framework, stressing functional relations in *both* directions—upward from the more molecular components in human physiology and downward from the more molar elements in social life and culture. With this model, we would expect to obtain the most penetrating findings not from the smallest pieces of physical reality alone but together in their patterning with larger elements in our environment. This two-directional model, up and down, would offer a new way of comprehending ourselves and the nature of reality (Sperry, 1995). In more familiar terms, it would move away from the contemporary emphasis on reductionism to include more holistic concerns, concentrating on systems analysis and the patterning of factors at various levels of complexity.

In conclusion, these persistent issues—the scientist-practitioner split, relations with allied fields, and prospects for a paradigm—are major components of psychology's identity problems. They reflect psychology's growing pains—not a surprising condition in a young, vigorous, growing field—and they raise questions about forthcoming developments. But growing pains are rarely lethal, and they often become instructive (Rychlak & Struckman, 2000). In fact, they can be regarded as favorable signs.

In any case, psychology's emphasis on empiricism should continue; in fact, it is often cited as the field's unifying characteristic. And productive empiricism requires rationalism, promoting psychology's theoretical achievements. These twin themes—empiricism and rationalism—appear throughout the field, along with the concept of multiple causality. In historical perspective, psychology reflects these three themes. Its most prominent schools of thought have emerged in this context, each with its particular leadership, times, and settings.

Summary

Multiple Bases of Behavior

The various perspectives address the complexity of human behavior in diverse ways, and their findings remain probabilistic, indicating the likelihood that one condition is associated with another or causes another. Hence, advancements in knowledge occur through convergent evidence, in which different investigations and perspectives point to the same conclusion. Multiple causality states that behavior is typically influenced by several factors both inside and outside an individual.

Key Terms: **aggression, fallacy of the single cause, multiple causality, convergent evidence, meta-analysis, probabilistic findings**

The Perspectives Revisited

Biological and cognitive psychology maintain a quantitative research orientation, evident in predominantly nomothetic goals, experimental methods, and statistical analyses. Behaviorism and evolutionary psychology do so with less emphasis on traditional experimental methods. Traditional psychoanalysis and humanistic psychology maintain a more qualitative research orientation, commonly with idiographic goals, descriptive methods, and thematic analyses. Many practitioners today use these perspectives in an eclectic fashion.

Key Terms: **quantitative orientation, qualitative orientation, contextual thinking, eclecticism, multimodal therapy, cognitive behavior therapy**

Psychology in the Making

Human nature is viewed as negative in psychoanalysis, positive in humanistic psychology, nonexistent in behaviorism, and multifaceted in evolutionary psychology, an outlook generally compatible with findings and theories in biological and cognitive psychology. Questions about psychology's future concern the breach between its scientific and applied dimensions, its eventual relationships with allied fields, and its progression toward further perspectives or perhaps a paradigm.

Key Terms: **human nature, systems analysis**

Critical Thinking

1. A man planning to purchase a car reads numerous consumer reports. Indicate how contextual thinking may underlie his eventual choice.

2. Describe human sexual behavior from the viewpoint of multiple causality. Make reference to at least four psychological perspectives.

3. Explain how the idea of systems analysis reflects approaches to the mind-brain mechanism proposed in biological, cognitive, and evolutionary psychology. Cite the central concept in each case.

References

Aanstoos, C. M. (2003). The relevance of humanistic psychology. *Journal of Humanistic Psychology, 43*, 121–132.

Adler, A. C. (1927). *The practice and theory of individual psychology*. New York: Harcourt, Brace, & World.

Agras, W. S. (2000). Eating disorders. In A. E. Kazdin (Ed.), *Encyclopedia of psychology* (Vol. 3). New York: Oxford University Press.

Allport, G. W. (1962). The general and the unique in psychological science. *Journal of Personality, 30*, 405–421.

Ambady, N., & Rosenthal, R. (1993). Half a minute: Predicting teacher evaluations from thin slices of nonverbal behavior and physical attractiveness. *Journal of Personality and Social Psychology, 64*, 431–441.

American Psychiatric Association (1994). *Diagnostic and statistical manual of mental disorders* (4th ed.). Washington DC: Author.

Anand, B. K., & Brobeck, J. R. (1951). Hypothalamic control of food intake. *Yale Journal of Biological Medicine, 24*, 123–140.

Anastasi, A., & Schaefer, C. E. (1969). Biographical correlates of artistic and literary creativity in adolescent girls. *Journal of Applied Psychology, 53*, 267–273.

Anderson, C. A. (2000). Violence and aggression. In A. E. Kazdin (Ed.), *Encyclopedia of psychology* (Vol. 8). New York: Oxford University Press.

Anderson, C. A., & Bushman, B. J. (2002). Human aggression. *Annual Review of Psychology, 53*(1), 27–51.

Anderson, M. C., & Neeley, J. H. (1996). Interferences and inhibition in memory retrieval. In E. L. Bjork & R. A. Bjork (Eds.), *Handbook of perception and cognition: Memory* (2nd ed.). San Diego: Academic Press.

Archer, J. (1994). *Male violence*. London: Routledge.

Archer, J. (1996). Sex differences in social behavior: Are the social role and evolutionary explanation compatible? *American Psychologist, 51*, 909–917.

All citations follow the standards of the American Psychological Association. Unless otherwise noted, all quotations attributed to Bertha Pappenheim prior to 1883 are from Breuer (1895). All others are from Edinger (1968) or Guttmann (2001).

Aserinsky, E., & Kleitman, N. (1953). Regularly occurring periods of eye motility and concomitant phenomena during sleep. *Science, 118,* 273–274.

Aserinsky, E., & Kleitman, N. (1955). Two types of ocular motility during sleep. *Journal of Applied Physiology, 8,* 1–10.

Avons, S. E., Ward, G., & Russo, R. (2000). The dangers of taking capacity limits too literally. *Behavioral and Brain Sciences, 24,* 114–115.

Axline, V. M. (1964). *Dibs: In search of self.* New York: Ballantine.

Bachelder, B. L. (2000). The magical number 4=7: Span theory on capacity limitations. *Behavioral and Brain Sciences, 24,* 116–117.

Baddeley, A. D. (1992). Working memory. *Science, 255,* 556–559.

Baddeley, A. D., Thompson, N., & Buchanan, M. (1975). Word length and the structure of short-term memory. *Journal of Verbal Learning and Verbal Behavior, 14,* 575–589.

Bales, R. F. (1958). Task roles and social roles in problem-solving groups. In E. E. Maccoby, T. M. Newcomb, & E. L. Hartley (Eds.), *Readings in social psychology* (3rd ed.). New York: Holt.

Balota, D. A., & Cortese, M. J. (2000). Cognitive psychology: Theories. In A. E. Kazdin (Ed.), *Encyclopedia of psychology* (Vol. 2). New York: Oxford University Press.

Banaji, M. R., & Prentice, D. A. (1994). The self in social contexts. *Annual Review of Psychology, 45,* 297–332.

Bandura, A. (1986). *Social foundations of thought and action: A social cognitive theory.* Englewood Cliffs, NJ: Prentice Hall.

Bandura, A., Grusec, J. E., & Menlove, F. L. (1967). Vicarious extinction of avoidance behavior. *Journal of Personality and Social Psychology, 5,* 16–23.

Bargh, J. A. (1997). The automaticity of everyday life. In R. S. Wyer, Jr. (Ed.), *The automaticity of everyday life: Advances in social cognition* (Vol. 10). Mahwah, NJ: Erlbaum.

Baum, W. M. (1994). *Understanding behaviorism: Science, behavior, and culture.* New York: Harper Collins.

Baumrind, D. (1964). Some thoughts on ethics of research: After reading Milgram's "Behavioral study of obedience." *American Psychologist, 19,* 421–423.

Beaman, C. P. (2000). The size and nature of a chunk. *Behavioral and Brain Sciences, 24,* 1180.

Beck, A. T. (1991). Cognitive therapy: A thirty-year retrospective. *American Psychologist, 46,* 368–375.

Benet-Martinez, V. (1999). Exploring indigenous Spanish personality constructs with a combined emic-etic approach. In J. C. Lasry, J. G. Adair, & K. L. Dion (Eds.), *Contributions to cross-cultural psychology.* Lisse, The Netherlands: Swets & Zeitliner.

Ben-Shahar, T. (2002). *The question of happiness: On finding meaning, pleasure, and the ultimate currency.* New York: Writers Club Press.

Bentler, L. E. (1991). Have all won and must all have prizes? Revisiting Luborsky et al.'s verdict. *Journal of Consulting and Clinical Psychology, 59,* 226–232.

Berry, J. W. (2000). Culture: Cultural foundations of human behavior. In A. E. Kazdin (Ed.), *Encyclopedia of psychology* (Vol. 2, pp. 392–400). New York: Oxford University Press.

Berwin, C. R. (1996). Theoretical foundations of cognitive-behavioral therapy for anxiety and depression. *Annual Review of Psychology, 47,* 33–57.

Betz, N. E., & Fitzgerald, L. F. (1993). Individuality and diversity: Theory and research in counseling psychology. *Annual Review of Psychology, 44,* 343–481.

Billingham, R. E., Bland, R., & Leary, A. (1999). Dating violence at three time periods: 1986, 1992, and 1996. *Psychological Reports, 85,* 574–578.

Binder, L. M., Dixon, M. R., & Ghezzi, P. M. (2000). A procedure to teach self-control to children with attention deficit hyperactivity disorder. *Journal of Applied Behavior Analysis, 33,* 233, 237.

Blass, T. (2000). *Obedience to authority: Current perspectives on the Milgram paradigm.* Mahwah, NJ: Erlbaum.

Bloch, D. A. (1984). The family therapy of Anna O.: Other times, other paradigms. In M. Rosenbaum & M. Muroff (Eds.), *Anna O.: Fourteen contemporary reinterpretations.* New York: Free Press.

Block, J. (1961). *The Q-sort method in personality assessment and psychiatric research.* Springfield, IL: Charles C. Thomas.

Blumenthal, A. L. (1975). A reappraisal of Wilhem Wundt. *American Psychologist, 30,* 1081–1088.

Blumenthal, A. L. (1997). Wilhelm Wundt. In W. G. Bringmann, H. E. Luck, R. Miller, & C. E. Early (Eds.), *A pictorial history of psychology.* Chicago: Quintessence Publishing Company.

Boden, M. A. (1979). *Jean Piaget.* New York: Viking Press.

Bond, M. H., & Smith, P. B. (1996). Cross-cultural social and organizational psychology. *Annual Review of Psychology, 47,* 205–235.

Boneau, C. A. (1990). Psychological literacy: A first approximation. *American Psychologist, 45,* 891–900.

Borch-Jacobsen, M. (1996). *Remembering Anna O.: A century of mystification.* New York: Routledge.

Boring, E. G. (1950). *A history of experimental psychology.* New York: Appleton-Century-Crofts.

Boring, E. G. (1957). *A history of experimental psychology* (2nd ed.). Englewood Cliffs, NJ: Prentice Hall.

Botwin, M., Buss, D. M., & Shackelford, T. K. (1997). Personality and mate preferences: Five factors in mate selection and marital satisfaction. *Journal of Personality, 65,* 107–136.

Bower, G. H. (1981). Mood and memory. *American Psychologist, 36,* 129–148.

Bowlby, J. (1965). *Child care and the growth of maternal love* (2nd ed.). Harmondsworth, England: Penguin Books.

Branden, N. (1994). *The six pillars of self-esteem.* New York: Bantam Books.

Brandes, J. M. (1967). First trimester nausea and vomiting as related to outcome of pregnancy. *Obstetrics and Gynecology, 30,* 427–431.

Breland, K., & Breland, M. (1961). The misbehavior of organisms. *American Psychologist, 16,* 681–684.

Breuer, J. (1882). Case history [of Bertha Pappenheim] compiled by Josef Breuer and the report of her treatment in Bellevue Sanatorium. In A. Hirschmuller (1989), *The life and work of Josef Breuer,* Appendix D 23. New York: New York University Press.

Breuer, J. (1895). Fraulein Anna O. In J. Strachey (Ed. & Trans.), *The standard edition of the complete works of Sigmund Freud* (Vol. 2, 1955). London: Hogarth Press.

Breuer, J., & Freud, S. (1895). On the psychical mechanism of hysterical phenomena. In J. Strachey (Ed. & Trans.), *The standard edition of the complete works of Sigmund Freud* (Vol. 2, 1995). London: Hogarth Press.

Brewin, C. R. (1996). Theoretical foundations of cognitive-behavioral therapy for anxiety and depression. *Annual Review of Psychology, 47,* 33–57.

Brown, R. W. (1973). *A first language: The early stages.* Cambridge, MA: Harvard University Press.

Bruner, J. S. (1986). *Actual minds, possible worlds.* Cambridge, MA: Harvard University Press.

Bruner, J. S. (1990). *Acts of meaning.* Cambridge, MA: Harvard University Press.

Bruner, J. S., & Goodman, C. C. (1947). Value and need as organizing factors in perception. *Journal of Abnormal and Social Psychology, 42,* 33–44.

Buss, D. M. (1995a). Evolutionary psychology: A new paradigm for psychological science. *Psychological Inquiry, 6,* 1–30.

Buss, D. M. (1995b). Psychological sex differences: Origins through sexual selection. *American Psychologist, 50,* 164–168.

Buss, D. M. (1996a). Evolutionary psychology of human social strategies. In E. T. Higgins & A. W. Kruganski (Eds.), *Social psychology: Handbook of basic principles.* New York: Guilford Press.

Buss, D. M. (1996b). Social adaptation and five major factors of personality. In J. S. Wiggins (Ed.), *The five-factor model of personality.* New York: Guilford Press.

Buss, D. M. (1999). *Evolutionary psychology: The new science of the mind.* Needham Heights, MA: Allyn & Bacon.

Buss, D. M. (2000). Evolutionary psychology. In A. E. Kazdin (Ed.), *Encyclopedia of psychology* (Vol. 3). New York: Oxford University Press.

Buunk, B. P., Angleitener, A., Oubaid, V., & Buss, D. M. (1996). Sex differences in jealousy in evolutionary and cultural perspective: Tests from the Netherlands, Germany, and the United States. *Psychological Science, 7,* 359–363.

Byrnes, J. P., & Fox, N. A. (1998). The educational relevance of research in cognitive neuroscience. *Educational Psychology Review, 10,* 297–342.

Cacioppo, J. T., Berntsen, G.G., & Crites, S. L. (1996). Social neuroscience: Principles of psychophysiological arousal and response. In E. T. Higgins & A. W. Kruglanski (Eds.), *Social psychology: Handbook of basic principles.* New York: Guilford Press.

Campbell, A. (1993). *Men, women, and aggression.* New York: Basic Books.

Campbell, D. T., & Stanley, J. C. (1963). *Experimental and quasi-experimental designs for research.* Boston: Houghton Mifflin.

Cangelosi, D., & Schaefer, C. E. (1992). Psychological needs underlying the creative process. *Psychological Reports, 71,* 321–322.

Cannon, D. F. (1989). *Explorer of the human brain.* New York: Henry Schuman.

Carberry, M. S., Khalib, H. M., Leathrum, J. F., & Levy, L. S. (1979). *Foundations of computer science.* Potomac, MD: Computer Science Press.

Carey, S. (1990). Cognitive development. In D. N. Osherson & E. E. Smith (Eds.), *An invitation to cognitive science: Thinking* (Vol. 3). Cambridge, MA: MIT Press.

Catania, A. C. (1998). *Learning* (4th ed.). Upper Saddle River, NJ: Prentice Hall.

Cautela, J. R., & Ishaq, W. (1996). *Contemporary issues in behavior therapy: Improving the human condition.* New York: Plenum Press.

Chen, S. C. (1938). Social modification of the activity of ants in nest building. *Physiological Zoology, 19,* 420–436.

Chiesa, M. (1994). *Radical behaviorism: The philosophy and the science.* Boston, MA: Authors Cooperative, Inc.

Chomsky, N. (1957). *Syntactic structures.* The Hague: Mouton.

Chomsky, N. (1959). Review of "Verbal Behavior" by B. F. Skinner. *Language, 35,* 26–58.

Chomsky, N. (1972). *Language and mind.* New York: Harcourt, Brace, Jovanovich.

Cialdini, R. B. (1993). *Influence: Science and practice* (3rd ed.). New York: HarperCollins.

Cole, M. (1996). *Cultural psychology: A once and future discipline.* Cambridge, MA: Harvard University Press.

Coleman, A.M. (2001). Brain imaging techniques. In *Dictionary of psychology.* New York: Oxford University Press.

Compton, W. C. (2001). The values problem in subjective well-being. *American Psychologist, 56,* 84.

Cooper, R. M., & Zubeck, J. P. (1958). Effects of enriched and restricted early environments on the learning ability of bright and dull rats. *Canadian Journal of Psychology, 12,* 159–164.

Cornell, D. G. (1997). Post hoc explanation is not prediction. *American Psychologist, 51,* 1380.

Cosmides, L., & Tooby, J. (1992). Cognitive adaptation for social exchange. In J. H. Barkow, L. Cosmides, & J. Tooby (Eds.), *The adapted mind: Evolutionary psychology and the generation of culture.* New York: Oxford University Press.

Cosmides, L., Tooby, J., & Barkow, J. H. (1992). Introduction: Evolutionary psychology and conceptual integration. In J. H. Barkow, L. Cosmides, & J. Tooby (Eds.), *The adapted mind: Evolutionary psychology and the generation of culture.* New York: Oxford University Press.

Costa, P. T., & McCrae, R. R. (1992). *The NEO-PI-R professional manual.* Odessa, FL: Psychological Assessment Resources.

Cowan, N. (2000). The magical number 4 in short-term memory: A reconsideration of mental storage capacity. *Behavioral and Brain Sciences, 24,* 87–180.

Cramer, P. (1997). Identity, personality, and defense mechanisms: An observer-based study. *Journal of Research in Personality, 31,* 58–77.

Cramer, P. (2000). Defense mechanisms in psychology today. *American Psychologist, 55,* 637–646.

Creswell, J. W. (1998). *Qualitative inquiry and research design.* Thousand Oaks, CA: Sage.

Crews, F. C. (1998). *Unauthorized Freud: Doubters confront a legend.* New York: Viking.

Daly, M., & Wilson, M. (1988). *Homicide.* Hawthorne, NY: Aldine.

Damasio, H., Grabowski, T., Frank, R., Galabruda, A. M., & Damasio, A. R. (1994, May 20). The return of Phineas Gage: Clues about the brain from the skull of a famous patient. *Science, 264* (5162), 1102–1105.

Darwin, C. (1859). *The origin of species* (6th ed., 1872). New York: Merrill and Baker.

Darwin, C. (1876). Charles Darwin's autobiography. In F. Darwin (Ed.), *Charles Darwin's autobiography: With his notes and letters depicting the growth of* The Origin of Species (1950). New York: Schuman.

Dasen, P. R. (1975). Concrete operational development in three cultures. *Journal of Cross-Cultural Psychology, 6,* 156–172.

Davis, K. L., Kahn, R. S., & Ko, G. (1991). Dopamine in schizophrenia: A review and reconceptualization. *American Journal of Psychiatry, 148,* 1474–1486.

de Castro, J. M. (1991). Social facilitation of the spontaneous meal size of humans occurs on both weekdays and weekends. *Physiology and Behavior, 49,* 1289–1291.

DeGrandpre, R. J., & Buskist, W. (2000). Behaviorism and neobehaviorism. In A. E. Kazdin (Ed.), *Encyclopedia of psychology* (Vol. 1). New York: Oxford University Press.

Dement, W. C., & Vaughan, C. (1999). *The promise of sleep: A pioneer in sleep medicine explores the vital connection between health, happiness, and a good night's sleep.* New York: Dell Publishing.

Dempster, F. N. (1988). Retroactive interference in the retention of prose: A reconsideration and new evidence. *Applied Cognitive Psychology, 2,* 97–113.

de Paula Ramos, S. O. (2003). Revisiting Anna O.: A case of chemical dependence. *History of Psychology, 6,* 239–250.

Devos, T., & Banaji, M. R. (2005). American = white? *Journal of Personality and Social Psychology, 88,* 447–466.

Dickens, G., & Trethowan, W. H. (1971). Cravings and aversions during pregnancy. *Journal of Psychosomatic Research, 15,* 259–267.

Dindia, K., & Allen, M. (1992). Sex differences in self-disclosure: A meta-analysis. *Psychological Bulletin, 112,* 106–124.

Distinguished Scientific Awards. (1989). Early career contribution to psychology: 1988. David M. Buss. *American Psychologist, 44,* 636–638.

Dixon, M. R., & Holcomb, S. (2000). Teaching self-control to small groups of dually diagnosed adults. *Journal of Applied Behavior Analysis, 33,* 611–614.

Donald, M. (1997). The mind considered from a historical perspective. In D. M. Johnson & C. E. Erneling (Eds.), *The future of the cognitive revolution.* New York: Oxford University Press.

Dozier, M., & Kobak, R. R. (1992). Psychophysiology in attachment interviews. Converging evidence for deactivating strategies. *Child Development, 63,* 1473–1480.

Dresner, R. R. (1954). *Bertha Pappenheim: The contribution of a German Jewish pioneer social reformer to social work, 1859–1936.* Unpublished master's thesis, Fordham University, New York.

Driver-Linn, E. (2003). Where is psychology going? *American Psychologist, 58,* 269–278.

Eagly, A. H. (1995). The science and politics of comparing women and men. *American Psychologist, 50,* 145–158.

Eagly, A. H., Mladinic, A., & Otto, S. (1991). Are women evaluated more favorably than men? An analysis of attitudes, beliefs, and emotions. *Psychology of Women Quarterly, 15,* 203–216.

Eagly, A. H., & Wood, W. (1999). The origins of sex differences in human behavior: Evolved dispositions versus social roles. *American Psychologist, 54,* 408–442.

Earhard, M. (1967). Subjective organization and list organization as determinants of free-recall and serial-recall memorization. *Journal of Verbal Learning and Verbal Behavior, 6,* 501–507.

Edinger, D. (1968). *Bertha Pappenheim: Freud's Anna O.* Highland Park, IL: Congregation Solel.

Eisenberg, N. (2000). Empathy. In A. E. Kazdin (Ed.), *Encyclopedia of psychology* (Vol. 3). New York: Oxford University Press.

Ekman, P. (1992). Facial expressions of emotion: New findings, new questions. *Psychological Science, 3,* 34–38.

Ekman, P., & Friesen, W. V. (1975). *Unmasking the face.* Englewood Cliffs, NJ: Prentice Hall.

Elkin, I., Shea, M.T., Watkins, J. T., Imber, S. D., Sotsky, S. M., Collins, J. F., et al. (1989). NIMH treatment of depression collaborative research program: General effectiveness of treatments. *Archives of General Psychiatry, 46,* 971–982.

Ellenberger, H. F. (1970). *The discovery of the unconscious.* New York: Basic Books.

Ellis, A. (1991). The revised ABC's of rational-emotive therapy. *Journal of Rational-Emotive and Cognitive-Behavioral Therapy, 9,* 139–172.

Ellis, A. (1999). Why rational-emotive therapy to rational emotive behavior therapy? *Psychotherapy, 36,* 154–160.

Ellis, B. J. (1992). The evolution of sexual attraction: Evaluative mechanisms in women. In J. H. Barkow, L. Cosmides, & J. Tooby (Eds.), *The adapted mind: Evolutionary psychology and the generation of culture.* New York: Oxford University Press.

Elmes, D. G. (2000). Experimental psychology. In A. E. Kazdin (Ed.), *Encyclopedia of psychology* (Vol. 3). New York: Oxford University Press.

Epstein, S. (1973). The self concept revisited: Or a theory of a theory. *American Psychologist, 28,* 404–416.

Erdelyi, M. H. (2000). Repression. In A. E. Kazdin (Ed.), *Encyclopedia of psychology* (Vol. 7). NewYork: Oxford University Press.

Erikson, E. (1963). *Childhood and society* (2nd ed.). New York: Norton.

Eron, L. D. (1982). Parent-child interaction, television violence, and aggression of children. *American Psychologist, 37,* 197–211.

Eron, L. D. (2000). A psychological perspective. In V. B. Van Hasselt, M. Herson, et al. (Eds.), *Aggression and violence: An introductory text.* Boston: Allyn & Bacon.

Estes, W. K. (1991). Cognitive architectures from the standpoint of an experimental psychologist. *Annual Review of Psychology, 42,* 1–28.

Euler, H., & Weitzel, B. (1996). Discriminative grandparental solicitude as reproductive strategy. *Human Nature, 7,* 39–59.

Evans, M. G., & Chang, Y. C. (1998). Cheater detection and altruistic behaviour: An experimental and methodological exploration. *Management and Decision Economics, 19,* 467–480.

Eysenck, H. J. (1988). Skinner, Skinnerism, and the Skinnerian in psychology. *Counseling Psychology Quarterly, 1,* 299–301.

Fernald, A. (1992). Human maternal vocalizations to infants as biologically relevant signals: An evolutionary perspective. In J. H. Barkow, L. Cosmides, & J. Tooby (Eds.), *The adapted mind: Evolutionary psychology and the generation of culture.* New York: Oxford University Press.

Fernald, A., Taeschner, T., Dunn, J., Papousek, M., de Boyson-Bardies, B., & Fukui, I. (1989). A cross-language study of prosodic modifications in mothers' and fathers' speech to preverbal infants. *Journal of Child Language, 16,* 477–501.

Fernald, L. D. (1984). *The Hans legacy.* Hillsdale, NJ: Erlbaum.

Fernald, L. D. (1987). Of windmills and rope dancing: The instructional value of narrative structures. *Teaching of Psychology, 14,* 214–216.

Fernald, L. D. (1997). *Psychology.* Upper Saddle River, NJ: Prentice-Hall.

Fernald, L. D., & Fernald, P. S. (1985). *Introduction to psychology* (5th ed.). Dubuque, IA: W. C. Brown.

Fernald, P. S. (1995). Preparing psychology graduate students for the professoriate. *American Psychologist, 50,* 421–427.

Festinger, L., Riecken, H. W., & Schachter, S. (1956). *When prophecy fails.* Minneapolis: University of Minnesota Press.

Fisher, D. B. (2003). People are more important than pills in recovery from mental disorder. *Journal of Humanistic Psychology, 43,* 65–68.

Flick, U. (2006). *An introduction to qualitative research* (3rd ed.). Thousand Oaks, CA: Sage.

Flombaum, J. I., Santos, L. R., & Hauser, M. D. (2002). Neurology and psychological modularity. *TRENDS in Cognitive Science, 6,* 106–108.

Fodor, J. A. (1983). *The modularity of mind: An essay on faculty psychology.* Cambridge, MA: MIT Press.

Frankl, V. E. (1963). *Man's search for meaning: An introduction to logotherapy.* New York: Washington Square Press.

Freeman, L. (1972). *The story of Anna O.* New York: Paragon House.

Freud, S. (1895). Studies on hysteria. In J. Strachey (Ed. & Trans.), *The standard edition of the complete works of Sigmund Freud* (Vol. 2). London: Hogarth Press.

Freud, S. (1900). The interpretation of dreams. In J. Strachey (Ed. & Trans.), *The standard edition of the complete works of Sigmund Freud* (Vol. 4). London: Hogarth Press.

Freud, S. (1901). The psychopathology of everyday life. In J. Strachey (Ed. & Trans.), *The standard edition of the complete works of Sigmund Freud* (Vol. 6). London: Hogarth Press.

Freud, S. (1905). Three essays on the theory of sexuality. In J. Strachey (Ed. & Trans.), *The standard edition of the complete works of Sigmund Freud* (Vol. 7). London: Hogarth Press.

Freud, S. (1907). The sexual enlightenment of children. In J. Strachey (Ed. & Trans.), *The standard edition of the complete works of Sigmund Freud* (Vol. 9). London: Hogarth Press.

Freud, S. (1909). Five lectures on psycho-analysis. In J. Strachey (Ed. & Trans.), *The standard edition of the complete works of Sigmund Freud* (Vol. 11). London: Hogarth Press.

Freud, S. (1915). Repression. In J. Strachey (Ed. & Trans.), *The standard edition of the complete works of Sigmund Freud* (Vol. 14). London: Hogarth Press.

Freud, S. (1916). Dreams. In J. Strachey (Ed. & Trans.), *The standard edition of the complete works of Sigmund Freud* (Vol. 15). London: Hogarth Press.

Freud, S. (1917). The development of the libido and the sexual organization. In J. Strachey (Ed. & Trans.), *The standard edition of the complete works of Sigmund Freud* (Vol. 16). London: Hogarth Press.

Freud, S. (1925a). Josef Breuer. In J. Strachey (Ed. & Trans.), *The standard edition of the complete works of Sigmund Freud* (Vol. 19). London: Hogarth Press.

Freud, S. (1925b). Psycho-analysis. In J. Strachey (Ed. & Trans.), *The standard edition of the complete works of Sigmund Freud* (Vol. 20). London: Hogarth Press.

Freud, S. (1926). The question of lay analysis. In J. Strachey (Ed. & Trans.), *The standard edition of the complete works of Sigmund Freud* (Vol. 20). London: Hogarth Press.

Freud, S. (1927). Concluding remarks on the question of lay analysis. *International Journal of Psycho-Analysis, 8*, 392–401.

Freud, S. (1930). Civilization and its discontents. In J. Strachey (Ed. & Trans.), *The standard edition of the complete works of Sigmund Freud* (Vol. 21). London: Hogarth Press.

Fritsch, G. & Hitzig, E. (1870). Uber die elekrische Erregbarkeit des grosshirns. *Arch. F. Anat. Physiol. Und wissenschaftl medis.*, 300–332. (Reprinted as On the electrical excitability of the cerebrum. In G. von Bonin (Trans.), *Some papers on the cerebral cortex.* Springfield, IL: Charles C. Thomas).

Froh, J. J. (2004). The history of positive psychology: Truth be told. *NYS Psychologist, 16*, 18–20.

Fuchs, A. H. (1998). Psychology and "The Babe." *Journal of the History of the Behavioral Sciences, 34*, 153–165.

Futuyma, D. J. (1983). *Science on trial: The case for evolution.* New York: Pantheon Books.

Gage, F. H. (2003, September). Brain, repair yourself. *Scientific American*, 46–53.

Gage, N. F. (1952). Judging interests from expressive behavior. *Psychological Monographs, 66*, (18, Whole No. 350.)

Garcia, J., & Koelling, R. A. (1966). Relation of cue to consequence in avoidance learning. *Psychonomic Science, 4*, 123–124.

Garfield, S. L. (2000). Scientist-practitioner model. In A. E. Kazdin (Ed.), *Encyclopedia of psychology* (Vol. 7). New York: Oxford University Press.

Gilbert, D. T. (1989). Thinking lightly about others: Automatic components of the social inference process. In J. S. Uleman & J. A. Bargh (Eds.), *Unintended thought*. New York: Guilford Press.

Gilbert, D. T., & Malone, P. S. (1995). The correspondence bias. *Psychological Bulletin, 117*, 21–38.

Gleaves, D. H., & Hernandez, E. (1999). Recent reformulations of Freud's development and abandonment of his seduction theory. *History of Psychology, 2*, 324–354.

Godden, D. R., & Baddeley, A. D. (1975). Context-dependent memory in two natural environments: On land and underwater. *British Journal of Psychology, 66*(3), 325–331.

Gordon, T., Grummon, D. L., Rogers, C. R., & Seeman, J. (1954). *Developing a program of research in psychotherapy and personality change.* Chicago: University of Chicago Press.

Gray, P. (1996). Incorporating evolutionary theory into the teaching of psychology. *Teaching of Psychology, 23*, 207–214.

Greenberg, M. S. (2004, July 7). *Biological psychology: An approach to the brain.* Unpublished lecture presented in Fong Auditorium, Boylston Hall, at Harvard University, Cambridge, MA.

Greenfield, P. M., Keller, H., Fuligni, A., & Maynard, A. (2003). Cultural pathways through universal development. *Annual Review of Psychology, 54*, 461–490.

Greening, T. (2001). Commentary. *Journal of Humanistic Psychology, 41*(1), 4–7.

Greenough, W. T., & Chang, F. F. (1989). Plasticity of synapse structure and pattern in the cerebral cortex. *Cerebral Cortex, 7*, 391–440.

Greenwood, J. D. (1999). Understanding the "cognitive revolution" in psychology. *Journal of the History of the Behavioral Sciences, 35*, 1–22.

Grissom, R. J. (1996). The magical number .7±.2: Meta-meta-analysis of the probability of superior outcome in comparisons involving therapy, placebo, and control. *Journal of Consulting and Clinical Psychology, 64*, 973–982.

Grotstein, J. S. (1990). The mirror in the frame. *Society for Psychoanalytic Psychotherapy Bulletin, 5*, 21–33.

Guttmann, M. G. (2001). *The enigma of Anna O.: A biography of Bertha Pappenheim.* Wickford, RI: Moyer Bell.

Haggbloom, S., Warnick, R., Warnick, J., Jones, V., Yarbrough, G., Russell, T., et al. (2002). The 100 most eminent psychologists of the 20th century. *Review of General Psychology, 6*(2), 139–152.

Hakel, M. D., & Herring, L. (2000). American Psychological Society. In A. E. Kazdin (Ed.), *Encyclopedia of psychology* (Vol. 1). New York: Oxford University Press.

Hardy, C., & Latane, B. (1986). Social loafing on a cheering task. *Social Science, 71,* 165–172.

Harlow, H. F. (1932). Social facilitation of feeding in the albino rat. *Journal of Genetic Psychology, 41,* 211–221.

Harlow, H. F., & Harlow, M. K. (1966). Learning to love. *American Scientist, 54,* 244–272.

Harlow, J. M. (1869). *Recovery from the passage of an iron bar through the head.* Boston: David Clapp & Son.

Hebben, N. (2005, May 9). *Introduction to neuropsychological assessment.* Unpublished seminar presentation in Sever Hall at Harvard University, Cambridge, MA.

Hellige, J. B. (1990). Hemispheric asymmetry. *Annual Review of Psychology, 41,* 55–80.

Hermans, H. J. M., & Kempen, H. J. G. (1998). Moving cultures: The perilous problems of cultural dichotomies in a globalizing society. *American Psychologist, 53,* 1111–1120.

Herskovits, M. J., Campbell, D. T., & Segall, M. H. (1969). *A cross-cultural study of perception.* Indianapolis: Bobbs-Merrill.

Hesse-Biber, S. N., & Leavy, P. (2006). *The practice of qualitative research.* Thousand Oaks, CA: Sage.

Heyman, G. M. (2004). The sense of conscious will. *Behavioral and Brain Sciences, 27,* 663–664.

Hilgard, E. R. (1988). Reflections on the last 50 years of psychology. In E. R. Hilgard (Ed.), *Fifty years of psychology: Essays in honor of Floyd Ruch.* Glenview, IL: Scott Foresman.

Hirschfeld, L. A., & Gelman, S. A. (1994). Toward a topography of the mind. In L. A. Hirschfeld & S. A. Gelman (Eds.), *Mapping the mind.* New York: Cambridge University Press.

Hirschmüller, A. (1989). *The life and work of Josef Breuer: Physiology and psychoanalysis.* New York: New York University Press.

Hoberman, H. M. (1990). Study group report on the impact of television violence on adolescents. *Journal of Adolescent Health Care, 11,* 45–49.

Hogan, R., Curphy, G. J., & Hogan, J. (1994). What we know about leadership: Effectiveness and personality. *American Psychologist, 49,* 493–504.

Holt, R. (1962). Individuality and generalization in the psychology of personality. *Journal of Personality, 30,* 377–404.

Holyoak, K. J., & Spellman, B. A. (1993). Thinking. In L. W. Porter & M. R. Rosenzweig (Eds.), *Annual Review of Psychology, 44,* 265–315.

Holzman, P. S. (1984). The case of Anna O.: Then and now. In M. Rosenbaum & M. Muroff (Eds.), *Anna O.: Fourteen contemporary reinterpretations.* New York: Free Press.

Holzman, P. S. (2000, May 20). *Less is truly more: Reductivism in psychopathology research.* Paper presented at the Principles of Experimental Psychopathology: A Festschrift in Honor of Professor Brendan A. Maher, Harvard University, Cambridge, MA.

Homans, G. C. (1961). *Social behavior: Its elementary forms.* New York: Harcourt, Brace, World.

Houlihan, D., Schwartz, C., Miltenberger, R., & Heuton, D. (1993). Rapid treatment of a young man's balloon (noise) phobia using in vivo flooding. *Journal of Behavior Therapy and Experimental Psychiatry, 24*(3), 233–240.

Hyde, J. S., & Plant, E. A. (1995). Magnitude of psychological gender differences. *American Psychologist, 50,* 203–216.

Ito, M. (2004). How neuroscience accounts for the illusion of conscious will. *Behavioral and Brain Sciences, 24,* 664–665.

James, W. (1890). *Principles of psychology.* New York: Holt.

Janus, S. S., & Janus, C. L. (1993). *The Janus report on sexual behavior.* New York: John Wiley & Sons.

Jenkins, J. G., & Dallenbach, K. M. (1924). Obliviscence during sleep and waking. *American Journal of Psychology, 35,* 605–612.

Jensen, E. (1970). Anna O—A study of her later life. *Psychoanalytic Quarterly, 39,* 269–293.

Jones, E. (1953). *Life and work of Sigmund Freud* (Vol. 1). New York: Basic Books.

Jordan, E. A. (1996). Skinner at Harvard: Intellectual or mandarin? In L. D. Smith & W. R. Woodward (Eds.), *B. F. Skinner and behaviorism in American culture.* Bethlehem, PA: Lehigh University Press.

Jung, C. G. (1928). *Contributions to analytic psychology.* New York: Harcourt.

Kagan, J. (2006). *An argument for mind.* New Haven, CT: Yale University.

Kahneman, D., & Tversky, A. (1984). Choices, values, and frames. *American Psychologist, 39,* 341–350.

Kaplan, M. A. (1984). Anna O. and Bertha Pappenheim: An historical perspective. In M. Rosenbaum & M. Muroff (Eds.), *Anna O.: Fourteen contemporary reinterpretations.* New York: Free Press.

Karlins, M., Coffman, T. L., & Walters, G. (1969). On the fading of social stereotypes. *Journal of Personality and Social Psychology, 13,* 1–6.

Karpe, R. (1961). The rescue complex in Anna O.'s final identity. *Psychoanalytic Quarterly, 30,* 1–27.

Kashdan, T. B., & Steger, M. F. (2004). Approaching psychological science with Kuhn's eyes. *American Psychologist, 59,* 272–273.

Katz, A. N. (2000). Mental imagery. In A. E. Kazdin (Ed.), *Encyclopedia of psychology* (Vol. 5). New York: Oxford University Press.

Kelley, H. H. (1992). Common-sense psychology and scientific psychology. *Annual Review of Psychology, 43,* 1–23.

Kelley, T. M. (2004). Positive psychology and adolescent mental health: False promise or true breakthrough? *Adolescence, 39,* 254–278.

Kendall, P. C., Krain, A. L., & Henin, A. (2000). Cognitive-behavioral therapy. In A. E. Kazdin (Ed.), *Encyclopedia of psychology* (Vol. 2). New York: Oxford University Press.

Kerr, N.L., & Tindale, R. S. (2004). Group performance and decision making. In S. T. Fiske, D. L. Schacter, & C. Zahn-Walker (Eds.), *Annual Review of Psychology, 55,* 623–655.

Kim, H., & Markus, H. R. (1999). Deviance or uniqueness, harmony or conformity? A cultural analysis. *Journal of Personality and Social Psychology, 77,* 785–800.

Kimball, M. M. (2000). From "Anna O." to Bertha Pappenheim: Transforming private pain into public action. *History of Psychology, 3,* 20–43.

Kimble, G. A. (1984). Psychology's two cultures. *American Psychologist, 39,* 833–839.

Kinnier, R. T., Kernes, J. L., Tribbensee, N. E., & van Puymbroeck, C. M. (2003). What eminent people have said about the meaning of life. *Journal of Humanistic Psychology, 43,* 105–118.

Kinsey, A.C., Pomeroy, W. B., & Gebhard, P. H. (1953). *Sexual behavior in the human female.* Philadelphia: Saunders.

Kinsey, A. C., Pomeroy, W. B., & Martin, C. E. (1948). *Sexual behavior in the human male.* Philadelphia: Saunders.

Klebanoff, M. A., Koslowe, P. A., Kaslow, R., & Rhoades, G. G. (1985). Epidemiology of vomiting in early pregnancy. *Obstetrics and Gynecology, 66,* 612–616.

Koenig, L. J., & Wasserman, E. L. (1995). Body image and dieting failure in college men and women: Examining links between depression and eating problems. *Sex Roles, 32,* 225–248.

Kohn, A. (1993). *Punished by rewards.* Boston: Houghton Mifflin.

Kohn, A., & Kalat, J. W. (1992). Preparing for an important event: Demonstrating the modern view of classical conditioning. *Teaching of Psychology, 19,* 100–102.

Kolb, B., Gibb, K., & Robinson, T. E. (2003). Brain plasticity and behavior. *Current Directions in Psychological Science, 12,* 1–5.

Kosslyn, S.M., & Koenig, O. (1992). *Wet mind: The new cognitive neuroscience.* New York: Free Press.

Kramer, T. A. M. (2000). Polypharmacy. *The Prescriber: Medscape Mental Health, 5*(3) 6–7.

Kuhn, T. S. (1970). *The structure of scientific revolutions* (2nd ed.). Chicago: University of Chicago Press.

Leahey, T. H. (2000). Psychology: Renaissance through the enlightenment. In A. E. Kazdin (Ed.), *Encyclopedia of psychology* (Vol. 6). New York: Oxford University Press.

Leary, M. R., & Tangney, J. R. (2003). The self as an organizing construct in the behavioral and social sciences. In M. R. Leary & J. R. Tangney (Eds.), *Handbook of self and identity.* New York: Guilford Press.

LeDoux, J. E. (1995). Emotion: Clues from the brain. *Annual Review of Psychology, 46,* 209–235.

LeDoux, J. E. (2002). *Synaptic self: How our brains become who we are.* New York: Penguin.

Lehman, D. R., Chiu, C., & Schaller, M. (2004). Psychology and culture. *Annual Review of Psychology, 55,* 689–714.

Lerman, D. W., Iwata, B. A., & Wallace, M. D. (1999). Side effects of extinction. *Journal of Applied Behavior Analysis, 32,* 1–8.

Lilienfeld, S. O. (2000). Psychopathology. In A. E. Kazdin (Ed.), *Encyclopedia of psychology* (Vol. 6). New York: Oxford University Press.

Linton, R. (1949). The personality of peoples. *Scientific American, 181*(2), 11–15.

Lipsey, M. W., & Wilson, D. B. (1993). The efficacy of psychological, educational, and behavioral treatment: Confirmation from meta-analysis. *American Psychologist, 48,* 1181–1209.

Littlepage, G. E., Morris, L. W., & Poole, J. R. (1991). Components of state anxiety as mediators of social interference in a coaction situation. *Journal of Social Behavior and Personality, 6,* 377–386.

Lopez, S. R., & Guarnaccia, P. J. (2000). Cultural psychopathology: Uncovering the social world of mental illness. *Annual Review of Psychology, 51,* 571–598.

Luborsky, L., Singer, B., & Luborsky, L. (1975). Comparative studies of psychotherapies. *Archives of General Psychiatry, 32,* 995–1008.

Lucas, M. (2004). Existential regret: A crossroads of existential anxiety and existential guilt. *Journal of Humanistic Psychology, 44,* 58–70.

Maddi, S. R. (2004). Hardiness: An operationalization of existential courage. *Journal of Humanistic Psychology, 44,* 279–298.

Malinowski, B. (1927). *Sex and repression in savage society.* New York: Harcourt Brace.

Malinowski, B. (1929). *The sexual life of savages in north-western Melanesia.* New York: Harcourt Brace.

Mandler, G. (1985). *Cognitive psychology: An essay in cognitive science.* Hillsdale, NJ: Erlbaum.

Mantell, D. M. (1971). The potential for violence in Germany. *Journal of Social Issues, 27,* 101–112.

Margolin, G., & Gordis, E. B. (2000). The effects of family and community violence on children. *Annual Review of Psychology, 51,* 445–479.

Marjoriebanks, K. (1997). Parents' and young adults' individualism-collectivism: Ethnic group differences. *Psychological Reports, 80,* 934–936.

Marks, I. M. (1969). *Fears and phobias.* Oxford: Academic Press.

Markus, H. (1978). The effect of mere presence on social facilitation: An unobtrusive test. *Journal of Experimental Social Psychology, 14,* 389–397.

Markus, H. R., & Kitayama, S. (1991). Culture and the self: Implications for cognition, emotion and motivation. *Psychological Review, 98*(2), 224–253.

Marmor, J., & Gorney, R. (1999). Instinctual sadism: A recurrent myth about human nature. *Journal of the American Academy of Psychoanalysis, 2*(1), 1–6.

Marshall, C., & Rossman, G. B. (2006). *Designing qualitative research.* Thousand Oaks, CA: Sage.

Martorano, J. T. (1984). The psychopharmacological treatment of Anna O. In M. Rosenbaum & M. Muroff (Eds.), *Anna O.: Fourteen contemporary reinterpretations.* New York: Free Press.

Maslow, A. H. (1954). *Motivation and personality.* New York: Harper.

Maslow, A. H. (1970). *Motivation and personality* (2nd ed.). New York: Harper.

Maxon, S. C. (1998). Homologous genes, aggression, and animal models. *Developmental Neuropsychology, 14,* 143–156.

Maxwell, J. A. (2005). *Qualitative research design: An interactive approach* (2nd ed.). Thousand Oaks, CA: Sage.

May, R. (1994). *Escape from freedom*. New York: Holt.

Mayer, J. (1956, November). Appetite and obesity. *Scientific American*, 108–116.

Mazur, A., & Booth, A. (1999). The biosociology of testosterone in men. In D. D. Franks, T. S. Smith, et al. (Eds.), *Mind, brain and society: Toward a neurosociology of emotion* (Vol. 5). Stamford, CT: Jai Press.

McAdams, D. P., & Pals, J. L. (2006). A new big five: Fundamental principles for an integrative science of personality. *American Psychologist, 61*, 204–217.

McArthur, L. Z. (1972). The how and what of why: Some determinants and consequences of causal attribution. *Journal of Personality and Social Psychology, 22*, 171–193.

McCrae, R. R., Costa, P. T., Jr., del Pilar, G. H., Rolland, J. P., & Parker, W. D. (1998). Cross-cultural assessment of the five-factor model: The revised NEO Personality Inventory. *Journal of Cross-Cultural Psychology, 29*(1), 171–188.

McGovern, T. V., Furomoto, L., Halpern, D., Kimball, G. A., & McKeachie, W. J. (1991). Liberal education, study in depth, and the arts and sciences major—psychology. *American Psychologist, 46*, 598–605.

McGuffin, P., & Thapar, A. (1998). Genetics and antisocial personality disorder. In T. Millon, E. Simonsen, M. Birket-Smith, & R. D. Davis (Eds.), *Psychopathy: Antisocial, criminal, and violent behavior*. New York: Guilford Press.

McNally, R. J. (1987). Preparedness and phobias: A review. *Psychological Bulletin, 101*, 283–303.

Messer, S. C., & Gross, A. M. (1995). Childhood depression and family interaction: A naturalistic observation study. *Journal of Clinical Child Psychology, 24*, 77–88.

Micale, M. S. (2000, July). The decline of hysteria. *Harvard Mental Health Letter*, 4–6.

Michaels, J. W., Blommel, J. M., Brocato, R. M., Linkous, R. A., & Rowe, J. S. (1982). Social facilitation and inhibition in a natural setting. *Replications in Social Psychology, 2*, 21–24.

Milgram, S. (1974). *Obedience to authority*. New York: Harper & Row.

Miller, G. A. (1956). The magical number seven, plus or minus two: Some limits on our capacity for processing information. *Psychological Review, 63*, 81–97.

Miller, G. A., & Gildea, P. (1987). How children learn words. *Scientific American, 257*, 94–99.

Miller, J. G. (1999). Cultural psychology: Implications for basic psychological theory. *Psychological Science, 10*, 85–91.

Miller, L. T., & Vernon, P. A. (1997). Developmental changes in speed of information processing in young children. *Developmental Psychology, 33*, 549–554.

Miller, N. E., Bailey, C. J., & Stevenson, J. A. F. (1950). Decreased "hunger" but increased food intake resulting from hypothalamic lesions. *Science, 12*, 256–259.

Milner, B. (1965). Memory disturbances after bilateral hippocampus lesions. In B. Milner & S. Glickman (Eds.), *Cognitive processes and the brain*. Princeton, NJ: Van Nostrand.

Milner, B., Corkin, S., & Teuber, H. L. (1968). Further analysis of the hippocampal amnesic syndrome. *Neurobiology, 6*, 215–234.

Mitchell, S. A. (2000). Object relations theory. In A. E. Kazdin (Ed.), *Encyclopedia of psychology* (Vol. 5). New York: Oxford University Press.

Moraglia, G. (2004). On facing death: Views of some prominent psychologists. *Journal of Humanistic Psychology, 44,* 337–357.

Motschnig, R., & Nykl, L. (2003). Toward a cognitive-emotional model of Rogers' person-centered approach. *Journal of Humanistic Psychology, 43,* 8–45.

Muroff, M. (1984). Anna O.: Psychoanalysis in group process theory. In M. Rosenbaum & M. Muroff (Eds.), *Anna O.: Fourteen contemporary reinterpretations.* New York: Free Press.

Murray, J. P. (2000). Media effects. In A. E. Kazdin (Ed.), *Encyclopedia of psychology* (Vol. 5). New York: Oxford University Press.

Myers, D. G. (2000). The funds, friends, and faith of happy people. *American Psychologist, 55,* 56–67.

Myers, D. G., & Diener, E. (1996). The pursuit of happiness. *Scientific American, 274*(5), 70–72.

Neisser, U. (1967). *Cognitive psychology.* New York: Appleton-Century-Crofts.

Neisser, U. (2000). Cognition. In A. E. Kazdin (Ed.), *Encyclopedia of psychology* (Vol. 2). New York: Oxford University Press.

Newell, A., Shaw, J. C., & Simon, H. A. (1958). Elements of a theory of human problem solving. *Psychological Review, 65,* 151–166.

Nies, A. S., & Spielberg, S. P. (1996). Principles of therapeutics. In J. G. Hardman & L. E. Limbird (Eds.), *Goodman & Gilman's The pharmacological basis of therapeutics* (9th ed.). New York: McGraw-Hill.

Nisbett, R. E., Caputo, C., Legant, P., & Marecek, J. (1973). Behavior as seen by the actor and as seen by the observer. *Journal of Personality and Social Psychology, 27,* 154–164.

Norman, W. T. (1963). Toward an adequate taxonomy of personality attributes: Replicated factor structure in peer nomination personality ratings. *Journal of Abnormal and Social Psychology, 66,* 574–583.

Noshpitz, J. D. (1984). Anna O. as seen by a child psychiatrist. In M. Rosenbaum & M. Muroff (Eds.), *Anna O.: Fourteen contemporary reinterpretations.* New York: Free Press.

O'Hara, M., & Taylor, E. (2000). Humanistic psychology. In A. E. Kazdin (Ed.), *Encyclopedia of psychology* (Vol. 4). New York: Oxford University Press.

Overholser, J. C., & Moll, S. H. (1990). Who's to blame: Attributions regarding causality in spouse abuse. *Behavioral Sciences and the Law, 8,* 107–120.

Ozer, D. J. (2000). Nomothetic and idiographic orientations. In A. E. Kazdin (Ed.), *Encyclopedia of Psychology* (Vol. 5). New York: Oxford University Press.

Pappenheim, B. (1882). Letter to Robert Binswanger, November 8. In A. Hirschmüller (1989), *The life and work of Josef Breuer,* Appendix D 34. New York University Press.

Pappenheim, B. (1890). In der Trodelbude (In the junk shop). Published under the pseudonym P. Berthold. In A. Hirschmüller (1989), *The life and work of Josef Breuer.* New York University Press.

Pappenheim, B. (1899). Frauenrecht (Women's rights). Published under the pseudonym P. Berthold. In A. Hirschmüller (1989), *The life and work of Josef Breuer.* New York University Press.

Pappenheim, B. (1923). Letter to Felix Warburg, November 23. In D. Edinger (1968), *Bertha Pappenheim.* Highland Park, IL: Congregation Solel.

Pappenheim, B. (1924). Letters from abroad, 1911–1912. From *Sysyphus Arbeit.* In D. Edinger (1968), *Bertha Pappenheim.* Highland Park, IL: Congregation Solel.

Pappenheim, B. (1989). Kleine geschichte fur kinder (Little stories for children). In A. Hirschmüller (1989), *The life and work of Josef Breuer.* New York: New York University Press.

Paris, B. J. (2000). Karen D. Horney. In A. E. Kazdin (Ed.), *Encyclopedia of psychology* (Vol. 4). New York: Oxford University Press.

Pascual-Leone, J. (1997). Meta-subjective processes: The missing "lingua franca" of cognitive science. In D. M. Johnson & C. E. Erneling (Eds.), *The future of the cognitive revolution.* New York: Oxford University Press.

Pavlov, I. P. (1927). *Conditional reflexes* (G. V. Anrep, Trans.). New York: Oxford University Press.

Perry, W. G. (1970). *Forms of intellectual and ethical development in the college years.* New York: Holt.

Pessin, J. (1933). The comparative effects of social and mechanical stimulation on memorizing. *American Journal of Psychology, 45,* 263–270.

Pessin, J., & Husband, R. W. (1933). Effects of social stimulation on human maze learning. *Journal of Abnormal and Social Psychology, 28,* 148–154.

Pfungst, O. (1911). *The horse of Mr. von Osten (Clever Hans)* (C. L. Rahn, Trans.). New York: Holt.

Phelps, M. E., & Mazziotta, J. C. (1985). Positron emission tomography: Human brain function and biochemistry. *Science, 228,* 799–809.

Piaget, J. (1950). *The psychology of intelligence.* New York: Harcourt Brace.

Piaget, J. (1952a). Jean Piaget. In E.G. Boring, H. S. Langfeld, H. Werner, & R. M. Yerkes (Eds.), *A history of psychology in autobiography* (Vol. 4). New York: Appleton Century Crofts.

Piaget, J. (1952b). *The origins of intelligence in children.* New York: International University Press.

Piaget, J. (1954). *The construction of reality in the child* (M. Cook, Trans.). New York: Basic Books.

Pinker, S. (2002). *The blank slate.* New York: Viking.

Pollock, G. H. (1984). Anna O.: Insight, hindsight, and foresight. In M. Rosenbaum & M. Muroff (Eds.), *Anna O.: Fourteen contemporary reinterpretations.* New York: Free Press.

Postle, B. R., & Corkin, S. (1998). Impaired word-stem completion priming but intact perceptual identification priming with novel words: Evidence from the amnesic patient, H. M. *Neuropsychologia, 36,* 421–440.

Premack, D. (1965). Reinforcement theory. In D. Lewis (Ed.), *Nebraska Symposium on Motivation.* Lincoln, NE: University of Nebraska Press.

Profet, M. (1992). Pregnancy sickness as adaptation: A deterrent to maternal inges-tion of teratogens. In J. H. Barkow, L. Cosmides, & J. Tooby (Eds.), *The adapted mind: Evolutionary psychology and the generation of culture.* New York: Oxford University Press.

Pullum, G. K. (1991). *The great Eskimo vocabulary hoax, and other irreverent essays on the study of language.* Chicago: University of Chicago Press.

Rachlin, H. (1991). *Introduction to modern behaviorism* (3rd ed.) New York: Freeman.

Rakos, R. F. (2004). The belief in free will as a biological adaptation: Thinking inside and outside the behavior analytic box. *European Journal of Behavior Analysis, 5*(2), 95–103.

Ramon y Cajal, S. (1989). *Recollections of my life.* Cambridge, MA: MIT Press.

Rapoport, A. (1968). General systems theory. In D. L. Sills (Ed.), *International ency-clopedia of the social sciences* (Vol. 15). New York: Macmillan.

Rasinski, K. A. (1989). The effect of question wording on public support for govern-ment spending. *Public Opinion Quarterly, 53,* 388–394.

Rescorla, R. A. (1988). Pavlovian conditioning: It's not what you think it is. *American Psychologist, 43,* 151–160.

Rescorla, R. A. (1992). Hierarchical associative relations in Pavlovian conditioning and instrumental cotraining. *Current Directions in Psychological Science, 1,* 66–70.

Rice, C. E. (1997). The scientist-practitioner split and the future of psychology. *American Psychologist, 52,* 1173–1181.

Robins, R. W., Gosling, S. D., & Craik, K. H. (1999). An empirical analysis of trends in psychology. *American Psychologist, 54,* 117–128.

Rogers, C. R. (1942). *Counseling and psychotherapy: Newer concepts in practice.* Boston: Houghton Mifflin.

Rogers, C. R. (1951). *Client-centered therapy: Its current practice, implications, and research.* Boston: Houghton Mifflin.

Rogers, C. R. (1961). *On becoming a person: A therapist's view of psychotherapy.* Boston: Houghton Mifflin.

Rogers, C. R. (1967). Carl R. Rogers. In E. G. Boring & G. Lindzey (Eds.), *A history of psychology in autobiography* (Vol. 5). New York: Appleton Century Crofts.

Rogers, C. R. (1971). Learning to be free. In C. R. Rogers & B. Stevens (Eds.), *Person to person: The problem of being human.* New York: Pocket Books.

Rogers, C. R. (1980). *A way of being.* Boston: Houghton Mifflin.

Rogers, C. R. (1989). *The Carl Rogers reader.* Boston: Houghton Mifflin.

Rogers, C. R., & Dymond, R. F. (1954). *Psychotherapy and personality change: Coordinated studies in the client-centered approach.* Chicago: University of Chicago Press.

Rogers, C. R., & Russell, D. (2002). *Carl Rogers: The quiet revolutionary.* Roseville, CA: Penmarin Books.

Rosch, E. A. (1973). On the internal structure of perceptual and semantic categories. In T. E. Moore (Ed.), *Cognitive development and the acquisition of language.* New York: Academic Press.

Rosen, D. H. (2000). Carl Gustav Jung. In A. E. Kazdin (Ed.), *Encyclopedia of psy-chology* (Vol. 4). New York: Oxford University Press.

Rosenbaum, M. (1984a). Anna O. (Bertha Pappenheim): Her history. In M. Rosenbaum & M. Muroff (Eds.), *Anna O.: Fourteen contemporary reinterpretations.* New York: Free Press.

Rosenbaum, M. (1984b). Introduction. In M. Rosenbaum & M. Muroff (Eds.), *Anna O.: Fourteen contemporary reinterpretations.* New York: Free Press.

Rosenthal, R. (Ed.). (1907). *Clever Hans: The horse of Mr. von Osten.* New York: Holt.

Rosenzweig, M. R., Leiman, A. L., & Breedlove, S. M. (1996). *Biological psychology.* Sunderland, MA: Sinauer Associates.

Roser, M., & Gazzaniga, M. S. (2004). Automatic brains—interpretive minds. *Current Directions in Psychological Science, 13,* 56–59.

Rotman, B. (1977). *Jean Piaget: Psychologist of the real.* Ithaca, NY: Cornell University Press.

Rowe, D. C., Almeida, D. M., & Jacobson, K. C. (1999). School context and genetic influences on aggression in adolescence. *Psychological Science, 10,* 277–280.

Runyan, W. M. (1984). *Life histories and psychobiography.* New York: Oxford University Press.

Rychlak, J. F., & Struckman, A. (2000). Psychology: Post-World-War II. In A. E. Kazdin (Ed.), *Encyclopedia of psychology* (Vol. 6). New York: Oxford University Press.

Sales, B., & Folkman, S. (Eds.) (2000). *Ethics in the conduct of research with human participants.* Washington, DC: American Psychological Association.

Sarbin, T.R. (1986). *Narrative psychology: The storied nature of human conduct.* New York: Praeger.

Schlosser, G., & Wagner, G. P. (2004). Introduction: The modularity concept in developmental and evolutionary biology. In G. Schlosser & G. Wagner (Eds.), *Modularity in development and evolution.* Chicago: University of Chicago Press.

Schmolck, H., Buffalo, E., & Squire, L. R. (2000). Memory distortions develop over time. *Psychological Science, 11,* 39–45.

Schorske, C. E. (1979). *Fin-de-siecle Vienna.* New York: Vintage.

Schwartz, W. (2003, December 1). *Pre-empirical psychology, psychoanalysis, and therapy.* Unpublished seminar presentation in Sever Hall at Harvard University, Cambridge, MA.

Schweder, R. A. (1990). Cultural psychology—what is it? In J. W. Stigler, R. A. Shweder, & G. Herdt (Eds.), *Cultural psychology.* New York: Cambridge University Press.

Scott, T. R. (1991). A personal view of the future of psychology departments. *American Psychologist, 46,* 975–976.

Seligman, M. E. P. (1991). *Learned optimism.* New York: Knopf.

Seligman, M. E. P. (2002). *Authentic happiness.* New York: Free Press.

Seligman, M. E. P., & Csikszentmihalyi, M. (2000). Positive psychology: An introduction. *American Psychologist, 55,* 5–14.

Shackelford, T. K., Buss, D. M., & Bennett, K. (2002). Forgiveness or breakup: Sex differences in responses to a partner's infidelity. *Cognition and Emotion, 16,* 299–307.

Simon, H. A. (1980). Herbert A. Simon. In G. Lindzey (Ed.), *A history of psychology in autobiography* (Vol. 7). San Francisco: W. H. Freeman.

Singer, D. G., & Revenson, T. A. (1978). *A Piaget primer: How a child thinks*. New York: New American Library.

Singh, D. (1995). Female judgment of male attractiveness and desirability for relationships: Role of waist-to-hip ratio and financial status. *Journal of Personality and Social Psychology, 69*, 1089–1101.

Singh, D., & Young, R. K. (1995). Body weight, waist-to-hip ratio, breasts, and hips: Role in judgments of female attractiveness and desirability for relationships. *Ethology & Sociobiology, 16*, 483–507.

Skeels, H. M. (1966). Adult status of children with contrasting early life experiences: A follow-up study. *Monographs of the Society for Research in Child Development, 31*(3, Whole No. 105).

Skeels, H. M., & Dye, H. B. (1939). A study of the effects of differential stimulation on mentally retarded children. *Proceedings and Addresses of the American Association on Mental Deficiency, 44*, 114–136.

Skinner, B. F. (1938). *The behavior of organisms*. New York: Appleton-Century-Crofts.

Skinner, B. F. (1945, October). Baby in a box. *Ladies Home Journal*, 98–104.

Skinner, B. F. (1948). *Walden two*. New York: Macmillan.

Skinner, B. F. (1953). *Science and human behavior*. New York: Macmillan.

Skinner, B. F. (1967). B. F. Skinner. In E. G. Boring & G. Lindzey (Eds.), *A history of psychology in autobiography* (Vol. 5). New York: Appleton Century Crofts.

Skinner, B. F. (1971). *Beyond freedom and dignity*. New York: Knopf.

Skinner, B. F. (1976). *Particulars of my life*. New York: Knopf.

Skinner, B. F. (1987). *Upon further reflection*. Englewood Cliffs, NJ: Prentice Hall.

Skinner, B. F. (1989). The origins of cognitive thought. *American Psychologist, 44*, 114–136.

Smith, M. B. (1959). Research strategies toward a conception of positive mental health. *American Psychologist, 14*, 673–681.

Smith, M. L., & Glass, G. V. (1977). Meta-analysis of psychotherapy outcome studies. *American Psychologist, 32*, 752–760.

Smith, N. W. (2001). *Current systems in psychology*. Belmont, CA: Wadsworth.

Smith, S. M., Brown, H. O., Toman, J. E. P., & Goodman, L. S. (1947). The lack of cerebral effects of d-tubocurarine. *Anesthesiology, 8*, 1–14.

Smith, T. C., & Thompson, T. L. (1993). The inherent, powerful value of a good physician-patient relationship. *Psychosomatics: Journal of Consultation Liaison Psychiatry, 34*, 166–170.

Snape, D., & Spencer, L. (2003). The foundations of qualitative research. In J. Ritchie & J. Lewis (Eds.), *Qualitative research practice*. Thousand Oaks, CA: Sage.

Spelke, E. S., Breinlinger, K., Macomber, J., & Jacobson, K. (1992). Origins of knowledge. *Psychological Review, 99*, 605–632.

Sperry, R. W. (1995). The future of psychology. *American Psychologist, 50*, 505–506.

Stasiewicz, P. R., & Maisto, S. A. (1993). Two-factor avoidance theory. *Behavior Therapy, 24*, 337–356.

Sternberg, R. J. (2000). Thinking: An overview. In A. E. Kazdin (Ed.), *Encyclopedia of psychology* (Vol. 8). New York: Oxford University Press.

Sternberg, R. J., & Dennis, M. J. (1997). Elaborating cognitive psychology through linkages to psychology as a helping profession. *Teaching of Psychology, 24,* 246–249.

Stewart, A. E. (2000). Alfred Adler. In A. E. Kazdin (Ed.), *Encyclopedia of psychology* (Vol. 1). New York: Oxford University Press.

Strachey, J. (1955). Editor's introduction. In J. Breuer & S. Freud (1895), Studies in hysteria. In J. Strachey (Ed. & Trans.), *The standard edition of the complete works of Sigmund Freud* (Vol. 2). London: Hogarth Press.

Strobel, M. G. (1972). Social facilitation of operant behavior in satiated rats. *Journal of Comparative and Physiological Psychology, 80*(3), 502–508.

Stumpf, C. (1930). Carl Stumpf. In E. Murchison (Ed.), *A history of psychology in autobiography* (Vol. 1). Worcester, MA: Clark University Press.

Symonds, D. (1979). *The evolution of human sexuality.* New York: Oxford University Press.

Tagler, M. J. (2000). Neuroscience and mainstream psychology. *American Psychologist, 55,* 271.

Tierson, F. D., Olsen, C. L., & Hook, E. B. (1986). Nausea and vomiting of pregnancy and association with pregnancy outcome. *American Journal of Obstetrics and Gynecology, 155,* 1017–1022.

Tinbergen, N. (1953). *Social behavior in animals.* New York: Wiley.

Tolpin, M. (2000). A cure with a defect: A previously unpublished letter by Freud concerning Anna O. *International Journal of Psychoanalysis, 81,* 357–359.

Tooby, J., & Cosmides, L. (1992). The psychological foundations of culture. In J. H. Barkow, L. Cosmides, & J. Tooby (Eds.), *The adapted mind: Evolutionary psychology and the generation of culture.* New York: Oxford University Press.

Triandis, H. C., & Suh, E. M. (2002). Cultural influences on personality. *Annual Review of Psychology, 53,* 133–160.

Tversky, A., & Kahneman, D. (1974). Judgment under uncertainty: Heuristics and biases. *Science, 185,* 1124–1131.

Valsiner, J. (2000). Cultural psychology. In A. E. Kazdin (Ed.), *Encyclopedia of psychology* (Vol. 2). New York: Oxford University Press.

Villejo, R. E., Humphrey, L. L., & Kirschenbaum, D. S. (1997). Affect and self-regulation in binge eaters: Effects of activating family images. *International Journal of Eating Disorders, 21,* 237–249.

Virgin, C. E., & Sapolsky, R. M. (1997). Styles of male social behavior and their endocrine correlates among low-ranking baboons. *American Journal of Primatology, 42*(1), 25–39.

Viscusi, W. K. (1992). *Smoking: Making the risky decision.* New York: Oxford University Press.

Wachtel, P. L. (2000). Integrative psychotherapy. In A. E. Kazdin (Ed.), *Encyclopedia of psychology* (Vol. 4). New York: Oxford University Press.

Wagener, J. J., & Laird, J. D. (1980). The experimenter's foot-in-the-door: Self-perception, body weight, and volunteering. *Personality and Social Psychology Bulletin, 6*(3) 441–446.

Wahlsten, D. (2000). Behavior genetics. In A. E. Kazdin (Ed.), *Encyclopedia of psychology* (Vol. 1). New York: Oxford University Press.

Watson, R. I. (1967). Psychology: A prescriptive science. *American Psychologist, 22,* 435–443.

Weakley, M. M., Petti, T. A., & Karwisch, A. (1997). Case study: Chewing gum treatment of rumination in an adolescent with an eating disorder. *Journal of American Academy of Child and Adolescent Psychiatry, 36,* 1124–1127.

Wegner, D. M. (2002). *The illusion of conscious will.* Cambridge, MA: MIT Press.

Welty, J. C. (1934). Experiments in group behavior of fishes. *Physiological Zoology, 7,* 85–128.

Wertheimer, M. (1972). *Fundamental issues in psychology.* New York: Holt, Rinehart, Winston.

Westen, D. (1998). The scientific legacy of Sigmund Freud: Toward a psychodynamically informed psychological science. *Psychological Bulletin, 124*(3), 333–371.

Westen, D. (1999). The scientific status of unconscious processes: Is Freud really dead? *Journal of the American Psychoanalytic Association, 47*(4), 1061–1106.

Whorf, B. L. (1956). *Language, thought, and reality.* Cambridge, MA: MIT Press.

Wilkins, W. (1986). Placebo problems in psychotherapy research: Social-psychological alternatives to chemotherapy concepts. *American Psychologist, 41,* 551–556.

Wollstonecraft, M. (1792). *A vindication of the rights of women.* London: J. Johnson.

Wolpe, J. (1961). The systematic desensitization treatment of neurosis. *Journal of Nervous and Mental Disease, 132,* 189–203.

Wood, W., Wong, F. Y., & Cachere, J. G. (1991). The effects of media violence on viewers' aggression in unconstrained social interaction. *Psychological Bulletin, 109*(3), 371–383.

Wrangham, R., & Peterson, D. (1996). *Demonic males.* Boston: Houghton Mifflin.

Wundt, W. (1874/1904). *Principles of physiological psychology* (E. B. Titchener, Trans.). New York: Macmillan. (English translation published in 1904)

Yalom, I. D. (1980). *Existential psychotherapy.* New York: Basic Books.

Zajonc, R. B. (1965). Social facilitation. *Science, 149,* 269–274.

Zimring, F. (1990). A characteristic of Rogers' response to clients. *Person-Centered Review, 5,* 433–448.

Index

About the Author

Dodge Fernald is Lecturer on Psychology in the Department of Psychology at Harvard University. He received his PhD in Counseling/Clinical Psychology from Cornell University and has served as Associate Professor at Bowdoin College, a Fulbright Lecturer at the University of Madrid and as a Visiting Professor at Wellesley College and Cornell University. His basic textbook, *Introduction to Psychology,* has been published in several editions, and he has written other books (*The Hans Legacy: A Story of Science, Walking Tour of Walden Two*). He has received the Petra T. Shattuck Award for Excellence in Teaching in the Harvard Extension School, and he is a Fellow of the American Psychological Association Division Two—Society for the Teaching of Psychology. His areas of special interest include psychological measurement, clinical practice, and instructional methods in psychology.